# CHILD FORENSIC PSYCHOLOGY

# Child Forensic Psychology

## Victim and Eyewitness Memory

Edited by

Robyn E. Holliday

and

Tammy A. Marche

palgrave
macmillan

First published 2013 by
PALGRAVE MACMILLAN

Palgrave Macmillan in the UK is an imprint of Macmillan Publishers Limited,
registered in England, company number 785998, of Houndmills, Basingstoke,
Hampshire RG21 6XS.

Palgrave Macmillan in the US is a division of St Martin's Press LLC,
175 Fifth Avenue, New York, NY 10010.

Palgrave Macmillan is the global academic imprint of the above companies
and has companies and representatives throughout the world.

Palgrave® and Macmillan® are registered trademarks in the United States,
the United Kingdom, Europe and other countries

ISBN: 978–0–230–57708–4

This book is printed on paper suitable for recycling and made from fully
managed and sustained forest sources. Logging, pulping and manufacturing
processes are expected to conform to the environmental regulations of the
country of origin.

A catalogue record for this book is available from the British Library.

A catalog record for this book is available from the Library of Congress.

10  9  8  7  6  5  4  3  2  1
22 21 20 19 18 17 16 15 14 13

Printed in China

*This book is dedicated to those who introduced us to the intricacies of human memory.*

# Contents

# Illustrations

**Figure**

**Table**

# Acknowledgments

We are deeply indebted to the contributors to this book for their dedication to contributing chapters that reflect the current state of knowledge and research in child forensic psychology. Thanks to Jaime Marshall, Paul Stevens, Jenny Hindley and Cecily Wilson at Palgrave Macmillan, and team at Newgen Knowledge Works, whose valuable skills and direction also made this book possible, and to St. Thomas More College, for its publication grant. We would also like to thank the reviewers for their constructive comments and suggestions. Also, special thanks to our current and former graduate and undergraduate students for their many questions, discussions, and for their passion, all of which continue to drive our interest and learning in this area. Lastly, we thank our families for their encouragement during the writing of this book.

# Contributors

**Patricia Bauer** is Senior Associate Dean for Research in Emory College, and is the Asa Griggs Candler Professor of Psychology. She received her PhD from Miami University in 1985 and was a post-doctoral fellow at the University of California, San Diego, from 1985 to 1989. She was on the faculty of the Institute of Child Development at the University of Minnesota from 1989 to 2005. Her research focuses on the development of memory from infancy through childhood, with special emphasis on the determinants of remembering and forgetting, and links between social, cognitive, and neural developments and age-related changes in autobiographical or personal memory.

**Daniel Bederian-Gardner** is a graduate student in developmental psychology at the University of California, Davis. He obtained his BA in Psychology from Concordia University, Montreal, Quebec, Canada. He previously received a BCommerce in accounting from Concordia University and spent several years in municipal finance. His research to date has included studies of jury decision-making, false memory development, and foster care services in California. Other interests include the role of emotion in forensic psychology as well as the role of individual difference factors in lie-telling behavior. He has published several papers on child maltreatment and child witnesses.

**Charles J. Brainerd** is Professor and Chair of the Department of Human Development and Psychology at Cornell University, USA. He is a fellow of the Division of General Psychology, the Division of Experimental Psychology, the Division of Developmental Psychology and the Division of Educational Psychology of the American Psychological Association, and the American Psychological Society. He holds BS, MA and PhD degrees in Experimental and Developmental Psychology. He has published over 200 research articles and chapters, and more than 20 books. His research covers human memory and decision-making, neuroscience, neurocognitive impairment, mathematical modeling, cognitive development, and psychology and the law. His current research program centers on the relation between memory and higher reasoning, on false-memory phenomena, and on neurocognitive impairment. He is the co-developer of fuzzy-trace theory, a model of the relation between memory and higher reasoning, which has been widely applied within medicine and law.

**Stephen J. Ceci** is H. L. Carr Chaired Professor of Developmental Psychology at Cornell University where he conducts research on child testimonial issues. His research has been cited by courts in America, including the U.S. Supreme Court. He is a frequent lecturer to judges about the reliability risks of young witnesses. Ceci has received numerous professional awards and honors including three lifetime achievement awards from major scientific societies.

**Jonathan C. Corbin** is a third year PhD candidate in the Human Development program at Cornell University. He has a BA in Psychology from the University of North Carolina, Asheville and an MA in Experimental Psychology from Appalachian State University. He currently works in Dr. Valerie Reyna's Laboratory for Rational Decision-Making. His research interests include cognitive development, and the relationships between human memory, decision-making and individual differences in cognition.

**Jason J. Dickinson** is Associate Professor of Psychology at Montclair State University. He holds a PhD in Legal Psychology from Florida International University. His research interests include child and adult eyewitness testimony and children's disclosure of sexual abuse. His research on children's testimony has been funded by grants from the National Science Foundation. He regularly works with child protection groups to help translate empirical findings into evidence based practices for interviewing children.

**Vicki Gier** is Assistant Professor of Psychology at Mississippi State University Meridian. She received her BS and MS in Psychology from the University of Central Missouri and a PhD from the University of Nevada, Reno. Her work focuses on educational psychology and recognition of missing children.

**Gail S. Goodman** is Distinguished Professor of Psychology and Director of the Center for Public Policy Research at the University of California, Davis. She obtained her PhD in Developmental Psychology from UCLA and conducted postdoctoral studies at the University of Denver and the Université René Descartes in Paris, France. She has received many awards, including the Association for Psychological Science James McKeen Cattell Award for Lifetime Outstanding Contributions to Applied Psychological Research, the Urie Bronfenbrenner Award for Lifetime Contribution to Developmental Psychology, and two Distinguished Contribution awards from the American Psychological Association (the Distinguished Contributions to Research in Public Policy Award and the Distinguished Professional Contributions to Applied Research Award). Goodman is the upcoming president of Division 7 (Developmental Psychology) of the American Psychological Association and has served as the president of several other divisions, including the American

Psychology-Law Society. She has published widely and has received many federal, state, and foundation grants. Her research has been cited repeatedly in U.S. Supreme Court decisions. Goodman's Center for Public Policy Research brings science to policy on behalf of children and families. Her research concerns memory development, child maltreatment, trauma and memory, and children in the legal system.

**Robyn E. Holliday** is Senior Lecturer in Psychology at the University of Leicester, United Kingdom. She holds an Honors degree and a PhD in Experimental, Forensic and Developmental Psychology from the University of Newcastle, Australia. Her current research centers on the processes underlying true and false memories across the lifespan, particularly of children and the elderly; child and elderly eyewitness testimony, including identification abilities; and forensic interview protocols. She is registered with the Health Professions Council as Chartered Forensic Psychologist and Chartered Scientist. She is a member of a number of professional societies. She regularly provides expert testimony for criminal cases in the United Kingdom.

**Mark L. Howe** is Professor of Psychology and University Research Chair (Developmental Psychology) at Lancaster University, United Kingdom. Howe is a fellow of the Association for Psychological Science, the American Psychological Association, and the British Psychological Society. His professional career has spanned the academic and public communities particularly those areas concerned with children and the law. Howe's major research interests lie in the formulation of an integrative and adaptive theory of memory development, one that spans both normal and atypical development. His current work focuses on the origins of autobiographical memory, the development of false memories, and the origins of adaptive memory.

**J. Zoe Klemfuss** is a post-doctoral researcher in the Department of Psychology and Social Behavior at the University of California, Irvine, where she studies the impact of individual differences and social context on the content and quality of children's memory reports. She is also interested in the practical implications of this work in the areas of children's autobiographical development, psychological well-being, and eyewitness abilities. She completed her PhD in Developmental Psychology in 2011 in the Department of Human Development at Cornell University. Her dissertation focused on young children's competency to provide legal testimony, and predicting individual children's testimonial accuracy. She has received numerous awards including the Flora Rose, Martha Foulk, Ethel, Rebecca Quin Morgan, and Olin graduate fellowships.

**James Michael Lampinen** is Professor of Psychological Science at the University of Arkansas. He received his BS in Psychology from Elmhurst College and a PhD in Cognitive Psychology from Northwestern University. He is a recipient of the Fulbright College of Arts and Sciences Master Researcher Award. Lampinen's research focuses on prospective person memory (the ability to spot missing or wanted individuals in the environment), false memories, and eyewitness identification.

**Michael J. Lawler** is Dean and Professor, School of Health Sciences, University of South Dakota. Previously, he served as Director of the Center for Human Services and co-director of the Center for Public Policy Research at the University of California, Davis. Lawler has 30 years of experience as a social work practitioner, administrator, and educator. He holds a PhD in Human Development from the University of California, Davis and MSW from the University of California, Berkeley. He was awarded the 2011 Career Achievement Award from the National Staff Development and Training Association of the American Public Human Services Association and the 2010 James H. Meyer Distinguished Achievement Award from the University of California, Davis. His research areas include child welfare services, juvenile justice, foster care, parent–child relationships, and professional education.

**Tammy A. Marche** is a cognitive developmental psychologist specializing in memory development and is a faculty member in the Psychology Department at St. Thomas More College, University of Saskatchewan. Research in her lab aims to advance the experimental and theoretical literature on memory as well as extend this research to more applied settings (e.g. false memories, memory for emotional experiences).

**Timothy N. Odegard** is Associate Professor of Psychology at the University of Texas Arlington. His research interests include the cognitive neuroscience of human memory and learning and their application to real world settings. Other research includes neuroimaging of memory processes using fMRI. Basic research interests also include the identification of core cognitive processing deficits in dyslexic children and adult. Applied research includes forensic interviewing of children and the treatment of dyslexia.

**Christopher S. Peters** is a graduate student in Psychological Science at the University of Arkansas. He received a BA in Psychology from University of North Texas and an MA in Clinical Psychology from Western Carolina University. Peters' research focuses on the use of multiple posters in prospective person memory situations as well as entrapment defenses during jury trials.

**Debra Ann Poole** is Professor of Psychology at Central Michigan University. After completing a PhD from the University of Iowa in Developmental and Experimental Child Psychology, she focused her research on the interface between basic research in cognitive psychology and social policy issues. A fellow of the Association for Psychological Science, Poole has served on investigative interviewing protocol committees in two states, where she helps interdisciplinary groups promote evidence-based practice. Studies in her laboratory, funded by grants from the National Science Foundation, address questions raised by practitioners as well as concerns suggested by emerging research on children's capabilities and limitations.

**Joanna D. Pozzulo** is Professor in the Department of Psychology at Carleton University, Canada. She is also a child clinical psychologist registered with the Ontario College of Psychologists. Her research and teaching falls under the domain of Forensic Psychology (borrowing from developmental, social, and cognitive psychology). Pozzulo is focused on understanding the development of face memory and the procedures that police can use to increase the reliability of face identification from lineups with an emphasis on children's identification evidence.

**Valerie F. Reyna** is Professor of Human Development and Psychology at Cornell University, USA, and a codirector of the Center for Behavioral Economics and Decision Research. She has been elected as a fellow of the American Association for the Advancement of Science. She is also a fellow of the Division of Experimental Psychology, the Division of Developmental Psychology, the Division of Educational Psychology and the Division of Health Psychology of the American Psychological Association, and the American Psychological Society. She holds a PhD in Experimental Psychology from Rockefeller University. Her research encompasses human judgment and decision-making, numeracy and quantitative reasoning, risk and uncertainty, medical decision-making, social judgment, and false memory. She is a developer of fuzzy-trace theory, a model of the relation between mental representations and decision-making that has been widely applied in law, medicine and public health. She publishes regularly in journals such as *Psychological Review* and *Psychological Science*.

**Karen Salmon** is Associate Professor of Psychology and worked as a clinical psychologist for 12 years before embarking on a PhD (University of Otago, New Zealand) focusing on interview strategies that can enable young children to remember and report full and accurate accounts of their experiences. She held an academic appointment at the University of New South Wales (Sydney, Australia) for 10 years, before returning to New Zealand and Victoria University of Wellington in 2007. Salmon's research focuses on the role of children's memory (in particular, emotional memory) in psychopathology and psychological well-being. For example, she has investigated the influence of everyday conversations between adults and children on the children's memory for their emotional experiences and on their developing emotion competence, and currently, is focusing on the role of specific memory biases in children and adolescents' psychological functioning.

**Lindsey N. Sweeney** is a graduate student in Psychological Science at the University of Arkansas. She received her BA in Psychology with a minor in Criminal Justice from the University of South Carolina in 2008 and her MA in Experimental Psychology from the University of Arkansas in 2011. Sweeney's current work focuses on the role of visual attention in prospective person memory.

**Michael P. Toglia** is Chair and Professor in the Department Psychology at the University of North Florida (UNF). He is the winner of a Fulbright Senior Specialist grant (Mexico) as well as a fellow in Division 3 (Experimental), and Division 41 (Psychology and the Law) of the American Psychological Association. He also holds fellow status in the Association for Psychological Science and the Midwestern Psychological Association. He has over 70 scientific publication books to his credit. He has testified and/or consulted in numerous cases involving eyewitness lineup identification and the suggestibility of memory, been interviewed by several national newspapers.

**Evan A. Wilhelms** is a PhD student in the department of Human Development at Cornell University. He earned his BS in Psychology and Philosophy at Baldwin-Wallace College, and is currently working in Dr. Valerie Reyna's Laboratory for Rational Decision-Making. His research interests include behavioral economics and cognitive development, including the relationships between decision-making and affective outcomes as well as their societal applications.

# Introduction

Robyn E. Holliday and Tammy A. Marche

There has been an explosion of research on eyewitness testimony in the last 25 years. Much of this research has been concerned with obtaining accurate testimony from child witnesses and victims of crime. We have brought together world-leading researchers to present and review the latest scientific knowledge on children's memory and eyewitness testimony. Both theoretical and applied aspects of child forensic psychology are covered. The over-arching themes of this book are: (1) the current state of scientific knowledge of memory in children from infancy to adolescence, and (2) how that knowledge is applied practically to children's eyewitness testimony. The question of central concern throughout this book is: How reliable are children's memories and testimony for events that they have witnessed or experienced? The answer is: It depends! A number of factors determine the accuracy of children's eyewitness testimony. To help illustrate some of these factors, which are discussed in various chapters throughout the book, we begin with three cases of child eyewitness testimony.

## Case 1: R. v Steven Barker

A young girl made an unprompted allegation to her foster carer at the age of 2 years 11 months concerning numerous indecent acts of a sexual nature, including anal intercourse, committed by Steven Barker. Three months later, she repeated these complaints unprompted to a child psychiatrist. Three months after this, she repeated the complaints to a pediatrician and a family therapist. By the time she was given an Achieving Best Evidence (ABE) video-recorded interview by police, six months had elapsed since she had made the original complaints. The trial was delayed by 13 months because Barker was on trial for the homicide of the girl's brother Peter.

Barker was convicted of the rape of a child of less than 3 years of age and sentenced to life imprisonment, with a minimum of 12 years to be served. An appeal was lodged on the basis of competence of the child to testify and the

1

passage of time between the initial ABE interview and the trial. The appeal judge found that due course was given by the trial judge in establishing competence. The appeal was dismissed. This case can be seen as a watershed for young witnesses. Cooper and Wurzel (2010) noted that this case "has made it clear that children have the right to be heard in the criminal courts. Whether they are competent is a matter for the Judge, having regard to the particular child and the particular circumstances. Whether they are reliable is a matter for the jury, having regard to all the evidence. Each case still turns on its own facts."

## Case 2: R. v Edwards

In this case, the trial judge instructed counsel to avoid using the traditional methods of cross-examination with the young witness. To the best of our knowledge, this is a first for a criminal trial in the United Kingdom with a very young child witness. Despite the recommendations of the Pigot Report (1989) that cross-examination of vulnerable witnesses be prerecorded on video similar to evidence-in-chief (ABE interview), the legal profession has strenuously opposed any such changes.

On July 16, 2009, C1 (Child 1), then aged 5, was taken to hospital complaining of stomach pain. She had been vomiting throughout that day and her mother had become concerned after seeing blood in the vomit. Tests revealed that blood was leaking from C1's kidneys into her abdomen. She had a large bruise to her lower abdomen and groin. C1's step-father was arrested and charged with cruelty to a person under 16 years of age. The prosecution case was that Edwards had punched C1 in the stomach and that, having been aware that he had caused her injury or pain, had done nothing to help her. The defendant denied the charges. In her ABE interview played to the court, C1 stated that the defendant had punched her in the stomach because she had not eaten her porridge quickly enough. The trial judge informed the jury that the traditional form of cross-examination would not occur when questioning C1, but would instead be restricted to asking only necessary questions. He directed that the defendant's counsel should not ask C1 challenging questions; rather they should ask open-ended questions only. Before deliberation, the judge directed the jury in his summing up to make proper and fair allowances for the difficulty faced by counsel for the defendant in asking questions of a child witness. The defendant was convicted.

Edwards appealed his conviction on the basis that the judge had wrongly restricted the cross-examination of the child, rendering the child's testimony to be more reliable than it actually was, had defense counsel been allowed to perform more rigorous cross-examination. The appeal was dismissed.

[The judgment is available at: [2011] EWCA Crim 3028 Court of Appeal, All England Reporter, 2011].

## Case 3: R. v Powell

The child in this case was also very young and the trial was held nine months after the alleged assault. However, in contrast to the previous case, the child was not ABE interviewed until nine weeks after the alleged offence, despite the fact that she made the allegations soon after she said it occurred. The trial judge in this case did not instruct defense counsel to avoid challenging questions in cross-examination of the child.

Here is a synopsis of the case. A 3½-year old girl (we will call Child 2) told her mother that the defendant, Powell, had licked her genitals during a birthday party. Powell's DNA was found inside and outside the girl's panties. He was convicted of indecent assault of a young child. He subsequently appealed on the basis of the witness's age, arguing that she was too young to provide reliable testimony. The girl was interviewed nine weeks after the party. The trial was seven months later, that is nine months after the alleged assault. The trial judge ruled that the child was competent to give evidence and her ABE interview was played for the court. The defense argued that the girl did not demonstrate competence during cross-examination – that she did not fully understand the questions (Hoyano, 2010). The defendant was convicted and subsequently lodged an appeal.

It was the Appeal Judge's opinion that the child was competent at the time of the ABE video interview, but not at cross-examination at trial. His opinion was that the trial judge should have found C2 not competent at cross-examination, because the child was not able to answer questions in cross-examination in any coherent manner. Furthermore, this judge noted that the form of the crucial question, which demonstrated the child's incompetence, was posed by defense counsel,

Q: "No man licked your nunny, did he? C: Shook her head." The appeal was allowed.

These cases raise a number of questions about the ability of children to provide reliable eyewitness testimony. What effect does age have on a child's memory and ability to provide testimony? How young is too young? How do delay and repeated questioning and repeated interviewing influence what children report? Could the child in Case 1, at 4 years of age, provide an accurate and reliable account of what happened to her, given that she was under 3 years of age at the time of the rape and the numerous delays? What evidence should be present for children to be deemed competent to give testimony? In Case 2, would the child's responses to the counsel's questions at cross-examination have been different if the judge had *not* required only open, non-challenging questions? Would the young girl in Case 3 be deemed competent, as the judge decided she was, based on the current scientific understanding of children's competency? What impact do suggestive questions have on children's accuracy and suggestibility?

Next, we present outlines of the chapters in this book. Each of the chapters attempts to answer a number of these questions.

In Chapter 1, *Theory and Processes in Memory Development: Infancy and Early Childhood*, Patricia Bauer discusses the characteristics of event memory and memory development from infancy to toddlerhood (0 to 2 years). Do infants have long-term memories? If so, how are their preverbal memories tested? Bauer describes the methods that have been used to measure memory during this period of rapid development in cognition, such as the novelty preference, conjugate reinforcement, and elicited and deferred imitation paradigms. She outlines the age-related changes in the encoding, storage and retrieval of information observed in the literature. She discusses the research findings and theories that have been proposed to explain them as well as the mechanisms of developmental changes. Bauer concludes her chapter with a discussion of an apparent discontinuity in memory between infancy and early childhood, that between nonverbal and verbal accessibility of early memories. Understanding the developmental changes that take place in memory across infancy and toddlerhood speaks to the question of how young is too young in terms of children's ability to reliably recount experiences that have happened to them or that they have witnessed. Based on what we know about memory development during this age period, was the child in Case 1, who was 2 years 11 months at the time of the event, capable of providing a forensically relevant account of what she experienced?

Similar to the issues raised in the first chapter, Chapter 2, Mark Howe's *Feats of Early Memory: Courtroom Tales of What Adults Claim to Remember about Early Childhood Events*, speaks to what memory is not capable of during the first two years of life, during the "infantile amnesia period", which again address how young is too young in terms of children's ability to provide reliable memoires of their experiences and of older children and adult's ability to recount experiences from that developmental period. It is often the case that these kinds of memories form the bases of criminal prosecutions. The problem is how do we know whether or not such allegations are true or false? What do scientific studies tell us about this important issue? Howe discusses the characteristics of the types of memories recalled, and the conditions under which many of these recollections are produced. One important point to mention here is that many of these kinds of allegations of historical sexual abuse are reported by the claimant to have occurred in the first four or five years of life, when most people cannot remember much if anything about their lives, a phenomenon called "infantile amnesia".

In Chapter 3, *Theory and Processes in Memory Development: Childhood to Adolescence,* Jonathan Corbin, Evan Wilhelms, Valerie Reyna and Charles Brainerd focus on the theory and empirical evidence that drive existing models of memory processes and the age-related changes in memory across childhood to adolescence. They begin with a comprehensive account of the basic methods used to measure true memory, false memory and misinformation effects in both recall and recognition memory-testing paradigms. They then move on to evaluate foundational theories of memory, namely *constructivism* and *schema theory* that paved the way for more recent theories of memory and development. Next they present an overview of the theory behind the source monitoring framework (SMF) and demonstrate how it conflicts with another major theory of memory development, namely, fuzzy-trace theory (FTT). The SMF proposes that false memories, including misinformation effects, are due to errors in identification of the correct source of the memory. Source confusions are predicted to decline with age. FTT is a dual-processes theory of memory development, which proposes two independent memory processes, one that focuses on storage of surface details (i.e. verbatim memory), and a second process that focuses on the bottom-line meaning of information (i.e. gist memory). Verbatim and gist memory have differing developmental trajectories. Young children are heavily reliant on verbatim memory, which decays rapidly. On the other hand, the ability to extract the gist or meaning of information improves with age from childhood to adolescence. Corbin et al. give the reader a good sense of how and why children's memories improve with age, and of the factors that can impair their memory, such as the deleterious impact of delay. What impact did the delay between the initial report and the trial have on the child's memories in Case 3?

In Chapter 4, *Children as Eyewitnesses: Historical Background and Factors Affecting Children's Eyewitness Testimony,* Timothy Odegard and Michael Toglia present the historical context of children's eyewitness testimony and the scientific debates surrounding the reliability of children's memories of abuse. In the decade 1982–1992, a number of high-profile cases involving very young children's allegations of sexual and ritual abuse brought the spotlight on whether the claims they had made could be true or false. Factors such as interviewer biases, repeated questioning, and the use of props such as puppets and dolls led to numerous claims by young children of ritual and sexual abuse allegedly perpetrated by daycare centre workers in the United States, United Kingdom, Australia and New Zealand. Notably, the majority of these cases began with a single claim made by a parent to authorities that they suspected their child had been assaulted by workers at the child's daycare centre.

Moreover, in these cases, one initial allegation of abuse spread like a forest fire amongst other parents until, in some cases, more than 200 children made allegations. It should be noted that in many of these cases children did not make allegations until they had experienced numerous interviews that were "facilitated" by interviewers who used anatomically detailed dolls and puppets. Odegard and Toglia also critically evaluate empirical and theoretical issues underlying suggestibility and misinformation effects in children.

In Chapter 5, *Children's Memory for Emotionally Negative Experiences: An Eyewitness Memory Perspective*, Tammy Marche and Karen Salmon present the latest research on the complex relationship between emotion and memory, particularly eyewitness memory, and the implications these findings have for children's eyewitness testimony. They argue that the particular interaction of biological, psychological and social factors relating to the child, his/her experience and the circumstances of the forensic interview(s) influence the child's arousal and emotion regulation, which directly impacts what will be reported. That is, children's recall is influenced by predisposing factors that sway children to interpret and respond to events, by precipitating factors that affect how they respond during emotionally negative events as well as by perpetuating factors that influence children's memory retention and reconstruction. Thus, there are multiple pathways through which individual differences in arousal and subsequent emotional regulation attempts affect children's memories for distressing events in their lives. Marche and Salmon indicate that child witnesses can provide forensically relevant accounts of their experiences and that there are conditions under which stress and negative emotion might enhance children's recall. Some children may, however, experience difficulties recalling emotionally negative events. They argue that it is critical that those carrying out forensic interviews, as well as experts who testify in court, take into account all the important factors that influence children's memory for stressful experiences and how these factors might be manifested in children's accounts. In Case 1, the child was raped anally, a horrible and painful experience for such a young child. Marche and Salmon discuss the impact that such an emotionally negative experience has on children's memory and testimony.

The manner in which a witness is interviewed is crucial for criminal investigations and successful prosecutions. In Chapter 6, *Investigative Interviews of Children*, Debra Ann Poole and Jason Dickinson discuss the key issues surrounding interviewing child witnesses and the empirical research which underpins current investigative interview protocols, and summarize the similarities and differences among a set of well-known investigative protocols (e.g. Cognitive Interview, NICHD [National Institute of Child Health and Human Development] protocol, MOGP [Memorandum of Good Practice] interview). They outline three topics they believe will define the future direction of interview protocol development, namely, (1) the use of props, (2) physical evidence and (3) modifying existing suspect-oriented protocols for broader child protection purposes.

In Chapter 7, *The Law and Science of Children's Testimonial Competence*, J. Zoe Klemfuss and Stephen Ceci discuss the important issue of whether a child is competent to provide testimony that is useful to the court. They explain that competence is not to be confused with the accuracy or completeness of testimony. If a child shows that she is of sufficient intelligence to demonstrate memories of an event and can communicate these details, then she is likely to be deemed competent to give evidence. In the United Kingdom, a child witness is required to demonstrate competence in all aspects of testimony, including cross-examination. The trial judge is the person who decides whether or not a particular child witness is competent to give evidence-in-chief and evidence in cross-examination. As discussed earlier, in Cases 2 and 3, competence is at the heart of every trial that involves child witnesses.

In Chapter 8, *Child Eyewitness Person Descriptions and Lineup Identifications*, the latest research on eyewitness identification by children is presented. Joanna Pozzulo notes that there are many crimes in which a child is the sole witness, for example, in sexual and/or physical abuse, robberies and public order offences. She discusses the well-publicized case of the kidnapping of 14-year-old Elizabeth Smart, in June 2002, from her bedroom that she shared with her younger sister Mary Katherine, aged 9 years. Mary Katherine, who witnessed the kidnapping whilst pretending to be asleep, gave police a detailed description of the offender and the events that transpired in the bedroom that night. The Smart family had a facial sketch drawn up based on Mary Katherine's description. The chapter focuses on the characteristics of descriptions of offenders provided by child witnesses in terms of accuracy and completeness and types of details. Pozzulo also discusses the status of the scientific knowledge about the accuracy and the reliability of lineup identification decisions by child eyewitnesses and recommendations for conducting "best practice" lineup identification with child witnesses. Although not a primary issue in our highlighted cases in the Introduction, as it is in some other cases, the child had to, in fact, identify the perpetrator.

In Chapter 9, *The Psychology of the Missing: Missing and Abducted Children*, James Lampinen, Christopher Peters, Vicki Gier and Lindsey Sweeney present a relatively new area of research about a long-established problem for law enforcement – that of the recovery of missing and abducted children. Lampinen et al. point out that two types of person memory are implicated in missing children cases, *prospective memory* and *retrospective memory*. Prospective person memory is accessed if one sees a child in person, for example in the mall, or on the street, whose picture one has seen previously on a missing child poster, AMBER Alert or other public notification system. Missing child notification systems also rely on retrospective person memory. Retrospective person memory in this instance refers to situations where a member of the general public has encountered a missing or wanted person in the past, and later encounters an alert concerning the person. Given that one of the factors that determines a successful outcome in cases of missing and abducted children is the reliability of memory of those who last saw the child, and that sometimes apprehension of the perpetrator rests on the missing or abducted child's memory of her experiences, Lampinen et al. describe our current psychological understanding of "the missing".

Chapter 10, *Conclusions and Next Steps for Researchers and Practitioners*, is a summing up of the key points discussed in the preceding chapters, and areas in which there is a need for further scientific study. In this chapter, Michael Lawler, Daniel Bederian-Gardner and Gail Goodman demonstrate how the topics in this book reconcile current practices in law, law enforcement, social work and psychology with some of the best-known scientific research and suggest areas of additional examination to further refine research frameworks and evidence bases of practice.

This book presents up-to-date information from the major researchers of developmental child forensic psychology. To this end, we believe that the book will be of interest and practical use to all who are involved with children in forensic contexts. We hope you enjoy it.

# References

Cooper, J., & Wurzel, D. (February 13, 2010). Criminal Law & Justice Weekly. Downloaded 5/3/12 from www.vulnerablewitness.co.uk/?p=192.

Hoyano, L. (2010). "And What's Your Name Rebecca?" Child and Other Vulnerable Witnesses and Defendants: Competence and Special Measures. Paper presented at the Criminal Bar Association Spring Conference, Bristol, United Kingdom.

Pigot, Judge (1989). Report of the Advisory Group on Video Evidence. Home Office: London, United Kingdom.

# CHAPTER I

# Theory and Processes in Memory Development: Infancy and Early Childhood

PATRICIA BAUER

The development of memory has been a topic of interest at least since Freud's (1905/1953) observations of the "great intellectual accomplishments" (p. 64) of which infants and young children are capable. Yet it was not until 80 years after this observation that empirical evidence on age-related changes in memory began to accrue. Prior to the 1980s, it was widely assumed that infants lacked the ability to encode, store and later retrieve memories of specific past events, and that very young children's memories were generally weak and poorly organized. These perspectives stemmed from Piaget's (1952) theory of genetic epistemology. A major tenet of the theory was that for the first 18 to 24 months of life, infants lacked symbolic capacity and, thus, the ability to mentally *re-present* objects and events. Instead, they were thought to live in a here-and-now world of physically present entities that had no past and no future. Preschoolers were assumed to have constructed the capacity for mental representation, yet were thought to be without the cognitive structures that would permit them to organize events along coherent dimensions that would make the events memorable. Consistent with this suggestion, in retelling fairy tales, children as old as 7 years made errors in temporal sequencing (Piaget, 1926, 1969).

Methodological issues also contributed to the impression that infants were mnemonically challenged. In older children and adults, memory typically is examined through a verbal report of a list of words, a story or a personal experience, for example. For infants and young children, verbal report is not a viable alternative: It is not until age 3 years that children provide even minimally coherent reports about past events. It was viewed as more than coincidence that the earliest memories of adults typically are from roughly the same age, namely, 3 to 3.5 years (see Bauer, 2007; and West & Bauer, 1999, for reviews). These two observations – one from children and the other from adults – "conspired" to create the impression that age 3 marked the onset of the ability to remember.

In this chapter, I summarize some of the developments that have led to revision of the perspective that infants and young children are unable to remember the past. Because much of the research attention has been focused on whether very young children are able to create, retain, and later retrieve coherent memories of specific past experiences, this type of memory (i.e. long-term memory for specific events or episodes) is featured (see Bauer, in press; and Oakes, Ross-Sheehy, & Luck, 2007, for discussions of changes in short-term or working memory). After describing some of the techniques used to examine long-term event memory in infancy and young children, I turn to a review of some of the data generated from the paradigms, and summarize developmental changes in the temporal extent and robustness of memory across the first years of life. I then discuss mechanisms of development change, including age-related changes in the encoding, consolidation and retrieval of memory traces, and how the changes relate to development of the neural substrate that subserves memory. The chapter concludes with discussion of an apparent discontinuity in memory between infancy and early childhood, namely, between nonverbal and verbal accessibility of early memories, and its implications for our understanding of early memory.

Though the first chapter in a volume concerning the accuracy of children's memories and their reliability as witnesses, this chapter is not about accuracy or eyewitness testimony. Yet the chapter should be of substantial interest to researchers, scholars and students of these issues, nonetheless. It is highly relevant to these concerns because it chronicles the early emergence of the ability to recall the past, and thus establishes the lower limit on children's abilities to report on the events of their lives. Moreover, the discussion of the processes of memory formation, preservation and subsequent retrieval – though discussed in the context of infancy and early childhood – is relevant for the memories of individuals of any age. In an absolute sense, these basic mnemonic processes determine what there is to remember about a past event and, thus, are of fundamental importance to issues of accuracy and reliability. Finally, discussion of the later verbal accessibility of early memories is of central importance to anyone who ponders the fates of early, preverbal memories, and whether they ever can be retrieved and reported once language is available. Thus, the chapter concerns fundamental questions about basic memory processes, memory products, and the determinants of remembering and forgetting, thereby establishing the boundary conditions for what we may expect in terms of later accuracy of testimony.

# Assessing memory in infancy and early childhood

The 1980s was the source of challenges to the perspective that infants were unable to recall or re-present past events, yet did not feature the first evidence of memory in infancy or among young children. It has long been clear that infants learn and otherwise benefit from past experience: they recognize their caregivers over changes in time and context, they learn motor skills such as walking and feeding themselves, and they make great strides in learning language, for example. Infants also demonstrate their memory abilities in experimental paradigms such as *visual paired comparison* or *habituation* and the operant conditioning paradigm of *mobile conjugate reinforcement*. Studies using these paradigms have revealed evidence of strikingly robust memory, from very young infants. Yet, as discussed in Bauer (2006), these findings were not what prompted revision of the suggestion that the first years of life were devoid of the ability to mentally re-present objects or events and thereby recall them. That distinction is reserved for findings from a third infant memory paradigm, *elicited* and *deferred imitation*, a nonverbal analogue to verbal report. Before summarizing some of the major findings from each of these paradigms, I introduce an important distinction in the memory litera-ture – between non-declarative and declarative memory – that is essential to adequate description of developmental changes, as well as their explanation.

## Distinguishing non-declarative and declarative memory

Although it is not universally accepted (see Rovee-Collier, 1997) by both developmental and adult cognitive scientists, it is widely believed that memory is not a unitary trait but is comprised of different systems or processes, which serve distinct functions, and are characterized by fundamentally different rules of operation (e.g. Schacter, Wagner, & Buckner, 2000; Squire, 1987). The type of memory termed *non-declarative* represents a variety of non-con-scious abilities, including the capacity for learning habits and skills, priming and some forms of conditioning (see Lloyd & Newcombe, 2009; Parkin, 1997, for reviews). Common features of non-declarative memory are that acquisi-tion of information is relatively slow (it accrues with practice or experience), yet the result is long lasting. In addition, the impact of experience is made evident through a change in behavior or performance, but the products of the change are not consciously accessible and cannot be verbally described (Zola-Morgan & Squire, 1993). In contrast, the type of memory termed *declarative* (or explicit) captures most of what we think of when we refer to "memory" or "remembering" (Zola-Morgan & Squire, 1993). It involves the capacity for rapid, even one-trial, learning. The products of learning are names, places, dates, events and so forth. They are consciously accessible and, as such, can support explicit recognition or recall.

The distinction between different types of memory originally was derived from the adult cognitive and neuroscience literatures. It is based on data from patient populations, animal models of trauma and disease, and from neuroimaging studies. The data from these different sources converge to suggest patterns of breakdown and sparing, and patterns of activation and co-activation across different neural structures that sort themselves along lines consistent with the major division between non-declarative and declarative memory systems. One memory system seems specialized for acquisition of information at a slower rate, yet seemingly permits more robust retention, whereas the other seems specialized for rapid encoding of information that is subject to equally rapid forgetting. Computer simulations have revealed that these specializations are actually incompatible with one another. That is, a system that is good at maintaining old inputs has difficulty "learning" new things. Conversely, a system that can change rapidly to accept new inputs has difficulty maintaining old inputs (e.g. McClelland, McNaughton, & O'Reilly, 1995). This analysis suggests that complementary memory systems work in concert in order to avoid interference with existing knowledge, yet still maintain flexibility. The different memory systems may have evolved in order to deal with competing demands for different kinds of information storage. Alternatively, nature may have taken fair advantage of structures that had evolved for others reasons, in order to deal with the demands.

The distinction between an unconscious non-declarative form of memory and a conscious declarative form of memory presents challenges in the developmental literature. Chief among them is the fact that it is difficult to evaluate whether preverbal infants and newly verbal children are conscious of the contents of their minds. Yet the distinction between different memory systems is vitally important for developmental scientists, because non-declarative and declarative memory rely on different neural substrates that have different courses of development. A variety of brain regions are implicated in support of non-declarative memory, including neocortex (priming), striatum (skill learning) and cerebellum (conditioning; see Toth, 2000, for a review). These regions are thought to develop early and, as a result, to support early emergence of non-declarative memory (see Nelson, 1997, for a review). In contrast, as described in more detail later, declarative memory depends on a multi-component neural network including temporal and cortical structures (e.g. Zola & Squire, 2000). Whereas some components of the network develop early, other aspects undergo a protracted developmental course. The entire circuit begins to coalesce near the end of the first year of life and continues to develop for years thereafter, contributing to pronounced changes in declarative memory (see Bauer, 2007, 2009; Bachevalier, 2001; Nelson, de

Haan, & Thomas, 2006; Richman & Nelson, 2008, for reviews). The major findings from the three main infant memory paradigms are consistent with these expectations.

## Visual paired comparison or habituation

*Visual paired comparison* involves showing infants pairs of pictures of a stimulus and then presenting the now "familiar" picture along with a novel one, and observing where the infants look. A variant of the technique, *visual habituation*, involves presenting a sequence of pictures and then, after some criterion is reached (typically, a 50 percent decrease in looking time), introducing a novel picture and noting changes in looking. In both techniques, differential looking to novel and familiar stimuli is taken as evidence of recognition memory. After only a short familiarization time, infants tend to look longer at familiar stimuli. With longer periods of familiarization (or habituation), they tend to look longer at novel stimuli (see Bahrick & Pickens, 1995, for a review). The amount of familiarization required to produce a novelty response also interacts with age, with older infants (6.5-month-olds) requiring less time relative to younger infants (e.g. 3.5-month-olds; Rose, Gottfried, Melloy-Carminar, & Bridger, 1982).

Patterns of looking to familiar and novel stimuli most often are examined over relatively short periods, such as seconds to minutes. For example, between 3 and 12 months of age, the length of time over which a novelty response was apparent increased from 5–10 seconds to 10 minutes (Rose, Feldman, & Jankowski, 2001). Visual attention also has been used to examine retention over as many as three months. Over such long intervals, the evidence for recognition comes in the form of more visual attention to familiar stimuli (e.g. Bahrick & Pickens, 1995). The change in distribution of attention (from greater attention to novel to greater attention to familiar) is taken as evidence of the differential status of mnemonic traces over time. The assumption is that on the basis of a "fresh" memory trace (i.e. after a short retention interval), infants need not spend time processing familiar stimuli and, consequently, spend more time attending to novel stimuli. As memory fades (with increasing delay), infants devote attentional resources to reconstruction of the trace for the once-familiar stimulus (see Bahrick, Hernandez-Reif, & Pickens, 1997; Courage & Howe, 1998, for discussion).

Attentional preference techniques clearly measure changes in infants' responses to previously encountered stimuli. However, it is unclear whether they measure the same type of recognition, as evidenced when adults explicitly affirm that they have seen a particular stimulus before. Snyder (2007) made a compelling argument that the shift in attention from an old to a new stimulus may be the result of *repetition suppression* – a reduction of neuronal responses in the occipital-temporal visual pathway that occurs in response to stimulus repetition – rather than of explicit recognition. This argument is consistent with one by C. A. Nelson (1995, 1997), who suggested that early in development, attention to novel stimuli is driven by the frequency with which stimuli are presented rather than their novelty or familiarity (see Nelson & Collins, 1991, 1992, for discussion; see also Mandler, 1998, for a related argument). In sum, although changes in the distribution of infant attention as a result of prior exposure *may* be based on explicit recognition memory, because such judgments are not required to produce the response (e.g. McKee & Squire, 1993), they cannot be assumed, especially in light of alternative candidate explanations.

## Operant conditioning

The second major technique used to test retention in early infancy is conditioning in general, and the operant conditioning paradigm of mobile conjugate reinforcement in particular. In this paradigm, an attractive mobile is suspended above an infant's crib or playpen. After measuring the baseline rate at which the infants kick (which they do spontaneously), researchers "tether" the infant's leg to the mobile such that, as the infant kicks, the mobile moves. Infants quickly learn the contingency between kicking and the movement of the mobile. After a delay, the mobile again is placed above the infant but the infant's leg is not attached to the mobile. If the post-training rate of kicking is greater than the baseline rate of kicking (i.e. before the infant experienced the contingency), memory is inferred (see Rovee-Collier & Cuevas, 2009, for a description of this and related procedures).

The mobile conjugate reinforcement paradigm has been quite productive, yielding many important findings. For example, it is clear that the length of time the conditioned response is retained increases from 1–3 days at 2 months of age to 14 days by 6 months of age (Hill, Borovsky, & Rovee-Collier, 1988). "Reminding" infants of the mobile during the delay extends the length of time over which behavior towards the mobile is retained (Rovee-Collier et al., 1980). The time over which the conditioned response can be retained is also influenced by the amount of training that infants receive, the distribution of training and even the affect that they display during training (see Rovee-Collier & Cuevas, 2009, for a review). A salient characteristic of memory as evidenced by this paradigm is its specificity. For example, young infants fail to recognize the training mobile if even a single element of it is changed. Minor changes to the fabric that lines the crib or playpen (e.g. changing the shape of the figures on the liner) also disrupts performance (e.g. Borovsky & Rovee-Collier,

1990; Rovee-Collier, Schechter, Shyi, & Shields, 1992). It is only as details of the original stimulus are forgotten that infants generalize from the stimulus or context associated with the learning episode to other similar stimuli.

The specificity of memory in the mobile conjugate reinforcement paradigm is one feature that has led to the suggestion that the type of memory measured by this technique is different from that assessed through verbal report and other declarative memory paradigms. Rather, as argued by Mandler (1998), the patterns of generalization, extinction and reinstatement are similar to those observed across species in other operant conditioning paradigms. In addition, although the neural substrate that supports the behavior has not been elucidated, C. A. Nelson's (1997) analysis of the paradigm implicates cerebellum and the hippocampus, but not the balance of the temporal-cortical network that supports declarative memory. For these reasons, the memory demonstrated in mobile conjugate reinforcement is thought to be reflective of implicit learning, rather than of declarative memory (e.g. Mandler, 1990; Nelson, 1997; Schneider & Bjorklund, 1998; Squire, Knowlton, & Musen, 1993; although, see Rovee-Collier, 1997, for a different view).

## Deferred imitation

*Deferred imitation* originally was suggested by Piaget (1952) as a hallmark of the development of symbolic thought. Beginning in the mid-1980s, the technique was developed as a test of memory ability in infants and young children (e.g. Bauer & Mandler, 1989; Bauer & Shore, 1987; Meltzoff, 1985). It involves using props to produce a single action or a multi-step sequence, and then, either immediately (elicited imitation), after a delay (deferred imitation), or both, inviting the infant or young child to imitate.

As discussed in detail elsewhere (e.g. Bauer, 2007; Bauer, DeBoer, & Lukowski, 2007; Carver & Bauer, 2001; Mandler, 1990; Meltzoff, 1990; Squire et al., 1993), the conditions of learning and later testing in deferred imitation are conducive to formation of declarative memories but not of non-declarative memories, and the resulting mnemonic behaviors share characteristics of declarative memories. First, infants learn and remember on the basis of a single experience (e.g. Bauer & Hertsgaard, 1993). Rapid learning is a hallmark of declarative memory. Second, as discussed in more detail later, once children acquire the linguistic capacity to do so, they talk about multi-step sequences they experienced as preverbal infants (e.g. Bauer et al., 1998; Cheatham & Bauer, 2005). In contrast, non-declarative memories are not accessible to language.

Third, imitation-based tasks pass the "amnesia test". McDonough, Mandler, McKee and Squire (1995) tested adults with amnesia (in whom declarative memory processes are impaired) and control participants in an imitation-based task using multi-step sequences. Whereas normal adults produced the model's actions even after a delay, patients with amnesia did poorly, performing no better than did control participants who had never seen the events demonstrated. Older children and young adults who were rendered amnesic as a result of pre- or peri-natal insults also show decreased performance on imitation-based tasks (Adlam, Vargha-Khadem, Mishkin, & de Haan, 2005). These findings strongly suggest that although imitation-based tasks are behavioral rather than verbal; they tap declarative memory. For this reason, the data from imitation-based tasks have forced revision of the assumption of a mnemonically incompetent infant. In the next section, I review some of the key developmental changes in infant memory.

## Developments in event memory in infancy

The remainder of this chapter is focused on early development of a particular type of declarative memory, namely, memory for events. As defined by K. Nelson (1986), events "involve people in purposeful activities, and acting on objects and interacting with each other to achieve some result" (p. 11). This definition includes the activities in which individuals engage in a typical day as well as the unique experiences that ultimately define us as individuals: who we are is who we were and what we did. This definition also specifies what there is to be remembered about events, namely, actors, actions, objects and the orders in which the elements combine to achieve specific goals. There are numerous behavioral changes relevant to event memory that occur across infancy and very early childhood. I focus on two of the most salient.

### Changes in temporal extent

Perhaps the most salient change in memory over the first two years of life is in the length of time over which it is apparent. Because like any complex behavior, the length of time an episode is remembered is multiply determined; there is no "growth chart" function that specifies that children of X age should remember for Y long. Nonetheless, across numerous studies there has emerged evidence that with increasing age, infants tolerate lengthier retention intervals. For example, at 6 months of age, infants remember an average of one action of a 3-step sequence (taking a mitten off a puppet's hand, shaking the mitten which, at the time of demonstration, held a bell that rang, and replacing the mitten) for 24 hours (Barr, Dowden, & Hayne, 1996). Collie and Hayne (1999) found that 6-month-olds remembered an average of one out of five possible actions over a 24-hour delay. However, without reminding or reinstatement treatments, the memories of 6-month-old infants do not last beyond a day.

By 9 to 11 months of age, the length of time over which memory for laboratory events is apparent has increased substantially. Nine-month-olds remember individual actions over delays from 24 hours (Meltzoff, 1988b) to five weeks (Carver & Bauer, 1999, 2001). By 10 to 11 months of age, infants remember over delays as long as three months (Carver & Bauer, 2001; Mandler & McDonough, 1995). Thirteen- to fourteen-month-olds remember actions over delays of four to six months (Bauer, Wenner, Dropik, & Wewerka, 2000; Meltzoff, 1995). By 20 months of age, children remember the actions of event sequences over as many as 12 months (Bauer et al., 2000).

Infants also recall the temporal order of actions in multi-step sequences, though retaining order information presents a cognitive challenge to young infants, in particular, as evidenced by low levels of ordered recall and substantial within-age-group variability in the first year. Although 67 percent of 6-month-olds in Barr et al. (1996) remembered some of the actions associated with the puppet sequence over 24 hours, only 25 percent of them remembered actions in the correct temporal order. Collie and Hayne (1999, Experiment 1) reported no ordered recall after 24 hours by 6-month-olds. Among 9-month-olds, approximately 50 percent of infants exhibited ordered reproduction of sequences after a five-week delay (Bauer et al., 2003; Bauer, Wiebe, Waters, & Bangston, 2001; Carver & Bauer, 1999). By 13 months of age, the substantial individual variability in ordered recall has resolved: 78 percent of 13-month-olds exhibit ordered recall after one month. Nevertheless, throughout the second year of life, there are age-related differences in children's recall of the order in which actions of multi-step sequences unfolded. The differences are especially apparent under conditions of greater cognitive demand, such as when less support for recall is provided, and after longer delays (Bauer et al., 2000).

## Changes in the robustness of memory

Over the first two years, there are also changes in the robustness of memory for specific events. For instance, there are changes in the number of experiences that seem to be required in order for infants to remember. In Barr et al. (1996), at 6 months of age, infants required six exposures to events in order to remember these 24 hours later. If, instead, they saw the actions demonstrated only three times, they showed no memory after 24 hours (i.e. the performance of infants who had experienced the puppet sequence did not differ from that of naïve control infants). By 9 months of age, the number of times actions need to be demonstrated to support recall after 24 hours has reduced to three (e.g. Meltzoff, 1988b). Indeed, 9-month-olds who see sequences modeled as few as two times within a single session recall individual actions of them one week later (Bauer et al., 2001). However, over the same delay, ordered recall was observed only among infants who had seen the sequences modeled a total of six times, distributed over three exposure sessions. Three exposure sessions also supports ordered recall over the longer delay of one month. By the time infants are 14 months of age, a single exposure session is all that is necessary to support recall of multiple different single actions over four months (Meltzoff, 1995). Ordered recall of multi-step sequences is apparent after as long as 6 months for infants who received a single exposure to the events at the age of 20 months (Bauer, unpublished data).

Another index of the robustness of memory is the extent to which it is disrupted by interference. One form of interference that has been studied in infancy is changes in context between encoding and retrieval. Reports on infant's sensitivity to contextual changes are mixed. There are some suggestions that recall is disrupted if between exposure and test the appearance of the test materials is changed. For example, in research by Hayne, MacDonald, and Barr (1997), when 18-month-olds experienced the puppet sequence demonstrated on a cow puppet and then were tested with the same puppet, they showed robust retention over 24 hours. However, when they experienced the sequence modeled on a cow puppet and then were tested with a duck puppet, they did not show evidence of memory. Twenty-one-month-olds remembered the sequence whether tested with the same or a different puppet (see also Hayne, Boniface, & Barr, 2000; Herbert & Hayne, 2000).

There also are reports indicating that infants' memories are robust to changes from encoding to test. Infants have been shown to recall events even when there are changes in (a) the size, shape, color, and/or material composition of the objects experienced at encoding versus test (e.g. Bauer & Dow, 1994; Bauer & Fivush, 1992; Lechuga, Marcos-Ruiz, & Bauer, 2001); (b) the appearance of the room at the time of demonstration of modeled actions and at the time of memory test (e.g. Barnat, Klein, & Meltzoff, 1996; Klein & Meltzoff, 1999); (c) the setting for demonstration of the modeled actions and the test of memory for them (e.g. Hanna & Meltzoff, 1993; Klein & Meltzoff, 1999); and (d) the individual who demonstrated the actions and the individual who tested for memory for the actions (e.g. Hanna & Meltzoff). Infants are even able to use 3-dimensional objects to produce events that they have only seen modeled on a television screen (Meltzoff, 1988a; although see Barr & Hayne, 1999). Evidence of flexible recall extends to infants as young as 9 to 11 months of age (e.g. Baldwin, Markman, & Melartin, 1993; Lukowski, Wiebe, & Bauer, 2009; McDonough & Mandler, 1998).

Critically, as tested in imitation-based tasks, the flexibility of memory is not born of forgetting of the features of the original event context. Even as they demonstrate memory using new objects and in different settings, infants remember the features of events. For example, in Bauer and Dow (1994), 16- and 20-month-olds showed above-chance levels of selection of the props used to produce events, even when tested with highly confusable (i.e. functionally equivalent) distracter props. By 20 months of age, memory for the specific objects used to produce multi-step sequences predicts how well the events will be remembered one month later (Bauer & Lukowski, in press). In summary, whereas there is evidence that with age, infants' memories as tested in imitation-based paradigms become more flexible (e.g. Herbert & Hayne, 2000), there is substantial evidence that from an early age, infants' memories survive changes in context and stimuli. As reviewed earlier, with increasing age, infants' memories also last for longer and longer periods of time.

## Mechanisms of age-related changes in event memory

Ultimately, several sources of variance will be implicated in the explanation of age-related changes in event memory. They will range from changes in the neural systems and basic mnemonic processes that permit memories to be formed, retained and later retrieved, to the social forces that shape what children come to view as important to remember and even how they express their memories. In this section, I illustrate some of these mechanisms of change, beginning with a brief review of the neural network understood to subserve event memory in the adult and what is known about its development. I then examine the basic mnemonic processes of encoding, consolidation and retrieval, and evaluate their contributions to age-related changes in long-term recall of events.

### Neural structures supporting declarative memory

Studies of patients with specific types of lesions and disease and animal models thereof, as well as neuroimaging studies, have made clear that registration of experience and formation of event memory traces involve multi-stage processes that depend on networks of neural structures. Specifically encoding, consolidation and later retrieval of declarative memories depends on a multi-component network involving temporal (hippocampus, and entorhinal, parahippocampal and perirhinal cortices) and cortical (including prefrontal and other association areas) structures (e.g. Eichenbaum & Cohen, 2001; Markovitsch, 2000; Zola & Squire, 2000).

Formation or *encoding* of a new declarative memory begins as the elements that constitute an experience register across primary sensory areas (e.g. visual and auditory). Inputs from primary cortices are projected to unimodal association areas where they are integrated into whole percepts of what objects look, feel and sound like. Unimodal association areas, in turn, project to polymodal prefrontal, posterior and limbic association cortices where inputs from the different sense modalities are integrated and maintained over brief delays (see: e.g. Petrides, 1995). For maintenance of traces of experience over delays of longer than a few seconds or minutes, the inputs to the association areas must be stabilized or *consolidated*, a task attributed to medial-temporal structures, in concert with cortical areas (McGaugh, 2000). Specifically, information from association areas converges on perirhinal and parahippocampal structures, from which it is projected to entorhinal cortex and, in turn, to hippocampus. Within the hippocampus, conjunctions and relations among the elements of experience are stabilized into a single event. Association areas share the burden of consolidation, by integrating new memories into long-term storage. Finally, behavioral and neuroimaging data implicate prefrontal cortex in the *retrieval* of memories from long-term storage (see Gilboa, 2004, for a review).

## Development of the neural substrate supporting declarative memory

Developments in the neural substrate supporting declarative memory are summarized in several sources (e.g. Bauer, 2007, 2009, in press; Nelson, 2000; Nelson et al., 2006; Richman & Nelson, 2008). In brief, there are a number of indicators suggesting that, in the human, many components of the medial temporal lobe develop early. For instance, as reviewed by Seress and Abraham (2008), the cells that make up most of the hippocampus are formed in the first half of gestation and virtually all are in their adult locations by the end of the prenatal period. The neurons in most of the hippocampus also begin to connect early in development: synapses are present as early as 15 weeks gestational age. The number and density of synapses both increase rapidly after birth, and reach adult levels by approximately 6 postnatal months. Perhaps as a consequence, glucose utilization in the temporal cortex reaches adult levels at the same time (i.e. by about 6 months: Chugani, 1994; Chugani & Phelps, 1986). Thus, there are several indices of early maturity of major portions of the medial temporal components of the network.

In contrast to early maturation of most of the hippocampus, development of the dentate gyrus of the hippocampus is protracted (Seress & Abraham,

2008). At birth, the dentate gyrus includes only about 70 percent of the adult number of cells. Thus, roughly 30 percent of the cells are produced post-natally. Indeed, neurogenesis in the dentate gyrus of the hippocampus continues throughout childhood and adulthood (Tanapat, Hastings, & Gould, 2001). It is not until 12 to 15 postnatal months that the morphology of the structure appears adult-like. Maximum density of synaptic connections in the dentate gyrus is also delayed, relative to that in the other regions of the hippocampus. In humans, synaptic density increases dramatically (to well above adult levels) beginning at 8 to 12 postnatal months and reaches its peak at 16 to 20 months. After a period of relative stability, excess synapses are pruned until adult levels are reached at about 4 to 5 years of age (Eckenhoff & Rakic, 1991).

The association areas also undergo a protracted course of development (Bachevalier, 2001). For example, it is not until the seventh prenatal month that all six cortical layers are apparent. Synaptic density in prefrontal cortex increases dramatically at eight postnatal months, and peaks between 15 and 24 months. Pruning to adult levels does not begin until late childhood; adult levels are not reached until late adolescence or early adulthood (Huttenlocher, 1979; Huttenlocher & Dabholkar, 1997; see Bourgeois, 2001, for discussion). In the years between, in some cortical layers there are changes in the size of cells and the lengths and branching of dendrites (Benes, 2001). Although the maximum density of synapses may be reached as early as 15 postnatal months, it is not until 24 months that synapses develop adult morphology (Huttenlocher, 1979). There also are changes in glucose utilization and blood flow over the second half of the first year and into the second year: blood flow and glucose utilization increase above adult levels by 8 to 12, and 13 to 14 months of age, respectively (Chugani, Phelps, & Mazziotta, 1987). Other maturational changes in pre-frontal cortex, such as myelination, continue into adolescence, and adult levels of some neurotransmitters are not seen until the second and third decades of life (Benes, 2001). It is not until adolescence that neurotransmitters such as acetylcholine reach adult levels (discussed in Benes, 2001).

Although much of the attention to developmental changes has focused on the medial-temporal and prefrontal regions, there also are age-related changes in the lateral temporal and parietal cortices. Cortical gray matter changes occur earlier in the frontal and occipital poles, relative to the rest of the cortex, which matures in a parietal-to-frontal direction. The super-ior temporal cortex is last to mature (though the temporal poles mature early; Gogtay et al., 2004). The late development of this portion of cortex is potentially significant for memory, as it is one of the polymodal asso-ciation areas that plays a role in integration of information across sense modalities.

## Functional consequences of development of the neural substrate

Because the full network that supports declarative memory in the human involves medial temporal and cortical components, it can be expected to function as an integrated whole only once each of its components, as well as the connections between them, has reached a level of functional maturity. "Functional maturity" may be said to be reached as the number of synapses reaches its peak; "full maturity" is achieved as the number of synapses is pruned to adult levels (Goldman-Rakic, 1987). Adoption of this metric leads to the prediction of the emergence of declarative memory by late in the first year of life, with significant development over the course of the second year, and continued development for years thereafter (see Barbas, 2000; Fuster, 2002, for discussion). The time frame is based on increases in synaptogenesis from 8 to 20 months in the dentate gyrus (Eckenhoff & Rakic, 1991), and from 8 to 24 months in the prefrontal cortex (Huttenlocher, 1979; Huttenlocher & Dabholkar, 1997). The expectation of developmental changes for months and years thereafter stems from the schedule of protracted pruning both in the dentate gyrus (until 4 to 5 years; e.g. Eckenhoff & Rakic, 1991) and in the prefrontal cortex (throughout adolescence; e.g. Huttenlocher & Dabholkar, 1997), as well as continued age-related changes in both gray and white matter volume and connectivity throughout the first two decades of life (e.g. Caviness et al., 1996; Giedd et al., 1999; Gogtay et al., 2004; Sowell et al., 2004).

What are the consequences for behavior of the slow course of development of the neural network that supports declarative memory? At a general level, we may expect concomitant behavioral development: As the neural substrate develops, so does behavior (and vice versa, of course). But precisely how do changes in the medial temporal and cortical structures, and their interconnections, produce changes in behavior? In other words, how do they affect memory representations? To address this question, we must consider the basic processes involved in memory trace formation, encoding, storage and retrieval, and how the "recipe" for a memory might be affected by changes in the underlying neural substrate. In other words, we must consider how developmental changes in the substrate for memory relate to changes in the efficacy and efficiency with which information is encoded and stabilized for long-term storage and in the reliability and ease with which it is retrieved.

## Basic cognitive and mnemonic processes

The main "stages" in the life of a memory are encoding, consolidation and retrieval. With developmental changes in the neural substrate that supports these processes, we may expect concomitant behavioral changes. Although the processes are difficult to separate cleanly from one another (e.g. when encoding ends and consolidation begins is a challenging question to address), they do build on one another and, thus, are described in the nominal order in which they occur: encoding, consolidation and retrieval.

## *Encoding*

As just described, association cortices are involved in the initial registration and temporary maintenance of experience. Because prefrontal cortex, in particular, undergoes considerable postnatal development, it is reasonable to expect that neurodevelopmental changes in it relate to age-related changes in the speed and efficiency with which information is encoded into long-term storage. Consistent with this suggestion, in a longitudinal study, my colleagues and I (Bauer et al., 2006) found age-related changes in the robustness of encoding as measured by event-related potentials (ERPs). At each of two ages – 9 months of age and 10 months of age – infants were exposed to event sequences, and immediately thereafter we used ERP to test their recognition of the props used to produce the events, as a measure of encoding. One month later, we tested the infants' recall of the events. Relative to their responses as 9-month-olds, 10-month-olds showed more robust recognition responses to familiar stimuli immediately after experience of them. The infants also showed more robust long-term recall of events encoded at 10 months of age, relative to events encoded at 9 months of age. Behavioral data also indicate developments in encoding throughout the second year of life. For example, relative to 15-month-olds, 12-month-olds require more trials to learn multi-step events to a criterion (learning to a criterion indicates that the material was fully encoded). In turn, 15-month-olds are slower to achieve criterion, relative to 18-month-olds (Howe & Courage, 1997). Indeed, across development, older children learn more rapidly than do younger children (Howe & Brainerd, 1989).

## *Consolidation*

As reviewed earlier, medial-temporal structures are implicated in the processes by which new memories become "fixed" for long-term storage; cortical association areas are the presumed repositories for long-term memories. In a fully mature, intact adult, the changes in synaptic connectivity associated with memory trace consolidation continue for hours, weeks, and even months, after an event. Memory traces are vulnerable throughout this time: lesions inflicted during the period of consolidation result in deficits in memory, whereas lesions inflicted after a trace has been consolidated do not (e.g. Kim & Fanselow, 1992; Takehara, Kawahara, & Kirino, 2003).

For the developing organism, the road to a consolidated memory trace may be a bumpier one, relative to that traveled by the adult. Not only are some of the implicated neural structures relatively undeveloped (i.e. dentate gyrus and prefrontal cortex), but the connections between them are still being sculpted and, thus, are less than fully effective and efficient. As a consequence, even once children have successfully encoded an event, as evidenced by achievement of a criterion level of learning, for example, they remain vulnerable to forgetting. Younger children may be more vulnerable to forgetting, relative to older children (Bauer, 2004, 2005).

To examine the role of consolidation processes in long-term memory in 9-month-old infants, Bauer et al. (2003) combined ERP measures of immediate recognition (as an index of encoding), ERP measures of one-week delayed recognition (as an index of consolidation), and deferred imitation measures of recall after one month. After the delay, 46 percent of the infants evidenced ordered recall of the sequences, and 54 percent did not. At the immediate ERP test, regardless of whether they subsequently recalled the events, the infants evidenced recognition: Their ERP responses were different with the old and new stimuli. This strongly implies that the infants had encoded the events. Nevertheless, one week later, at the delayed recognition test, the infants who would go on to recall the events recognized the props, whereas infants who would not evidence ordered recall did not. Thus, in spite of having encoded the events, a subset of 9-month-olds failed to recognize them after one week and subsequently failed to recall them after one month. Moreover, the size of the difference in delayed-recognition response predicted recall performance one month later. Thus, infants who had stronger memory representations after a one-week delay exhibited higher levels of recall one month later. The pattern is a replication of Carver, Bauer and Nelson (2000). These data strongly imply that at 9 months of age, consolidation and/or storage process are a source of individual differences in mnemonic performance.

In the second year of life, there are behavioral suggestions of between-age group differences in consolidation and/or storage processes, as well as a replication of the finding among 9-month-olds that intermediate-term consolidation and/or storage failure relates to recall over the long term. In Bauer, Cheatham, Cary and Van Abbema (2002), 16- and 20-month-olds were exposed to multi-step events and tested for recall immediately (as a measure of encoding) and after 24 hours. Over the delay, the younger children forgot a substantial amount of the information they had encoded: they produced only 65 percent of the target actions and only 57 percent of the ordered pairs of actions that they had learned just 24 hours earlier. For the older children, the amount of forgetting over the delay was not statistically reliable. It is not until 48 hours that children 20 months of age exhibit significant forgetting (Bauer, Van Abbema, & deHaan, 1999). These observations suggest age-related differences in the vulnerability of memory traces during the initial period of consolidation.

The vulnerability of memory traces during the initial period of consolidation is related to the robustness of recall after one month. This is apparent from another of the experiments in Bauer et al. (2002), one involving 20-month-olds only. The children were exposed to multi-step events and were then immediately tested for memory for some of the events, then for some of the events after 48 hours (a delay after which, based on Bauer et al., 1999, some forgetting was expected), and some of the events after one month. Although the children exhibited high levels of initial encoding (as measured by immediate recall), they nevertheless exhibited significant forgetting after both 48 hours and one month. The robustness of memory after 48 hours predicted 25 percent of the variance in recall one month later; variability in level of encoding did not predict significant variance. This effect is a conceptual replication of that observed with 9-month-olds in Bauer et al. (2003; see Bauer, 2005, and Howe & Courage, 1997, for additional evidence of a role for post-encoding processes in long-term recall). The findings that infants who are "good consolidators" have high levels of long-term recall are reminiscent of Bosshardt et al. (2005) with adults: fMRI activations one day after learning were predictive of forgetting one month later.

## Retrieval

Retrieval of memories from long-term storage sites is thought to depend on prefrontal cortex. Prefrontal cortex undergoes a long period of postnatal development, making it a likely candidate source of age-related differences in long-term recall. Yet although retrieval processes are a compelling candidate source of developmental differences in long-term recall, there are few data with which to evaluate their contribution. A major reason is that most studies do not allow for assignment of relative roles of the processes that take place before retrieval, namely, encoding and consolidation. As discussed in the section on encoding, older children learn more rapidly than younger children. Yet age-related differences in encoding effectiveness rarely are taken into account. In fact, in many studies of long-term recall, no measures of encoding or initial learning are obtained (i.e. imitation is deferred until the long-term recall test). In addition, with standard testing procedures, it is difficult to know whether a memory representation has lost its integrity and become unavailable (consolidation and storage failure) or whether the memory trace remains intact but has become inaccessible with the cues provided (retrieval failure). Implication of retrieval processes as a source of developmental change requires that encoding be controlled and that memory be tested under conditions of high support for retrieval.

In the infancy period, one of the studies that permits assessment of the contributions of consolidation and/or storage relative to retrieval processes is Bauer et al. (2000; see also Bauer et al., 2003, described earlier). The study provided data on children of multiple ages (13, 16, and 20 months) tested over a range of delays (one to 12 months). Because immediate recall of half of the events was tested, measures of encoding are available. Because the children were given what amounted to multiple test trials, without intervening study trials, there were multiple opportunities for retrieval. As discussed by Howe and his colleagues (e.g. Howe & Brainerd, 1989; Howe & O'Sullivan, 1997), the first test trial could be expected to initiate a retrieval attempt. If a memory trace remained and was at a reasonably high level of accessibility, the event would be recalled. If, on the other hand, a memory trace remained but was relatively inaccessible, the retrieval would strengthen the trace and route to retrieval of it, increasing accessibility on the second test trial. Conversely, lack of improvement across test trials would imply that the trace was no longer available (although see Howe & O'Sullivan, 1997, for multiple nuances of this argument). Third, relearning was tested immediately after the recall tests. That is, after the second test trial, the experimenter demonstrated each event once, and allowed the children to imitate. Since Ebbinghaus (1885), relearning has been used to distinguish between an intact but inaccessible memory trace and a trace that has disintegrated. Specifically, if the number of trials required to relearn a stimulus was smaller than the number required to learn it initially, savings in relearning was said to have occurred. Savings presumably accrues because the products of relearning are integrated with an existing (though not necessarily accessible) memory trace. Conversely, the absence of savings is attributed to storage failure: there is no residual trace upon which to build. In developmental studies, age-related differences in relearning would suggest that the residual memory traces available to children of different ages are differentially intact.

To eliminate encoding processes as a potential source of developmental differences in long-term recall, in a re-analysis of the data from Bauer et al. (2000), subsets of 13- and 16-month-olds and subsets of 16- and 20-month-olds were matched for levels of encoding (as measured by immediate recall; Bauer, 2005). The amount of information the children forgot over the delays then was examined. For both comparisons, even though they were matched for levels of encoding, younger children exhibited more forgetting relative to older children. The age effect was apparent on both test trials. Moreover, in both cases, for older children, levels of performance after the single relearning trial were as high as those at initial learning. In contrast, for younger children, performance after the relearning trial was lower than at initial learning. Together, the findings of age-related differential loss of information over time and of age effects in relearning strongly implicate storage, as opposed to retrieval processes, as the major source of age-related differences in long-term recall.

This line of reasoning implies that we should reconsider the role in memory development played by age-related changes in prefrontal cortex (Bauer, 2007). Rather than on retrieval processes, a major effect of developments in prefrontal structures may be on consolidation processes. Consolidation is an interactive process between medial-temporal and cortical structures. As such, changes in cortical structures may be as important to developments in consolidation processes as are changes in medial-temporal structures. Moreover, the ultimate storage sites for long-term memories are the association cortices. Prefrontal cortex is thought to play an especially significant role in storage of information about the *where* and *when* of events and experiences, the very features that distinguish experiences from one another. Thus, developmental changes in prefrontal cortex may play their primary role in supporting more efficient and effective consolidation; their role in improving retrieval processes may be secondary.

## Later verbal accessibility of early event memories

As noted at the beginning of this chapter, historically, it was thought that there was substantial discontinuity in memory development, such that pre-school age and older children had the ability to remember past events, whereas infants did not. Data indicating long-term declarative memory in infants make clear that this assumption was unwarranted: by the end of the second year of life, declarative memory is both long-term and robust. Moreover, by some metrics, the neural substrate that supports declarative memory can be considered to be functionally (though not fully) mature (with functional maturity marked by the rise to peak number of synapses in the neural structures that subserve declarative memory: Goldman-Rakic, 1987). These observations beg the question of the source of a major apparent discontinuity between early and later memory, namely, between nonverbal and verbal accessibility of memories formed early in life. By the time children are 3 years of age, they demonstrate verbal recall of past events. Yet verbal children do not use their language to talk about events from the time before language. It is as if events and experiences encoded without the benefit of language remain inaccessible to it. And, of course, verbal inaccessibility of early memories among adults is one of the hallmarks of infantile or childhood amnesia.

Historically, the difference in the mode of expression of memory – exclusively verbal in infancy and primarily verbal in childhood – has had profound implications for conclusions about the continued accessibility of very early memories. Following Nelson and Ross (1980), Pillemer and White (1989,

p. 321) argue that, if young children are able to recall specific past events over long periods of time, then their "memories should not only be express-ible through behavior, they also should become verbally expressible when the child has the ability to reconstruct preverbal events in narrative form." What evidence bears on the issue of children's ability to express their early mem-ories verbally? It is clear that children can provide verbal reports of events experienced in the distant past (see Fivush, 1997, for a review). Indeed, it was in part this fact that provided the original impetus for research on pre- and early-verbal children's event memory. However, a striking characteristic of these early reports is the amount of work that an interviewer must do to obtain them. In Hamond and Fivush (1991), for example, fully 78 percent of the information provided by the 3- to 5-year-old participants was elicited in response to direct questions and prompts provided by the interviewer.

Evidence of the difficulty that even younger children have verbally express-ing their memories of past events is apparent in Peterson and Rideout (1998). The researchers interviewed children about their memories for emergency room procedures necessitated by accidents. The accidents occurred when the children were between 13 and 35 months of age; the interviews were con-ducted shortly after the children's visits to the emergency room, and then again 6 months, 12 months, and 18 or 24 months later. Children who were 26 months of age or older at the time of the experience were able to provide ver-bal reports at all of the delays. Although they had not been able to talk about their experiences at the time, children who were injured at between 20 and 25 months were able to provide verbal reports at the six-month interview. Some of the children maintained verbal accessibility of their memories over subse-quent delays between interviews. In contrast, children who were 18 months of age or younger at the time of their injuries were unable to provide verbal accounts of their experiences, even though, at the later interviews, they had the language ability to do so. These data seem to suggest that, regardless of later verbal facility, children younger than 18 months at the time of experi-ence are not able to talk about past events. Children slightly older are able to, but there is no assurance that verbal accessibility will be maintained.

Young children's difficulty in talking about the past stands in sharp con-trast to their rapidly developing ability to talk about the "here and now". This has led to the suggestion that it is the decontextualized nature of the circum-stances under which verbal reports of the past typically are elicited that makes it difficult for young children to produce them (Bauer & Wewerka, 1997). Consider that in Peterson and Rideout (1998), as in most studies of verbal expression of memory, at the time of the report, the children were not only temporally, but also spatially, separated from the to-be-recalled material. The children were provided a verbal prompt about the event but there is evidence to suggest that verbal prompts alone may not be effective retrieval cues for children younger than 3 (Hudson, 1991, 1993). If it is the decontextualized nature of the activity that limits young children's ability to talk about the past, then "contextualizing" the task, by allowing children to return to the physical location of a previous experience, for example, should facilitate verbal expression of memory.

Although relevant data are not plentiful, there is evidence that with contextual support, children are able to talk about events from the distant past. For example, in Bauer et al. (1998; see also Bauer & Wewerka, 1995, 1997), we analyzed the spontaneous verbal expressions of some of the 16- and 20-month-olds who had taken part in Bauer et al. (2000). At the time of test, the children were between 22 and 32 months of age. Although the researchers did not elicit them, the children spontaneously produced verbalizations over the course of the session. Some of the verbalizations were indicative of memory for the past events. Thus, in supportive context, even after long delays, children spontaneously expressed their memories (see Myers, Clifton, & Clarkson, 1987, for another example of verbal expression of preverbal memory; and Nelson & Ross, 1980, and Todd & Perlmutter, 1980, for examples derived from parental diary reports of early mnemonic behavior). Measures of concurrent verbal fluency accounted for 35 percent of the variance in spontaneous mnemonic expression.

Suggestively, age at the time of experience of an event may take on an increasingly important role as the interval between experience of an event and verbal expression of it increases. At 36 to 42 months of age, the children who participated in Bauer et al. (1998) returned to the supportive context of the laboratory once again. This time, they were explicitly probed for verbal memories of the events. The children who had been enrolled at 16 months of age did not maintain verbally accessible memories into the fourth year of life. In contrast, the children who had been 20 months at the time of the original experience subsequently provided verbal reports about the events. What predicted verbal expression was not concurrent language ability, but previous mnemonic expression. Thus, when memory is queried in decontextualized circumstances, age or verbal fluency at the time of experience may be a major determinant of later verbal accessibility (e.g. Peterson & Rideout, 1998). In contrast, in supportive context, concurrent verbal facility permits linguistic augmentation of event representations originally encoded without the benefit of language; previous verbal mnemonic expression aids in the long-term maintenance of verbal accessibility (Bauer et al., 1998). These data clearly indicate that the transition from explicitly nonverbal to primarily verbal expression of memory is not reflective of a fundamental change in the nature of memory. Declarative memory develops early in life and, under the right circumstances, memories from infancy persist into the preschool years and can be expressed through language.

# Conclusion

Historically, declarative memory was thought to be relatively late to develop. Research in the last decades of the twentieth century made clear that the assumption was unwarranted. Contrary to earlier suggestions that children of preschool age were poor mnemonists and to speculations that younger children and infants were no mnemonists at all, it now is clear that from early in life, the human organism stores information over the long term and that the effects of prior experience are apparent in behavior. In the first months of life, infants exhibit recognition memory for all manner of natural and artificial stimuli. Recognition memory is apparent over delays of as long as three months (e.g. Bahrick, Hernandez-Reif, & Pickens, 1997; Bahrick & Pickens, 1995; Courage & Howe, 1998). Whether or not the recognition memory behaviors exhibited by very young infants index the same type of memory as tapped by verbal recognition paradigms used with older children and adults (see Mandler, 1998; and Nelson, 1997; Snyder, 2007; for discussion), the mnemonic feats that they perform make clear that the human organism is, from birth, exquisitely prepared to benefit from its experiences.

Elicited and deferred imitation procedures provide a means of examining questions of continuity and discontinuity in mnemonic processes from infancy through early childhood and beyond. By 6 months of age, infants demonstrate recall memory over the short term (Barr et al., 1996). By 9 months of age, they not only demonstrate retention over long delays, but a substantial number of infants also evidence ordered recall (Bauer et al., 2003, 2006; Carver & Bauer, 1999). Over the course of the second year of life, there are age-related changes in the temporal extent and robustness of event memory, suggesting the coalescence of declarative mnemonic processes (Bauer et al., 2000).

Like any complex behavior, the development of declarative memory is multiply. One of the rate-limiting variables in its development is the neural substrate that permits new memories to be encoded, consolidated and later retrieved. Aspects of the substrate develop early whereas others have a more protracted developmental course. The functional consequences of changes in the neural substrate are apparent in age-related differences in encoding and consolidation processes throughout the first and second years of life. Though retrieval processes long have been a compelling candidate source of developmental differences in long-term recall, currently available data imply that substantial variance is explained by the earlier-stage processes. It will be left to future research to chronicle the dynamic contributions of each stage in the life of a memory over the course of development.

A vitally important question about early memories is whether they later are verbally accessible. Although the body of relevant research is small, that which does exist suggests that when children are required to report on experiences without the benefit of contextual support for recall, verbal ability at the time of experience of an event determines whether it later will be verbally accessible (e.g. Peterson & Rideout, 1998). When children are permitted to report on experiences supported by props and a familiar context, later verbal accessibility is determined by concurrent language ability and by previous verbal mnemonic expression (Bauer et al., 1998). These findings inform the question of why so few memories from early in life later are verbally accessible: Rarely is the context in which an event occurred re-experienced. Because a rather restricted range of conditions effectively reinstate memories for younger children (e.g. Hudson & Sheffield, 1998), it is uncommon for the representation of an event and newly acquired language to describe it to be available at the same time (see Bauer, 2007, for discussion).

What are the implications of the work reviewed in this chapter for the accuracy and reliability with which very young children can be expected to report on past events? In infancy, the length of time over which events are remembered is restricted, as are the conditions under which memories later are retrieved and "translated" for verbal report. Moreover, there are strong suggestions that the lack of later accessibility is not due to difficulties with retrieval alone. Instead, it seems that the very processes by which experiences are translated into enduring memory traces are not as efficient in infancy as they are in older children and adults, due to immaturity of the neural substrate supporting recall. As a result, transient patterns of neural activation that correspond to events and experiences are not effectively consolidated into enduring traces that become incorporated into long-term memory. In other words, memory fails because storage fails and when storage fails, there is no trace to retrieve (see Bauer, 2005, for discussion). These outcomes are not absolute – some memories do endure, even over long periods of time. Yet, in general, the younger the infant or child at the time of experience, the more imposing the limits on memory trace formation and later accessibility.

The singular noun – *memory* – gives the impression that memory is a unitary construct. On the contrary, there are many different types and kinds of memory, each with its own characteristics and developmental course. Continued progress in understanding memory and its development requires careful consideration of the type of memory under study and its determinants. As we work to explain remembering and forgetting, we must keep in mind that its determinants likely shift over the course of development. Recognition of the fact that just as behavior changes, so, too, do the explanatory mechanisms, stands to improve the questions that we ask and as a result, the answers that we achieve.

# References

Adlam, A-L. R., Vargha-Khadem, F., Mishkin, M., & de Haan, M. (2005). Deferred imitation of action sequences in developmental amnesia. *Journal of Cognitive Neuroscience, 17*, 240–248.

Bachevalier, J. (2001). Neural bases of memory development: Insights from neuropsychological studies in primates. In C. A. Nelson & M. Luciana (Eds), *Handbook of Developmental Cognitive Neuroscience* (pp. 365–379). Cambridge, MA: The MIT Press.

Bahrick, L. E., Hernandez-Reif, M., & Pickens, J. N. (1997). The effect of retrieval cues on visual preferences and memory in infancy: Evidence for a four-phase attention function. *Journal of Experimental Child Psychology, 67*, 1–20.

Bahrick, L. E., & Pickens, J. N. (1995). Infant memory for object motion across a period of three months: Implications for a four-phase attention function. *Journal of Experimental Child Psychology, 59*, 343–371.

Baldwin, D. A., Markman, E. M., & Melartin, R. L. (1993). Infants' ability to draw inferences about nonobvious object properties: Evidence from exploratory play. *Child Development, 64*, 711–728.

Barbas, H. (2000). Connections underlying the synthesis of cognition, memory, and emotion in primate prefrontal cortices. *Brain Research Bulletin, 52*, 319–330.

Barnat, S. B., Klein, P. J., & Meltzoff, A. N. (1996). Deferred imitation across changes in context and object: Memory and generalization in 14-month-old children. *Infant Behavior and Development, 19*, 241–251.

Barr, R., Dowden, A., & Hayne, H. (1996). Developmental change in deferred imitation by 6- to 24-month-old infants. *Infant Behavior and Development, 19*, 159–170.

Barr, R., & Hayne, H. (1999). Developmental changes in imitation from television during infancy. *Child Development, 70*, 1067–1081.

Bauer, P. J. (in press). Memory. To appear in P. D. Zelazo (Ed.), *Oxford Handbook of Developmental Psychology*. New York, NY: Oxford University Press.

Bauer, P. J. (2004). New developments in the study of infant memory. In D. M. Teti (Ed.), *Blackwell Handbook of Research Methods in Developmental Science* (pp. 467–488). Oxford, United Kingdom: Blackwell Publishing.

Bauer, P. J. (2005). Developments in declarative memory: Decreasing susceptibility to storage failure over the second year of life. *Psychological Science, 16*, 41–47.

Bauer, P. J. (2006). Event memory. In D. Kuhn & R. Siegler (Volume Editors) *Cognition, Perception, and Language*, Volume 2, of W. Damon & R.M. Lerner (Editors-in-Chief). *Handbook of Child Psychology*, Sixth Edition (pp. 373–425). Hoboken, NJ: John Wiley & Sons, Inc.

Bauer, P. J. (2007). *Remembering the Times of Our Lives: Memory in Infancy and Beyond.* Mahwah, NJ: Erlbaum.

Bauer, P. J. (2009). The cognitive neuroscience of the development of memory. In M. L. Courage and N. Cowan (Eds), *The Development of Memory in Infancy and Childhood*, Second Edition (pp. 115–144). New York, NY: Psychology Press.

Bauer, P. J., Cheatham, C. L., Cary, M. S., & Van Abbema, D. L. (2002). Short-term forgetting: Charting its course and its implications for long-term remembering. In S. P. Shohov (Ed.), *Advances in Psychology Research*. Volume 9 (pp. 53–74). Huntington, NY: Nova Science Publishers.

Bauer, P. J., DeBoer, T., & Lukowski, A. F. (2007). In the language of multiple memory systems, defining and describing developments in long-term declarative memory. In L. M. Oakes & P. J. Bauer (Eds), *Short- and Long-term Memory in Infancy and Early Childhood: Taking the First Steps toward Remembering* (pp. 240–270). New York, NY: Oxford University Press.

Bauer, P. J., & Dow, G. A. A. (1994). Episodic memory in 16- and 20-month-old children: Specifics are generalized, but not forgotten. *Developmental Psychology, 30,* 403–417.

Bauer, P. J., & Fivush, R. (1992). Constructing event representations: Building on a foundation of variation and enabling relations. *Cognitive Development, 7,* 381–401.

Bauer, P. J., & Hertsgaard, L. A. (1993). Increasing steps in recall of events: Factors facilitating immediate and long-term memory in 13.5- and 16.5-month-old children. *Child Development, 64,* 1204–1223.

Bauer, P. J., Kroupina, M. G., Schwade, J. A., Dropik, P. L., & Wewerka, S. S. (1998). If memory serves, will language? Later verbal accessibility of early memories. *Development and Psychopathology, 10,* 655–679.

Bauer, P. J., & Lukowski, A. F. (in press). The memory is in the details: Relations between memory for the specific features of events and long-term recall in infancy. *Journal of Experimental Child Psychology.*

Bauer, P. J., & Mandler, J. M. (1989). One thing follows another: Effects of temporal structure on one- to two-year-olds' recall of events. *Developmental Psychology, 25,* 197–206.

Bauer, P. J., & Shore, C. M. (1987). Making a memorable event: Effects of familiarity and organization on young children's recall of action sequences. *Cognitive Development, 2,* 327–338.

Bauer, P. J., Van Abbema, D. L., & de Haan, M. (1999). In for the short haul: Immediate and short-term remembering and forgetting by 20-month-old children. *Infant Behavior and Development, 22,* 321–343.

Bauer, P. J., Wenner, J. A., Dropik, P. L., & Wewerka, S. S. (2000). Parameters of remembering and forgetting in the transition from infancy to early childhood. *Monographs of the Society for Research in Child Development, 65* (4), Serial No. 263.

Bauer, P. J., & Wewerka, S. S. (1995). One- to two-year-olds' recall of events: The more expressed, the more impressed. *Journal of Experimental Child Psychology, 59,* 475–496.

Bauer, P. J., & Wewerka, S. S. (1997). Saying is revealing: Verbal expression of event memory in the transition from infancy to early childhood. In P. van den Broek, P. J. Bauer, & T. Bourg (Eds), *Developmental Spans in Event Comprehension and Representation: Bridging Fictional and Actual Events* (pp. 139–168). Mahwah, NJ: Erlbaum.

Bauer, P. J., Wiebe, S. A., Carver, L. J., Lukowski, A. F., Haight, J. C., Waters, J. M., & Nelson, C. A. (2006). Electrophysiological indices of encoding and behavioral indices of recall: Examining relations and developmental change late in the first year of life. *Developmental Neuropsychology, 29,* 293–320.

Bauer, P. J., Wiebe, S. A., Carver, L. J., Waters, J. M., & Nelson, C. A. (2003). Developments in long-term explicit memory late in the first year of life: Behavioral and electrophysiological indices. *Psychological Science, 14,* 629–635.

Bauer, P. J., Wiebe, S. A., Waters, J. M., & Bangston, S. K. (2001). Re-exposure breeds recall: Effects of experience on 9-month-olds' ordered recall. *Journal of Experimental Child Psychology, 80,* 174–200.

Benes, F. M. (2001). The development of prefrontal cortex: The maturation of neurotransmitter systems and their interaction. In C. A. Nelson & M. Luciana (Eds), *Handbook of Developmental Cognitive Neuroscience* (pp. 79–92). Cambridge, MA: The MIT Press.

Borovsky, D., & Rovee-Collier, C. (1990). Contextual constraints on memory retrieval at six months. *Child Development, 61,* 1569–1583.

Bosshardt, S., Degonda, N., Schmidt, C. F., Boesiger, P., Nitsch, R. M., Hock, C., & Henke, K. (2005). One month of human memory consolidation enhances retrieval-related hippocampal activity. *Hippocampus, 15,* 1026–1040.

Bourgeois, J.-P. (2001). Synaptogenesis in the neocortex of the newborn: The ultimate frontier for individuation? In C.A. Nelson & M. Luciana (Eds), *Handbook of Developmental Cognitive Neuroscience* (pp. 23–34). Cambridge, MA: The MIT Press.

Carver, L. J., & Bauer, P. J. (1999). When the event is more than the sum of its parts: Nine-month-olds' long-term ordered recall. *Memory, 7*, 147–174.

Carver, L. J., & Bauer, P. J. (2001). The dawning of a past: The emergence of long-term explicit memory in infancy. *Journal of Experimental Psychology: General, 130*, 726–745.

Carver, L. J., Bauer, P. J., & Nelson, C. A. (2000). Associations between infant brain activity and recall memory. *Developmental Science, 3*, 234–246.

Caviness, V. S., Kennedy, D. N., Richelme, C., Rademacher, J., & Filipek, P. A. (1996). The human brain age 7–11 years: A volumetric analysis based on magnetic resonance images. *Cerebral Cortex, 6*, 726–736.

Cheatham, C. L., & Bauer, P. J. (2005). Construction of a more coherent story: Prior verbal recall predicts later verbal accessibility of early memories. *Memory, 13*, 516–532.

Chugani, H. T. (1994). Development of regional blood glucose metabolism in relation to behavior and plasticity. In G. Dawson & K. Fischer (Eds), *Human Behavior and the Developing Brain* (pp. 153–175). New York: Guilford.

Chugani, H. T., & Phelps, M. E. (1986). Maturational changes in cerebral function determined by 18FDG positron emission tomography. *Science, 231*, 840–843.

Chugani, H. T., Phelps, M., & Mazziotta, J. (1987). Positron emission tomography study of human brain functional development. *Annals of Neurology, 22*, 487–497.

Collie, R., & Hayne, H. (1999). Deferred imitation by 6- and 9-month-old infants: More evidence of declarative memory. *Developmental Psychobiology, 35*, 83–90.

Courage, M. L., & Howe, M. L. (1998). The ebb and flow of infant attentional preferences: Evidence for long-term recognition memory in 3-month-olds. *Journal of Experimental Child Psychology, 70*, 26–53.

Ebbinghaus, H. (1885). *On memory* (H. A. Ruger & C. E. Bussenius, Translators). New York: Teachers' College, 1913. Paperback edition, New York: Dover, 1964.

Eckenhoff, M., & Rakic, P. (1991). A quantitative analysis of synaptogenesis in the molecular layer of the dentate gyrus in the rhesus monkey. *Developmental Brain Research, 64*, 129–135.

Eichenbaum, H. & Cohen, N. J. (2001). *From Conditioning to Conscious Recollection: Memory Systems of the Brain*. New York: Oxford University Press.

Fivush, R. (1997). Event memory in early childhood. In N. Cowan (Ed.), *The Development of Memory in Childhood* (pp. 139–161). Hove East Sussex: Psychology Press.

Freud, S. (1905/1953). Childhood and concealing memories. In *The basic writings of Sigmund Freud* (A. A. Brill, Trans. & Ed.). New York: The Modern Library.

Fuster, J. M. (2002). Frontal lobe and cognitive development. *Journal of Neurocytology, 31*, 373–385.

Giedd, J. N., Blumenthal, J., Jeffries, N. O., Castellanos, F. X., Liu, H., & Zijdenbos, A., Paus, T., Evans, A. C., & Rapoport, J. L. (1999). Brain development during childhood and adolescence: A longitudinal MRI study. *Nature Neuroscience, 2*, 861–863.

Gilboa, A. (2004). Autobiographical and episodic memory – one and the same? Evidence from prefrontal activation in neuroimaging studies. *Neuropsychologia, 42*, 1336–1349.

Gogtay, N., Giedd, J. N., Lusk, L., Hayashi, K. M., Greenstein, D., Vaituzis, A. C., Nugent, T. F., Herman, D. H., Clasen, L. S., Toga, A. W., Rapoport, J. L., & Thompson, P. M. (2004). Dynamic mapping of human cortical development during childhood through early adulthood. *PNAS, 101*, 8174–8179.

Goldman-Rakic, P. S. (1987). Circuitry of primate prefrontal cortex and regulation of behavior by representational memory. In F. Plum (Ed.), *Handbook of Physiology, the Nervous System, Higher Functions of the Brain*, Volume 5 (pp. 373–417). Bethesda, MD: American Physiological Society.

Hamond, N. R., & Fivush, R. (1991). Memories of Mickey Mouse: Young children recount their trip to Disneyworld. *Cognitive Development, 6*, 433–448.

Hanna, E., & Meltzoff, A. N. (1993). Peer imitation by toddlers in laboratory, home, and day-care contexts: Implications for social learning and memory. *Developmental Psychology, 29*, 702–710.

Hayne, H., Boniface, J., & Barr, R. (2000). The development of declarative memory in human infants: Age-related changes in deferred imitation. *Behavioral Neuroscience, 114*, 77–83.

Hayne, H., MacDonald, S., & Barr, R. (1997). Developmental changes in the specificity of memory over the second year of lie. *Infant Behavior and Development, 20*, 233–245.

Herbert, J., & Hayne, H. (2000). Memory retrieval by 18–30-month-olds: Age-related changes in representational flexibility. *Developmental Psychology, 36*, 473–484.

Hill, W.L., Borovsky, D., & Rovee-Collier, C. (1988). Continuities in infant memory development. *Developmental Psychobiology, 21*, 43–62.

Howe, M. L., & Brainerd, C. J. (1989). Development of children's long-term retention. *Developmental Review, 9*, 301–340.

Howe, M. L., & Courage, M. L. (1997). Independent paths in the development of infant learning and forgetting. *Journal of Experimental Child Psychology, 67*, 131–163.

Howe, M. L., & O'Sullivan, J. T. (1997). What children's memories tell us about recalling our childhoods: A review of storage and retrieval processes in the development of long-term retention. *Developmental Review, 17*, 148–204.

Hudson, J. A. (1991). Learning to reminisce: A case study. *Journal of Narrative and Life History, 1*, 295–324.

Hudson, J. A. (1993). Reminiscing with mothers and others: Autobiographical memory in young two-year-olds. *Journal of Narrative and Life History, 3*, 1–32.

Hudson, J. A., & Sheffield, E. G. (1998). Déjà vu all over again: Effects of reenactment on toddlers' event memory. *Child Development, 69*, 51–67.

Huttenlocher, P. R. (1979). Synaptic density in human frontal cortex: Developmental changes and effects of aging. *Brain Research, 163*, 195–205.

Huttenlocher, P. R. & Dabholkar, A. S. (1997). Regional differences in synaptogenesis in human cerebral cortex. *Journal of Comparative Neurology, 387*, 167–178.

Kim, J. J., & Fanselow, M. S. (1992). Modality-specific retrograde amnesia of fear. *Science, 256*, 675–677.

Klein, P. J., & Meltzoff, A. N. (1999). Long-term memory, forgetting, and deferred imitation in 12-month-old infants. *Developmental Science, 2*, 102–113.

Lechuga, M. T., Marcos-Ruiz, R., & Bauer, P. J. (2001). Episodic recall of specifics and generalisation coexist in 25-month-old children. *Memory, 9*, 117–132.

Lloyd, M. E., & Newcombe, N. S. (2009). Implicit memory in childhood: Reassessing developmental invariance. In M. L. Courage & N. Cowan (Eds), *The Development of Memory in Infancy and Childhood* (pp. 93–113). New York, NY: Taylor & Francis.

Lukowski, A. F., Wiebe, S. A., & Bauer, P. J. (2009). Going beyond the specifics: Generalization of single actions, but not temporal order, at nine months. *Infant Behavior and Development, 32*, 331–335.

Mandler, J. M. (1990). Recall of events by preverbal children. In A. Diamond (Ed.), *The Development and Neural Bases of Higher Cognitive Functions* (pp. 485–516). New York: New York Academy of Science.

Mandler, J. M. (1998). Representation. In D. Kuhn, & R. Siegler (Eds), *Cognition, Perception, and Language*, Volume 2, of W. Damon (Ed.), *Handbook of Child Psychology* (pp. 255–308). New York: John Wiley & Sons.

Mandler, J. M., & McDonough, L. (1995). Long-term recall of event sequences in infancy. *Journal of Experimental Child Psychology, 59*, 457–474.

Markovitsch, H. J. (2000). Neuroanatomy of memory. In E. Tulving and F. I. M. Craik (Eds), *The Oxford Handbook of Memory* (pp. 465–484). New York: Oxford University Press.

McClelland, J. L., McNaughton, B. L., & O'Reilly, R. C. (1995). Why there are complementary learning systems in the hippocampus and neocortex: Insights from the successes and failures of connectionist models of learning and memory. *Psychological Review, 102,* 419–457.

McDonough, L., & Mandler, J. M. (1998). Inductive generalization in 9- and 11-month-olds. *Developmental Science, 1,* 227–232.

McDonough, L., Mandler, J. M., McKee, R. D., & Squire, L. R. (1995). The deferred imitation task as a nonverbal measure of declarative memory. *Proceedings of the National Academy of Sciences, 92,* 7580–7584.

McGaugh, J. L. (2000). Memory-a century of consolidation. *Science, 287,* 248–251.

McKee, R. D., & Squire, L. R. (1993). On the development of declarative memory. *Journal of Experimental Psychology: Learning, Memory, and Cognition, 19,* 397–404.

Meltzoff, A. N. (1985). Immediate and deferred imitation in fourteen- and twenty-four-month-old infants. *Child Development, 56,* 62–72.

Meltzoff, A. N. (1988a). Imitation of televised models by infants. *Child Development, 59,* 1221–1229.

Meltzoff, A. N. (1988b). Infant imitation and memory: Nine-month-olds in immediate and deferred tests. *Child Development, 59,* 217–225.

Meltzoff, A. N. (1990). The implications of cross-modal matching and imitation for the development of representation and memory in infants. In A. Diamond (Ed.), *The Development and Neural Bases of Higher Cognitive Functions* (pp. 1–31). New York: New York Academy of Science.

Meltzoff, A. N. (1995). What infant memory tells us about infantile amnesia: Long-term recall and deferred imitation. *Journal of Experimental Child Psychology, 59,* 497–515.

Myers, N. A., Clifton, R. K., & Clarkson, M. G. (1987). When they were very young: Almost-threes remember two years ago. *Infant Behavior and Development, 10,* 123–132.

Nelson, C. A. (1995). The ontogeny of human memory: A cognitive neuroscience perspective. *Developmental Psychology, 31,* 723–738.

Nelson, C. A. (1997). The neurobiological basis of early memory development. In N. Cowan (Ed.), *The Development of Memory in Childhood* (pp. 41–82). Hove, East Sussex: Psychology Press.

Nelson, C. A. (2000). Neural plasticity and human development: The role of early experience in sculpting memory systems. *Developmental Science, 3,* 115–136.

Nelson, C. A, & Collins, P. F. (1991). Event-related potential and looking time analysis of infants' responses to familiar and novel events: Implications for visual recognition memory. *Developmental Psychology, 27,* 50–58.

Nelson, C. A., & Collins, P. F. (1992). Neural and behavioral correlates of recognition memory in 4- and 9-month-old infants. *Brain and Cognition, 19,* 105–121.

Nelson, C. A., de Haan, M., & Thomas, K. (2006). Neural bases of cognitive development. In D. Kuhn & R. Siegler (Volume Editors), *Cognition, Perception, and Language,* Volume 2, of W. Damon & R. M. Lerner (Editors-in-Chief), *Handbook of Child Psychology,* Sixth Edition (pp. 3–57). Hoboken, NJ: John Wiley & Sons.

Nelson, K. (1986). *Event knowledge: Structure and Function in Development.* Hillsdale, NJ: Erlbaum.

Nelson, K., & Ross, G. (1980). The generalities and specifics of long-term memory in infants and young children. In M. Perlmutter (Ed.), *New Directions for Child Development – Children's Memory* (pp. 87–101). San Francisco, CA: Jossey-Bass.

Oakes, L. M., Ross-Sheehy, S., & Luck, S. J. (2007). The development of visual short-term memory in infancy. In L. M. Oakes & P. J. Bauer (Eds), *Short- and Long-term Memory in Infancy and Early Childhood: Taking the First Steps toward Remembering* (pp. 75–102). New York: Oxford University Press.

Parkin, A. J. (1997). The development of procedural and declarative memory. In N. Cowan (Ed.), *The Development of Memory in Childhood* (pp. 113–137). Hove, UK: Psychology Press.

Peterson, C., & Rideout, R. (1998). Memory for medical emergencies experienced by 1 and 2-year-olds. *Developmental Psychology, 34*, 1059–1072.

Petrides, M. (1995). Impairments on nonspatial self-ordered and externally ordered working memory tasks after lesions of the mid-dorsal part of the lateral frontal cortex in monkeys. *The Journal of Neuroscience, 15*, 359–375.

Piaget, J. (1926). *The Language and Thought of the Child.* New York: Harcourt, Brace.

Piaget, J. (1952). *The Origins of Intelligence in Children.* New York: International Universities Press.

Piaget, J. (1969). *The Child's Conception of Time.* London: Routledge & Kegan Paul.

Pillemer, D. B., & White, S. H. (1989). Childhood events recalled by children and adults. In H. W. Reese (Ed.), *Advances in Child Development and Behavior,* Volume 21 (pp. 297–340). San Diego, CA: Academic Press.

Richman, J., & Nelson, C. A. (2008). Mechanisms of change: A cognitive neuroscience approach to declarative memory development. In C. A. Nelson & M. Luciana (Eds), *Handbook of Developmental Cognitive Neuroscience,* Second edition (pp. 541–552). Cambridge, MA: The MIT Press.

Rose, S. A., Feldman, J. F., & Jankowski, J. J. (2001). Visual short-term memory in the first year of life: Capacity and recency effects. *Developmental Psychology, 37*, 539–549.

Rose, S. A., Gottfried, A. W., Melloy-Carminar, P., & Bridger, W. H. (1982). Familiarity and novelty preferences in infant recognition memory: Implications for information processing. *Developmental Psychology, 18*, 704–713.

Rovee-Collier, C. (1997). Dissociations in infant memory: Rethinking the development of implicit and explicit memory. *Psychological Review, 104*, 467–498.

Rovee-Collier, C., & Cuevas, K. (2009). The development of infant memory. In M. L. Courage and N. Cowan (Eds), *The Development of Memory in Infancy and Childhood,* Second Edition (pp. 11–41). New York, NY: Psychology Press.

Rovee-Collier, C., Schechter, A., Shyi, G., & Shields, P. (1992). Perceptual identification of contextual attributes and infant memory retrieval. *Developmental Psychology, 28*, 307–318.

Rovee-Collier, C., Sullivan, M. W., Enright, M. K., Lucas, D., & Fagen, J. W. (1980). Reactivation of infant memory. *Science, 208*, 1159–1161.

Schacter, D. L., Wagner, A. D., & Buckner, R. L. (2000). Memory systems of 1999. In E. Tulving & F. I. M. Craik (Eds), *The Oxford Handbook of Memory* (pp. 627–643). New York: Oxford University Press.

Schneider, W., & Bjorklund, D. F. (1998). Memory. In D. Kuhn & R. S. Siegler (Volume Editors) *Cognition, Perception, and Language,* Volume 2, of W. Damon (Editor-in-Chief), *Handbook of Child psychology,* Fifth edition (pp. 467–521). New York: John Wiley & Sons.

Seress, L., & Abraham (2008). Pre- and postnatal morphological development of the human hippocampal formation. In C. A. Nelson & M. Luciana (Eds), *Handbook of Developmental Cognitive Neuroscience,* Second Edition (pp. 187–212). Cambridge, MA: MIT Press.

Snyder, K. A. (2007). Neural mechanisms of attention and memory in preferential looking tasks. In L. M. Oakes & P. J. Bauer (Eds), *Short- and Long-term Memory in Infancy and*

*Early Childhood: Taking the First Steps toward Remembering* (pp. 179–208). New York, NY: Oxford University Press.

Sowell, E. R., Thompson, P. M., Leonard, C. M., Welcome, S. E., Kan, E, & Toga, A. W. (2004). Longitudinal mapping of cortical thickness and brain growth in normal children. *Journal of Neuroscience, 24,* 8223–8231.

Squire, L. R. (1987). *Memory and Brain.* New York: Oxford University Press.

Squire, L. R., Knowlton, B., & Musen, G. (1993). The structure and organization of memory. *Annual Review of Psychology, 44,* 453–495.

Takehara, K., Kawahara, S., & Kirino, Y. (2003). Time-dependent reorganization of the brain components underlying memory retention in trace eyeblink conditioning. *Journal of Neuroscience, 23,* 9897–9905.

Tanapat, P., Hastings, N. B., & Gould, E. (2001). Adult neurogenesis in the hippocampal formation. In C. A. Nelson & M. Luciana (Eds), *Handbook of Developmental Cognitive Neuroscience* (pp. 93–105). Cambridge, MA: The MIT Press.

Todd, C.M., & Perlmutter, M. (1980). Reality recalled by preschool children. In M. Perlmutter (Ed.), *New directions for Child Development – Children's Memory* (pp. 69–85). San Francisco, CA: Jossey-Bass.

Toth, J. P. (2000). Nonconscious forms of human memory. In E. Tulving & F. I. M. Craik (Eds), *The Oxford Handbook of Memory* (pp. 245–261). New York, NY: Oxford University Press.

West, T. A., & Bauer, P. J. (1999). Assumptions of infantile amnesia: Are there differences between early and later memories? *Memory, 7,* 257–278.

Zola, S. M, & Squire, L. R. (1993). Neuroanatomy of memory. *Annual Review of Neuroscience, 16,* 547–563.

Zola, S. M., & Squire, L. R. (2000). The medial temporal lobe and the hippocampus. In E. Tulving and F. I. M. Craik (Eds), *The Oxford Handbook of Memory* (pp. 485–500). New York: Oxford University Press.

# CHAPTER 2

# Feats of Early Memory: Courtroom Tales of What Adults Claim to Remember about Early Childhood Events

MARK L. HOWE

When memory researchers serve as expert witnesses in legal cases where the main, or quite frequently the only, evidence consists of narrative accounts of early childhood memories, they are frequently confronted by what can only be described as astonishing cases of remembering. This is especially true in cases involving historic childhood sexual abuse. Here, the alleged abuse is said to have occurred sometime in the distant past, usually at least some 10 to 30 years earlier, and almost always went unnoticed by significant others (e.g. parents, teachers, friends) and was thus unreported at the time. In these cases, the main feature is adult recall of events from early childhood, many of which produce transcripts filled with amazing feats of alleged remembering that range from recall of being fondled while being bathed at the age of 1 year to being raped at an early age (sometimes at the age of 2 years or younger). Such descriptions often include considerable perceptual detail (e.g. the type of wallpaper in the room, the clothing that people were wearing) that is arguably peripheral to the central features of the event itself. Moreover, complainants frequently claim that they can clearly remember what appears to be verbatim recall of alleged conversations that occurred before, during and after the abuse experience. This clarity of recollection, including the extensive perceptual detail integrated in the memories themselves, is vehemently and confidently sworn to as being true by complainants. This despite the fact that other memories of equal vintage, regardless of whether they are positive (e.g. birthday parties, remembering best friends) or negative (e.g. the behavior of an abusive parent, failing a test at school), are admittedly faded and difficult if not impossible to remember.

Perhaps somewhat more puzzling is the claim that these memories have lain dormant for many years (usually two or more decades). Although I will sidestep the obvious question as to how one remembers that they have forgotten something (but see Abenavoli & Henkel, 2009; Herrmann, Sheets, Gruneberg, & Torres, 2005; Merckelbach et al., 2006), the claim is often made that these memories for early abusive experiences returned spontaneously to mind only very recently under somewhat curious circumstances. Sometimes these circumstances involve what might be considered very remote cues concerning abuse, such as watching one's own child (usually a daughter) playing in a park (e.g. swinging on a swing) and suddenly remembering that one had been abused at the same age. Other circumstances can involve cues that may seem more obvious, such as talking to a friend about his or her own abuse or reading an article in the popular press about the frequency of child abuse. Still other circumstances may involve considerably more "memory work" to "bring back" these alleged memories of abuse, usually in the service of accounting for current problematic issues in one's life (e.g. relationship problems, career failures), such as when one is involved in psychotherapeutic or religious counseling. Indeed, in many of these circumstances and regardless of how such "memories" are retrieved, these long-forgotten but now crystal-clear recollections are now believed to be at the root of the person's current and, sometimes, lifelong psychological distress (e.g. depression, relationship failures).

In this chapter, I review a selection of these feats of early memory as documented across a number of cases in North America and the United Kingdom. These feats of recollection are compared to what we know from the scientific study of memory, a contrast that permits an informed commentary on the plausibility of the memories they report, the reliability of such reports, and how such reports square with scientific evidence and theory. This critical commentary is important not only in terms of gaining a theoretical understanding of what can and cannot be remembered about early childhood experiences, but also because it contrasts the often naïve beliefs of triers of fact (e.g. lawyers, jurors, judges), beliefs that need to be amended and updated by scientific facts about the genesis and nature of early memory.

## Memory feats in the courtroom

I begin by describing some of the memories of early childhood experiences that are frequently encountered in courtroom testimony, especially in cases concerning alleged, historic sexual abuse.[1] People quite often report very specific and detailed recollections of alleged experiences from 10 to 30 years earlier. These narrative accounts include a variety of perceptual details, specific information about the surrounding environment in which the event(s) occurred, and even specific conversations that were heard before, during and after the abusive experience. For example, one complainant (SG) claimed to remember a number of experiences of early abuse, ones that occurred when she was 2 to 3 years old. These alleged memories, ones that had lain dormant for nearly 30 years, were very specific and included considerable detail. Indeed, her narrative account of these events included details concerning the exact words spoken by the accused during the event, what she and the accused were wearing, the precise time at night when the alleged events occurred, where everyone else was in the house, and finally, what the others in the house were doing during her abusive experiences. Of course, as discussed later in this chapter, such detailed memories are extremely unlikely to be formed at such a young age. Indeed, research has clearly demonstrated that it is usually only sparse fragments of early events that are remembered years later. For example, early recollections tend to be decontextualized segments of an experience, such as "I remembering sitting in my parents' bedroom, observing my mother as she did some cleaning. There is nothing else to the memory, but I remember having a very different perspective of the room at the time" (Bruce et al., 2005, p. 572).

What this example shows is that early memories are not rife with detail, although they do contain elements of the event that are central to the core of the experience itself. Interestingly, some cases of alleged historic child sexual abuse contain few of these ostensibly critical memory elements. That is, at the other end of this spectrum, there are those individuals who claim to have memories for very early events, despite the absence of details that might be expected. For example, PF claimed to have a memory of being raped when she was 3 to 4 years of age but provided very few details. Indeed, throughout her first interview concerning these events, she consistently maintained, even in the face of direct questioning, that the perpetrator of the alleged rape in question was a relative, TO. It was only later, when interviewed a second time, that she gives a different name, this time a relative named BH, who is now the accused in the case. Although one can certainly confuse names, such confusions are perhaps less likely in cases where the person has perpetrated a physical assault (i.e. rape) and is as well known to the victim as he is claimed to be in this allegation.

---

[1] In all of the descriptions in this chapter, fictitious initials are being used to protect the identities of those involved and in order that the cases being discussed remain anonymous.

Also during this second interview, PF has somewhat unexpected and considerable difficulty remembering what BH looked like. For example, when asked how old he was, she replied: "About 20 or about 15 or 13 or 16, I don't know." When asked what he looked like, she replied: "I can't remember." When asked what his hair was like, she replied: "all spiked up, or just normal, I don't know". Finally, when asked what color his hair was she replied: "It's blonde or black, or red brown. Or just, or just like, just bald, without no hair." Although, as we will see, autobiographical memories tend to contain primarily the central details or gist of events, given that BH was said to be familiar to PF, it is not clear why she cannot provide any details concerning this person's age or other physical characteristics. Yet, despite this lack of detail, PF claimed to be able remember events from 1 year of age: "about one year's old, I was in the pram and my dad was trying to pull me out, but before my dad took me out of the pram, one of my sisters got me out of the pram." Of course, such narrative accounts of events from such an early age (1 year old) have not been found in the scientific literature and are deemed by most, if not all, scientists to be impossible until at least two to three year of age, and even then, they are observed only very infrequently (for a review, see Howe, 2011).[2]

In addition to concerns about detail, both its absence as well as its overabundance, memory narratives for alleged childhood events have the curious habit of disappearing from memory, only to mysteriously reappear later in adulthood. For example, CP claimed that she did not remember the abuse that she now alleges happened to her when she was age 4 years until she was 15 or 16 years old: "I didn't start remembering this till I was 15, so it's, I kind of forgot all about it and it suddenly came back to me." When this memory did suddenly come to her, CP recounts conversational items, including "[he] told me to carry on watching TV" following the rape and that she was not to "tell anybody I did it, nobody would believe you and your mother will call you a liar and things. Nobody will believe you." Curiously, she also claims to remember that no contraception (specifically a condom) was used during this alleged rape.

---

[2] Although it is not always clear what constitutes a peripheral aspect of an event and how it differs from one that is central to that experience, it is arguably the case that central to most memories of sexual abuse is some detail concerning the perpetrator of the abuse. Indeed, in factually verified cases of sexual abuse, many complainants have an all too vivid recollection of their perpetrator. Of course the debate in PF's case concerns not only the centrality of the perpetrator to the veracity of this alleged memory, but also the juxtaposition of detail in an even earlier "memory" that has no obvious significance and the absence of detail in a more recent "memory" with more obvious significance. Indeed, the important point about PF's case is that she claims on the one hand to have a "memory" from the age of one year for a seemingly innocuous experience but little or no "memory" for an alleged sexual abuse experience that presumably occurred when she was older (aged three to four years).

Of course, CP's memories had some "help," both in terms of "getting them to return" as well as "recovering the specific details." For example, she had spoken with friends and relatives over the past year or two concerning their own abuse experiences prior to her "spontaneously remembering" her own abuse. Interestingly, these alleged abuse experiences that relatives and friends confided in her about were perpetrated by the same person that CP later accused of carrying out her own abuse. Moreover, CP had been in counseling for a considerable period of time (by some accounts for at least two years), and some of this counseling occurred during the period when these alleged sexual abuse memories started to surface. In fact, according to the counseling notes, part of this therapy involved the use of guided imagery and relaxation techniques, procedures that can foster and promote false recollections (e.g. Loftus & Davis, 2006). At the very least, the records indicated that "flashbacks" accompanied many of these "memories" as they returned. Although people can and do have intrusive thoughts about traumatic experiences, it is not well documented that memories of alleged abuse appear exclusively in the form of flashbacks (e.g. McNally, 2003).

Many similar cases involving the return of early childhood memories during therapy also exist. Sometimes, "memory work" is pursued wherein counselors can suggest that people should focus on certain objects, much as one would use any ordinary retrieval cue, to help them remember childhood experiences. For example, a particularly poignant example comes from a case involving MT. In one of the counts, she alleges a rape occurred in a wooded area in a red car. In the therapist's notes, "red cars" and "woods" are itemized as objects of fear for MT, and she is instructed to think about these items to see if any memory comes back involving them early in her childhood. Although at this time there is no mention of any rape event in a red car in the woods, one surely becomes apparent over the next few months. Counterintuitively, when MT is first asked to focus on these items, despite reporting intrusive thoughts at this time, these intrusions of events into conscious awareness do not include what would be an extremely traumatic event, the "rape in the red car." That this event is neither reported at this time nor does it exist as an intrusive thought, despite the presence of other intrusive thoughts, raised questions concerning the veracity of an early childhood memory for the alleged rape. Thus, these fears or "feelings" about red cars and woods predate any story about rape. As detailed later, given what we know about false memory formation, it is not unreasonable to assume that, with additional memory work with the therapist as well as the writings contained in MT's "feelings" diary, it is not outside the realm of possibility that MT might form a "rape story" that involved already fearful objects (red cars and woods).

Similar "memory work" may also explain several other counts found in MT's testimony, ones involving indecent assault during an evening babysitting session as well as an incident involving oral sex. These alleged event descriptions contained somewhat bizarre and unusual activities, including the use of a doll, and MT vomiting over the defendant after forced oral sex and her having to clean up the vomit. Although these would seem to be distinctive events, they are not included in correspondence with the therapist. That such events are not reported as intrusive thoughts, yet later become fully fledged assault events, is more consistent with continued "memory work" in the "feelings" diary.

As another example, consider MT's allegations concerning a computer. The computer appears first in the therapist's notes as another of MT's phobias (note that computer phobias were common in the mid-1990s when their use became more prevalent). In these notes, there is no mention of any abuse. Later, however, there is mention of abuse in MT's "feelings" diary and the severity of this abuse escalates. Although MT's computer phobia may be real, the growth in the severity of the alleged abuse incidents that include a computer, as well as the inconsistency of these allegations across different reports (including the original police report), suggests that these too may have emerged out of "memory work" and the "feelings" diary.

Overall, what comes out of this analysis of the accounts alleged by MT is that her "memories" of the alleged abuse are more likely false than true. This is because (a) there is a preexisting phobic base to many of her allegations (i.e. she had a longstanding fear associated with the woods, red cars, and computers that became embedded in her abuse scenarios), (b) there is clear evidence of the growth in the number and severity in the nature of abuse events/allegations across time/reports and therapeutic memory work, and (c) some of the most horrific and distinctive events, ones that should be very memorable, so memorable that if real they would be likely to have intruded into MT's consciousness (e.g. Hagenaars et al., 2010), are not "remembered" until much later in her statements. Moreover, that these events do not appear in her "feelings" diary and are not found in the therapist's notes would lead most reasonable memory scientists to conclude that these allegations are more consistent with what we know about the construction of false memories than what we know about true recall of traumatic experiences (e.g. Brainerd & Reyna, 2005; Davis & Loftus, 2007). Indeed, this is completely consistent with what we know about the growth of false memories over repeated recall attempts, regardless of whether those attempts are in aid of therapeutic processes, conversations, or for the purposes of forensic interviews.

There are myriad similar cases that many memory experts, particularly experts in early memory, have dealt with in the courts over the years. These can range from "remembering" alleged touching events (e.g. when being bathed as a baby) to more violent sexual assaults (e.g. forced oral or vaginal intercourse). Although there are may be more cases that involve true than false memories of early childhood sexual abuse, those that involve false recollections do conform to the patterns illustrated in these examples above. What these examples have in common is a variety of what I have called miraculous feats of recollection. That is, claimants frequently purport to remember events from very early in life, including during the period known as infantile amnesia (e.g. see Howe, Courage, & Rooksby, 2009). These event memories, ones that can vary markedly in their level of detail, frequently include exhaustive descriptions of seemingly peripheral and perhaps superfluous information. Such memories may even have lain dormant for 10 to 30 years, only to either spontaneously reappear in adulthood or sometimes require a little therapeutic urging to aid in their reappearance. Such feats, as I demonstrate in the next section, are not consistent with the scientific study of early memory.

## What the science of memory shows

In this section, I discuss what the science of memory has to say about the reliability of memory for autobiographical events from early childhood, the basis for the evidence provided in the cases reviewed earlier. As noted, the problem for triers of fact in such cases is that complainants base their accusations on "memories" that are said to have been formed very early in childhood (from 1 to 4 or 5 years of age, typically). Worse, these "memories" for the alleged events are usually 10 or more years old and may be ones that the complainant claims that they have never remembered before (i.e. they have not appeared in conscious awareness before). Finally, as the earlier examples illustrated, such "memories" are often "discovered" following a period of intense self-introspection, conversations with others about their abuse, reading information about abuse or attending some type of therapeutic intervention, all of which are factors that are known to give rise to false memories. What the presence of these factors does is raise a number of red flags concerning the veracity of the "memories" that form the basis for such allegations, ones that lead to a number of important questions. To begin, what can adults remember about their early childhood? That is, if the alleged events did take place, could a child as young as one to five years of age form an enduring memory of them at the time they occurred? Moreover, if these alleged events did not happen, what could make the complainant come to believe that they did?

In order to answer these (and other related) questions we need to know something about memory in young children, memory for traumatic experiences, memory and conscious recollection, and false memories and suggestibility, topics I review next. To anticipate the outcome of this review, it will be shown that the types of "memories" catalogued earlier that complainants base their narratives about the alleged events on, may be false rather than true. This is because complainants who claim to have these memories for very early experiences may have been at an age when stable and reliable memories of childhood events are not easily formed. Further, the manner in which these "memories" came about (i.e. they appeared relatively recently or perhaps in the form of dreams or "flashbacks") is not typical in the literature concerning memories for documented childhood sexual abuse (e.g. Alexander et al., 2005). In cases where there are gaps in memory (and many complainants admit to having a poor memory for childhood events), these gaps can be "filled in" using memory reconstruction (including collaborative recall, as when complainants reconstruct facts when discussing events with others), a process that can lead to false memories. This is particularly worrisome when people are trying to reconstruct their past because simply reflecting on one's life can lead to the creation of false memories, especially when a person repeatedly attempts to recall alleged abuse experiences across a variety of contexts.

## Memory in young children

What we saw from the earlier examples is that many of the alleged events are said to occur very early in life. Although young children can and do form memories, they are not the sorts of memories that are particularly enduring (for a recent review, see Howe, 2011). Indeed, the phenomenon of infantile or childhood amnesia limits our ability to remember experiences from our early childhood (Howe et al., 2009). Although age estimates vary concerning the offset of infantile amnesia, there is a general consensus that memories formed before the age of 4 or 5 are generally only poorly remembered, if at all, in later childhood or adulthood (Howe, 2011; Howe et al., 2009). Although it is not impossible to remember some events from perhaps 4 or 5 years of age, most memories at this age are not well preserved for future use. Thus, children would in all likelihood be too young to form lasting autobiographical memories of many of the alleged incidents found in most complainants' narratives. Of course, as we will see, this may depend on the nature of the events (rape v. touching), but in general, intact and accurately detailed memories are rarely seen until children are somewhat older (around 9 to 10 years of age, according to some; see below) and even then, only for particularly distinctive and memorable events.

Although it is not impossible to remember some events from this age range, as described earlier in this chapter, most early memories are fragmentary and are not well preserved for future use (e.g. Bruce et al., 2005, 2007). Complaints that involve events that are alleged to have happened when the person was 1 to 5 years old would, in all likelihood, involve children who would have been too young to form lasting autobiographical memories. In fact, according to some theorists, memories before the age of 8 years are readily forgotten and tend not to be remembered in later childhood or adulthood (e.g. see overview in the British Psychological Society's report, *Guidelines on Memory and the Law: Recommendations from the Scientific Study of Human Memory*, 2010). That is, more stable, adult-like memories are rarely seen until 9 to 10 years of age and even then, only for particularly distinctive and memorable events.

Thus, given what we know about the nature of early autobiographical memory, the claim that narrative accounts of early childhood abuse are based on intact memories for earlier events that actually happened is not strictly consistent with the scientific literature. This is especially true when these recollections are said to have appeared only recently and some (if not all) in the form of some kind of dreamlike reverie or "flashback." In one recent case, the complainant's recollections initially all reappeared to her following years of absence when she was dreaming or in a hypnagogic state. Later, as these "memories" became more detailed, they started to come to her in the form of "flashbacks" during waking states, something she took as an indication that they must be "real."

It is important to realize that whether one is recalling traumatic or non-traumatic experiences, all memories are subject to the same "laws" including "fading" with time, are subject to interference and intrusions from other similar events, and can be "tainted" by additional information, suggestion and repeated attempts to recall the event (see Brainerd & Reyna, 2005; Howe, 2011). That many complainants base their allegations on "memories" that are more than 20 years old means that there has been considerable opportunity for the natural forces of forgetting and reconstruction to alter what may have been encoded and stored some two decades earlier. What this means is that the narrative recall provided by such complainants about the alleged abuse incidents may bear little resemblance to any events that may have occurred. Even horrific and extremely traumatic events that have occurred many decades earlier are often misremembered after the passage of time (as seen, for example, in research that has been conducted with survivors of the holocaust; e.g. Wagenaar & Groeneweg, 1990).

These observations cast doubt on the authenticity of complainants' memories for these alleged events. Indeed, these observations are also consistent with the British Psychological Society's report, *Guidelines on Memory and the Law: Recommendations from the Scientific Study of Human Memory* (2010) where it is concluded:

(1) In general the accuracy of memories dating below the age of 7 years cannot be established in the absence of independent corroborating evidence; (p. 13)

(2) These findings lead to the conclusion that by approximately 9 to 10 years of age children have autobiographical memories that are adult in nature. (p. 14)

Thus, there is good scientific reason to doubt the veracity of complainants' "memories" for events alleged to have happened early in life.

## Memory for trauma

What about the fact that some complainants have "memories" for an event that is clearly traumatic (e.g. rape)? Do traumatic memories enjoy some kind of special status in the brain? Although some believe this is true (e.g. Nadel & Jacobs, 1998; Terr, 1988; van der Kolk & Fisler, 1995), the theoretical and empirical literatures on this topic are quite diverse (see Howe, 2011; Howe, Cicchetti, Toth, & Cerrito, 2004; Howe, Toth, & Cicchetti, 2011; McNally, 2003). However, there is an emerging consensus in the literature that traumatic experiences sometimes can be remembered better than nontraumatic and mundane experiences (e.g. Howe, 1998; Howe, Cicchetti, & Toth, 2006). Although this may be true, this same literature shows that memories of traumatic experiences behave in a manner very similar to that of all memories. That is, they are susceptible to the effects of infantile amnesia, they can be forgotten, they are subject to traditional misinformation effects that arise during questioning, and they can be distorted by other well-known processes that interfere with memory more generally (e.g. Howe, 1998, 2000, 2011; Howe et al., 2006; Loftus & Pickrell, 1995; McNally, 2003). Indeed, the longevity of traumatic memories pertains solely to their central details and not to extraneous information.

Curiously, many narratives about alleged abuse contain considerably more detail than would be anticipated, given the scientific literature. For example, one complainant claimed to remember many details not typical of what we know about recall of early childhood events or even recall of traumatic events. These details included remembering the clothes people were wearing ("I had a yellow nightie on and pink panties", "He had jeans on with a black leather belt and a silver buckle. And he had like, a tee shirt on"), specific conversations ("and he said, 'I'll show you how to make it good, so I like it'"; "He just said, 'Kiss it, I like it if you kiss it'"), and that the defendant's "penis looked dirty", despite claiming in earlier interviews that she never saw his penis as her eyes were always closed during the abuse itself. Contrary to the content of such narratives, it is well known that peripheral details are the first to disappear from our memory (e.g. see Brainerd & Reyna, 2005). Although details that may be considered peripheral by some people can be central to other people, taking on added importance and salience depending on a number of individual differences factors, it is generally accepted that the central or meaning-related elements of traumatic memories are what is best remembered. Indeed, the meaning-related aspects of events are the ones that last longer than more peripheral aspects of those same events (e.g. see Howe, Courage, & Peterson, 1995). Despite this, even traumatic experiences are not immune to the laws that govern memories more generally.

Although these are important conclusions, there remain several additional questions that must be addressed before we can understand the role of trauma in memory for the early experiences that routinely appear in cases in our courtrooms. Specifically, are these conclusions based on any studies involving memory for abuse and did any of the studies involve repeated events with people and locations that are well known to the rememberer? Moreover, are any of the events being studied of a sexual nature and are these events likely to induce conflicting emotions, emotions said to be common in cases of sexual abuse?

There are two important points here. First, although the longevity of memories can differ as a function of stress, trauma and distinctiveness of the event, the "laws" that govern how memory operates do not behave differently as a consequence of the event being remembered. Although the meaning of stressful and traumatic experiences tends to be remembered over longer intervals than that of more mundane events (as long as they are important and salient to the individual rememberer), they are still subject to the same principles that govern memory more generally (e.g. they are subject to decay, forgetting, interference and misinformation effects). So, the first answer to the question of whether stressful and traumatic events are remembered any better than other, more mundane experiences is *yes* – stressful events tend to be remembered at least as well as, and in some cases better than, more benign experiences (e.g. Fivush, 2002; Ornstein, 1995). However, they are subject to the same types of reconstructive errors found in all of memory (e.g. see chapters in Howe, Goodman, & Cicchetti, 2008) and, as we will see in a subsequent section, depending on whether event valence is measured within rather than across individuals, these differences in event memory between traumatic and positive experiences, can disappear. Another important caveat is that in some studies, children who experienced higher levels of stress are actually poorer at remembering the stressful event – that is, children who are more highly stressed by the experience can produce more memory errors than children who are not as stressed by that same experience (e.g. Goodman & Quas, 1997).

The second answer to this question is that yes, the scientific literature contains many studies involving traumatic events, some involving sexual abuse, physical abuse, as well as other horrific events that involved potentially conflicting emotions. This literature includes research on children's memory for naturally occurring events that are both unanticipated and traumatic. For example, children's recollections of sniper attacks (Pynoos & Nader, 1989; Schwartz & Kowalski, 1991), hurricanes (Ackil, van Abbema, & Bauer, 2003; Bahrick, Parker, Fivush, & Levitt, 1998; Shaw, Applegate, & Schorr, 1996), tornados (Bauer, Burch, van Abbema, & Ackil, 2008), earthquakes (Najarian et al., 1996), a fatal bus-train collision (Tyano et al., 1996), attacks during the Gulf War (Dyregov, Gjestad, & Raundalen, 2002; Laor et al., 1997), and imprisonment in Cambodia (Kinzie et al., 1986). In all of these cases, remembering tended to be accurate in terms of central or meaning-relevant features, but were also subject to reconstructive errors.

However, many of these studies have examined traumatic and nontraumatic event memory in different, rather than the same, children. What this means is that individual differences (e.g. in stress reactivity), as well as developmental differences, are confounded with event type. What is needed is research that compares the recollection of both traumatic and nontraumatic experiences in the same child. Fortunately, there are some studies that have examined recall of both traumatic and nontraumatic events in the same children. For example, Fivush et al. (2003) examined 5- to 12-year-old children's recollection of nontraumatic events, ones that included more positive experiences, such as parties and holidays, as well as their recollection of traumatic events, ones that included negative episodes, such as parental separation, serious illness and death. Here, regardless of the nature of the event (traumatic or not), children's recall was quantitatively similar in terms of the amount of detail remembered. As anticipated, the narratives differed qualitatively in terms of the type of information remembered, such that there was more recall of emotional states concerning the self or others with traumatic than nontraumatic events. However, it was clear that when individual differences were controlled by having the same children remember differently valenced events, traumatic events were no better remembered than were nontraumatic, and possibly more positive and less emotional, events.

## Memory and conscious recollection

As mentioned earlier, for some complainants, the "memories" for these alleged events seem to have suddenly appeared. For example, as one complainant put it, the memories appeared "...just all of a sudden; it's just come into my head" and "...that's come back on their own without me even thinking about it. They've just come in me head on me own, you know." It might be suggested that somehow these complainants were able to "record" the events in some kind of nonverbal, nonconscious memory that would somehow later lead to recollection, say, in a time of emotional distress (e.g. perhaps when trying to understand a recent relationship failure). Indeed, there are some writers who have suggested that memories may be retained by the body and that under highly stressful conditions such somatic memories may be routinely formed, ones that may not be accessible to conscious inspection (e.g. Rothschild, 2000). It has also been argued that these somatic "memories" can suddenly surface and cause emotional distress long after the actual trauma has been suffered.

Although this might be an interesting idea, there is absolutely no scientific evidence to back up the claim that such memories exist, or even if they did, that they could suddenly enter consciousness as autobiographical memories. Although implicit memories or implicit processes that operate on memories (ones that are not conscious) do exist, the research that does exist suggests that their behavior is very similar to explicit memories (ones that are conscious) (e.g. see Rovee-Collier, Hayne, & Columbo, 2001). Moreover, there is no research that suggests that implicit memory processes are specially adapted for traumatic experiences (see Howe, 2011; Rovee-Collier et al., 2001). Indeed, for many if not most traumatic experiences, memories are available to conscious inspection and frequently intrude into consciousness all too unexpectedly (e.g. see Brewin, 2003).

Indeed, the problem for many real abuse victims is not that they cannot remember the abusive experiences, but rather, that they can remember them all too well. This point was made poignant in a case in which I was testifying about the ability of adults to retain central details of traumatic experiences. This was a case in which there was corroborating evidence concerning the historic childhood sexual abuse, evidence that had been well documented over the years. As one complainant in a case explained to me, "...you are studying the wrong thing. You don't need to do anymore research that tells me that I can remember my abuse, because I know that each and every day. Instead, your time would be better spent doing research that helps me and the others in this case forget their experiences."

## False memories, repeated recall and suggestibility

Returning to the central issues in this chapter, if the memories of the complainants discussed earlier are unreliable, how might they have come to believe that the alleged incidents were actual memories? The scientific literature clearly shows that false memories are relatively common and are not the exception (Brainerd & Reyna, 2005). Indeed, the meaning-based processes that are used to form "true" memories are the very same as those used to form "false" memories (Howe, 2011). Recent evidence shows that false memories are just as likely to occur in children who have been maltreated as those who have not (Howe et al., 2004, 2011) and that they occur not just for mundane everyday events but also for negative, emotional information. This holds for both children (Brainerd et al., 2010; Howe, 2007; Howe et al., 2010) and adults (Brainerd et al., 2008; Budson et al., 2006). In fact, entire fictitious childhood events are very easily implanted in children and adults, even if those events are negative (Candel, Wade, & Howe, 2008; Otgaar, Candel, & Merckelbach, 2008). Worse, there is some evidence that whereas false memories for neutral information persist over retention intervals of one week and more, false memories for negatively valenced information actually increase over time (Howe et al., 2010).

Of course, there is as yet no single indisputable test that deciphers true from false memories (Bernstein & Loftus, 2009). This raises the possibility that the various techniques used to cue memory (e.g. self introspection, discussions with others, counseling) could actually lead to the "recovery" of a real memory. Although some authors (e.g. Cheit, 1998) claim to have found the existence of repressed memories that are subsequently recovered, these cases have not been without their detractors and are frequently fraught with serious methodological flaws. Indeed, most if not all cases of alleged repressed, recovered memories have been discredited (for an illustration of these problems, see perhaps one of the most famous examples of this, the case of "Who Abused Jane Doe?" – Loftus & Guyer, 2002a, 2002b). For example, when the 35 cases reported by Cheit (1998) were reevaluated, not one of the cases provided any scientific evidence in support of recovered memory (Piper, 1999). In fact, Piper noted that Cheit had failed to address important questions, such as whether a traumatic event happened in the first place (lack of corroborating evidence) or whether normal amnesia (either biologically based or due to infantile or childhood amnesia) could explain the lack of memory. In those cases where the authenticity of the event could be corroborated, McNally (2003) pointed out that evidence for forgetting the event was "…seriously flawed or can be more plausibly explained in ways other than an *inability* to remember" (p. 227). Although the number of cases of alleged repressed and later recovered memories continues to grow, in each and every case, not one of the instances has passed scientific scrutiny. Indeed, "…an analysis of studies involving corroborated traumatic events uncovered no convincing evidence that victims had forgotten, let alone repressed, their trauma" (McNally & Geraerts, 2009, p. 128).

Although it is clear that memories of abuse can be temporarily "forgotten" (usually through normal mechanisms of forgetting), it is also true that the majority of these memories are extremely difficult to forget (see the example in the last section, as well as Loftus & Davis, 2006). Indeed, some of the alleged forgetting of traumatic experiences may turn out to be failing to remember that you remembered the event at some earlier point in time (see McNally & Geraerts, 2009). As noted earlier in this chapter, it is not clear whether the event (or events) has been genuinely forgotten or the person simply forgot that they had remembered it at some earlier point in time.

How might complainants come to believe that such events were memories if indeed they were not? It is possible that such narratives are created as the result of self-introspection or questioning by others. Thinking about or discussing abuse (real or not) with others can lead to rumination and the creation of false memories (e.g. Davis & Loftus, 2007). When individuals attempt to recall instances of abuse from memory (e.g. after reading about abuse in the newspaper or hearing about abuse from others), or when such instances are repeatedly queried across interviews or talked about in conversations with others (e.g. family and friends), scientific studies have shown that there is an increase in the likelihood of false memories. For example, Brainerd and Reyna (2005) state that, "even if suggestive techniques are not used,…repeated interviewing encourages reconstructive remembering of events that cannot be clearly recollected, which…is a source of false memory reports" (p. 304).

Adding to this concern is some recent work by Davis and Loftus (2007, p. 219) who point out:

> Although attempts to retrieve information are often themselves sufficient to impair or distort memory, perhaps even greater problems occur as a result of conversational recountings. Even the simple act of repeating a statement can increase the strength of one's belief in its truth.…Furthermore, even in the absence of any input from a conversational partner (such as alternative accounts, leading or misleading questions, feedback, therapeutic suggestions and procedures, etc.), persons asked to describe witnessed materials or events (a) bias their descriptions to reflect their own goals (for example, entertainment, deception, or informing accurately) or characteristics of the listener (for example, toward consistency with the listener's known attitudes or toward selective inclusion of aspects of interest to the listener); (b) subsequently report believing these biased descriptions; and (c) falsely recall the original stimuli as consistent with their biased descriptions.

Moreover,

> Such biased reports of witnessed events take place in a wide variety of social interactions, such as parent-child interactions, professional interviews with victims and suspects, therapeutic interactions, and the many conversations that might take place between co-witnesses or between a victim and supportive friends and family prior to police reports. Indeed, the more informal conversations, which no doubt take place in greater numbers and variety, may shape accounts more powerfully than the professional interactions…Once

these distorting conversations have taken place, subsequent memory is biased in the direction of the distorted reports (Davis & Loftus, 2007, p. 220).

Finally, Davis and Loftus (2007, p. 221) also point out that: "Over time, a witness who discusses witnessed events with others can be expected to provide biased reports to those others and ultimately to come to believe the distorted accounts and report these false recollections to still others." Of course, many cases involve conversations (informal and formal) with others over a fairly lengthy time frame.

Other important factors that contribute to false memories include delay – delay between the time of an experience and reporting it is important because as time passes, spontaneous false reports increase and people are more likely to accept false suggestions as true (Brainerd & Reyna, 2005). Indeed, over time, as was already mentioned, although true recollections of negative events can worsen, false memories concerning negative information can actually increase for both children and adults (e.g. Howe et al., 2010). The reporting (and presumably the "remembering") in many cases is considerably delayed from the alleged time of the original experience and is thus susceptible to these delay effects.

## Ecological validity and the science of false memory

There are two concerns that have been raised concerning the forensic relevance of the studies used to form opinions about false memories of sexual abuse that must be clarified in this chapter. First, it has been suggested in the clinical literature that the research just discussed on false memory lacks 'ecological' validity. That is, some of the conclusions about false memories have been made on the basis of research that has simply examined people's memory for word lists and not real life events. Here, people falsely remember a single word that had not been presented earlier but which is related to the theme of the words on the list. Criticisms by Freyd and Gleaves (1996) and by Pezdek and Lam (2007) suggest that the forensic implications of these findings are potentially constrained by the fact that the emotional content of the materials are, by ethical necessity, mild in comparison to the events of serious crimes (e.g. murders, horrific traffic accidents, or frightening injuries from assaults and childhood maltreatment). Indeed, these authors and many others have argued that even the study of memory for emotional words is not the same as memory for real-life events and that the effects of valence and arousal may be qualitatively and quantitatively different.

Importantly, Rubin and Talarico (2009) recently rejected conjectures such as these. They found that participants' emotional reactions were the same to real-life events, autobiographical memories, and lists of words that varied in valence and arousal. Similarly, in the very same issue of the journal *Consciousness and Cognition* that the Pezdek and Lam (2007) critique was published, Wade et al. (2007) also suggested that the differences between recollections of real-life events and memories studied in the laboratory are of little consequence "... if the study has strict experimental control, that is, high internal validity, and addresses basic theoretical questions, then it makes little difference whether the study is conducted in the laboratory or in the field, with ecologically interesting materials or with derived stimuli" (p. 25). Indeed, it has been demonstrated repeatedly that false memories for words on a list as studied in the laboratory are created by the same memory mechanisms as those used to generate false memories for entire events, events that most of us would agree did not take place, despite the persons' sincere and emotionally convincing narrative attesting to their belief that it happened (e.g. being abducted by aliens in a UFO – see Clancy et al., 2002). Interestingly, this also holds for people who have post-traumatic stress disorder (Bremner, Shobe, & Kihlstrom, 2000; Brennen, Dybdahl, & Kapidzic, 2007; Zoellner, Foa, Brigidi, & Przeworski, 2000), people who report recovered memories for past lives (e.g. Meyersburg, Bogdan, Gallo, & McNally, 2009), and those women who report recovered memories of childhood sexual abuse (Clancy, Schacter, McNally, & Pitman, 2000). Indeed, people reporting recovered memories of childhood sexual abuse exhibit *higher* false memory rates than people reporting no abuse history or people who report never forgetting the childhood abuse they experienced (Geraerts et al., 2005).

Thus, when the entire literature on the ecological validity of false memories is considered, it is not the case that the relevance of such studies to false memories of actual events is unclear. To the contrary, the rich literature on this topic indicates that the study of false memories, even false memories as simple as those created using word lists, are very similar to the matters being discussed in many of the cases outlined earlier in this chapter. Indeed, this research bears directly on issues concerning how people can come to believe that parts of events, or even entire events that never happened to them, can become "memories" they subsequently believe did happen to them.

Second, there are claims that events that have been used in implanted memory studies are not comparable to implanting entirely false memories of repeated sexual abuse (e.g. Pezdek & Lam, 2007). There are two points to be made here, one concerning the similarity of events and the other concerning event plausibility. On the one hand, concerning the similarity of implanted events and the events alleged to have occurred in the cases reviewed earlier, it should be obvious that for ethical reasons researchers are constrained in the types of events that can be implanted and, therefore, do not attempt to implant memories that are too horrific. Although people themselves appear to be able to "self-implant" events that can be horrific (e.g. as in those who believe they have been abducted by aliens in a UFO, memories that most would agree are impossible, and that often contain painful experiences such as medical exams, probes, and even some form of sexual behavior with aliens), researchers should not attempt to implant painful memories, as often people cannot forget them once they are implanted (e.g. Loftus & Bernstein, 2005).

However, this does not mean that events that are similar to ones in many court cases have not been implanted, ones that involve negative emotions and painful procedures. For example, adult participants have been led to believe that at age 5 or 6 they had been lost in a shopping mall for an extended period of time, were very upset, but were then rescued and reunited with their family (Loftus & Pickrell, 1995). Other research has shown participants can be led to believe that they had been hospitalized overnight or that they had an accident at a family wedding (Hyman, Husband, & Billings, 1995). False memories that are even more traumatic have been implanted, including having been the victim of a vicious animal attack (Porter, Yuille, & Lehman, 1999), or having nearly drowned and had to be saved by a lifeguard (Heaps & Nash, 2001). Although not all participants come to believe that these events actually happened, across a number of different studies an average of 31 percent or almost one-third of all participants produced false memories (see Lindsay et al., 2004). When doctored photographs are included as part of the induction procedure, this rate rises to 65 percent or almost two-thirds of all participants formed false memories for events that never happened to them (Lindsay et al., 2004). As Lindsay et al. (2004, p. 153) pointed out:

> These findings are particularly dramatic in that the subjects judged as having false memories gave quite high ratings of the extent to which they felt they were remembering the event, of the extent to which remembering the event was like reliving it, and of their confidence that the event had actually occurred.

There is also considerable evidence that people can come to have memories for traumatic events that they could not possibly have witnessed. For example, Crombag, Wagenaar and van Koppen (1996) studied people's memory for the October 1992 El Al Boeing 747 crash into an 11-story apartment building in Amsterdam, which killed the crew of four and 39 people inside the building. While there were no television crews there to film the actual crash, they did record the ensuing fire and rescue of survivors from the building. Ten months after the crash, the Dutch participants were questioned about their memories, including the leading question, "Did you see the television film of the moment the plane hit the apartment building?" Interestingly, as in the implanted memory studies above, 66 percent or two-thirds of the respondents said they had seen a TV film of the plane crashing into the apartment building. Other examples of false memories for traumatic events include misremembering the 1986 explosion of the space shuttle *Challenger* (Neisser & Harsch, 1992), the 9/11 attacks on the Trade Center in New York in 2001 (Hirst et al., 2009; Schmidt, 2004), and the death of Princess Diana (Ost, Vrij, Costall, & Bull, 2002). In this latter study, almost half (45 percent) of the British participants reported they had seen a nonexistent film of the actual car crash. Thus, people frequently misremember important parts of personally and historically significant traumatic events and add critical details in their memory narratives about key components of these events that were not present in what they witnessed (Nourkova, Bernstein, & Loftus, 2004).

The final point concerning the similarity of the scientific study of implanted, false memories and the types of memories we are dealing with in the cases outlined earlier is that some suggest that it is not simply the emotions such as trauma and fear that are not well studied, something we have seen is not true, but that the emotions related to shame, disgust and embarrassment of childhood sexual abuse that is absent in the scientific study of false memories. Although not studied in as much depth as other emotional reactions, these other emotions have been examined scientifically. Indeed, when these emotions are examined, it turns out that emotional elaboration of events that give rise to negative emotions such as disgust, embarrassment, being upset and angry, even resentful leads to *heightened susceptibility* to the formation of false memories (e.g. Drivdahl, Zaragoza, & Learned, 2009). In fact, "... emotional elaboration leads to higher false memory than other types of meaningful elaboration, thus providing evidence that the emotional content of the elaboration plays a role in promoting false memory development" (Drivdahl et al., 2009, p. 13).

On the other hand, concerning the ease of implanting implausible events, the previous literature reveals that people can come to believe that they can remember things that are impossible. Other examples include research showing that people can come to believe that they saw "Bugs Bunny" (a Warner Brothers character) at a Disney resort (e.g. Braun, Ellis, & Loftus, 2002). Unlike the suggestion that it is more difficult to implant false memories of an implausible than a plausible event, there is evidence that implausible events (e.g. having tea with Prince Charles – Strange, Sutherland, & Garry, 2006; or being abducted by a UFO – Otgaar, Candel, Merckelbach, & Wade, 2009) are relatively easy to implant in both children and adults.

Taken together, when the entire literature on implanted memories is considered, it is not the case that implanted memory studies are not comparable with implanting entirely false memories of repeated sexual abuse. To the contrary, the rich literature on this topic indicates that implanted memories are very similar to the matters being discussed in many of the court cases elaborated earlier in this chapter and bear direct relevance to the issue of how people can come to believe that events that never happened to them did happen to them, whether they are negative or positive, plausible or implausible.

## Conclusion

As reviewed in this chapter, there is considerable scientific evidence to indicate that memory, even memory for traumatic events, is reconstructive and is prone to a variety of different types of errors that can lead to misremembering at best and false memories at worst. This is particularly true for narratives concerning alleged early memories of events that must have been formed decades earlier. These memory facts are consistent with the rather large theoretical and empirical literatures on children's and adults' traumatic memory and is consistent with all of the scientific evidence reviewed to date. Regardless of whether the events were or were not traumatic, recollections of decades-old memories of alleged events, ones that would have been formed early in childhood, cannot be considered accurate and errorless, especially in the absence of corroborating evidence. Indeed, even if one were to accept the proposition that some parts of our reconstructions are true and other parts false, it is impossible to tell which is which. Is the claim that we were abused the true part, with the filling in of the sensory and perceptual details the false part, or is the initial presumption that we had been abused false, and some of the details (e.g. the people we mention, the house we lived in, the clothes we wore) true?

To illustrate the problem, recall that early memories are said to be decontextualized fragments from our early experiences. If true, then how do such fragments get translated into coherent memories? In many cases, such memories must be reinterpreted in the current context (our current needs and motivations) in which we find ourselves (e.g. Howe, 2011). That is, these memories are no longer the simple vestiges of events that remain in our faded memories, but can become full-blown episodes we come to believe are a part of our past. For example, one woman recounted what she said was a very vivid memory from her early childhood. In this recollection, she remembers being in a room that was both dark and hot, lying head down and naked in a crib. Her buttocks were raised because she was on her knees in the crib and she remembered seeing a shadowy figure behind her. This is the extent of the memory, but she admitted that she had needed to create a memory for childhood abuse, that this recollection would certainly have served her well. Instead, she asked her mother whether she could remember anything like this happening to her as a child. Her mother replied yes, that when she was young she had pneumonia, was laid in the position she remembered in order for her chest to drain, had to be kept in a warm room with a vaporizer, and that her temperature had to be monitored until her fever broke.

Importantly, what this example shows is that although she could remember a fragment of an early childhood experience, one that was confirmed by her mother, this fragment was not properly contextualized in her memory. If she had created a memory for early childhood sexual abuse based on this fragment, that part of the memory would certainly be true. However, the further contextualization of the fragment into a sexual abuse narrative would have been false. The problem is, once this narrative has been created, we the memory experts and those who are the triers of fact can never be certain, without additional corroborating evidence, which of the parts of this alleged experience were true and which of the parts were false.

Given that such narrative accounts are emblematic of historic childhood sexual abuse cases in which there exists no other evidence than one person's memory, including the cases outlined at the beginning of this chapter , how could we evaluate the veracity of such claims? To the extent that these cases exhibit inconsistencies with what we know about the nature of autobiographical recollection of early childhood experiences (e.g. they are contextualized narratives about complex event sequences), we can be reasonably certain that such recollections are not consistent with what the scientific literature would anticipate. If so, then we have to answer the equally difficult question concerning how it is that these complainants come to believe that their allegations are based on a recollection of events that actually happened? The literature on reconstructive memory processes gives some indication as to how people can form false memories, as well as how repeated recall attempts can influence this process. As noted, it is relatively easy to implant false memories for entire events (even negative ones), particularly when the person believes these events to be plausible. Apparently, complainants believe these events to be within the realm of plausibility, making it entirely possible that many of these allegations are based on false, not true, memories.

So herein lies the problem that confronts the early memory researcher in the courtroom–complainants believe they have experienced childhood sexual abuse and provide narratives describing this alleged abuse and the alleged abuser. Without independent corroboration from another person or hard evidence that the abuse occurred (e.g. a medical report verifying and detailing the abuse), how can we determine if the memory is real? As I mentioned earlier, there is no litmus test that will tell us whether a memory is true or false (see Bernstein & Loftus, 2009). However, we know that there are a number of important factors that can make a false memory feel and appear real. On this basis, we can examine the evidence and attempt to determine whether what we see is consistent with the scientific evidence concerning recall of memories we know to be true or recall of memories that we know to be false. Given the age at which many of these events are said to have taken place, it is unlikely that the complainants discussed earlier would have formed an enduring memory for these events that would be suddenly remembered (or appear as a flashback) some decades later. Indeed, even if there is an element of the memory that may have occurred earlier in the person's life (e.g. lying in a crib), the scientific evidence points to the possibility that many of these complainants' narratives contain a substantial number of features that may be false, not true. Thus, there is the possibility that the foundation for many of these allegations are more consistent with what we know about false memories than true memories and are, therefore, likely to be unreliable as evidence of an alleged assault.

# References

Abenavoli, R., & Henkel, L. A. (2009). Remembering when we last remembered our childhood experiences: Effects of age and context on retrospective metamemory judgments. *Applied Cognitive Psychology, 23,* 717–732.

Ackil, J. K., van Abbema, D. L., & Bauer, P. J. (2003). After the storm: Enduring differences in mother-child recollections of traumatic and nontraumatic events. *Journal of Experimental Child Psychology, 84,* 286–309.

Alexander, K. W., Quas, J. A., Goodman, G. S., Ghetti, S., Edelstein, R. S., Redlich, A. D., et al. (2005). Traumatic impact predicts long-term memory for documented child sexual abuse. *Psychological Science, 16,* 33–40.

Bahrick, L. E., Parker, J. F., Fivush, R., & Levitt, M. (1998). The effects of stress on young children's memory for a natural disaster. *Journal of Experimental Psychology: Applied, 4,* 308–331.

Bauer, P. J., Burch, M. M., van Abbema, D. L., & Ackil, J. K. (2008). Talking about twisters: How mothers and children converse about a devastating tornado. In M. L. Howe, G. S. Goodman, & D. Cicchetti (Eds), *Stress, Trauma, and Children's Memory Development: Neurobiological, Cognitive, Clinical, and Legal Perspectives* (pp. 204–235). New York: Oxford University Press.

Bernstein, D. M., & Loftus, E. F. (2009). How to tell is a particular memory is true or false. *Perspectives on Psychological Science, 4,* 370–374.

Brainerd, C. J., Holliday, R. E., Reyna, V. F., Yang, C., & Toglia, M. P. (2010). Developmental reversals in false memory: Effects of emotional valence and arousal. *Journal of Experimental Child Psychology, 107,* 137–154.

Brainerd, C. J., & Reyna, V. F. (2005). *The Science of False Memory.* NY: Oxford University Press.

Brainerd, C. J., Stein, L. M., Silveira, R. A., Rohenkohl, G., & Reyna, V. F. (2008). How does negative emotion cause false memories? *Psychological Science, 19,* 919–925.

Braun, K. A., Ellis, R., & Loftus, E. F. (2002). Make my memory: How advertising can change our memories of the past. *Psychology and Marketing, 19,* 1–23.

Bremner, J. D., Shobe, K. K., & Kihlstrom, J. F. (2000). False memories in women with self-reported childhood sexual abuse: An empirical study. *Psychological Science, 11,* 333–337.

Brennen, T., Dybdahl, R., & Kapidzic, A. (2007). Trauma-related and neutral false memories in war-induced posttraumatic stress disorder. *Consciousness and Cognition, 16,* 877–885.

Brewin, C. R. (2003). *Post-traumatic Stress Disorder: Malady or Myth?* New Haven, CT: Yale University Press.

Bruce, D., Phillips-Grant, K., Wilcox-O'Hearn, L. A., Robinson, J. A., & Francis, L. (2007). Memory fragments as components of autobiographical knowledge. *Applied Cognitive Psychology, 21,* 307–324.

Bruce, D., Wilcox-O'Hearn, L. A., Robinson, J. A., Phillips-Grant, K., Francis, L., & Smith, M. C. (2005). Fragment memories mark the end of childhood amnesia. *Memory & Cognition, 33,* 567–576.

Budson, A. E., Todman, R. W., Chong, H., Adams, E. H., Kensinger, E. A., Krangel, T. S., & Wright, C. I. (2006). False recognition of emotional word lists in aging and Alzheimer disease. *Cognitive and Behavioral Neurology, 19,* 71–78.

Candel, I., Wade, K., & Howe, M. L. (2008). *The role of plausibility and valence in the development of children's implanted false memories.* Technical Report, University of Maastricht, Maastricht, The Netherlands.

Cheit, R. E. (1998). Consider this, skeptics of recovered memory. *Ethics and Behavior, 8,* 141–160.

Clancy, S. A., McNally, R. J., Schacter, D. L., Lenzenweger, M. F., & Pitman, R. K. (2002). Memory distortion in people reporting abduction by aliens. *Journal of Abnormal Psychology, 111,* 455–461.

Clancy, S. A., Schacter, D. L., McNally, R. J., & Pitman, R. K. (2000). False recognition in women reporting recovered memories of sexual abuse. *Psychological Science, 11,* 26–31.

Crombag, H. F. M., Wagenaar, W. A., & van Koppen, P. J. (1996). Crashing memories and the problem of 'source monitoring'. *Applied Cognitive Psychology, 10,* 95–104.

Davis, D., & Loftus, E. F. (2007). Internal and external sources of misinformation in adult witness memory. In M. P. Toglia, J. D. Read, D. F. Ross, & R. C. L. Lindsay (Eds), *Handbook of Eyewitness Psychology.* Volume 9, *Memory for Events* (pp. 195–237). Mahwah, NJ: Erlbaum.

Drivdahl, S. B., Zaragoza, M. S., & Learned, D. M. (2009). The role of emotional elaboration in the creation of false memories. *Applied Cognitive Psychology, 23,* 13–25.

Dyregov, A., Gjestad, R., & Raundalen, M. (2002). Children exposed to warfare: A longitudinal study. *Journal of Traumatic Stress, 15,* 59–68.

Fivush, R. (2002). Scripts, schemas, and memory for trauma. In N. L. Stein, P. J. Bauer, & M. Rabinowitz (Eds), *Representation, Memory, and Development: Essays in Honor of Jean Mandler* (pp. 53–74). Mahwah, NJ: Erlbaum.

Fivush, R., Hazzard, A., Sales, J. M., Sarfati, D., & Brown, T. (2003). Creating coherence out of chaos? Children's narratives of emotionally positive and negative events. *Applied Cognitive Psychology, 17,* 1–19.

Freyd, J. J., & Gleaves, D. H. (1996). 'Remembering' words not presented in lists: Relevance to the current recovered/false memory controversy. *Journal of Experimental Psychology: Learning, Memory, and Cognition, 22,* 811–813.

Geraerts, E., Smeets, E., Jelicic, M., van Heerden, J., & Merckelbach, H. (2005). Fantasy proneness, but not self-reported trauma is related to DRM performance of women reporting recovered memories of childhood sexual abuse. *Consciousness and Cognition, 14,* 602–612.

Goodman, G. S., & Quas, J. A. (1997). Trauma and memory: Individual differences in children's recounting of a stressful experience. In N. L. Stein, P. A. Ornstein, B. Tversky, & C. J. Brainerd (Eds), *Memory for Everyday and Emotional Events* (pp. 267–294). Mahwah, NJ: Erlbaum.

Hagenaars, M. A., Brewin, C. R., van Minnen, A., Holmes, E. A., & Hoogduin, K. A. L. (2010). Intrusive images and intrusive thoughts as different phenomena: Two experimental studies. *Memory, 18,* 76–84.

Heaps, C. M., & Nash, M. (2001). Comparing recollective experience in true and false autobiographical memories. *Journal of Experimental Psychology: Learning, Memory, and Cognition, 27,* 920–930.

Herrmann, D., Sheets, V., Gruneberg, M., & Torres, R. (2005). Are self reports of memory failure accurate? *Applied Cognitive Psychology, 19,* 821–841.

Hirst, W., Phelps, E. A., Buckner, R. L., Budson, A. E., Cuc, A., Gabrieli, J. D. E., et al. (2009). Long-term memory for the terrorist attack of September 11: Flashbulb memories, event memories, and the factors that influence their retention. *Journal of Experimental Psychology: General, 138,* 161–176.

Howe, M. L. (1998). Individual differences in factors that modulate storage and retrieval of traumatic memories. *Development and Psychopathology, 10,* 681–698.

Howe, M. L. (2000). *The fate of early memories: Developmental science and the retention of childhood experiences.* Washington, DC: American Psychological Association.

Howe, M. L. (2007). Children's emotional false memory. *Psychological Science, 18,* 856–860.

Howe, M. L. (2011). *The nature of early memory: An adaptive theory of the genesis and development of memory.* New York: Oxford University Press.

Howe, M. L., Candel, I., Otgaar, H., Malone, C., & Wimmer, M. C. (2010). Valence and the development of immediate and long-term false memory illusions. *Memory, 18,* 58–75.

Howe, M. L., Cicchetti, D., & Toth, S. L. (2006). Children's basic memory processes, stress, and maltreatment. *Development and Psychopathology, 18,* 759–769.

Howe, M. L., Cicchetti, D., Toth, S. L., & Cerrito, B. M. (2004). True and false memories in maltreated children. *Child Development, 75,* 1402–1417.

Howe, M. L., Courage, M. L., & Peterson, C. (1995). Intrusions in preschoolers' recall of traumatic childhood events. *Psychonomic Bulletin & Review, 2,* 130–134.

Howe, M. L., Courage, M. L., & Rooksby. M. (2009). The genesis and development of autobiographical memory. In M. Courage and N. Cowan (Eds), *The Development of Memory in Infancy and Childhood* (pp. 177–196). Hove, UK: Psychology Press.

Howe, M. L., Goodman, G. S., & Cicchetti, D. (Eds) (2008). *Stress, Trauma, and Children's Memory Development: Neurobiological, Cognitive, Clinical, and Legal Perspectives.* New York: Oxford University Press.

Howe, M. L., Toth, S. L., & Cicchetti, D. (2011). Can maltreated children inhibit true and false memories for emotional information? *Child Development, 82,* 967–981.

Hyman, I. E., Husband, T. H., & Billings, F. J. (1995). False memories of childhood experiences. *Applied Cognitive Psychology, 9,* 181–197.

Kinzie, J. D., Sack, W. H., Angell, R. H., Manson, S., & Rath, B. (1986). The psychiatric effects of massive trauma on Cambodian children: I. The children. *Journal of the American Academy of Child and Adolescent Psychiatry, 25,* 370–376.

Laor, N., Wolmer, L., Mayes, L. C., Gershon, A., Weizman, R., & Cohen, D. J. (1997). Israeli preschool children under Scuds: A 30-month follow-up. *Journal of the American Academy of Child and Adolescent Psychiatry, 36,* 349–356.

Lindsay, D. S., Hagen, L., Read, J. D., Wade, K. A., & Garry, M. (2004). True photographs and false memories. *Psychological Science, 15,* 149–154.

Loftus, E. F., & Bernstein, D. M. (2005). Rich false memories: The royal road to success. In A. F. Healy (Ed.), *Experimental Cognitive Psychology and its Applications* (pp. 101–113). Washington, DC: American Psychological Association.

Loftus, E. F., & Davis, D. (2006). Recovered memories. *Annual Review of Clinical Psychology, 2,* 469–498.

Loftus, E. F., & Guyer, M. (2002a). Who abused Jane Doe? The hazards of a single case history: Part I. *Skeptical Inquirer, 26,* 24–32.

Loftus, E. F., & Guyer, M. (2002b). Who abused Jane Doe? The hazards of a single case history: Part II. *Skeptical Inquirer, 26,* 37–40.

Loftus, E. F., & Pickrell, J. E. (1995). The formation of false memories. *Psychiatric Annals, 25,* 720–725.

McNally, R. J. (2003). *Remembering Trauma.* Cambridge, MA: Harvard University Press.

McNally, R. J., & Geraerts, E. (2009). A new solution to the recovered memory debate. *Perspectives on Psychological Science, 4,* 126–134.

Merckelbach, H., Smeets, T., Geraerts, E., Jelicic, M., Bouwen, A., & Smeets, E. (2006). I haven't thought about this for years. Dating recent recalls of vivid memories. *Applied Cognitive Psychology, 20,* 33–42.

Meyersburg, C. A., Bogdan, R., Gallo, D. A., & McNally, R. J. (2009). False memory propensity in people reporting recovered memories of past lives. *Journal of Abnormal Psychology, 118,* 399–404.

Nadel, L., & Jacobs, W. J. (1998). Trauma memory is special. *Current Directions in Psychological Science, 7,* 154–157.

Najarian, L. M., Goenjian, A. K., Pelcovitz, D., Mandel, E., & Najarian, B. (1996). Relocation after a disaster: Posttraumatic stress disorder in Armenia after the earthquake. *Journal of the American Academy of Child and Adolescent Psychiatry, 35,* 374–383.

Neisser, U., & Harsch, N. (1992). Phantom flashbulbs: False recollections of hearing the news about the *Challenger.* In E. Winograd & U. Neisser (Eds), *Affect and Accuracy in Recall: Studies of Flashbulb Memories* (pp. 9–31). New York: Cambridge University Press.

Nourkova, V., Bernstein, D. M., & Loftus, E. F. (2004). Altering traumatic memory. *Cognition and Emotion, 18,* 575–585.

Ornstein, P. A. (1995). Children's long-term retention of salient personal experiences. *Journal of Traumatic Stress, 8,* 581–605.

Ost, J., Vrij, A., Costall, A., & Bull, R. (2002). Crashing memories and reality monitoring: Distinguishing between perceptions, imaginations and 'false memories'. *Applied Cognitive Psychology, 16,* 125–134.

Otgaar, H., Candel, I., & Merckelbach, H. (2008). Children's false memories: Easier to elicit for a negative than for a neutral event. *Acta Psychologica, 128,* 350–354.

Otgaar, H., Candel, I., Merckelbach, H., & Wade, K. A. (2009). Abducted by a UFO: Prevalence information affects young children's false memories for an implausible event. *Applied Cognitive Psychology, 23,* 115–125.

Pezdek, K., & Lam, S. (2007). What research paradigms have cognitive psychologists used to study "False memory," and what are the implications of these choices? *Consciousness and Cognition, 16,* 2–17.

Piper, A. (1999). A skeptic considers, then responds to Cheit. *Ethics and Behavior, 9,* 277–293.

Porter, S., Yuille, J. C., & Lehman, D. R. (1999). The nature of real, implanted, and fabricated memories for emotional childhood events: Implications for the recovered memory debate. *Law and Human Behavior, 23,* 517–537.

Pynoos, R. S., & Nader, K. (1989). Children's memory and proximity to violence. *Journal of the American Academy of Child and Adolescent Psychiatry, 28,* 236–241.

Rothschild, B. (2000). *The Body Remembers: The Psychophysiology of Trauma and Trauma Treatment.* New York: Norton.

Rovee-Collier, C., Hayne, H., & Columbo, M. (2001). *The Development of Implicit and Explicit Memory.* Philadelphia: John Benjamins.

Rubin, D. C., & Talarico, J. M. (2009). A comparison of dimensional models of emotion: Evidence from emotions, prototypical events, autobiographical memories, and words. *Memory, 17,* 802–808.

Schmidt, S. R. (2004). Autobiographical memories for the September 11th attacks: Reconstructive errors and emotional impairment of memory. *Memory & Cognition, 32,* 443–454.

Schwartz, E. D., & Kowalski, J. M. (1991). Malignant memories: PTSD in children and adults after a school shooting. *Journal of the American Academy of Child and Adolescent Psychiatry, 30,* 936–944.

Shaw, J. A., Applegate, B., & Schorr, C. (1996). Twenty-one month follow-up study of school-age children exposed to Hurricane Andrew. *Journal of the American Academy of Child and Adolescent Psychiatry, 35,* 359–364.

Strange, D., Sutherland, R., & Garry, M. (2006). Event plausibility does not determine children's false memories. *Memory, 14,* 937–951.

Terr, L. (1988). What happens to early memories of trauma? A study of twenty children under age five at the time of documented events. *Journal of the American Academy of Child and Adolescent Psychiatry, 27,* 96–104.

Tyano, S., Iancu, I., Solomon, Z., Sever, J., Goldstein, I., Touveianna, Y. et al. (1996). Seven-year follow-up of child survivors of a bus-train collision. *Journal of the American Academy of Child and Adolescent Psychiatry, 35,* 365–373.

van der Kolk, B. A., & Fisler, R. (1995). Dissociation and the fragmentary nature of traumatic memories: Overview and exploratory study. *Journal of Traumatic Stress, 8,* 505–525.

Wade, K. A., Sharman, S. J., Garry, M., Memon, A., Mazzoni, G., Merckelbach, H., & Loftus, E. F. (2007). False claims about false memory research. *Consciousness and Cognition, 16,* 18–28.

Wagenaar, W. A., & Groeneweg, J. (1990). The memory of concentration camp survivors. *Applied Cognitive Psychology, 4,* 77–87.

Zoellner, L. A., Foa, E. B., Brigidi, B. D., & Przeworski, A. (2000). Are trauma victims susceptible to "false memories"? *Journal of Abnormal Psychology, 109,* 517–524.

# CHAPTER 3

# Theory and Processes in Memory Development: Childhood to Adolescence

JONATHAN C. CORBIN, EVAN A. WILHELMS,
VALERIE F. REYNA, AND CHARLES J. BRAINERD

This chapter focuses on the theory and basic science that is currently driving understanding of children and adolescents' memory processes relevant to forensic settings. Developmental changes in memory are particularly relevant to situations in which children and adolescents are the only witnesses and victims to crimes, which is often the case for crimes such as child sexual abuse and domestic violence. In many instances, the child's testimony is the major source of evidence for or against a defendant. Assessment of the accuracy of children and adolescents' testimony in such cases depends on implementing lessons from research into memory processes, of which experiments pertaining to false memory and suggestibility represent the most important studies of that literature for the forensic context (Reyna, Mills, Estrada, & Brainerd, 2007).

We begin this chapter with an overall assessment of the current techniques that are being used to measure true memory, false memory and misinformation effects. This section serves as a guide for the tasks and terminology that we refer to throughout the rest of the chapter, including description of both recall and recognition testing paradigms. Next, we introduce constructivism and schema theory, which are foundational theories of memory that paved the way for more recent theories of memory and development. These theories rose from experiments that led to the conclusion that memory is reconstructed from one's individual experience, and that memory does not necessarily reflect a true experience, but rather one's interpretation of it. It was also predicted that as people age, their memory of an experience should improve.

Later research has proven these claims to be incomplete (namely, that memory for exact events can be measured and, under specific circumstances, it is possible for children to show more accurate memory than adults). These conflicting findings lead into an analysis of two recent theories of memory: the *source-monitoring framework* (SMF) and *fuzzy-trace theory* (FTT).

Following a review of constructivism/schema theory, we give an overview of the theory behind SMF. Specifically, we address the fundamental assumption of SMF that memory errors are primarily caused by source confusions (Johnson, 2006), and the prediction that source confusions will decline with age (Foley, Johnson, & Raye, 1983). We also address the limitations of SMF as a cognitive model with respect to other evidence. After reviewing this evidence for basic memory models, we will briefly address how these discoveries have influenced applied research in spontaneous and misinformation studies, as well as how such application pertains to children in forensic contexts.

We discuss fuzzy-trace theory, which postulates two independent memory processes, one that focuses on storage of surface details (i.e. *verbatim memory*) and a second process that focuses on the bottom-line meaning of information (i.e. *gist memory*; Reyna & Brainerd, 1995). We describe how verbatim and gist memory develop with age and how these processes account for true and false-memory performance, including misinformation effects (Reyna & Kiernan, 1994), as well as the prediction that false memory does increase with age in contexts in which related meaning is a salient factor (Brainerd, Reyna, & Ceci, 2008). We also discuss further predictions made by FTT regarding how individual differences in the ability to process semantic information, negative emotions, and manipulations of verbatim and gist memory impact true and false memory in children and adolescents.

## How true and false memory is measured

Memory experiments tend to follow a similar format, in that participants are exposed to a list of memory targets – such as words, sentences, pictures or narratives – and are then required to recognize the targets among distractors on recognition tests, or freely recall the original targets (Reyna et al., 2006). As a result, studies of false memory are studies of true memory as well, because measures of accuracy can be obtained. Both memory accuracy and memory errors are necessary to reveal a comprehensive theory of memory, the mechanism of which will be detailed below.

There are two basic paradigms for testing memory: recognition and recall. Recognition tests contain test probes that are either the original target words or unpresented items. Unpresented distractors can be further divided into two groups: items that in some salient way are similar to the targets, usually in a meaningful, associative or semantic way (i.e. related distractors), and items that do not share meaningful qualities with targets (i.e. unrelated distractors). For example, a list of memory targets may be a list of items in some taxonomic group, such as musical instruments (flute, piano, drums), in which case a related distractor could be a musical instrument not on the list (banjo), and an unrelated distractor would not be a member of that taxonomic group (sheep). Recall tests are administered in a more straightforward manner, in which the index of false memory is simply the rate at which unpresented items are claimed by the participant to have been presented. Such erroneously recalled items are referred to as intrusions.

Much of the research on children's false memory has centered on the "misinformation effect," which typically uses a three-stage procedure (Loftus, Miller, & Burns, 1978). This procedure consists of an initial phase, in which targets are first presented (a red hat), then a misinformation phase, in which participants are given a distractor (a green hat), and then a test phase (was the hat red or green?) (Ceci, Ross, & Toglia, 1987). Before a decade ago, most of the research done on false memories in children was conducted in this paradigm, which included a misinformation phase that suggested information to the subject that is contrary to the facts (see Bruck & Ceci, 1999 for a review).

## Theories of memory and development

Although there are numerous theories of memory in the literature, most of these, such as schema theory, have been discredited by recent evidence (e.g. Alba & Hasher, 1983). Successful aspects of these theories survive in more contemporary theories discussed here, which have also been applied in forensic contexts. In addition, we wish to focus on theories that address mechanisms for both true and false memory, as both are relevant to forensic settings. Two specific theories that stand out in the false memory and forensic research literature are the source-monitoring framework and fuzzy-trace theory. These theories both have well-established predictions for how memory develops with age. We will briefly introduce constructivism as an antecedent to these theories.

### *Constructivism and schema theory*

Both source-monitoring theory and fuzzy-trace theory obtain their theoretical roots from the constructivist theory of memory (Mitchell & Johnson, 2000; Reyna & Brainerd, 1995), which states that information – both true and false – is constructed at the point of encoding (Paris & Carter, 1973). In a classic study, Bransford and Franks (1971) demonstrated false recognition in adults based on the semantic consistency between presented and unpresented sentences. Some example sentences included statements such as, "The ants ate the sweet jelly," and, "The sweet jelly was on the table." When presented with other sentences of varying length, participants falsely believed they had been presented with the statement, "The ants ate the sweet jelly that was on the table," a statement which is semantically consistent but not presented. Subjects' confidence in the false belief was often higher than for originally presented statements. The explanation at the time for results such as these was that memory is constructive and based on schemata. This assertion, which is similar to the claim made by Piaget and Inhelder (1973, p. 382) that "the schemata used by the memory are borrowed from the intelligence," would logically predict that these false identifications would increase with age, as the intelligence from which schemata is borrowed would likewise increase with age. This prediction, however, met with mixed results in practice.

This conclusion that memory is schematic or constructive was found to be subject to the confounding of word familiarity with semantic relationship: that is, when in the above experiments unpresented distractor sentences are listed, they contain words that were in the original statements, whereas false sentences – those which are contrary to the schema of the original sentences – contain new words. The confound of this previous research is that it is impossible to determine from these studies alone whether the semantic congruence of the distractor sentences or the mere familiarity of the words used in the sentences was the cause of the false recognition.

Reyna and Kiernan (1994) conducted research in which these variables were unconfounded. In this study, 6- and 9-year olds were presented with stories that varied in being either the expression of spatial relationships (e.g. a bird is in a cage under a table), or of linear relationships (e.g. cocoa is hotter than tea, which is hotter than coffee). Test sentences varied based on whether they were factually true or not based on the stated premise, whether they contained an original premise or an inference based on that premise, and whether or not the premise or inference contained novel words (e.g. "cooler" instead of "hotter"). Subjects were instructed to say no to any sentences in which anything was different from the original sentence. Distractor sentences representing true inferences were falsely recognized at a lower rate among older children. These results contradict the previously mentioned prediction that naturally rises from constructivist theory – that older children should exhibit memory errors for sentences that preserve meaning at a higher rate than younger children do – in fact, the opposite was found.

These experiments also revealed a critical element to accurately measuring false memories, namely, that explicit instructions to reject meaning-consistent distractors are necessary. Alba and Hasher (1983) had previously found that subjects presume that their responses should be based on the meaning behind the verbatim text rather than the verbatim text itself, as often occurred in experiments in the constructivist paradigm. The possibility, then, is that memories may appear constructive when in reality participants merely misunderstood the task. In the above experiments (Reyna & Kiernan, 1994, 1995), examples of true sentences that were not verbatim replicates of targets were given before testing, with the instruction that such sentences were to be rejected. The issue of task misunderstandings being mistaken for constructive memories was thus avoided. Again, that mistakes can be reduced with careful instruction is of particular relevance to forensic settings, such as in interrogations and interviews in which witnesses are required to remember the exact wording of statements, not just meaning-consistent wordings (see Reyna, Holliday, & Marche, 2002).

It has also been noted that constructivism fails to predict the storage of details that are not meaningful to the individual and thus cannot be schematically encoded (Alba & Hasher, 1983). To whit,

> At least some schematically unimportant information is stored. At least some details are stored no matter what the extent of a person's prior knowledge, and no matter whether that knowledge is activated at encoding, lexical and syntactic information, along with semantic information, are all accorded representation in memory. Memory of a topic does not seem to consist of a tightly integrated set of all relevant information. Although subjects may impose their own interpretations on incoming stimuli, they appear to do so less often than schema theory would suggest. When people do generate interpretations, source identifying markers are not necessarily lost. (Alba & Hasher, 1983, p. 225)

Constructivism thus had the limitation that it depended upon existing schema for encoding, whereas evidence shows that information can be encoded without an existing schema. Both source-monitoring framework and fuzzy-trace theory address this limitation.

## Source-monitoring framework

Source-monitoring framework (SMF) is a theory that describes memories as judged to be either true or false based on attribution of the source of the memory (Johnson, 2006). A memory is generally deemed to be true when the level of detail for the memory is high. Misidentification of memories occurs through increasing the similarity of memories from different sources (Johnson, 2006). For example, in the case of a false memory, the sources being confused are the external event as it occurred in reality, and internal thoughts that are similarly related, yet untrue. When the amount of detail in memory traces is similar between these two sources, the false memory is mistakenly deemed to be accurate. Given that the details in memory generally improve with age (Brainerd & Reyna, 2001; Brainerd, Reyna, & Ceci, 2008), this framework makes clear developmental predictions regarding decreases of monitoring errors with age.

Herein we will briefly discuss the origin of source monitoring, followed by reviewing the terms and constructs of the SMF and describing the processes that SMF proposes to occur during the encoding and retrieval of memories. We will then review the developmental predictions that the theory makes, as well as the evidence regarding these predictions.

# Background theory

## Monitoring at encoding and retrieval

According to SMF, the monitoring of source occurs during both encoding and retrieval of memories. Evidence that monitoring can occur during encoding is found by priming participants before study of target materials that source mistakes can result in the possibility of false memories (Gallo, Roediger, & McDermott, 2001). Warning participants of the effect at this time point has a resultant decline in false recognition of distractor items, an effect that was not replicated when the warning was given after study but before testing.

Despite this, however, source monitoring has been a process primarily associated with retrieval (Mitchell & Johnson, 2000; Johnson 2006). SMF proposes a monitoring mechanism that discriminates between representations of actual events and presentations from reality and those that were merely imagined. This distinction is referred to as a discrimination between internal and external memories (Johnson, Hashtroudi, & Lindsay, 1993). Furthermore, this process must also monitor distinctions between multiple external sources as well as multiple internal sources (e.g. distinctions between what may be thought at different points in time or in different contexts). In all cases, this mechanism relies on characteristics of the memories in making judgments about them. Including previously discussed phenomenological details, judgments can be based on:

> records of perceptual information (e.g. sounds and color), contextual information (spatial and temporal), semantic detail, affective information (e.g. emotional reactions), and cognitive operations (e.g. records of organizing, elaborating, retrieving, and identified) that were established when the memory was formed. (Johnson et al., 1993, p. 4)

## Distinctiveness effect

As previously mentioned, it has been proposed that when memories are recovered along with details of the phenomenological experience of the original presentation of materials, these can generally be thought to be memories of actual past events (although this can often be a mistaken conclusion; see Jacoby, Kelley, & Dywan, 1989). This ability to discern true memories from the level of detail associated with them is referred to as the *distinctiveness effect*, and is generally seen in adults. For example, if a subject recalls seeing a word on a word list, and additionally remembers where the word was on the page and what typeface it was printed in, this level of detail would generally indicate that the event – seeing the original word on the page – happened in reality. Details of the phenomenological experience could refer to aspects of the event that were in the periphery (e.g. it was rainy that evening and a streetlamp was blinking on and off), or specific details about the situation (e.g. the robber was wearing glasses, and a digital watch on his left wrist). The distinctiveness effect can be seen in elements of associated false responses other than the phenomenological character. For example, if a distractor word on a false recognition test just happens to be longer than many of the target words, then they are easily rejected by the monitoring process as being distinctively different from the memorized targets (Roediger, Watson, McDermott, & Gallo, 2001).

*Heuristic and systematic processes.* The theoretical claim is that the monitoring process of evaluating information about source is most often automatic, rapid and unconscious, in that one makes these decisions while remembering the memories these decisions are about, without this process entering into one's awareness. Such evaluations can also occur deliberatively, in cases in which plausibility of memories must be consciously evaluated, and in these situations supporting memories can be brought to mind. Within the source-monitoring paradigm, these divergent processes are referred to as "heuristic" and "systematic," respectively (Johnson, 2006). Both processes require thresholds of detail for the above-named characteristics (e.g. perceptual information, contextual information, etc.). An event is deemed to have occurred by this process, for example, if the level of phenomenological detail exceeds this certain threshold. Criteria for the systematic process might be, for example, that the memory of an event meets a certain threshold of consistency with other events that are known to have occurred (specifically, other memories brought to mind in deliberation).

As these two examples illustrate, the evaluations made by the heuristic and systematic components of the source-monitoring process may produce opposing results. For example, the phenomenological detail of the memory trace has reached the threshold necessary to be considered an event that actually occurred, but the memory trace may be implausible when compared to other memories brought to mind. This illustrates that in monitoring judgments, various characteristics are implicitly given more weight than others, perhaps in this example that the implausibility of the memory would supersede the fact that the detail has reached its requisite threshold, and that the monitoring process would in turn reject the memory trace as having been a likely event in reality.

Indeed, even the thresholds of systematic and heuristic evaluations may be altered based on social context, which is a point of particular interest to the subject of memory in law. Specifically, it is presumed that the threshold of both these processes can be raised – e.g. that more phenomenological detail is required, or a higher standard of consistency with other memory traces is required for the memory to be deemed a representation of an actual event in reality – in the context of a testimony in a courtroom, when compared to the thresholds when recounting a story to a friend. In all the above illustrations of judgments of source, the conclusions are based on the qualities of memory traces themselves, which is dependent on the processes that occur during the encoding of the initial experience. It is easy to conceive of processing being compromised either at the point of encoding (e.g. stress or distraction prevents an individual from processing details, which will later impair one's ability to recognize the true incidence of the event) or at the point of deliberation (e.g. stress, distraction or time pressure could prevent an individual from retrieving information that would deem a specific memory trace implausible) (Johnson, Hashtroudi, & Lindsay, 1993; Johnson, 2006).

## Developmental predictions

A major prediction of SMF is that, as memories for source details will improve with age, ability to discriminate accurately between sources will also improve with age, and susceptibility to false memories will decline. For example, Foley, Johnson and Raye (1983) found that, though 6-year-olds and 17-year-olds were equally accurate in discriminating true memories of what they themselves said from what others had said, 6-year-olds were not as good at discriminating between what they said and what they merely thought (but see Sugrue, Strange, & Hayne, 2009). This was also despite the 6-year-olds being equally adept as older children at discrimination between external sources, as well as discrimination between their own thoughts and external sources. The source-monitoring framework identifies this finding as justification for the idea that the ability to monitor sources differentiated between self and other emerges earlier than the same ability between thought and action.

SMF also predicts that when untrue memory traces are imagined in greater detail, they are more difficult to differentiate from actually perceived realities (Johnson, 2006). For example, Segovia and Bailenson (2009) performed a study in which preschoolers (mean age = 4.96) and elementary school children (mean age = 6.46) were presented with a verbal narrative (e.g. a story of swimming with a whale) and then either guided through a virtual experience of that narrative, imagined participation in the same narrative or remained idle. The youngest children reported more false memories in the imagining and virtual conditions than in the idle condition, whereas no effect of condition was found in the older children. This evidence was used to indicate that the richness of imagery created difficulty in distinguishing between memories from the physical world and those that came merely from a mental or simulated image.

In a related study, Ghetti, Castelli and Lyons (2010) performed research that required participants aged 7–9, as well as adults, to either engage in, imagine or confabulate about (imagine and describe) actions that were designated as either common or bizarre. Bizarre actions involved common objects though they were engaged in an uncommon way (e.g. smelling a wall), whereas common actions consisted of common objects used conventionally (e.g. jumping rope). After taking a recognition test in which they were instructed to identify those actions that were actually enacted, participants indicated how confident they were in each answer, and also indicated how memorable each recognition prime was (or would be, for unrecognized primes). All age groups indicated higher confidence in accurate responses, though younger children were unable to exhibit high confidence in rejecting bizarre distractors. This was taken to indicate that the young children were not monitoring the memorability of actions, and that deficits in monitoring were specific rather than general.

Finally, the theory predicts that instructing individuals to explicitly make judgments about the source of memories (i.e. cuing the systematic process) should reduce the incidence of false recognition and recall (Reyna & Lloyd, 1997). This prediction was borne out in a study (Lindsay & Johnson, 1989) in which participants were presented with a picture of an office scene, followed by either a misleading text that described items that were actually in the scene with other items that fit the theme of the scene but were not actually present, or a control text that only described items that were actually in the scene. Furthermore, some subjects received a source-monitoring test in which they were instructed to think carefully about whether the item was present only in the picture, only in the text, both, or neither. Those who did not receive this prompt merely took the same yes/no recognition test regarding items in the original picture. As predicted, those who received a prompt to deliberately monitor the source of the memory were able to reduce the incidence of false recognition when compared to those in the misinformation group who did not receive the source-monitoring prompt.

Regarding these explicit prompts about source judgments, it should be noted that false recognition tends not to disappear completely when individuals are presented with such prompts, though reductions do occur (Reyna & Lloyd, 1997). One key factor in the magnitude of the effect has been demonstrated to be the instruction to visualize distractor cues, which SMF argues increases false memory through source misattribution, since the traces of misleading cues contain greater detail upon deliberate visualization. SMF offers no single clear explanation for this effect. Within the framework, it may be that the improvement in source judgment that accompanies the source-monitoring prompt is derived from either a more conservative criteria in judgment (i.e. that the threshold to deem a memory trace as representing an event in reality is raised) or from deliberately bringing to mind cognitive and perceptual cues as well as supporting memory traces (Johnson, Hashtroudi, & Lindsay, 1993).

The source-monitoring framework, in summary, is effective in describing many false-memory effects that deal with suggestibility. It is, however, more easily understood as a description of an effect rather than an explicit cognitive model. The theory does accurately predict that memory for source will improve with age, and thus source confusions will decrease with age. SMF predicts, however, that similarities between sources will only be confusing, though similarity between targets and distracters has also been found to be distinctive (Reyna, 2000). Although SMF predicts that memory for source will increase with age, and thus, false memory based on source-misattribution will decrease with age, it is important to mention that the studies described here noting the accuracies of predictions of the source-monitoring paradigm tend to be either source confusions between external sources (e.g. between heard and seen sources), or contain a deliberate suggestion phase in which the participants are instructed to imagine objects or events. Few studies are performed in the paradigm in which false memories occur without external source confusion or an imaginative prime, and thus, source-monitoring theory would have difficulty explaining effects that are commonly observed in spontaneous false memory, such as increases in incidence of false recognition and recall with age (Reyna & Lloyd, 1997).

## Fuzzy-trace theory

Fuzzy-trace theory is a dual-process memory model that integrates constructivist ideas with ideas from the verbal learning association tradition (Reyna & Brainerd, 1995). By dual-process theory, we mean that there are two memory representations that are encoded independently and simultaneously – gist memory (episodic memory for an item's semantic content) and verbatim memory (episodic memory traces for an item's surface form) (Reyna & Kiernan, 1994, 1995). Simply put, verbatim traces (a memory of seeing the suspect threatening his wife with a knife) are stored separately from episodic memory for an item's semantic content, or gist traces (a memory that the suspect was seen having a heated disagreement with his wife). Though constructivism relies upon a single memory operation (i.e. the integration of experience and inference) and SMF relies upon a single judgment operation (Johnson et al., 1993), FTT has shown gist and verbatim memory to be statistically independent (Reyna, 2002; Reyna & Brainerd, 1990). The independence of verbatim and gist representations reconciles the competing results that have challenged models in the past, and it leads to novel predictions about specific conditions that can increase and decrease true and false memories (Brainerd & Reyna, 2007; Brainerd, Reyna, & Ceci, 2008; Reyna & Kiernan, 1994; Reyna & Lloyd, 1997).

In this section, we begin by describing the development of the two memory representations (i.e. verbatim and gist) in FTT through childhood and adolescence. We show evidence for a rapid improvement of verbatim development and a more gradual improvement in gist memory as children age. We discuss how FTT theory explains source-misattribution in situations whereby verbatim memories have disintegrated, as well as situations involving gist-consistent suggestion. Then we explain how gist memory, verbatim memory and age interact, allowing for the FTT prediction of developmental reversals in false memory (younger children being less susceptible to false memories than older children, adolescents and adults; Reyna, 2011). We then extend developmental reversal findings to misinformation paradigms involving active suggestibility, showing that under conditions where only gist memory is available, contrary to SMF predictions, source-misattributions can increase with age.

We also discuss the importance of taking individual differences in ability within age groups into account, and how learning disabilities can influence memory (Reyna et al., 2002). Specifically, we show that even within age groups, children with learning disabilities are less able to encode gist than same-age children who do not display learning disabilities. This leads to the prediction that when gist memories are cued, children with learning disabilities should show lower levels of false memory than those without learning disabilities.

Another key aspect that FTT addresses is how emotion affects memory in children and adolescents. This topic is especially relevant to areas within the law and forensics, due to the fact that witnessing a crime is an emotionally charged event. In FTT, emotion is incorporated as an aspect of gist memory, and therefore is predicted to increase susceptibility to false memories.

In this section, we demonstrate that valence (how good or bad something feels), especially impacts susceptibility to false memory, and that this effect is more pronounced as individuals age.

Finally, we discuss FTT predicted manipulations that can increase younger children's ability to encode gist, as well as manipulations that decrease older children and adolescents' ability to encode gist. Using these manipulations, FTT predicts that one can increase false memories in young children and decrease false memories in older children and adolescents, respectively. The implications of these manipulations with respect to theoretical and forensic relevance are discussed further in this section.

## Verbatim memory and development

Many experiments have now shown that verbatim memory improves with age between early childhood and young adulthood, with marked improvements between preschool and early elementary school (Brainerd & Reyna, 1998, 2001; Brainerd, Reyna, & Ceci, 2008; Reyna & Brainerd, 1995; Reyna & Kiernan, 1994, 1995). Although in most instances, it is okay to misstate some details when you are telling a story, verbatim memory is important in the law because witnesses must recall the exact details of an event. This is especially important because memory reports are the most common form of evidence in criminal law (Brainerd & Reyna, 2005).

Though younger children's verbatim memories are less developed than are those of older children, they do have the capability of recalling verbatim detail. All things being equal, older children will have better access to verbatim traces. Furthermore, verbatim memory degrades fairly rapidly (Reyna & Kiernan, 1994; Brainerd & Reyna, 1996); therefore, in typical court cases in which it may take months before witnesses take the stand, it is likely that the vast majority of verbatim representations will have decayed, no matter what the child's age. Though access to verbatim memories decline rapidly with time (and more so in younger children), people can retain access to certain elements of verbatim memory and not others. This allows for the possibility of source-misattribution as described by SMF. One such instance is that memory for a face may remain accessible, but source information for where one initially saw that person may be lost. The obvious issue here is when an eyewitness is able to recall a face, but not whether they saw the face at the scene of the crime, or if it was from several days later when they made the identification at a line-up.

Due to the rapid disintegration of verbatim memory, it is likely that witnesses interviewed immediately after the event will have access to more accurate memories. Even so, questioning must remain open-ended and avoid suggestion as to cue verbatim retrieval rather than gist memory. Also, early memory testing (i.e. testing people's memory immediately after an event) has been shown to reinforce verbatim memory in both children and adults (Brainerd & Ornstein, 1991; Reyna, 1992) and consequently decrease susceptibility to misleading questions (Warren & Lane, 1995).

## Gist memory and development

Although verbatim memory improves with age, therefore giving older children the upper hand in rejecting familiar but false items or events, gist memory (which promotes the acceptance of familiar items or events) also improves with age (Reyna & Kiernan, 1994, 1995). Despite the fact that young children are able to extract the gist of a specific item (a Labrador is a type of dog), it takes a number of years before one is able to connect the gist across multiple exemplars (labrador, German shepherd, poodle, golden retriever is a list of dog names) (Reyna & Lloyd, 1997). In Reyna and Kiernan (1994), 9-year-olds were better than 6-year-olds when it came to extracting the sentence and story level meaning from three-sentence vignettes that were previously studied. In this experiment, between ages 6 and 9, the improvements in meaning connection at both the sentence and story level roughly doubled.

What this means for FTT predictions regarding memory accuracy and development is that even without access to verbatim memory, as children age they should be better able to encode and retrieve general principles regarding what they experienced (i.e. the husband and wife were having some kind of disagreement). This means that older children are therefore better equipped to reject suggestions that are inconsistent with their gist than are younger children who are less likely to have encoded a gist for the experience. Unlike constructivism or SMF, FTT makes the prediction that when a suggestion is consistent with the gist of an experience, and verbatim memory is unavailable, individuals are more likely to accept the suggestion as they age through adolescence into young adulthood.

## Developmental reversals in false memory

Given that both verbatim and gist memory improve with age, FTT predicts that under certain conditions, false memory should increase with age (Brainerd & Reyna, 1998; Ceci & Bruck, 1998). Specifically, situations where age increases in false memory occur should have two features: (a) false memories arise from people's propensity to connect meaning across distinct events that share meaning and (b) it is difficult to use verbatim traces of

actual events to suppress those distortions. This finding that false memories might actually increase between early childhood and young adulthood is
such a counterintuitive prediction, that it is called a "developmental reversal"
prediction.

In this section, we show that developmental reversals have been demonstrated in a number of conditions that all share the common theme of emphasizing the cuing of gist through meaning connection. We begin with the
original paradigm used to demonstrated developmental reversals: the Deese-
Roediger-McDermott illusion. In order to generalize this effect beyond a
single paradigm, we discuss studies that have found developmental reversals within the misinformation paradigm, using multiple methodologies. It
is important to note that the findings discussed in this section can only be
accounted for by FTT, and that SMF cannot account for decreases in memory accuracy with age.

One experimental procedure that happens to be of the most exten-
sively studied paradigms in false-memory literature is the Deese/Roediger/
McDermott (DRM; Deese, 1959; Roediger & McDermott, 1995) illusion.
In this paradigm, the list of target materials is a list of 12–15 words, all
of which are associates of a critical missing word. For example, a list of
12 words containing the examples "bed," "rest," "snooze," and "awake,"
among others, are all forward associates of the critical missing word "sleep."
In this paradigm, the relationship between the target words can vary: it may
be that the targets are synonyms or antonyms, or they could be exemplars
of a taxonomic category named by the critical lure. These lists encourage
meaning connections between list words to be formed while overwhelming
the ability to accurately recall each individual word due to list length, therefore setting up the ideal conditions necessary for high levels of false memory. It might be tempting to criticize the DRM task on the basis that a word
list task would not generalize well to real-life situations. Brainerd, Reyna,
Ceci and Holliday (2008) point out that DRM word lists are actually ideal
for simulating the conditions that exists in criminal court, because both
situations force people to remember items that are richly interconnected by
meaning.

Use of the DRM paradigm in children began in 2002. Two studies published within two months of each other (Brainerd, Reyna, & Forrest, 2002;
and Ghetti, Qin, & Goodman, 2002) contained results that appeared to be
contradictory. Specifically, Brainerd et al. (2002) reported experiments in
which false memory for both recall and recognition appeared to increase with
age, whereas Ghetti et al. reported stable false memory across age groups for
recognition, with a decrease in false memory in recall with age. Subsequent
analysis (Reyna, Mills, Estrada, & Brainerd, 2007) on the data from the
Ghetti et al. experiment revealed that false recall and recognition did not vary

with age (though true recall and recognition did increase with age). A simple restriction of range explained the lack of a developmental reversal, in that the typical DRM word list contains 12–15 words, whereas Ghetti et al. used word lists with 7 words. The smaller word lists allowed for adults to have better access to verbatim traces, which would naturally lead to an increased ability to reject gist-consistent distracters, resulting in low levels of false memory (a result predicted by fuzzy-trace theory).

Brainerd et al. (2002) reported a total of three experiments, all of which contained a free-recall portion, and the third of which also contained a recognition portion. The first experiment consisted of 10 DRM lists, each with 12 words, presented auditorily to 5-year-olds, alternating with one minute of free recall after each list. The second experiment was similar, and used 16 DRM lists (15 words per list), which were divided among those that have been previously shown to produce particularly high levels of false recall in adults and those that have been shown to produce particularly low levels of recall. In this second experiment, two age groups (5- and 7-year-olds) were compared. Intrusions from prior DRM lists were more likely for 5-year-olds, and 7-year-olds showed a mix of intrusions from previously presented lists as well as intrusions of words that had a similar meaning as the DRM list words. Importantly, 7-year-olds did not show an increase in critical unpresented words, which is the pattern that emerged for adults. Whether the list was categorized as high or low for adults – which in adults has generated drastic differences between high and low lists, around 60 percent for high and 20 percent for low – did not produce any similar effect in children. The final experiment compared 5-year-olds, 11-year-olds and young adults on the 16 lists that were used in experiment 2, and as previously mentioned, included a recognition test in order to achieve a more sensitive measure of false memory. False memory for the critical word nearly tripled across this age range, and the high and low lists did not produce different levels of false memory in young children, but did produce the expected pattern of higher false memory for high lists in adults and 11-year-olds (only for critical distracters) with no effect on memory for target items (see Figure 3.1). The results of this study support FTT's prediction that the ability to connect meaning across items drives false-memory generation and that younger children lack this ability. In fact this study shows that it is not until around 11-years-old that this effect begins to show, with increases in false memory into adulthood.

Subsequently, many more studies have been conducted that apply the DRM illusion to child development. The developmental reversal has been found in DRM studies measuring recall and recollection in a variety of countries (Dewhurst & Robinson, 2004; Howe, 2005; Howe, Cicchetti, Toth, & Cerrito, 2004). A recent review by Brainerd, Reyna and Zember (2011) documented

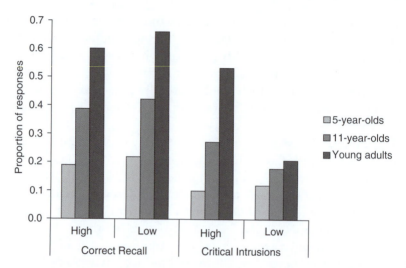

**Figure 3.1** Proportions of true recall and critical intrusions between age groups (5-year-olds, 11-year-olds, and young adults). High = DRM lists that have previously shown high levels of false memory in adults; Low = DRM lists that have previously shown low levels of false memory in adults. Adapted from 'Are young children susceptible to the false memory illusion?' by C. J. Brainerd, V. F. Reyna, and T. J. Forrest, 2002, *Child Development, 73,* pp. 1363–1377. Copyright 2002 by the Society for Research in Child Development Incorporated.

55 experiments in which DRM performance has been compared across age groups, and 53 of the 55 experiments detected developmental increases in false recall and/or recognition. This is more than ample evidence for the basic trend of developmental reversals in false memory.

The development reversal effect not only applies to word lists with many semantic relations (i.e. DRM lists), but also applies to other materials highlighting meaning consistency. One example is if an investigator needs to know if an abused child can recall a specific type of clothing that his/her attacker was wearing during the attack. Although the DRM procedure lists forward associates of a target exemplar, researchers have also given memory tests using categorized materials that consist of study lists that contain multiple exemplars of one or more categories (e.g. ballcap, cabbie hat, raincoat, boots, scarf) and false memories that consist of unpresented exemplars (fedora, peacoat), or unpresented labels (clothing). This procedure has been utilized with word lists (Howe, 2006) as well as lists of categorized pictures (Fisher & Sloutsky, 2005; Sloutsky & Fisher, 2004a; Sloutsky & Fisher, 2004b; Wilburn & Feeney, 2008) and has obtained developmental reversals in false memory using both.

# Misinformation effects and developmental reversals

Once the common trend of developmental reversals of false memory had been clearly identified in the literature regarding studies of spontaneous false memory, similar studies emphasizing meaning-consistent false memories have been conducted within the domain of suggested false memories. Unlike SMF, which relies heavily on the misinformation paradigm and only predicts age decreases in false memory, the experiments below support FTT's prediction that by cuing gist memory, older children are more susceptible to memory suggestions than younger children even in a paradigm that emphasizes source discrimination.

In a study conducted by Connolly and Price (2006), false memory was found to increase with age after a misinformation phase. A sample consisting of preschoolers and first graders was split among single-play- and repeated-play-session conditions, the latter of which were scheduled two times a day over two days. Play sessions consisted of eight activities, each of which contained two details that were the subject of later misinformation. For example, one of the play activities involved making up a story about a $500 bill while thinking about the color white, from which the critical details were the $500 bill and the color white. In each case, the critical details were explicitly mentioned three times. After two weeks, all groups were subjected to a biasing interview. The biasing interview consisted of questions in which the critical details from play were contradicted. For example, a child might have been asked, "My next questions are about the story that you made about a piano on cape day. I heard the story was pretty neat. Do you like to make up stories?" Control questions resembled biasing questions but without the misleading details. A day later, free and cued recall tests were administered based only on what happened during the original play sessions. When misleading details had meanings that were strongly associated with the original detail (e.g. when pretending to be a "dog" was replaced with pretending to be a "fly," another animal), the older age group was three times as likely to falsely report the detail in a free-recall test, and was four times as likely to do so on a cued recall test.

The same developmental reversal was found in a study of subjects aged 5 to 12 in which eyewitness identification was a key element (Ross et al., 2006). Participants were shown a video in which a female teacher is depicted reading to children, followed by the same teacher leaving a wallet on a cafeteria table so a (male) thief is able to steal the money from inside. Half of the participants saw an altered video (the bystander condition), such that another male bystander was in the initial scene with the teacher, sitting and reading, visible for the same duration that the actual thief was visible. After watching the video, participants were instructed to select the thief from a five-person line-up that contained the bystander, but not the thief. Children were also informed that they could answer that they do not know if the thief was among the line-up, or that the thief was explicitly not among the line-up. For children in the bystander condition, false identification of the bystander steadily increased across this age range, from an initial probability of misidentification of .18 for 5-year-olds to a probability of .64 for 12-year-olds. The rate of misidentification in the bystander condition was only significantly different from the control condition among the older age group (11- and 12-year-olds). Incidentally, net accuracy (the ratio of true memory to total memory) across both the control and bystander conditions declined with age. Thus, the same developmental reversal in false memory was found in child witness misidentification.

Ceci, Papierno and Kulkofsky (2007) implemented another study in which an increase in false memory over age was evoked by meaning connection in materials. Four- and 9-year-old children were presented with many triads of color pictures of common objects. The children were instructed to identify which of the three objects did not belong, and explain why. These data were used to identify the semantic difference between all the objects (22 in all) depicted in the triads, as indicated by each of the age groups. Participants were then divided into control and misinformation groups. In this phase of the study, the children were presented with stories accompanied by pictures. The story contained eight critical items taken from the original 22 objects from the first phase of the study. The misinformation group then also experienced a semantically related suggestion regarding four of the eight critical items in an interview. For example, in a story that depicted a girl and a boy seeing an eagle at a zoo, it was suggested that the bird was a robin. The control group received a similar interview without misinformation. Days later, participants responded to a recognition test in which the objects were represented pictorially, and the eight critical items were presented, along with the four related distractors as well as other items from the original 22 objects and other unrelated items. Generally, likelihood of false recognition of a semantically related distractor was related to the strength of its relationship to the critical item as determined in phase 1. It was also found that, when critical items were paired with their semantically related distractor (e.g. eagle with bird) in cases in which the relationship was stronger among 9-year-olds than among 4-year-olds, false recognition of the distractor roughly doubled across age groups. When pairs were identified in which the relationship was stronger for 4-year-olds than for 9-year-olds, a decline in false recognition was detected. As predicted by fuzzy-trace theory, opposite trends were thus discovered when the trends in meaning connection were also opposed.

In a final study in which meaning generated an increase in suggestibility with age, Fazio and Marsh (2008) presented 5-, 6- and 7-year-old children with four fictional stories that revolved around a theme (e.g. a trip to the

Eiffel Tower, or a skunk that learned to defend himself). Integrated into the four stories were six world facts that were age-appropriate for the sample, such as the French translation of "thank you," and the name of a mother sheep. However, for each of these facts, an erroneous version was created. For example, a child might be told that "autumn" is another word for "spring" instead of "fall." Half the facts in each story were correct and half were not, and the fact format was counterbalanced. After hearing these stories, children responded to a general knowledge test consisting of 24 questions, half of which directly assess the aforementioned facts. Contrary to the intuitive assertion that general world knowledge would increase with age and, thus, older children would avoid being misled, Fazio and Marsh predicted that susceptibility to the misrepresented facts would increase with age. In fact, despite the intuitive expectation, older children had more erroneous intrusions:

> Hearing misinformation in a story increased the likelihood that children of all ages would choose the misinformation answer on a later multiple-choice general knowledge test. Only the older children (7-year-olds), however, reproduced the stories' errors on a cued recall test. The children's suggestibility on the cued recall test was not due to difficulties with source memory. (Fazio & Marsh, 2008, p. 1087)

Thus, when suggestibility studies emphasize common meaning between true and misleading information, developmental reversals – increases in false memory with age – are easily borne out in evidence.

The current section has made clear that developmental reversals have been demonstrated across the spectrum of false-memory methods: from DRM tasks, which are devoid of explicit suggestion, to misinformation paradigms, which provide a high level of suggestibility. As demonstrated above, developmental reversals have appeared in studies using word lists, categorized items, eyewitness identification procedures, stories and video presentations. The evidence presented in this section gives ample support for developmental reversals in a variety of contexts. When interviewing children as witnesses, one must consider the degree to which older children and adolescents are more likely to respond based on gist memory. Though age differences are a common measurement of development in the literature, it is also important to consider whether other measures of development (such as intelligence) can show similar effects within age groups as those between age groups.

## Memory development and ability

As age can be used as a predictor of levels of false memory in many tasks, an important point to keep in mind for forensic contexts is the fact that not all children are the same with respect to ability level. There can be large differences between ability ranging from children who are learning disabled to children who just may have trouble with certain types of comprehension. FTT predicts that even between children of the same age group, children with worse semantic processing skills should show lower levels of false memory when compared to children with better semantic processing skills of the same age group.

Brainerd, Forrest, Karibian and Reyna (2006) compared DRM performance between 7- and 11-year-old children who were classified as learning-disabled, and children of the same age who were not. Children with learning-disabled classification are typically reading- or language-disabled have been found to have deficiencies in their ability to process semantic relations among word list items (see various chapters in Obrzut & Hynd, 1991). Brainerd et al. (2006) confirmed that although learning-disabled children showed lower levels of true memory than some age non-disabled children, learning-disabled children also showed lower levels of false memory than some age non-disabled children. Another approach was taken by Weekes, Hamilton, Oakhill and Holliday (2007), who matched children for age and general intelligence, but differed with respect to reading comprehension and found that false recall was higher in children with normal semantic processing (high reading comprehension) than children with low semantic processing (low reading comprehension). These findings highlight the theoretical and forensic importance of recognizing that even children of the same age will show differences in false memory based on their individual ability to connect meaning.

## Impacts of emotion on memory throughout development

Thus far, the experiments discussed have established the fact that memories tested in the laboratory are similar to those that eyewitnesses may be asked to recall (i.e. filled with meaningful connections and, in some cases, repeated events). Recently, researchers have begun to look at another key aspect of witnessing a crime – the fact that the memories are emotionally charged.

Budson et al. (2006) created a DRM methodology whereby participants were given either lists in which the critical distractors were emotionally neutral words (e.g. chair, foot, teacher), or lists in which the critical distractors were emotional words (e.g. anger, cry, sick). Though it may be tempting to assume that the impact of emotional word lists on memory cannot approach the impact of witnessing a crime, note that a study by Rubin and Talarico (2009) found that participants' emotional reactions were similar for real-life events, autobiographical memories, and words that varied in valence and arousal.

Howe (2007) and Howe, Candel, Otgaar, Malone, and Wimmer (2010) used Budson et al.'s (2006) method to test the impact of emotional DRM lists on false memory in children. Howe (2007) administered the lists to 5-, 7-, and 11-year-olds and Howe et al. (2010) administered them to 8- and 11-year-olds and found that false-alarm rates for critical distractors were higher for emotional lists in recognition tests and developmental increases in false memory were comparable between lists. Howe et al. (2010) also looked at the effect these lists had over time and discovered that though target hit rates declined over a week, false-alarm rates did not, critical distractor false-alarm rates were higher for emotional lists than for neutral lists and developmental trends in false memory were comparable between emotional and neutral lists. These findings provide support for Reyna and Brainerd's (1995) conclusions, in that children's false memories can be more stable than true memories, and suggest that this finding is especially robust with respect to emotional gist memories.

Brainerd, Holliday, Reyna, Yang and Toglia (2010) took this approach a step further and tested children ages 7 and 11 as well as young adults using DRM lists with words that were either high/low for arousal and positively/negatively valenced. This allowed valence and arousal to be manipulated factorially, going beyond the measurement of emotional words on memory. FTT predicts that the presence of negative emotion should increase false memory, due to the fact that gist memories incorporate emotional information. FTT theory has gone further in distinguishing emotion into arousal and valence and predicts that valence should have a larger impact on memory as people age, since it is a kind of an emotional gist (an example is that the word trash "feels" negative and hug "feels" positive). Brainerd et al. (2010) found the typical developmental reversal for false memory and that net accuracy (the ratio of true memory to total memory) decreased with age. These effects were more pronounced for negatively valenced and high arousal words than positively valenced materials and low arousal words. As predicted by FTT, valence had a larger effect on the developmental increases than arousal.

It is important to keep in mind that although it is vital to be aware of the effects of suggestibility when questioning a witness (especially a child witness), one must also keep in mind the impact of the event itself on a child's memory as they age. The research cited above suggests that as children grow older, they may be more likely to have access to the gist of what they witnessed, which could lead them to retrieve false information that has been affected by the emotional nature of the situation itself even before the child is questioned. Also, Howe et al. (2010) point out that the emotional nature of witnessing crimes can increase the likelihood of retrieving (gist-consistent) false information as time passes.

## Gist and verbatim manipulations

We have seen that by creating a situation in which study items all represent the same meaning, we can increase false memories with age. This is because gist memory improves with age, meaning that older children will be increasingly better at encoding a gist between similar items than younger children. In order to test whether the ability to connect meaning could be increased in younger children through the cuing of gist, Holliday, Brainerd and Reyna (2008) studied 7-, 9-, 11-, 13- and 15-year-olds using six 14-word DRM lists. Children did separate recall tasks for each list and were assigned to either a control condition or the gist cuing condition. The children in the gist cuing condition were told that the words in the list would have very similar meanings and were given the theme of the list before presentation. False recall increased with age in the control condition whereas in the gist cuing condition, intrusions increased for the 9- and 11-year-olds. Brainerd, Reyna and Estrada (2006) found similar results to Holliday et al. (2008) with 6-, 11-, and 14-year-olds in a DRM experiment with a more in-depth cuing procedure. Specifically, false recall notably increased for 11-year-olds in the gist cuing condition whereas there were unreliable increases for the other age groups.

Another way to cue gist is to present the information in a narrative form rather than just presenting word lists. This is exactly what Dewhurst, Pursglove and Lewis (2007) did, giving children ages 5, 8, and 11 either 14 DRM lists followed by a recognition task, or 14 narratives that incorporated the words from the DRM lists into a story. The words in the *doctor* DRM list were presented as follows:

> The nurse had written a prescription for Sally because she was sick. Her mum, who was a lawyer, told Sally she had to take the medicine because it would improve her health. She said if Sally did not take it she would have to go to the hospital. Sally hated them more than the dentist. Sally saw a physician the last time she was ill. She went into his office and he listened to her heart with a stethoscope. She then went to a different clinic in which she saw a surgeon who gave her the treatment she needed to cure her. (p. 378)

In the control condition, false recognition increased with age, as expected, but in the narrative condition, the false-alarm rate rose for 5-year-olds (from .5 to .8), but did not affect 8- or 11-year-olds. The story allowed 5-year-olds to make meaning connections that would not otherwise occur, and thus increased false memory in that age group.

These results indicate that although younger children are generally unable to encode connected gist representations to the extent that older children do, with the correct cues, children even as young as 5-years-old can show increased false memory due to gist cuing. This is forensically relevant in that it demonstrates the basic processes that can underlie many different types of suggestibility techniques that occur in eyewitness interviews. Even when interviewing a young child, it is therefore possible to influence that child with a particular theme that can lead them to remember things that they may not have experienced (especially when it is unlikely that the young child retains access to much of verbatim memory). The previous few studies have given evidence that even young children can show elevated levels of false memory when given the gist (thereby decreasing their net accuracy of memory responses). FTT also predicts that if you make the gist unavailable to older children and adolescents, you can lower their levels of false memory (thereby increasing their net accuracy).

Whereas the previous studies confirmed that gist cuing is sufficient to increase false memory in young children, it is also important to test whether taking away meaning connection can decrease false memory in older participants. This requires one to interfere with the formation of meaning connections in those who generally make these connections spontaneously (i.e. adolescents). Brainerd and Reyna (2007) tested this by having a control condition in which only one semantically related target was presented (i.e. participants were not given multiple words expressing the same meaning). When participants between the ages of 6- and 14-years-old were given blocks of eight exemplars of categories, false recognition of unpresented category exemplars rose from age 6 to 14. In the condition with only one exemplar, false recognition fell from age 6 to 14. By decreasing the number of semantically related items in the word lists so that no meaning connections could be made, older children's levels of false memory were drastically reduced.

Another method of testing for the necessity of semantic relations was created by Holliday and Weekes (2006), whereby participants were given words that were phonologically similar in a DRM format, and given recognition tests with related distractors that sounded like the studied words. Since even young children easily connect phonological similarity across targets (because of improvements with age in verbatim memory), it was predicted that net false memory would actually decrease with age. In this experiment, false-alarm rates for related distractors declined from .42 for 8-year-olds to .3 (age 11) to .29 (age 13). Finally, in Holliday, Brainerd and Reyna (2011), 7- and 11-years-old were either given normal DRM lists or DRM lists with word fragments and then were tested for their memory of the words. The word fragment condition lowered levels of false memory by roughly two-thirds in 11-year-olds, while lowering it by only 6 percent in 7-year-olds.

The above experiments support FTT's prediction that false memories can be increased in younger children and decreased in older children all with the manipulation of one's access to gist and verbatim memory. These results emphasize the importance not only of understanding the developmental trajectories of gist and verbatim memory (they both improve with age), but that gist and verbatim memory can be manipulated, regardless of age to increase or decrease true or false memory. Specifically, it is critical to understand that in situations where even though older children and adolescents are typically more susceptible to spontaneous false memories than younger children, it is possible to create conditions through gist cuing in which you can increase false memories in children and adolescents. It is also possible to increase true memory and subsequently decrease false memory in both children and adolescents by creating conditions that preferentially cue verbatim memory. A conceptual understanding of the developmental trends of gist and verbatim memory are important to those working in the law, but even more so, a basic theoretical understanding of the mechanisms (i.e. gist and verbatim memory) underlying true and false memory, and how they respond in differing contexts can give those working in the law the ability to size up forensic situations with a critical eye.

## Conclusion

Study of memory in children and adolescence has been of particular significance to a number of forensic situations, not the least of which is the case of child sexual abuse, in which a single child is often the only witness, and often no other physical evidence is left. This places a great deal of importance on evaluating the quality and accuracy of the memory of this witness, as what results in a false recognition in the lab may result in a false conviction in practice. Conversely, and perhaps more importantly, failure to acquire accurate information from child witnesses can result in failure to apprehend abusers, who then reoffend. However, the impact of these findings can extend to other contexts: cases regarding dissolution of marriage, custody hearings and domestic violence crimes, as well as cases for which the child is the suspect or defendant. In all such cases, the risk of false testimony may be high, even when suggestive or coercive tactics are not used. The ability to judge based on the context of the original crime and subsequent interrogation, and the reliability of witness testimony is at once both complex and critical.

As previously mentioned, the past decade saw a shift in the general trend of research performed on false memory in children, which was a shift from studies that focus on suggestibility and misinformation paradigms to studies that focus on spontaneous generation of false memories from related meaning. A key motivation for this shift is that practices of investigation with children have evolved towards a focus on reliability of children's memory, having turned from suggestive questioning towards interview protocols that can produce an abundance of information from child witnesses. Much of this change was the result of public outrage towards the treatment of child witnesses in the 1990 case, the *State of California v. Buckley*, in which, for example, one child was subjected to a 17-day embarrassing and fatiguing cross-examination (Brainerd & Reyna, 2005). As a result, some reforms were widely adopted, including increased permission of unsworn out-of-court statements, simplifying children's involvement in pretrial investigations and making the courtroom environment more attuned for child testimony. Those working in science and the law both should keep in mind the crucial lessons that are being learned with respect to the social pressures that lead to distorted child witness testimony (Bruck, Ceci, & Hembrooke, 2002), as well as the cognitive factors that underlie these memory reports, including witness reports of crimes.

In the context of this shift in interview protocols, one should also note the discovery of the important effect of memory instructions as demonstrated in experiments done by Reyna and Kiernan (1994, 1995). It is important to note that these experiments showed that children do have memory for verbatim information, therefore lending credibility to the claim that they should be allowed to testify. They also showed that if individuals are not explicitly instructed to reject details that are meaning-consistent, individuals will report based on encoded meaning (i.e. gist) as a default, rather than based on verbatim memory. This is a trend that only increases as children grow older into adulthood. Although such instruction is not typically found in much of day-to-day life, because exact verbatim testimony is not required, it is this sort of protocol one must follow when giving eyewitness testimony. That is, to the best of their ability, witnesses must attempt to report the facts as they experienced them, not their interpretations or inferences about the meaning of the facts. That basic research had assimilated this nuance of legal procedures will be to its advantage when the ecological validity of lab experiments is questioned.

With respect to theoretical explanations for the reviewed phenomena, it shall be noted that the source-monitoring framework does identify useful effects to the forensic context. Illustrations of source confusion are demonstrated easily when witnesses and suspects are repeatedly interrogated. The effects of an increase in false memory following detailed imagining and repeated suggestion in this context are often borne out. The source-monitoring framework also provides a helpful manipulation for this context, that warning individuals of the possibility of source confusion can reduce the incidence of false reports.

As a cognitive model, however, SMF falls short in predicting often-seen effects in the development of memory – specifically that spontaneous false recall and recognition can increase with age, as well as numerous other effects that contradict predictions of SMF (see Reyna, 2000; Reyna & Lloyd,

1997). Another specific example can be found in Brainerd, Reyna and Kneer (1995), in which participants were primed with targets just before they were given the related distractors in a memory test (e.g. CAT is a target and is presented just before ANIMAL, which is a related distractor). In this experiment, participants misrecognized related distractors less frequently than unrelated distractors, even though unrelated distractors are more distinctive. This effect, and its modulation by factors such as repeated study, is predicted by FTT's distinction between verbatim and gist memories (see Reyna & Brainerd, 1995).

As a dual-process model, FTT can also explain the often-seen decrease in source-monitoring errors with age that SMF has identified. That is, both gist and verbatim memory improve with age. Phenomenological details that are used to identify source are verbatim traces, and without a gist or meaning that would lead to spontaneous inference, the advantage older children have in maintaining verbatim traces will lead to fewer source confusions. FTT holds an advantage in that it can also explain increases in false memory with age when verbatim traces are unavailable, and the situation allows for an easily encoded gist, even in a paradigm where suggestibility is present. Furthermore, FTT relies on the same gist/verbatim distinction to predict that children with superior semantic processing skills will show higher levels of false memory than will those with worse semantic processing under specific conditions.

FTT has inspired further developmental research in the relationship between emotion and memory, and researchers have discovered that negative emotion (particularly negative valence) also promotes increases in false memory with age (Brainerd et al., 2010). This result confirms FTT prediction that gist memory includes emotional input from one's experience, and follows the natural FTT prediction that as individuals grow older, they are more likely to encode gist. Though it may be tempting to assume that this result means that younger children are less impacted by emotionally negatively charged events, two reminders are warranted. First, it is important to recall that experiments rarely replicate the true emotional intensity of witnessing a crime. Secondly, even as data suggest that young children may not be able to fully encode the gist of an emotionally charged crime, FTT has demonstrated that gist does develop with age and is robust against forgetting. In following the actual theoretical predictions of FTT, children who may not grasp the gist of an emotionally traumatic event immediately will develop the ability to gain an understanding with age, and are not likely to forget the overall "feel" of the event. This also means they may be more susceptible to false memories, as verbatim traces disintegrate with time and gist traces develop (Howe et al., 2010).

The evidence explored in this chapter leads to the conclusion that future studies in the area of false memory, be they social or cognitive in nature, must take memory mechanisms informed through theoretically motivated research into account. Basic research in the area of false memory continues to light the way towards an overall understanding of how these processes work. Future studies must be vigilant in addressing the role that meaning plays in memory throughout the aging process.

In criminal cases, physical evidence plays little role in the final decision made by the trier of fact, mainly because such evidence is not available (Horvath & Meesig, 1996, 1998). This means that the outcome of criminal cases commonly depends on memory reports (in many cases, even physical evidence is presented through testimony). Since it is ultimately up to the trier of fact to weigh the presented evidence, it is critical that they are informed by up-to-date theory driven research on memory in order to weigh it properly. Basic research has the potential to better calibrate triers of fact as they weigh evidence. More fundamentally, the results of rigorously conducted research should replace common myths and misconceptions regarding memory in children and adolescents.

# References

Alba, J. W., & Hasher, L. (1983). Is memory schematic? *Psychological Bulletin, 93,* 203–231. doi:10.1037/0033–2909.93.2.203.

Brainerd, C. J., Forrest, T. J., Karibian, D., & Reyna, V. F. (2006). Development of the false-memory illusion. *Developmental Psychology, 42,* 662–679.

Brainerd, C. J., Holliday, R. E., Reyna, V. F., Yang, Y., & Toglia, M. P. (2010). Developmental reversals in false memory: Effects of emotional valence and arousal. *Journal of Experimental Child Psychology, 107,* 137–154.

Brainerd, C. J., & Ornstein, P. A. (1991). Children's memories for witnessed events: The developmental backdrop. In J. Doris (Ed.), *The Suggestibility of Children's Recollections* (pp. 10–20). Washington, DC, US: American Psychological Association.

Brainerd, C. J., & Reyna, V. F. (1996). Mere memory testing creates false memories in children. *Developmental Psychology, 32,* 467–476.

Brainerd, C. J., & Reyna, V. F. (1998). Fuzzy-trace theory and children's false memories. *Journal of Experimental Child Psychology, 71,* 81–129.

Brainerd, C. J., & Reyna, V. F. (2001). Fuzzy-trace theory: Dual processes in memory, reasoning, and cognitive neuroscience. *Advances in Child Development and Behavior, 28,* 49–100.

Brainerd, C. J., & Reyna, V. F. (2005). *The Science of False Memory*. New York: Oxford University Press.

Brainerd, C. J., & Reyna, V. F. (2007). Explaining developmental reversals in false memory. *Psychological Science, 18,* 442–448.

Brainerd, C. J., Reyna, V. F., & Ceci, S. J. (2008). Developmental reversals in false memory: A review of data and theory. *Psychological Bulletin, 134,* 343–382.

Brainerd, C. J., Reyna, V. F., Ceci, S. J., & Holliday, R. E. (2008). Understanding developmental reversals in false memory. *Psychological Bulletin, 134,* 343–382.

Brainerd, C. J., Reyna, V. F., & Estrada, S. (2006). Recollection rejection of false narrative statements. *Memory,* 14(6), 672–691.

Brainerd, C. J., Reyna, V. F., & Forrest, T. J. (2002). Are young children susceptible to the false memory illusion? *Child Development, 73,* 1363–1377.

Brainerd, C. J., Reyna, V. F., & Zember, E. (2011). Theoretical and forensic implications of developmental studies of the DRM illusion. *Memory and Cognition, 39,* 365–380.

Bransford, J. D., & Franks, J. J. (1971). The abstraction of linguistic ideas. *Cognitive Psychology, 2,* 331–350.

Bruck, M., & Ceci, S. J. (1999). The suggestibility of children's memory. *Annual Review of Psychology 50,* 419–439.

Bruck, M., Ceci, S. J., & Hembrooke, H. (2002). The nature of children's true and false narratives. *Developmental Review, 22,* 520–554.

Budson, A. E., Todman, R. W., Chong, H., Adams, E. H., Kensinger, E. A., Krangel, T. S., & Wright, C. I. (2006). False recognition of emotional word lists in aging and Alzheimer disease. *Cognitive and Behavioral Neurology, 19,* 71–78.

Ceci, S. J., & Bruck, M. (1998). The ontogeny and durability of true and false memories: A fuzzy trace account. *Journal of Experimental Child Psychology, 71,* 165–169.

Ceci, S. J., Papierno, P. D., & Kulkofsky, S. (2007). Representational constraints on children's suggestibility. *Psychological Science, 18,* 503–509.

Ceci, S. J., Ross, D. F., & Toglia, M. P. (1987). Suggestibility of children's memory: Psycholegal implications. *Journal of Experimental Psychology: General, 116,* 38–49.

Connolly, D. A., & Price, H. L. (2006). Children's suggestibility for an instance of a repeated event versus a unique event: The effect of degree of association between variable details. *Journal of Experimental Child Psychology, 93,* 207–223.

Deese, J. (1959). On the prediction of occurrence of certain verbal intrusions in free recall. *Journal of Experimental Psychology, 58,* 17–22.

Dewhurst, S. A., Pursglove, R. C., & Lewis, C. (2007). Story contexts increase susceptibility to the DRM illusion in 5-year-olds. *Developmental Science, 10,* 782–786.

Dewhurst, S. A., & Robinson, C. A. (2004). False memories in children: Evidence for a shift from phonological to semantic associations. *Psychological Science, 15,* 782–786.

Fazio, L. K., & Marsh, E. J. (2008). Older, not younger, children learn more false facts from stories. *Cognition, 106,* 1081–108.

Fisher, A. V., & Sloutsky, V. M. (2005). When induction meets memory: Evidence for a gradual transition from similarity-based to category-based induction. *Child Development, 76,* 583–597.

Foley, M. A., Johnson, M. K., & Raye, C. L. (1983). Age-related changes in confusion between memories for thoughts and memories for speech. *Child Development, 54,* 51–60.

Gallo, D. A., Roediger, H. L., III, & McDermott, K. B. (2001). Associative false recognition occurs without strategic criterion shifts. *Psychonomic Bulletin & Review, 8,* 579–586.

Ghetti, S., Castelli, P., & Lyons, K. E. (2010). Knowing about not remembering: developmental dissociations in lack-of-memory monitoring. *Developmental Science,* 13(4), 611–621. doi:10.1111/j.1467-7687.2009.00908.x.

Ghetti, S., Qin, J., & Goodman, F. S. (2002). False memories in children and adults: Age, distinctiveness, and subjective experience. *Developmental Psychology, 38,* 705–718.

Holliday, R. E., Brainerd, C. J., & Reyna, V. F. (2008). Recall of details never experienced: Effects of age, repetition, and semantic cues. *Cognitive Development, 23,* 67–78.

Holliday, R. E., Brainerd, C. J., & Reyna, V. F. (2011). Developmentals reversals in false memory: Now you see them, now you don't! *Developmental Psychology, 47,* 442–449.

Holliday, R. E., & Weekes, B. S. (2006). Dissociated developmental trajectories for semantic and phonological false memories. *Memory, 14,* 624–636.

Horvath, F., & Meesig, R. (1996). The criminal investigation process and the role of forensic evidence: A review of empirical findings. *Journal of Forensic Sciences, 41,* 963–969.

Horvath, F., & Meesig, R. (1998). A content analysis of textbooks on criminal investigation: An evaluative comparison to empirical research findings on the investigative process and the role of forensic evidence. *Journal of Forensic Sciences, 43,* 133–140.

Howe, M. L. (2005). Children (but not adults) can inhibit false memories. *Psychological Science, 16,* 927–931.

Howe, M. L. (2006). Developmentally invariant dissociations in children's true and false memories: Not all relatedness is created equal. *Child Development, 77,* 1112–1123.

Howe, M. L. (2007). Children's emotional false memories. *Psychological Science, 18,* 856–860.

Howe, M. L., Candel, I., Otgaar, H., Malone, C., & Wimmer, M. C. (2010). The role of valence in the development of immediate and long-term false memory illusions. *Memory, 18,* 58–75.

Howe, M. L., Cicchetti, D., Toth, S. L., & Cerrito, B. M. (2004). True and false memories in maltreated children. *Child Development, 75,* 1402–1417.

Jacoby, L. L., Kelley, C. M., & Dywan, J. (1989). Memory attributions. In H. L. Roediger III & F. I. M. Craik (Eds), *Varieties of Memory and Consciousness: Essays in Honour of Endel Tulving* (pp. 391–422). Hillsdale, NJ: Erlbaum.

Johnson, M. K. (2006). Memory and reality. *American Psychologist, 61,* 760–771, doi: 10.1037/0003–066X.61.8.760.

Johnson, M. K., Hashtroudi, S., & Lindsay, D. S. (1993). Source monitoring. *Psychological Bulletin, 114,* 3–28.

Lindsay, S., & Johnson, M. K. (1989). The eyewitness suggestibility effect and memory for source. *Memory and Cognition 17,* 349–358. doi: 10.3758/BF03198473.

Loftus, E. F., Miller, D. G., & Burns, H. J. (1978). Semantic integration of verbal information into visual memory. *Journal of Experimental Psychology: Human Learning and Memory, 4,* 19–31.

Mitchell, K. J., & Johnson, M. K. (2000). Source monitoring: Attributing mental experiences. In E. Tulving & F.I.M. Craik (Eds), *The Oxford Handbook of Memory* (pp. 179–195). New York: Oxford University Press.

Obrzut, J., & Hynd, G. (Eds) (1991). *Advances in the Neuropsychology of Learning Disabilities.* New York: Academic Press.

Paris, S. G., & Carter, A. Y. (1973). Semantic and constructive aspects of sentence memory in children. *Developmental Psychology, 9,* 109–113.

Piaget, J., & Inhelder, B. (1973). Memory and intelligence. New York: Basic Books.

Reyna, V. F. (2000). Fuzzy-trace theory and source monitoring: An evaluation of theory and false memory data. *Learning and Individual Differences, 12,* 163–175.

Reyna, V. F. (2011) Across the lifespan. In B. Fischhoff, N. T. Brewer, J. S. Downs (Eds), *Communicating Risks and Benefits: An Evidence-based User's Guide* (pp. 111–119). U.S. Department of Health and Human Services, Food and Drug Administration. Retrieved from http://www.fda.gov/ScienceResearch/SpecialTopics/RiskCommunication/ default.htm.

Reyna, V. F., & Brainerd, C. J. (1995). Fuzzy-trace theory: An interim synthesis. *Learning and Individual Differences, 7,* 1–75.

Reyna, V. F., Holliday, R. E., & Marche, T. (2002). Explaining the development of false memories. *Developmental Review, 22,* 436–489.

Reyna, V. F., & Kiernan, B. (1994). Development of gist versus verbatim memory in sentence recognition: Effects of lexical familiarity, semantic content, encoding instructions, and retention interval. *Developmental Psychology, 30,* 178–191.

Reyna, V. F., & Kiernan, B. (1995). Children's memory and interpretation of psychological metaphors. *Metaphor and Symbolic Activity 10,* 309–331.

Reyna, V. F., & Lloyd, F. (1997). Theories of false memory in children and adults. *Learning and Individual Differences, 9,* 95–123.

Reyna, V. F., Mills, B. A., Estrada, S., & Brainerd, C. J. (2007). False memory in children: Data, theory, and legal implications. In M. P. Toglia, J. D. Read, D. F. Ross, & R. C. L. Lindsay (Eds), *The Handbook of Eyewitness Psychology*. Volume I, Memory for Events (pp. 473–510). Mahwah, NJ: Erlbaum.

Roediger, H. L., III & McDermott, K. B. (1995). Creating false memories: Remembering words not presented on lists. *Journal of Experimental Psychology: Learning, Memory, and Cognition, 21,* 803–814.

Roediger, H. L., III, Watson J. M., McDermott, K. B., & Gallo, D. A. (2001). Factors that determine false recall: A multiple regression analysis. *Psychonomic Bulletin & Review, 8,* 385–405.

Ross, D. F., Marsil, D. F., Benton, T. R., Hoffman, R., Warren, A. R., Lindsay, R. C. L., & Metzger, R. (2006). Children's susceptibility to misidentifying a familiar bystander from a lineup: When younger is better. *Law and Human Behavior, 30,* 249–257.

Rubin, D. C., & Talarico, J. M. (2009). A comparison of vector and circumplex models: Evidence from emotions, prototypical events, autobiographical memories, and words. *Memory, 17,* 802–808.

Segovia, K.Y., & Bailenson, J. N. (2009). Virtually true: Children's acquisition of false memories in virtual reality. *Media Psychology, 12,* 371–393. doi:10.1080/15213260903287267.

Sloutsky, V. M., & Fisher, A. V. (2004a). Induction and categorization in young children: A similarity-based model. *Journal of Experimental Psychology: General, 133,* 166–188.

Sloutsky, V. M., & Fisher, A. V. (2004b). When development and learning decrease memory. *Psychological Science, 15,* 553–558.

Sugrue, K., Strange, D., & Hayne, H. (2009). False memories in the DRM paradigm: Age-related differences in lure activation and source monitoring. *Experimental Psychology, 56,* 354–360. doi:10.1027/1618-3169.56.5.354.

Warren, A. & Lane, P. (1995). Effects of timing and type of questioning on eyewitness accuracy and suggestibility. In M. Zaragoza, J. R. Graham, G. C. N. Hall, R. Hirschman & Y. S. Ben-Porath (Eds), *Memory and Testimony in the Child Witness* (pp. 40–60). Thousand Oaks, CA: Sage.

Weekes, B. S., Hamilton, S., Oakhill, J., & Holliday, R. E. (2007). False recollection in children with reading comprehension difficulties. *Cognition, 106,* 222–233.

Wilburn, C. J. & Feeney, A. (2008). Do development and learning really decrease memory? On similarity and category-based induction in adults and children. *Cognition, 106,* 1451–1464.

# CHAPTER 4

# Children as Eyewitnesses: Historical Background, and Factors Affecting Children's Eyewitness Testimony

TIMOTHY N. ODEGARD AND MICHAEL P. TOGLIA

The capabilities of child witnesses to accurately recollect events and provide reliable testimony have been debated for more than a hundred years (Binet, 1900; Varendonck, 1911). Initially, children were branded as unreliable and even dangerous witnesses, with early studies observing them to be highly susceptible to producing distorted recollections of the past (Pear & Wyatt, 1914; Stern, 1910). Yet, this initial view was tempered by a lengthy debate concerning the child witness that continues to spark interesting research questions, which speak to developmental, cognitive, and social factors surrounding the vulnerability of child witnesses to suggestion and their propensity to create false memories. Collectively, researchers have identified critical factors that influence the ability of a child witness to accurately recollect an event. Of these factors, some are intrinsic to a child, such as age and past experience with a given topic, whereas other factors are extrinsic to the child, relating to external factors, such as the inclusion of misleading information during questioning and various forms of social pressure (Melnyk, Crossman, & Scullin, 2007).

Distorted recollections of the past provided by child witnesses can be viewed as stemming from a mixture of external and internal factors. We argue that the division of intrinsic and extrinsic factors allows for a powerful method of identifying means of helping to safeguard the veracity of a memorial report provided by a child witness. In particular, the identification of intrinsic factors provides a basis to evaluate the reliability of a child's memory, whereas the identification of extrinsic factors provides a basis to actively change the procedures used to interact with child witnesses in an effort to maximize the amount and accuracy of information obtained from them. This division is similar to a distinction drawn by Gary Wells when differentiating between estimator and system variables associated with eyewitness lineups (Well, 1978). In this framework, estimator variables, such as the witness's age, race and sex, were highlighted as being useful for postdicting the accuracy of an eyewitness' identification of a suspect in a lineup. These variables are not under the direct control of law enforcement personnel and, as such, can only be used to estimate the potential reliability of an eyewitness. These factors closely resemble factors intrinsic to a child, such as age, background knowledge and emotional reactivity. These factors are in contrast to factors extrinsic to the child that can be directly controlled, such as the manner in which a child is questioned, or the use of specific props during the interview process. These extrinsic variables resemble system variables that are under the direct control of the law enforcement community and, as such, can be modified to maximize the accuracy of lineup identifications. These include providing unbiased instructions (the suspect may be absent, you can decide not to choose or say "I don't know"), using double blind administration and preventing co-witness contamination.

The focus of this chapter is to first review the history of child witnesses from the perspective of psychology and the legal community, highlighting how a group once thought of as being unreliable and even detrimental to court proceedings are now viewed as potentially highly credible witnesses who can provide invaluable information. We will then review some of the intrinsic and extrinsic factors that influence the reliability of a child witness. It has been through the identification of these factors that practical recommendations have been made about how best to interact with child witnesses, allowing for more accurate eyewitness accounts to be obtained from children. Thus, in a concluding section, we will address applied implications and recommendations.

## History

The very early research on the child witness was reported a little more than a hundred years ago. Binet (1900; Binet & Simon, 1905) commented on children's suggestibility of memory and there soon followed a number of experimental papers. For example, in reports by Pear and Wyatt (1914), Stern (1910), Varendonck (1911), and others, it was concluded that young children were highly susceptible to producing distorted memories and, thus, should be considered the most dangerous of witnesses. Much of this early research was conducted in Europe and is reviewed in great detail, beyond the scope of the current chapter, by Siefried Sporer in a paper aptly titled *Lessons from the origins of eyewitness testimony research in Europe* (Sporer, 2008).

Interest in children's eyewitness memory experienced a renewed attention in the 1980s, spurred on in particular by a seminal set of research articles that were published in a special issue of the *Journal of Social Issues* in 1984 edited by Gail Goodman, and by the hysteria raised in several high profile daycare child abuse cases that had grabbed the public's attention (e.g. the McMartin Preschool sexual molestation case in Manhattan Beach, CA; the prosecution of Kelly Michaels for allegedly abusing her charges at the Wee Care Nursery School in Maplewood, New Jersey; and the trial of Betsy and Bob Kelly who ran the Little Rascals Day Care Center in Edenton, North Carolina, and were accused of sexual abuse as well as satanic ritual abuse; see Ceci & Bruck, 1995; Garven, Wood, Malpass, & Shaw, 1998).

Shortly thereafter, Ceci, Ross and Toglia published an influential article, while simultaneously introducing the first edited volume addressing the memory of child witnesses (Ceci, Toglia, & Ross, 1987). These authors noted that the "renewed" experimental work in this area tended to support the conclusions drawn in the studies from the early 1900s, while at the same time this newer research also raised serious concerns that the early work was compromised by methodological flaws and suffered from a lack of ecological validity. These problems alone justified replications. Unlike the very early work, the studies that have been conducted in the last 25 years have been more than empirical demonstrations. This research has been squarely grounded in theory, mindful of external validity, and has had an increasing impact on the criminal justice system.

During the last quarter century, a large number of well-designed studies have been published on the suggestibility of children's memory that have typically shown that very young children, compared to older children, are the most susceptible to suggestive, misleading questioning, as indexed in large part by inaccurate memories. Critically, such false recollections are often accompanied by changes in beliefs (Ceci & Bruck, 1993; Bruck & Ceci, 1999; Poole & Lamb, 1998), including beliefs held with high confidence (Reyna, Mills, Estrada, & Brainerd, 2007). In this regard Poole (2001) noted in a *Boston Herald* (2001) interview:

> It has nothing to do with lying and everything to do with the implanting of false memories. Studies have shown that children will vehemently defend the veracity of implanted memories. They recall reporting them, and those reports produce mental images of the events that these individuals cannot distinguish from their real experiences. But the kids are not responsible for that. The interviews are.

Similarly, in the same article run by the Boston Herald, Ceci offered the following two observations:

> Our review of typical interviews from the 1980s shows many investigators blindly pursued a single hypothesis: Sexual abuse occurred. They would reinforce that hypothesis to the children, who would be led to believe in it...It is essential to keep in mind now that most children with such implanted memories will have believed in their allegations of abuse for far longer than they were alive before those allegations first surfaced. Those "implanted" memories are no less visceral than real-life memories.

Yet, the same can be said of adults. Through suggestive questioning and other techniques, adults can come to believe that they were witnesses to events that did not actually occur (Davis & Loftus, 2009; Loftus, 2005).

At odds with the experiments of a hundred years ago, the experimental investigations since the mid-1980s have revealed important boundary conditions regarding the circumstances under which children can produce accurate reports and would therefore not be "dangerous witnesses." Perhaps the key circumstance that can promote high degrees of accuracy with young children is interviewing them in non-suggestive manners.

Paralleling the attention that children's testimony received at the turn of the twentieth century, it was also a hundred years ago or so that saw the emergence of research and essays on "legal psychology," which spoke to the relevance of psychological research to the law. A particularly vocal proponent of psychology's value to legal issues was Hugo Munsterberg. In his book *On the Witness Stand* (1908), Munsterberg reviewed available research studies on a variety of topics of importance to the criminal justice system, including the trustworthiness of eyewitness testimony, witness credibility and false confessions. The fact that some of his views on law and psychology were not confirmed by research findings hindered the selling of his main theme that experimental psychology had much to offer in the legal arena. A well-known severely critical piece on Munsterberg's book appeared the next year (Wigmore, 1909). A law professor at Cornell, Wigmore argued that Munsterberg overstated the evidence for psychology's application to the courtroom. Fortunately, Wigmore did not simply brush away the notion that psychology's experimental methodologies could be useful to the courts. Rather, he believed that "legal psychology" showed promise that had just not yet been delivered. As our chapter and the other chapters of this edited volume will illustrate, Psychological Science has come a long away in delivering theoretically grounded empirical research that clearly demonstrates the boundary conditions under which child eyewitness testimony can be deemed reliable.

Munsterberg (1908) was not alone in pursuing a relationship between psychology and law. Several psychologists (e.g. Binet, 1900; Cattell, 1895; Stern, 1902, 1910) investigated the bases and relevance of cognitive processes to criminal justice matters by conducting various applied investigations on memory, suggestibility, lie detection and false confessions. Whipple (1909, 1912) summarized some of these studies of this time period, and he noted various techniques used in the research of eyewitness testimony. These techniques included methods of presentation (picture test, rumor test, and expression via an event) as well as methods of report (interrogatory v. narrative). Through his analysis of this research, he identified multiple factors that could influence the testimony of eyewitnesses. These included "misdirected attention, mal-information ... errors of memory ... lack of caution [and] of zeal for accurate statement." Here we can clearly see parallels to factors identified as be critically important to the veracity of child eyewitness reports identified by more recent research.

Whipple also commented tersely on the testimony of child witnesses. He stated that, compared to adult reports, in children's reports "the range is small, the inaccuracy large, and since the assurance is high, the warranted assurance and reliability of assurance are both very low." He also identified children's suggestibility as being the primary reason for the weakness of their reports. He stated that at puberty, the available data indicated that children's reports saw a sharp increase in accuracy and reliability. As our review of the recent research in this area highlights, a similar trend is still observed today. In a follow-up paper, Whipple (1912) described studies that were prompted by earlier findings concerning the inaccuracies in the reports of eyewitnesses. These studies, referred to by Whipple in his 1912 paper, targeted methodologies designed to improve witness reports and testimony via various training techniques on the questioning of witnesses. Here we see a foreshadowing of modern-day studies and sets of guidelines concerned with appropriate interviewing.

During the same time period, the early twentieth century, legal scholars and practitioners were grappling with children's rights, and particularly with the role of child testimony in legal proceedings (Tanenhaus, 2005; Kaczorowski, 1987). In many ways, this struggle was simply a reflection of a broader movement towards liberal constitutionalism in America, which would ultimately shape the very foundations of the modern state (Hawes, 1991; Mason, 1994). Following the abolition of chattel slavery, lawmakers and members of the judiciary were forced to reexamine existing notions of social government and public order in order to transition into a system of governance based on individual rights and liberties (Novak, 1996). In doing so, it was necessary to reconceptualize the limits of parental authority and the power of the state acting as child guardian (Minow, 1995). Other important developments were the positive rights of social citizenship (e.g. shelter, clothing, nourishment and education; Katz, 2001) and individual privacy rights (Gordon, 1994).

These trends in constitutional jurisprudence had serious consequences for the legal rights of children. The more progressive aspects of this developing body of constitutional law imbued children with individual rights and ensured that they were entitled to protection under the law (Tanenhaus, 2005). At the same time, however, the 'parental rights' doctrine undermined the very protections afforded children during the liberal constitutionalism movement and oftentimes denied them the ability to meaningfully participate in the legal process (Willrich, 2003). Even today, the parental rights doctrine tends to limit children's due process rights and effectively deprive them of a real voice in legal proceedings (Woodhouse, 2001).

A hundred years ago, this approach to children's legal rights was only minimally informed by the social science research of the time. As mentioned above, prominent legal scholars only summarily weighed in on the intersection of psychology and law (e.g. Wigmore, 1909), while practitioners and jurists more or less ignored empirical research regarding the credibility of child witnesses in favor of an approach that viewed children as "dependent" or "helpless" individuals in need of guidance and instruction (e.g. Petition of Ferrier, 103 Ill. 367, 1882; *McLean v. Humphreys*, 104 Ill. 379, 1882). As such, it was not until the advent of Juvenile Courts in the 1920s that children regularly testified in open court and that such testimony was considered credible enough to determine guilt or innocence (Tanenhaus & Bush, 2007). This shift coincided with a growing body of literature in psychology and psychiatry that viewed cognitive development and memory in children as incremental, characterized by differing levels of emotional and intellectual capacities, and thus entitled to varying degrees of credibility (Goodman, 1984).

Contemporary jurisprudence, on the other hand, has taken great strides in embracing the contributions of psychology and psychiatry as it relates to child witnesses, and incorporating specific mechanisms to address the various problems cited by experts in both fields (Lyon, 2002). A growing body of scholarship, focused largely on child abuse cases, has effectively permeated our legal institutions and resulted in tangible changes to the way that children participate in legal matters (Ceci, Toglia, & Ross, 1987; Toglia, Read, Ross, & Lindsay, 2007). Juvenile Courts and diversion programs based on contemporary understandings of child development and psychology are now widespread and accepted as an effective mechanism for dealing with a whole host of issues ranging from family law to criminal charges (Gilstrap, Fritz, Torres, & Melinder, 2005). To the extent that our legal institutions have not yet embraced scientific findings or incorporated specific mechanisms consistent with those findings, it is clear that the legal community is attuned to the growing body of research in psychology regarding eyewitness testimony, and particularly to the role of children as witnesses (Marsil, Montoya, Ross, & Graham, 2002). Influential studies on suggestibility and false memory, for instance, have gained a great deal of traction in legal circles and enabled policymakers and practitioners to implement important changes to eyewitness interviewing techniques while simultaneously dispelling more antiquated notions of child competence (e.g. Toglia et al., 2007). This traction can also be seen outside of North America in many jurisdictions throughout Europe. As an example, Austria has moved to put in place legal reforms addressing the reduction of the frequency of interviews/interrogations of child witnesses (Sporer, 2008).

We now move from our historical sketch research on child witnesses and their changing role in the criminal justice system to an examination of factors that impact children who are eyewitnesses. As noted above, we categorize these into intrinsic and extrinsic factors that influence the accuracy of a child witness.

## Factors influencing child eyewitnesses

Many researchers have concluded that there is an identifiable developmental trajectory of decreasing suggestibility across childhood (preschoolers through about adolescence). This pattern is based on various forms of implanting memories (e.g. the Loftus misleading postevent information paradigm; Loftus, Miller, & Burns, 1978; Loftus, 1979; Toglia, Goodwin, & Neuschatz, 2009) that particularly impact younger children (Brainerd & Reyna, 2005; Ceci & Bruck, 1995; Holliday, Douglas, & Hayes, 1999; Holliday & Hayes, 2000). While implantation may be thought of as deliberate, on the part of an interviewer, *intent* is not a necessary condition for producing distorted reports from memory (Ceci & Bruck, 1993). For example, false memories can also arise from factors intrinsic to an individual, through a process generally known as *autosuggestion*. In either case, implanted false memories can be viewed as stemming from external "active" attempts to distort memory as well as "passive" internal factors.

Clearly, purposeful efforts to mislead a witness would be considered "active" efforts. However, so, too, would be instances when an interviewer questions a child in a suggestive manner without realizing it. Individuals are capable of unconscious forms of social cognition, such as implicit attitudes (for a review, see Greenwald & Banaji, 1995; Melnyk, Crossman, & Scullin, 2007). We can behave in biased fashions with motives that are outside of our conscious awareness. Such implicit forms of social cognition potentially can bias the manner in which an individual interviews a child eyewitness. Even though the *intent* is missing on the part of the questioner, the interviewee may be actively influenced, nonetheless. Active influence is especially likely in those instances when a child perceives the interviewer, who is typically an authority figure, to know more about the probed event than he or she does (see Ceci & Bruck, 1995, for a review). Note that a child's beliefs about the interviewing process may not imply that they realize the questions are inconsistent with the witnessed episode.

A recent research study on meta-suggestibility (London, Bruck, Poole, & Melnyk, 2011) is relevant to this notion. London and her colleagues define meta-suggestibility "as an awareness of factors and situations that can taint memory and/or event reports." One aspect of meta-suggestibility is whether or not there is an awareness that questions and assertions from someone can make someone else report their experiences inaccurately. These researchers examined children's ability to comprehend that conversational pressure can lead a child to give a false report because compliance with leading and suggestive questions and comments is a major cause of distortion of children's memory (e.g. Bruck & Ceci, 1999). They accomplished this by having children of various ages watch a video during which a young boy falsely claims to have been hit after being interviewed in a suggestive manner. In questioning of participants that followed watching the video, 6- and 7-year-olds performed poorly, revealing failures in meta-suggestibility, whereas 12- and 13-year-old children demonstrated a clear understanding of meta-suggestibility. Thus, developmental increases are observed in meta-suggestibility between 8 and 11 years of age, signaling that meta-suggestibility undergoes lengthy advancement well into late childhood.

There are also more "passive" forms of illusory memory, known as a spontaneous false memory (as in the DRM illusion, autosuggestion; Roediger & McDermott, 1995). Young children as less susceptible to this type of false memory than are older children and adults. Note that this is exactly the opposite developmental pattern as the one exhibited to the susceptibility to external factors. These spontaneous false memories and similar false memories develop slowly, reaching adult levels around early adolescence (Brainerd, Reyna, & Forrest, 2002; Brainerd, Holliday, & Reyna, 2004). This dissociation between implanted and spontaneous false memories has been addressed in large number of fairly recent studies showing developmental reversals (for a review, see Brainerd, Reyna, & Ceci, 2008).

Unlike false memories that arise from suggestions presented by external sources, false memories that arise from autosuggestion actually increase developmentally. Young children are, in fact, more immune to these false memories than are older children. In addition, these false memories are particularly difficult to spot as being erroneous. In many instances, individuals are highly confident of the veracity of these memories, and the memories are by their very nature consistent with the overall context of the situation in question, making it difficult for them to be identified as false by external observers. Clearly, these memorial issues implicate a variety of cognitive processes, with many cognitively driven theories having been advanced to explain the bases for creating false memories, the circumstances under which they are created, and how and why illusory recollections are sustained. In the sections that follow, we first highlight several factors intrinsic to a child that influence his or her accuracy/reliability as an eyewitness. Then, we highlight several factors external to the child that can influence his or her accuracy/reliability as an eyewitness.

## Intrinsic factor: age

To be clear, young children *can* remember past real-life events (Farrar & Goodman, 1990; Fivush, 1984; Hayne, Gross, McNamee, Fitzgibbon, & Tustin, 2011; Hudson, 1990; Hudson & Fivush, 1991; Hudson, Fivush, & Kuebli, 1992). As an aside, Hayne et al. showed that both 3- and 5-year-olds were capable of describing events that would happen in the near future. With respect to past events, for example, children between 3 to 4 years old remembered a considerable amount about the events prior to, during and following hurricane Andrew (Bahrick, Parker, Fivush, & Levitt, 1998; Fivush et al., 2004). In addition, children as young as 2 years old remembered having experienced a fire drill at their preschool after two weeks, and were still able to remember some aspects of this event seven years later (Pillemer, 1992). Similarly, 2-year-old children can remember a medical emergency (Peterson & Bell, 1996; Peterson & Rideout, 1998), and can do so even after a considerable amount of time has passed (Peterson, 1999; Peterson & Whalen, 2001). A number of related studies demonstrating good event memory by very young children one to two months after the episode are nicely reviewed and summarized by Pipe, Thierry and Lamb (2007).

Such data demonstrate that even very young children are capable of remembering past real-life events. Yet, there are important age-related differences that speak directly to how informative the eyewitness reports of younger children might be to forensic investigations. In particular, older children provide more-detailed reports than do younger children (Peterson & Bell, 1996). For example, children who were 4 years old at the time of a fire drill provided more-detailed accounts than did the younger children when later questioned about the event (Pillemer, Picariello, & Pruett, 1994). The amount of information provided is critical to moving forensic investigations forward. While the amount of information obtained from an eyewitness is crucial to the investigation, so, too, is the veracity of the information obtained. Yet, the research reviewed thus far does not speak to the accuracy of the children's memories for these real-life events. While the research reviewed thus far provides a great deal of information about the characteristics of children's memories for stressful, real-life events, it is often difficult, if not impossible, to ascertain the accuracy of the memory reports provided for these types of events. Given that accuracy is paramount in legal settings, there are limitations to the applicability of such research to forensic settings.

To overcome this obstacle, researchers have had children experience scripted events in controlled settings. Afterwards, in order to test the accuracy of their memory, children are questioned about what took place during these events. Preschool-aged children have been observed to accurately remember past events when such techniques are used. However, consistent with the studies cited at the beginning of this section, older children provide more details, and the details they provide are generally more accurate (Baker-Ward, Gordon, Ornstein, Larus, & Clubb, 1993; Ornstein, Baker-Ward, Gordon, Pelphrey, Tyler, & Gramzow, 2006; Ornstein, Merritt, Baker-Ward, Furtado, Gordon, & Principe, 1998; Quas, Goodman, Bidrose, Pipe, Craw, & Ablin, 1999). For example, Baker-Ward and her colleagues (1993) tested the ability of children between the ages of 3 to 7 years to remember a scripted medical check-up for which the events that transpired were known by the experimenter. Children in all of the age groups tested remembered an impressive number of events that took place during the medical examination. For instance, the 3-year-old children remembered roughly 80 percent of the events that took place when tested immediately after the medical exam. However, older children remembered a greater number of events than did younger children, even when children were initially tested after the medical exam. Additionally, older children reported more events when asked open-ended questions (e.g. Tell me what happened when you went to the doctor's office), whereas younger children required more cues to remember the past events (e.g. Did the doctor shine a light in your eye?) and forgot more information as time passed than did the older children. There is, however, some concern when examining memory for schematic activities and scripted events because schemas/scripts are built upon repeated events, often ones that occur with some degree of regularity. Thus, there is tendency for children (and adults, as well) to blend differences among events, leaving open the real possibility of misremembering a specific occurrence of the event in question (Lamb, Orbach, Warren, Esplin, & Hershkowitz, 2007).

In summary, as children age, there is an increase in the amount and accuracy of the information that they provide when questioned about an event. The amount of information provided is critical for two reasons. First, information is the key to moving an investigation forward, and investigating officers are motivated to seek it out. Second, past research illustrates that individuals conducting forensic interviews revert to close-ended, pointed questioning when initial probes about an event do not generate information. As such, younger children are at a greater risk of being asked pointed questions in comparison to older children. As will be discussed in following sections, the use of pointed questions and increased social pressure has detrimental effects on the accuracy of the information obtained from a child witness. This is extremely unfortunate. Although younger children do not provide as much information as do older children, the information younger children do provide to open-ended questions can be highly accurate.

## Intrinsic factor: prior knowledge

A factor related to age that appears to facilitate memory is the amount of prior knowledge that individuals have about an event (Ornstein et al., 1998, 2006; Ornstein, Gordon, & Larus, 1992; Peters, 1987; Saywitz, Goodman, Nicholas, & Moan, 1991; Quas et al., 1999). Arguably, older children are more likely to have prior knowledge of such events that could help them to reconstruct the detail of the past medical events. Yet, reconstructing the past based on prior knowledge can facilitate accurate memory of a past event, but it can also lead a child to falsely report the presence of details typical of an event that were not actually present (Ornstein et al., 2006).

To address this issue, researchers have asked children if specific details were present during a past medical examination. Some of the details were actually present during the exam, while other details were not. Of the details that did not take place, some were often typical of going to the doctor (e.g. Did the doctor give you a shot?), whereas other events that children are questioned about would likely not have happened at a doctor's office (e.g. Did the doctor cut your hair?). Baker-Ward and her colleagues observed 5-year-old children to falsely indicate having experienced roughly 10–25 percent of both types of events when tested immediately after the medical examination, and these rates remained relatively constant across the six-week period of questioning. In contrast, older children correctly rejected both types of items when interviewed immediately after the medical exam. Yet, the false acceptance of the typical events increased over the six-week period, but the same was not true of the events that were not likely to have occurred in that setting.

These findings demonstrate that younger and older children commit memory errors, but important systematic differences are observed between the types of errors committed by children of different ages. Younger children falsely accepted both typical and atypical events immediately after having completed the medical exam, and continue to do so over a delay, whereas the older children correctly rejected both typical and atypical events that had not occurred when tested immediately, but falsely accepted a greater number of typical events that had not occurred after a delay.

## Intrinsic factor: gist extraction and plausibility monitoring

Past research investigating the impact of prior knowledge on the veracity of the memory of children motivates the question as to the developmental trajectory of the processing the underlying meaning of event and forming global representation of their structure. The ability to form global representation of meaning is required in order to use this information to constrain memory reports to include information that is plausible with the overall nature of a given event or set of events. Indeed, children have been observed to include implausible events in their eyewitness accounts of the past. In her review of research on children's eyewitness testimony, Goodman (2006) discussed the *State of New Jersey v. Michaels* (1994), referred to earlier, in which Kelly Michaels was wrongly convicted of 115 counts of sexual abuse (Ceci & Bruck, 1995). Included in the testimonies obtained from 20 preschool-aged children were eyewitness accounts of implausible and/or bizarre events. For example, Michaels was accused of licking peanut butter off children's genitals, forcing children to drink her urine and eat her feces, and sexually assaulting the children with knives, forks and various toys. The Michaels case is just one among many cases that have emerged in which bizarre allegations have been reported by young children.

   Such cases raise the question as to why children include events that could not have realistically occurred in their eyewitness accounts (Goodman, 2006). Young children likely report implausible events due in part to external social factors present in forensic interviewing settings that will be discussed in the next section. Yet, cognitive factors intrinsic to an individual that allow him or her to gauge the plausibility of memory candidates also influence the tendency of a child to report implausible events (Odegard, Jenkins, & Koen, 2010).

   A cognitive factor that influences the tendency of children to include implausible events in their memory reports is their ability to extract a *global gist* representation that identifies connections across multiple events (Lampinen, Leding, Reed, & Odegard, 2006; Odegard, Holliday, Brainerd, & Reyna, 2008). In contrast to local gist, which is defined as the meaning of an event when considered in isolation, global gist represents relations observed across multiple events. For example, when studying a list of category exemplars – such as: *dog, cat, goldfish, turtle, cow, horse, pig, zebra, monkey, lion* – a child will likely extract the meaning of each item, even if there is a failure to note how the items relate to one another (Brainerd & Reyna, 2007). Yet, consider an instance in which an individual is presented with a series of numbers – such as 1, 7, 13, 21, 105, 159, etc. (see Brainerd & Reyna, 2005; Reyna & Brainerd, 1991, for additional examples). It is likely that the meaning of each individual item will be processed, but a child might also extract the global gist that the list contains a sequence of increasing odd numbers.

Access to a global gist representation of past events allows children to constrain memory responses to instances that are consistent with the overall nature of what happened (Odegard et al., 2010). Yet, older but not younger children are able to identify *meaning*-based relationships across multiple events. For example, in a false memory paradigm created by Deese (1959) and later reintroduced by Roediger and McDermott (1995), the DRM paradigm, participants are presented with a series of words, such as *nurse, sick* and *lawyer*, that are all semantically related to a critical non-presented word, in this instance, *doctor*. On a later memory test, older but not younger children recognize and recall non-presented critical lures (e.g. *doctor*) and studied items (e.g. *nurse*; Brainerd, Forrest, Karibian, & Reyna, 2006). When young children do recall items that were not presented on a list, they do not recall words consistent with the global gist of the list. Instead, they falsely recall words unrelated to the global gist, such as remembering *table* as having been part of the *doctor* list.

Such age differences in the ability of children to identify meaning-based relations across multiple events are not limited to the DRM paradigm. For example, Brainerd and Reyna (2007) presented 6-, 10- and 14-year-olds with categorical lists composed of either semantic or phonological associates and later tested their recognition memory. The oldest children falsely recognized non-presented exemplars from the semantic lists at far greater rates than the younger children. However, for those children who studied lists of phonologically related words, the youngest children falsely accepted more critical non-presented exemplars than the older children, demonstrating the youngest age group to have made connections across phonological but not semantic associates (for related results, see Dewhurst & Robinson, 2004; Holliday & Weekes, 2006).

## Internal factors: interim discussion

Several important age-related patterns of memory emerge from the extant literature in regards to intrinsic factors. First, it is clear that both younger and older children can remember past events. Moreover, when open-ended questions are used, the information provided can be highly accurate. However, older children provide more information to open-ended questions than do younger children, whereas young children require more cues and prompting in order to remember past events (Bahrick, Parker, Fivush, & Levitt, 1998;

Hudson et al., 1992; Lamb, Orbach, Hershkowitz, Esplin, &Horowitz, 2007; Odegard et al., 2009, Peterson & Bell, 1996; Peterson & Rideout, 1998).

Second, when asked pointed questions about events that did not occur, younger children are more prone to errors than are older children. Such questions may lead preschoolers to draw inferences about what might have occurred, resulting in false memories (Reyna et al., 2007). In addition, young children do not constrain their answers to events that are likely to have happened. Rather, they appear to be biased to indicate that even events that are unlikely to have occurred actually took place. They also are just as likely to do so when interviewed immediately after the events in question transpired as they are when questioned after a considerable amount of time has passed. However, older children are not inclined to accept events that likely would not have occurred. Rather, when these children make errors, they tend to falsely indicate events that likely would have occurred as having taken place (Baker-Ward et al., 1993; Ornstein et al., 1998, 2006).

Such age-related differences in the ability of children to remember past events are critically important to eyewitness memory. In forensic settings, the individuals conducting the interview do not know what happened, and an individual might be inclined to probe a child's memory with specific cues (Ceci & Bruck, 1995; Lamb, Orbach, Warren, Esplin, & Hershkowitz, 2007; Lamb, Sternberg, Orbach, Hershkowitz, Horowitz, & Esplin, 2002; Poole & Lamb, 1998). However, doing so increases the tendency for children of all ages to make errors, especially after time has passed and memories get fuzzier. Moreover, young children often assume the interviewer knows what happened, such that a proper interview can reduce this belief if the interviewer specifically tells the child up front that he/she does not know what happened, and needs the child to tell him/her what occurred.

Clearly, a balance must be achieved when probing a witness. The consequences of unreliable interviewing techniques are potentially twofold. First, they can result in the wrongful prosecution of an individual based on inaccurate information. Second, they can result in the testimony of a victim being judged as inadmissible, even in instances when the information provided might be largely accurate.

## Extrinsic factors: social factors and misleading questioning

The impact of biased questioning is exacerbated by the power structure inherent to interviews. Children are very knowledgeable of the status held by adults generally and authority figures in particular (e.g. parents, police officers and lawyers). Given the power dynamics that can be present when children are questioned, they can at times feel compelled to question their own memories of the past and defer to what they may perceive as the greater knowledge of what actually took place that is held by the person conducting the interview (Ceci, Ross, & Toglia, 1987; Holliday, 2003a, 2003b; Lampinen & Smith, 1995; Toglia et al., 1992). Furthermore, children may simply feel compelled to tell the authority figure what they think he or she wants to hear.

For example, Ceci, Ross and Toglia (1987) investigated the ability of children between 3- to 12-years-old to remember a series of events that took place during a story, accompanied by pictures, that was read to them about a girl named Loren. During an initial memory interview, some of the children in each age group were asked a series of unbiased questions about the events that took place in the story. Other children in each age group were asked a series of questions that contained biased information that presupposed details not present in the story to have taken place (e.g. suggesting that Loren ate cereal for breakfast, when in fact it was eggs). The 3- to 4-year-old children who were asked biased questions were the most likely to falsely indicate these items as having occurred during the story when questioned for the last time, doing so roughly 65 percent of the time. In contrast, the youngest children were just as capable of correctly rejecting events that were not present in the story when interviewed with unbiased questions. These data present a mixed story. They clearly indicate the preschool-age children to be more susceptible to biased forms of questioning relative to older children. However, when unbiased questions were used, the youngest children were very capable of remembering the details included in the story. These results are somewhat perplexing and raise an interesting question. What is causing the preschool-age children to have seemingly worse memories for the story when asked biased questions in the initial memory interview?

One possible explanation is that the youngest children are the most susceptible to social pressures. Thus, when the interviewer implies that Loren had a headache opposed to a stomachache during the initial interview, the youngest children defer to the information provided by the interviewer. When later asked, the children then report Loren to have had a headache opposed to a stomachache. To test this hypothesis, these researchers conducted another study in which 3- to 4-year-old children were presented with biased questions during the first memory interview by either an adult interviewer or by a 7-year-old child. Presumably, if the children are deferring to the adult as an authority figure, then they might be less likely to falsely report the misinformation when it is introduced by a source that is perceived to be a peer. Indeed, this was the principal finding. Children interviewed by the 7-year-old child falsely reported the misinformation included in the biased questions 20 percent less often than did the children interviewed by the adult. These findings were later replicated and extended by Lampinen and Smith (1995). These researchers observed 3- to 5-year-old children to have been less likely to falsely report misinformation introduced by another child or a *silly* adult than misinformation introduced by a *normal* adult. Such data suggest that even young children are quite adept at picking up on social cues of credibility and defer to credible sources when later reporting what took place in the past.

Based on the current review of previous research, it appears that there are important age-related differences in the ability of children to remember the past. Moreover, it also seems apparent that such differences are exacerbated by factors that can be introduced during the interview process. When care is taken to interview children with open-ended questions, past research seems to suggest that age-related differences in memory can be minimized. Such findings are promising and provide hope that structured interviewing techniques might be able to help ensure the credibility of the information obtained from even very young children.

## Extrinsic factors: repeated interviews and questions

Children are commonly repeatedly questioned on multiple occasions by their parents, therapists, child protective service agents and prosecuting attorneys. While it is not uncommon for children to be interviewed numerous times by different legal professionals and family members before a case goes to trial, such practices can negatively impact the accuracy of the information provided by child witnesses. But a distinction must be made between repeated interviews on different occasions and repeatedly questioning a child about a specific fact or detail during the same interview. Past research suggests that repeated requests for information within an interview may signal to a child that their earlier answer was incorrect. Young children in particular are apt to change their answers when questioned repeatedly and often feel compelled to provide an answer opposed to saying, "I don't know" (Holliday, 2003a, 2003b). This reluctance is particularly prominent when *yes/no* questions are asked (Bruck et al., 1995; Melnyk et al., 2007; Peterson & Biggs, 1997; Peterson, Dowden, & Tobin, 1999; Poole & White, 1993).

Yet, there are both positive and negative consequences of repeated interviews. On the positive side, repeated interviews may produce *hypermnesia*. Hypermnesia is a phenomenon by which individuals actually remember seemingly forgotten information by repeated interviews or tests. However, it is critical that repeated interview questions be open-ended (Peterson, Moores, & White, 2001; Reyna & Titcomb, 1997). When open-ended questions are not used and children are asked leading questions, the rate at which they report inaccurate information over a series of interviews increases (Bruck et al., 2002; Ceci et al., 1994; Powell, Jones, & Campbell, 2003). For example, over a sequence of five interviews, 4- to 5-year-old children were interviewed about a series of events, half of which were false (Bruck et al., 2002). During the initial interview children were simply asked unbiased questions (e.g. Did you ever see a man come into the daycare and steal something?). However, children were presented with biased questions about the events in the subsequent interviews. Initially, children correctly remembered events that actually occurred an overwhelming majority of the time (82 percent). Moreover, they were relatively good at correctly rejecting events that had not occurred, having done so 22 percent of the time. Yet, the false acceptance rate ballooned to 63 percent, 91 percent, 88 percent, and 78 percent during the remaining four interviews, which included different forms of biased questions. The findings demonstrate the negative impact that interviewing children multiple times can have on their tendency to report events that had not occurred. It must also be stressed, however, that the 4- to 5-year-old children in the study were relatively good at correctly rejecting events that had not occurred when questioned about them once using non-biased questioning.

Second, the children were interviewed about what took place on multiple occasions. Such practices can negatively impact the reliability of the memory reports provided by children by increasing the amount of false information mistakenly reported (Bruck, Ceci, & Hembrooke, 2002; Ceci, Loftus, Leichtman, & Bruck, 1994). Moreover, children can come to believe that they must somehow be mistaken because it is not typical for someone to continually ask a person about the same thing after an answer has been given. They might also feel that they are not mistaken, but nonetheless believe that they are expected to comply and provide the answer that the interviewer expects to hear (Bruck et al., 2002). Such feelings can be exacerbated by the power imbalance inherent to the social structure of the setting in which forensic interviews take place, which brings us to our third factor (i.e. social factors). Children view adults as authority figures and are typically taught to obey them. This can result in children feeling compelled to please the adult and tell them what they want to hear, which can intensify the negative effects of children being interviewed multiple times (Bruck et al., 2002; Ceci, Ross, & Toglia, 1987; Holliday, 2003a, 2003b; Lamb et al., 2007; Lampinen & Smith, 1995; Toglia, Ross, Ceci, & Hembrooke, 1992).

## Extrinsic factors: anatomical dolls

Suspicion first arose in the Michaels case, mentioned previously, when a 4-year-old child reported to a nurse who was taking his temperature rectally, "That's what my teacher does to me at school," and when questioned further he explained, "her takes my temperature." He was later interviewed by child protective services with the use of an anatomical doll. While being questioned, the child inserted two fingers into the rectum of the doll and indicated that this had happened to him and two other children. Anatomical dolls are used when interviewing children because they are thought to help overcome barriers that might prevent them from reporting abuse (Everson & Boat, 1994, 2002). Specifically, they are thought to help children to express themselves nonverbally, helping them to overcome their language barriers (Vivard & Tranter, 1988). Additionally, they are also thought to aid children in remembering past abuse by making retrieval cues explicitly available (Davies, 1991).

However, the use of anatomical dolls is also highly controversial because their use has been observed to increase the rate at which children falsely report information suggestive of abuse in field studies (Lamb, Hershkowitz, Sternberg, Boat, & Everson, 1996; Leventhal, Hamilton, Rededal, Tebano-Micci, & Eyster, 1989; Thierry et al., 2005) as well as laboratory studies (Bruck, Ceci, &Francoeur, 2000; Bruck et al., 1995; Goodman & Aman, 1990; Saywitz et al., 1991). In addition, children who have not been abused or inappropriately touched will perform sexually provocative or violent acts with the dolls when being questioned about innocuous events from their past (Bruck et al., 1995; Melnyk et al., 2007; Saywitz et al., 1991). We have described a series of factors, intrinsic and extrinsic, that impact children's reporting of events. This distinction is further leveraged in our discussion of implications that follow in the final section of this chapter.

## Conclusion

Children of today and of a hundred years ago are different in many ways, but arguably not when it comes to their memory capabilities. The frailties of memories continue to be a concern about young witnesses, and indeed witnesses of all ages (Wright & Holliday, 2007). However, we now know from a wealth of psychological research that young children can provide useful testimony, especially when the interviewing process does not taint their reports (Holliday, R. E., 2003a, 2003b; Lamb et al., 2002). Similarly, legal opinion and practice has shifted to this view of young witnesses. Thus, as we look back, both Munsterberg (1908) and Wigmore (1909) were on track. Though perhaps premature as Wigmore noted, Munsterberg's claim that psychological science could be of service to the legal system has largely turned out to be true. Neither could have predicted that this connection would be so slow to develop. But it has developed and in keeping in step with several of our theses, Sporer (2008) noted, and we agree, that, "Comparative historical and cross-national legal analyses may help to find solutions to pressing legal-psychological issues." In a related vein, Beresford (2005) has outlined recent cases involving child witnesses who come before international tribunals. The tribunals have weighed in on the accuracy of young witnesses, showing an awareness of the suggestibility literature, while critically dealing with the protection of child witnesses. In many of the tribunal cases worldwide, at issue are child combatants in wars who are witnesses to war crimes and violations of human rights. If these children, often as young as 10, testify, can they their memories be trusted and how should we insure their rights and insulate them from possible retaliation.

One of the seminal papers that finally ignited this connection was Wells (1978), whose study of lineup identification and the many factors that influence an identification led him to distinguish between estimator and system variables. We employed a variation on this distinction in casting effects upon children's eyewitness memory and testimony in terms of intrinsic and extrinsic factors. This dichotomy, we believe, is useful in framing past and current research, and in guiding future investigations relevant to the child witness. This distinction can also be employed as a schema for categorizing related phenomena, such as meta-suggestibility introduced above, as well as phenomena that we have not discussed including, for example, theory of mind (Meltzoff, 1995).

# References

Bahrick, L. E., Parker, J. F., Fivush, R., & Levitt, M. (1998). The effects of stress on young children's memory for a natural disaster. *Journal of Experimental Psychology: Applied, 4,* 308–331.

Baker-Ward, L., Gordon, B. N., Ornstein, P. A., Larus, D. M., & Clubb, P. A. (1993). Young children's Long-Term retention of a pediatric examination. *Child Development, 64*(5), 1519–1533.

Beresford, S. (2005). Child witnesses and the international criminal justice system. *Journal of International Criminal Justice, 3,* 721–748. doi: 10.1093/jicj/mqi031.

Binet, A. (1900). *La suggestibilité.* Paris, France: Librairie C. Reinwald.

Binet, A., & Simon, T. (1905). New methods for the diagnosis of the intellectual level of subnormals. *L'annee Psychologique, 12,* 191–244.

Boston Herald (July 8, 2001). *Memories Questioned, but Victim Still Certain of Evil – Studies Say Kids Can Be Easily Led.*

Brainerd, C. J., Forrest, T. J., Karibian, D., & Reyna, V. F. (2006). Development of false memory illusion. *Developmental Psychology, 42,* 962–979.

Brainerd, C. J., Holliday, R. E., & Reyna, V. F. (2004). Behavioral measurement of remembering phenomenologies: So simple a child can do it. *Child Development, 75,* 505–522.

Brainerd, C. J., & Reyna, V. F. (2007). Explaining developmental reversals in false memory. *Psychological Science, 18,* 442–448.

Brainerd, C. J., Reyna, V. F., & Ceci, S. J. (2008). Developmental reversals in false memory: A review of data and theory. *Psychological Bulletin, 134*(3), 343–382.

Brainerd, C. J., Reyna, V. F., & Forrest, T. J. (2002). Are young children susceptible to the False-Memory illusion? *Child Development, 73*(5), 1363–1377.

Bruck, M., & Ceci, S. J. (1999). The suggestibility of children's memory. *Annual Review of Psychology, 50*(1), 419–439.

Bruck, M., Ceci, S. J., & Francoeur, E. (2000). Children's use of anatomically detailed dolls to report genital touching in a medical examination: Developmental and gender comparisons. *Journal of Experimental Psychology: Applied, 6*, 74–83.

Bruck, M., Ceci, S. J., Francoeur, E., & Renick, A. (1995) Anatomically detailed dolls do not facilitate preschoolers' reports of a pediatric examination involving genital touching. *Journal of Experimental Psychology: Applied, 1*, 95–109.

Bruck, M., Ceci, S. J., & Hembrooke, H. (2002). The nature of children's true and false narratives. *Developmental Review, 22*(3), 520–554.

Cattell, J. M. (1895). Measurements of the accuracy of recollection. *Science, 2*(49), 761–766.

Ceci, S. J., & Bruck, M. (1993). Suggestibility of the child witness: A historical review and synthesis. *Psychological Bulletin, 113*(3), 403–439.

Ceci, S. J., & Bruck, M. (1995). *Jeopardy in the Courtroom: A Scientific Analysis of Children's Testimony.* Washington, DC: American Psychological Association.

Ceci, S. J., Loftus, E. F., Leichtman, M., & Bruck, M. (1994). The possible role of source misattributions in the creation of false beliefs among preschoolers. *International Journal of Clinical and Experimental Hypnosis, 42*, 304–320.

Ceci, S. J., Ross, D. F., & Toglia, M. P. (1987). Suggestibility of children's memory: Psycholegal implications. *Journal of Experimental Psychology: General, 116*(1), 38–49.

Davies, G. B. (1991). Research on children's testimony: Implications for interview practice. In C. R. Hollin, & K. Howells (Eds), *Clinical Approaches to Sex Offenders and Their Victims* (pp. 93–115). Chichester, England: Wiley.

Davis, D., & Loftus, E. F. (2009). Expectancies, emotion and memory reports for visual events. In J. R. Brockmore (Ed.), *The Visual World in Memory* (pp. 178–214). New York, NY: Psychology Press.

Deese, J. (1959). On the prediction of occurrence of particular verbal intrusions in immediate recall. *Journal of Experimental Psychology, 58*, 17–22.

Dewhurst, S. A., & Robinson, C. A. (2004). False memories in children: Evidence for a shift from phonological to semantic associations. *Psychological Science, 15*, 782–786.

Everson, M. D., & Boat, B. W. (1994). Putting the anatomical doll controversy in perspective: An examination of major doll uses and related criticisms. *Child Abuse and Neglect, 18*, 113–129.

Everson, M. D., & Boat, B. W. (2002). The utility of anatomical dolls and drawing in child forensic interviews. In M. L. Eisen, J. A. Quas, & G. S. Goodman (Eds), *Memory and Suggestibility in the Forensic Interview* (pp. 383–408). Mahwah, NJ: Erlbaum.

Farrar, M. J., & Goodman, G. S. (1990). Developmental differences in the relation between scripts and episodic memory: Do they exist? In R. Fivush, & J. A. Hudson (Eds), *Knowing and Remembering in Young Children* (pp. 30–64). New York, NY: Cambridge University Press.

Fivush, R. (1984). Learning about school: The development of kindergartners' school trips. *Child Development, 55*, 1697–1709.

Fivush, R., McDermott Sales, J., Goldberg, A., Bahrick, L., & Parker, J. (2004). Weathering the storm: Children's long-term recall of Hurricane Andrew. *Memory, 12*, 104–118.

Garven, S., Wood, J. M., Malpass, R. S., Shaw, J. S. (1998). More than suggestion: the effect of interviewing techniques from the McMartin Preschool case. *Journal of Applied Psychology, 83*, 347–359.

Goodman, N. (1984). *Of Mind and Other Matters.* Cambridge, MA: Harvard University Press.

Goodman, G. S. (2006). Children's eyewitness memory: A modern history and contemporary commentary. *Journal of Social Issues, 62,* 811–832.

Goodman, G. S., & Aman, C. (1990). Children's use of anatomically detailed dolls to recount an event. *Child Development, 61,* 1859–1871.

Gordon, L. H. (1994). PAIRS curriculum guide and training manual. Falls Church, VA: PAIRS.

Greenwald, A. G., & Banaji, M. R. (1995). Implicit social cognition: Attitudes, self esteem, and stereotypes. *Psychological Review, 102,* 4–27.

Hawes, J. M. (1991). *The Children's Rights Movement: A History of Advocacy and Protection.* Boston: Twayne Publishers.

Hayne, H., Gross, J., McNamee, S., Fitzgibbon, O., & Tustin, K. (2011). Episodic memory and episodic foresight inn 3-and 5-year old children. *Cognitive Development, 26,* 343–355.

Holliday, R. E. (2003a). The effect of a prior cognitive interview on children's acceptance of misinformation. *Applied Cognitive Psychology, 17,* 443–457.

Holliday, R. E. (2003b). Reducing misinformation effects in children with Cognitive interviews: dissociating recollection and familiarity. *Child Development, 74,* 728–751.

Holliday, R. E., Douglas, K., & Hayes, B. K. (1999). Children's eyewitness suggestibility: memory trace strength revisited. *Cognitive Development, 14,* 443–62.

Holliday, R. E., & Hayes, B. K. (2000). Dissociating automatic and intentional processes in children's eyewitness memory. *Journal of Experimental Child Psychology, 75,* 1–42.

Holliday, R. E., & Weekes, B. S. (2006). Dissociated developmental trajectories for semantic and phonological false memories. *Memory, 14,* 624–636.

Hudson, J. A. (1990). Constructive processing in children's event memory. *Developmental Psychology, 26,* 180–187.

Hudson, J. A., & Fivush, R. (1991). As time goes by: Sixth graders remember a kindergarten experience. *Applied Cognitive Psychology, 5,* 347–360.

Hudson, J. A., Fivush, R., & Kuebli, J. (1992). Scripts and episodes: the development of event memory. *Applied Cognitive Psychology, 6,* 483–505.

Katz, L. F. (2001). Physiological processes and mediators of the impact of marital conflict on children. In J. H. Grych & F. D. Fincham (Eds), *Interparental Conflict and Child Development: Theory, Research, and Applications* (pp. 188 –212). New York: Cambridge University Press.

Lamb, M. E., Hershkowitz, I., Sternberg, K. J., Boat, B., & Everson, M. D. (1996). Investigative interviews of alleged sexual abuse victims with and without anatomical dolls. *Child Abuse and Neglect, 20,* 1251–1259.

Lamb, M. E., Orbach, Y., Warren, A. R., Esplin, P. W., & Hershkowitz, I. (2007). Enhancing performance: Factors affecting the informativeness of young witnesses. In M. P. Toglia, J. D. Read, D. F. Ross & R. C. L. Lindsay (Eds), *The Handbook of Eyewitness Psychology.* Volume I, *Memory for Events* (pp. 429–451). Mahwah, New Jersey: Lawrence Erlbaum.

Lamb, M. E., Sternberg, K. J., Orbach, Y., Hershkowitz, I., Horowitz, D., & Esplin, P. W. (2002). The effects of intensive training and ongoing supervision on the quality of investigative interviews with alleged sex abuse victims. *Applied Developmental Science, 6,* 114–125.

Lampinen, J. M., Leding, J. K., Reed, K. B., & Odegard, T. N. (2006). Global gist extraction in children and adults. *Memory, 14,* 952–964.

Lampinen, J. M., & Smith, V. L. (1995). The incredible (and sometimes incredulous) child witness: Child eyewitness' sensitivity to source credibility cues. *Journal of Applied Psychology, 80,* 621–627.

Leventhal, J. M., Hamilton, J., Rededal, S., Tebano-Micci, A., Eyster, C. (1989). Anatomically correct dolls used in interviews of young children suspected of having been sexually abused. *Pediatrics, 84,* 900–906.

Gilstrap, L. L., Fritz, K., Torres, A. & Melinder, A. (2005). Child witnesses: Common ground and controversies in the scientific community. *William Mitchel Law Review, 32,* 59–79.

Loftus, E. F. (1979). *Eyewitness Testimony.* Cambridge MA: Harvard University Press.

Loftus, E. F. (2005). Planting misinformation in the human mind: A 30-year investigation of the malleability of memory. *Learning & Memory, 12,* 361–366.

Loftus, E. E, Miller, D. G., & Burns, H. J. (1978). Semantic integration of verbal information into visual memory. *Journal of Experimental Psychology: Human Learning and Memory, 4,* 19–31.

London, K., Bruck, M., Poole, D. A., & Melnyk, L. (2011). The development of metasuggestibility in children. *Applied Cognitive Psychology, 25* (1), 146–155.

Lyon, T. D. (2002). Applying suggestibility research to the real world: the case of repeated questions. *Law & Contemporary Problems, 65,* 97–126.

Marsil, D. F., Montoya, J., Ross, D. & Graham, L. (2002). Child witness policy: law interfacing with social science. *Law & Contemporary Problems,* 209–241.

Melnyk, L., Crossman, A. M., & Scullin, M. H. (2007). The suggestibility of children's memory. In M. P. Toglia, J. D. Read, D. F. Ross & R. C. L. Lindsay (Eds), *The Handbook of Eyewitness Psychology.* Volume I, *Memory for Events* (pp. 401–427). Mahwah, New Jersey: Lawrence Erlbaum.

Meltzoff, A. (1995). Understanding the intentions of others: Re-enactment of intended acts by 18-month-old children. *Developmental Psychology, 31,* 838–850.

Minow, M. (1995). What ever happened to children's rights? *Minnesota Law Review, 80,* 267–298.

Munsterberg, H. (1908). *On the Witness Stand: Essays on Psychology and Crime.* New York: Doubleday.

Odegard, T. N., Cooper, C. M., Lampinen, J. M., Reyna, V. F., & Brainerd, C. J. (2009). Children's eyewitness memory for multiple real life events. *Child Development, 80,* 1877–1890.

Odegard, T. N., Holliday, R. E., Brainerd, C. J., & Reyna, V. F. (2008). Attention to global gist processing eliminates age effects in false memories. *Journal of Experimental Child Psychology, 99,* 96–113.

Odegard, T. N., Jenkins, K. M., & Koen, J. D. (2010). Developmental differences in the use of recognition memory rejection mechanisms. *Developmental Psychology, 46,* 691–698.

Ornstein, P. A., Baker-Ward, L., Gordon, B. N., Pelphrey, K. A., Tyler, C. S., & Gramzow, E. (2006). The influence of prior knowledge and repeated questioning on children's long-term retention of the details of a pediatric examination. *Developmental Psychology, 42,* 332–344.

Ornstein, P. A., Gordon, B., & Larus, D. M. (1992). Children's memory for a personally experienced event: Implications for testimony. *Applied Cognitive Psychology, 6,* 49–60.

Ornstein, P. A., Merritt, K. A., Baker-Ward, L., Furtado, E., Gordon, B., & Principe, G. (1998). Children's knowledge, expectation, and long-term retention. *Applied Cognitive Psychology, 12,* 387–405.

Pear, T., & Wyatt, S. (1914). The testimony of normal and mentally defective children. *British Journal of Psychology, 3,* 388–419.

Peters, D. P. (1987). The impact of naturally occurring stress on children's memory. In S. J. Ceci, M. P. Toglia, & D. F. Ross (Eds), *Children's Eyewitness Memory* (pp. 1–23). New York, NY: Springer-Verlag.

Peterson, C. (1999). Children's memory for medical emergencies: 2 years later. *Developmental Psychology, 35,* 1493–1506.

Peterson C., & Bell, M. (1996). Children's memory for traumatic injury. *Child Development, 67*, 3045–3070.

Peterson, C., & Biggs, M. (1997). Interviewing children about trauma: Problems with "specific" questions. *Journal of Traumatic Stress, 10*, 279–290.

Peterson, C., Dowden, C., & Tobin, J. (1999). Interviewing preschoolers: Comparisons of yes/ no and wh-questions. *Journal of Law and Human Behavior, 23*, 539–555.

Peterson, C., Moores, L., & White, G. (2001). Recounting the same events again and again: Children's consistency across multiple interviews. *Applied Cognitive Psychology, 15*, 353–371.

Peterson, C., & Rideout, R. (1998). Memory for medical emergencies experienced by 1- and 2-year olds. *Developmental Psychology, 34*, 1059–1072.

Peterson, C., & Whalen, N. (2001). Five years later: Children's memory for medical emergencies. *Applied Cognitive Psychology, 15*, S7–S24.

Pillemer, D. B. (1992). Preschool children's memories of personal circumstances: The fire alarm study. In E. Winograd and U. Neisser (Eds), *Affect and Accuracy in Recall: Studies of 'Flashbulb' Memories*. New York: Cambridge University Press.

Pillemer, D. B., Picariello, M. L., & Pruett, J. C. (1994). Very long-term memories of a salient preschool event. *Applied Cognitive Psychology, 8*, 95–106.

Pipe, M., Thierry, K. L., & Lamb, M. E. (2007). The development of event memory: Implications for child witness testimony. In M. P. Toglia, J. D. Read, D. F. Ross & R. C. L. Lindsay (Eds), *The Handbook of Eyewitness Psychology*. Volume I, Memory for Events (pp. 453–478). Mahwah, New Jersey: Lawrence Erlbaum.

Poole, D. A., & Lamb, M. E. (1998). *Investigative Interviews of Children: A Guide for Helping Professionals*. Washington, DC: American Psychological Association Press.

Poole, D. A., & White, L. T. (1993). Two years later: Effects of question repetition and retention interval on the eyewitness testimony of children and adults. *Developmental Psychology, 29*, 844–853,

Quas, J. A., Goodman, G. S., Bidrose, S., Pipe, M., & Craw, S. (1999). Emotion and memory: Children's long-term remembering, forgetting, and suggestibility. *Journal of Experimental Child Psychology, 72*, 235–270.

Reyna, V. F., & Brainerd, C. J. (1991). Fuzzy-trace theory and children's acquisition of scientific and mathematical concepts. *Learning and Individual Differences, 3*, 27–60.

Reyna, V. F., Mills, B., Estrada, S., & Brainerd, C. J. (2007). False memory in children: Data, theory, and legal implications. In M. P. Toglia, J. D. Read, D. F. Ross & R. C. L. Lindsay (Eds), *The Handbook of Eyewitness Psychology*. Volume I, *Memory for Events* (pp. 479–507). Mahwah, New Jersey: Lawrence Erlbaum.

Roediger, H. L., III, & McDermott, K. B. (1995). Creating false memories: Remembering words not presented on lists. *Journal of Experimental Psychology: Learning, Memory, and Cognition, 21*, 803–814.

Saywitz, K. J., Goodman, G. S., Nicholas, E., & Moan, S. F. (1991). Children's memories of a physical examination involving genital touch: Implications for reports of child sexual abuse. *Journal of Consulting and Clinical Psychology, 59*, 682–691.

Sporer, S. L. (2008). Lessons from the origins of eyewitness testimony research in Europe. *Applied Cognitive Psychology, 22*, 737–757. doi: 10.1002/acp.1479.

Stern, L. W. (1902). *Zur Psychologie der Aussage. Experimentelle Untersuchungen über Erinnerungstreue*. Berlin: Guttentag.

Stern, L. W. (1910). Abstracts of lectures on the psychology of testimony and on the study of individuality. *The American Journal of Psychology, 21*, 270–282.

Tanenhaus, D. S. (2005). Between dependency and liberty: The conundrum of children's rights in the gilded age. *Law and History Review, 23*(2), 351–385.

Tanenhaus, D. S., & Bush, W. (2007). Toward a history of children as witnesses. *Indiana Law Journal, 82,* 1059–1075.

Thierry, K. L., Lamb, M. E., Orbach, Y., & Pipe, M. (2005). Developmental differences in the function and use of anatomical dolls during interviews with alleged sexual abuse victims. *Journal of Counseling and Clinical Psychology, 73,* 1125–1134.

Toglia, M. P., Goodwin, K. A., Neuschatz, J. S. (2009). Eyewitnesses: Suggestibility in adults. In A. Jamieson & A. Moenssens (Eds), *Wiley Encyclopedia of Forensic Science* (pp. 1065–1072). Chichester, UK: John Wiley & Sons.

Toglia, M. P., Read, J. D., Ross, D. F., & Lindsay, R. C. L. (Eds). (2007). *The Handbook of Eyewitness Psychology.* Volume I, *Memory for Events.* Mahwah, NJ: Lawrence Erlbaum.

Toglia, M. P., Ross, D. F., Ceci, S. J., & Hembrooke, H. (1992). The suggestibility of children's memory: A social-psychological and cognitive interpretation. In M. L. Howe, C. J. Brainerd, and V. F. Reyna (Eds), *Development of Long-Term Retention* (pp. 217–241). New York: Springer-Verlag.

Varendonck, J. (1911). Les temoignages d'enfants dans un proces retentissant. *Archives de psychologie, 11,* 129–171.

Vivard, E., & Tranter, M. (1988). Helping young children to describe experiences of child sexual abuse: General issue. In A. Bentovim, A. Elton, J. Hildebrand, M. Tranter, & E. Vizard (Eds), *Child Sexual Abuse within the family: Assessment and Treatment* (pp. 84–104). Bristol, England: John Wright.

Wells, G. L. (1978). Applied eyewitness-testimony research: System variables and estimator variables. *Journal of Personality and Social Psychology, 36*(12), 1546–1557.

Whipple, G. M. (1909). The observer as reporter: A survey of the psychology of testimony. *Psychological Bulletin, 6,* 153–170.

Whipple, G. M. (1912). Psychology of testimony and report. *Psychological Bulletin, 9,* 264.

Wigmore, J. H. (1909). Professor Munsterberg and the psychology of evidence. *Illinois Law Review, 3,* 399–445.

Willrich, M. (2003). *City of Courts: Socializing Justice in Progressive Era Chicago.* New York: Cambridge University Press.

Wright, A. M., & Holliday, R. E. (2007). Enhancing the recall of young, young-old, and old-old adults with cognitive interviews. *Applied Cognitive Psychology, 21,* 19–43.

# CHAPTER 5

# Children's Memory for Emotionally Negative Experiences: An Eyewitness Memory Perspective

TAMMY A. MARCHE AND KAREN SALMON

Over the past 30 years, an increasing number of children have faced the challenge of providing testimony in criminal proceedings. Typically, it is believed that the child has experienced or witnessed maltreatment or other forms of violence perpetrated against the child or others (Hanna et al., 2010; Quas & Sumaroka, 2011). Thus, the to-be-reported experience is likely negative and may well be emotionally charged. The quality of the information that can be obtained from the child during forensic interviews plays a pivotal role in whether or not prosecution of an alleged offender is successful, which, in turn, has significant implications for the safety of the individual child and of other children. Given these implications, researchers and interviewers alike must understand the full range of factors that can influence children's eyewitness reports. In this forensic context, understanding the associations between negative, emotionally arousing experiences and children's memory is particularly important, and is the focus of this chapter.

Memory is only one of many factors that determine children's responses in a forensic interview or courtroom (e.g. Pipe & Salmon, 2009). Yet how children remember does determine what they *can* report. Mindful, however, that our major concern is children's eyewitness testimony, we have restricted our review in several ways. First, we focus on the associations between negative emotions and children's recall. Further distinctions can also be made between experiences that are negatively valenced (e.g. sadness) and those that are also highly arousing or intense (e.g. fear; Hamm, Greenwald, Bradley,

& Lang, 1993). The sharpest point of the intersection between valence and arousal is children's recall of traumatic experiences. Strictly speaking, a *traumatic event* is one in which an individual experiences "actual or threatened death or serious injury," and, as a result, experiences intense fear, helplessness or horror (American Psychiatric Association, 2000). Research investigating the association between negative emotion and memory in children has tended to blur the distinction between valence and arousal, undoubtedly, at least in part, because of the difficulties involved in their disentanglement in all but laboratory-based experimental research using word-list stimuli (e.g. Brainerd et al., 2010; see also Yuille & Tollestrup, 1992, for similar comments regarding earlier research with adults). As a result, the concepts of "emotion," "stress," and "trauma" are often adopted interchangeably; we attempt to separate them here, when possible.

Second, we focus on the influence of negative emotions on children's explicit episodic memory, and in particular, their autobiographical memory, in contrast to implicit memory involving consciously inaccessible skills and habits (Bauer, 2009). *Autobiographical memory* is comprised of potentially verbalizable personal memories of specific events or episodes that concern the self and can be dated in time and place. *Episodic* or *autobiographical memory* is the memory "subtype" most obviously called upon in forensic interviews, where the task required of children is to provide highly specific details of their experiences, typically following delays of months or even years (e.g. Pipe & Salmon, 2009).

Finally, we focus on young people between 3 and around 18 years of age. One reason for our lower age limit is that after around age 3, children can provide at least a fledgling linguistic account of their experiences that may be of forensic relevance and, because of this, they do appear as witnesses under some circumstances, albeit relatively rarely (Hanna et al., 2010; Quas et al., 2010).

## Emotional memory: empirical findings and theoretical considerations

Memory for a number of emotionally negative experiences has been empirically examined. These have included, for example, documented cases of abuse (e.g. Bidrose & Goodman, 2000; Orbach & Lamb, 1999), inoculations (e.g. Alexander et al., 2002; Goodman, Bottoms, Schwartz-Kenney, & Ruth, 1991), painful medical procedures such as voiding cystourethrograms (VCUGs; Goodman et al., 1994, 1997; Merritt, Ornstein, & Spicker, 1994; Quas et al., 1999; Salmon, Price, & Pereira, 2002), emergency room treatments and injuries (Peterson, 1999; Peterson & Bell, 1996; Peterson &

Whalen, 2001), natural disasters such as hurricanes (Ackil, van Abbema, & Bauer, 2003; Bahrick, Parker, Fivush, & Levitt, 1998; Fivush et al., 2004; Shaw, Applegate, & Schorr, 1996), tornados (Bauer, Burch, van Abbema, & Ackil, 2007), and earthquakes (Najarian et al., 1996), as well as sniper attacks (Pynoos & Nader, 1989; Schwartz & Kowalski, 1991), a fatal bus-train collision (Tyano et al., 1996), the Gulf War (Dyregrov, Gjestad, & Raundalen, 2002; Laor et al., 1997), and imprisonment in Cambodia (Kinzie et al., 1986).

It is now well recognized, based on such research, that the relation between emotion and memory is far from straightforward (for reviews, see Quas & Fivush, 2009). According to earlier views, there is a direct association between emotion and memory, articulated in the question "do high levels of emotion or stress experienced during an event enhance or impair memory of that event?" (Bauer, 2009; Ceci & Bruck, 1993; Goodman, 2006). Because of findings that the degree of stress experienced by children and adults during emotionally negative events is both positively and negatively associated with memory for that event (see reviews in Howe, Goodman, & Cicchetti, 2008; Quas & Fivush, 2009), recent theoretical conceptualizations have refined this focus, highlighting how emotion differentially influences attention to, and recall of, different aspects of a stimulus or event. Thus, it is proposed that central, attention-grabbing aspects of an emotional experience are well remembered because they elicit arousal, but the consequence is a "memory narrowing" effect whereby other aspects, such as details that are spatially or contextually removed, are more likely to be forgotten (Goodman, Quas, & Ogle, 2010; Kensinger, 2009; Levine & Edelstein, 2009; Reisberg & Heuer, 2004). Indeed, convergent findings from behavioral and neuroimaging research with adults show that information that elicits arousal engages emotion-specific responses with respect to capturing attention and facilitating encoding, consolidation and, possibly, retrieval. These findings are over and above the additional rehearsal through conversation that an emotional experience might elicit (Hulse, Allan, Memon, & Read, 2007). In general, negative relative to positive valence confers a greater benefit to memory, and enhancement of central emotional information is stronger for negative than for positive experiences (Vaish, Grossmann, & Woodward, 2008).

Although much research supports this general pattern of findings (e.g. Bahrick et al., 1998; Christianson, 1992; Christianson & Loftus, 1991; Peterson & Whalen, 2001), there are inconsistencies in the expected results. For example, at times, emotion enhances memory for both central and peripheral information (e.g. Laney, Heuer, & Reisberg, 2003), and stress can have a generally deleterious effect on memory, rather than on central aspects only (Deffenbacher, Bornstein, Penrod, & McGorty, 2004; Levine & Edelstein, 2009). This is likely due to a range of factors, including different methods of defining stress and assessing memory (for further discussion, see Brewin, 2011). A further possible reason for these inconsistent findings is that emotionality is accorded to an event by the experiencer of that event; particular experiences engender emotional responses in particular individuals. Compas, Campbell, Robinson and Rodriguez (2009) argue that individuals respond to stress in two ways. The first is automatized reactions to stress, or stress reactivity, which differ substantially among individuals. People who are very sensitive to stress tend to experience extended physiological and emotional arousal after exposure to a stressful experience (e.g. Davidson, 2003). Furthermore, how one reacts to stress appears to be a stable individual difference apparent early in childhood (Kagan, Reznick, & Gibbons, 1989; Kagan, Reznick, & Snidman, 1987). The second way of responding to stress is controlled, effortful and purposeful (Compas et al., 2009), which is typically referred to as *coping*. Both arousal sensitivity or stress reactivity and coping or emotion regulation can influence event memory. For example, the strategies that are "launched" to reduce distress, particularly when they direct attention away from the experience, can impair memory for emotional events (Levine & Edelstein, 2009). Thus, arousal and regulation are two key factors emerging in the understanding of emotional memories across the lifespan (Kensinger, 2009; for reviews, see Goodman et al., 2010; Quas & Fivush, 2009).

Thus, to fully understand the various findings across studies, it is important to acknowledge that individual difference factors, such as stress reactivity and coping, play a considerable role in emotional memory. How an event is appraised (e.g. as negative or positive), how it relates to an individual's goals (that is, states that people wish to attain or avoid; Levine & Edelstein, 2009), and how these factors, in turn, are influenced by the individual's developmental pathway are also relevant to understanding emotional memory (Kensinger, 2009; Levine & Edelstein, 2009). Of note, Bauer (2009) queries whether the relations between stress and memory could be anything but complex, given the complexity of each. Memory itself is not a unitary construct but is comprised of different potential categorizations which may vary according to, for example, the duration of recall (seconds or years), the content (personal experiences, facts), and conceptualization/level of analysis (neural, physiological, psychological; Bauer, 2009). Moreover, as recognized by recent integrated models, emotional responses are determined by, and then influence, myriad interacting factors including psychological, neural and physiological ones (e.g. Alexander & O'Hara, 2009; Wallin, Quas, & Yim, 2009). The very mixed pattern of findings with respect to children's memory for emotional experiences is therefore likely to be explicable, at least in part, by the failure of earlier research to take into account the full range of relevant factors.

# Model of eyewitness memory

The idea that individual differences in stress reactivity and emotion regulation underlie the relationship between stress and memory is consistent with a model of eyewitness memory proposed by Herve, Cooper, and Yuille (2007). According to this model, threatening events increase autonomic nervous system arousal and, consequently, the saliency of memory traces, especially the core features of those traces. Because individuals differ in arousal sensitivity, so too will they differ in their event memory. Herve and colleagues argue that although more than a hundred years of research have been devoted to eyewitness memory, there is no comprehensive theory that explains the variability in eyewitnesses' accounts of crime-related events. To address this gap, Herve and company proposed a model of eyewitness testimony, focused on adult offenders' memory of a crime, which includes various biological, psychological, and social factors known to influence eyewitness memory. However, in the context of children's eyewitness testimony, developmental factors will influence all domains of functioning, including neurobiological maturity and information-processing capacity, as well as knowledge base, appraisals and interpretations of experiences, and emotion-regulation skills (the processes responsible for monitoring, evaluating, and modifying emotional reactions to facilitate goal accomplishment (Cicchetti & Dawson, 2002; Thompson, 2011).

There are, however, two unique features of the model that we particularly like as a framework for understanding the relationship between emotion and memory. First, as Herve et al. (2007) explain, their model is consonant with the predominant view that eyewitnesses' memories are heavily influenced by their emotional reactions, and they take account of the variety and complexity of these emotional reactions among individuals. Second, they provide a particularly useful structure for considering these diverse and complex variables by arguing that emotional reactions, and the memories that result, are influenced by interacting, and at times, overlapping, predisposing, precipitating and perpetuating biopsychosocial factors. *Predisposing factors* sway witnesses to respond to events in particular ways, *precipitating factors* affect how witnesses respond during events, and *perpetuating factors* influence memory retention and reconstruction. In the following, we outline a number of key predisposing, precipitating and perpetuating factors that influence children's memory for emotionally negative experiences.

## *Predisposing factors*

According to Herve and company (2007), *predisposing factors* are "either innate traits or experiences that occur prior to the event in question, and, as such, serve to delineate the typical response that someone will have to a stressful event" (p. 53). In our review of potentially relevant factors, we have expanded this definition to include two groups of factors related to the child and his or her experience that could influence what is reported during a forensic interview. The first group of factors relates to adverse experiences in childhood and their concomitants and sequelae: child maltreatment, psychopathology, problematic attachment relationships and impoverished parent–child conversation. The second group of factors concern those that might be considered relatively "fixed"; temperament and reactivity, intellectual ability and language ability. These overlapping factors influence the child's experience of emotion and arousal in relation to specific experiences, and potentially the emotion regulatory strategies adopted to manage this.

*Adverse childhood experiences and their sequelae*

**Child maltreatment.** The majority of children who undergo forensic interviews do so in relation to sexual assault, almost half of which are perpetrated by a family member (e.g. Hanna et al., 2010; Quas & McAuliff, 2009; Quas & Sumaroka, 2011). The age range varies, but children as young as 5 years, and less commonly even younger, are represented in current statistics (Hanna et al., 2010; Lamb et al., 2003; Quas & McAuliff, 2009; Zajac, Gross, & Hayne, 2003). This is not surprising, given findings from Trickett, Noll and Putnam's (2011) 23-year longitudinal study that the median age of onset of child sexual abuse is 7.5 years, and the median duration is approximately two years.

Research investigating the effects of child maltreatment on emotional memory has burgeoned over the past few years, with a range of paradigms adopted (e.g. memory for word lists using the Deese-Roediger-McDermott task, Howe, Cicchetti, & Toth, 2006, 2011; analog events or actual medical procedures, Eisen et al., 2007). There are, however, limitations to the conclusions that can be drawn (for a review, see Goodman et al., 2010). For example, maltreatment can vary widely from a single incident to multiple forms of abuse and associated risk factors (e.g. violence, poverty) associated with the "toxic relational environment" (Cicchetti & Toth, 2005, p. 810) within which maltreatment occurs (Azar & Wolfe, 2006; McMahon et al., 2003). Even within the narrower domain of sexual abuse, the adverse impact varies widely, depending on factors such as the severity, chronicity, developmental timing and relationship of the child to the perpetrator (Trickett et al., 2011). Moreover, there is a confound between maltreatment and other significant variables that are its common sequelae (as we discuss below), including past or current psychopathology. Careful research is beginning to tease out the differential effects of each of these important factors on memory, but in practice, emotional memory in maltreated children is likely to be multiply determined (e.g. Goodman et al., 2010).

Many maltreated children experience significant biological effects, which include disruption to cortisol levels, systemic brain changes in growth, maturation and neural development and plasticity (Kearney, Wechsler, Kaur, & Lemos-Miller, 2010), and it has, therefore, been of interest to establish whether these changes are reflected in alterations in basic memory functioning. Findings of experimental studies assessing maltreated children's ability to inhibit emotional or neutral information, and on tests assessing general memory and cognitive skills, reveal no pervasive and consistent deficits (e.g. Howe, Cicchetti, Toth, & Cerrito, 2004; Howe, Toth, & Cicchetti, 2011; Porter, Lawson, & Bigler, 2005; Valentino, Cicchetti, Rogosch, & Toth, 2008), although some suggestive findings highlight the importance of further work in this area (Goodman et al., 2011).

Research identifying the negatively cascading effects of maltreatment on children's functioning has, however, yielded important insights regarding potential effects on their explicit memory (Goodman et al., 2010). Noteworthy is that the sequelae have implications for children's level of arousal, the kind of information attended to, and the strategies adopted for emotion regulation. For example, early and severe stress, such as that associated with child sexual abuse, leads to an initial heightened stress response, which is attenuated over time; this may suggest suppression of an adaptive response to chronic exposure to glucocorticoids and their impact on brain function (Trickett et al., 2011). Moreover, in contrast to non-maltreated children, maltreated children exhibit a *negativity bias* on a number of psychological factors; they manifest negative emotions earlier, show earlier identification of anger and recall aggressive events better (Ayoub et al., 2006; Cicchetti & Toth, 2005; Pollak & Tolley-Schell, 2003). Within the context of unpredictable, intrusive parenting and insecure or disorganized attachment relationships, many children develop poor emotional and behavioral coping strategies, including subclinical dissociation (a failure of information processing in the face of trauma; Valentino et al., 2008) and other forms of functional avoidance, and heightened dysregulated and aggressive behavior (Ayoub et al., 2006; Cicchetti & Toth, 2005; Eisen et al., 2007; Shipman & Zeman, 1999; Shipman, Schneider, & Sims, 2005).

On reviewing research relating to maltreatment and memory, Goodman et al. (2010) drew two conclusions that underscore the importance of arousal and regulatory mechanisms. First, maltreated children remember stressful prior experiences and trauma-related information relatively well. Relevant factors may be their focus on salient information, heightened by their negative information processing bias and extended processing of negative material (e.g. Ayoub et al., 2006). Second, children with poorer emotion regulatory strategies tend to make more memory errors regarding negative emotional information. For example, Eisen et al. (2007) investigated maltreated children's recall of a stressful medical event during which a researcher was present, enabling the child's memory report to be compared with the checklist of event components. There were no pervasive effects of abuse status on recall, but higher levels of dissociation, a stronger cortisol response, and more self-reported trauma symptoms were associated with more memory errors (see also Cicchetti, Rogosch, Howe, & Toth, 2010). While these findings may indicate the deleterious effects of dissociation as an emotion-regulation strategy, it must be noted that not all researchers have found dissociation to be associated with poorer recall (Goodman et al., 2010; Eisen, Qin, Goodman, & Davis, 2002; Howe et al., 2006, 2011).

**Depression, anxiety, and Post-traumatic Stress Disorder (PTSD).** Consistent with many other findings, Trickett et al.'s (2011) longitudinal research has shown that at many points across their lifespan, sexually abused, relative to non-abused, females score higher on depression, anxiety, PTSD, dissociation, and behavioral problems such as aggression and delinquency. For example, rates of PTSD in children who have experienced sexual abuse exceed 50 percent, and this is even higher when they have also witnessed parental violence (Salmon & Bryant, 2002). Thus, many child witnesses will be recalling emotionally negative experiences in the context of depression, anxiety, and other forms of psychopathology. Note that although we discuss psychopathology as a predisposing factor, it is, of course, likely to infuse all factors (precipitating, perpetuating) relating to the child's testimony.

Theory and research suggests that each of these psychological disorders is associated with particular patterns of memory impairment (e.g. MacLeod, 2010), although the vast majority of studies have been conducted with adults. Most work with youth has focused on adolescents, and there is a paucity of research on the influence of psychopathology on younger children's memory. Indeed, there is evidence that, in children, high levels of anxiety, depression and aggression are each associated with attention to negative information, negative interpretation of ambiguous situations, and preferential recall of negative information (MacLeod, 2010; Reid, Salmon, & Lovibond, 2006). Thus, anxious adults and children preferentially attend to negative information; threatening stimuli capture their attention, rendering this kind of information easier to encode and identify (e.g. Hadwin & Field, 2010; Mitte, 2008). Less work has focused on anxiety and memory, although high relative to low anxious adults have been shown to manifest better recall (but not recognition) of threatening autobiographical information and poorer recall of positive information (Morgan, 2010). It might be expected, therefore, that highly anxious children would retain good information about abusive situations, consistent with the evidence presented above regarding maltreated children, but this remains in the realm of speculation. Of note, however, is evidence that trait anxiety is associated with exaggerations of negative experiences in memory. Rocha, Marche and von Baeyer (2009) found that children with higher levels of trait anxiety recalled that they had experienced greater pain during a dental procedure after a delay than they reported at the time, suggesting that these anxiety-prone children may have negatively distorted their memory of pain.

Research with adults suggests that depression is characterized primarily by difficulty disengaging attention from negative information in working memory and sustained processing and elaboration of negative material, resulting in negatively biased explicit (but not necessarily implicit) memory (Joormann, Hertel, LeMoult, & Gotlib, 2009; Mathews & MacLeod, 2005). Deficits in cognitive control may also contribute to the robust finding that depressed adults, and those experiencing PTSD, manifest overgeneral memory (OGM; i.e. recall of generic memories when requested to recall specific events) in response to positive and negative memory cues (Moore & Zoellner, 2007; Williams et al., 2007). The predominant theoretical perspective proposes that individuals truncate or limit their search during retrieval when only general descriptive information has been accessed, without moving "down" the hierarchy of their autobiographical memory system to the level of specific events. This is proposed to be due not only to reduced executive resources but also to the "capturing" of the memory search by rumination or negative self schemas (Conway & Pleydell-Pearce, 2000; for reviews, see Williams et al., 2007; Valentino, 2011). In this context, OGM is a form of functional avoidance that reduces the impact of negative affect or high arousal. Research with adolescents, and the few studies with children, similarly converge to demonstrate that referred samples of depressed relative to non-depressed adolescents generate disproportionately more OGM to positive and negative cue words, even when their depression is in remission (Drummond et al., 2006; Hipwell et al., 2010; Park, Goodyer, & Teasdale, 2002; Kuyken & Howell, 2006; Kuyken & Dalgleish, 2011; Sumner, Griffith, & Mineka, 2011; Swales, Williams, & Wood, 2001; Vrielynck, Deplus, & Piilippot, 2007).

Children experiencing PTSD may also have a greater tendency to retrieve overgeneral memories, although the evidence is much less consistent than for adults. Indeed, debate continues with respect to whether OGM is associated with a history of trauma or is more specific to depression and PTSD (e.g. Goodman et al., 2010; Johnson, Greenhoot, Glisky, & McCloskey, 2005). For example, maltreated children (aged 7 to 14 years) manifest greater difficulty retrieving specific memories in response to emotion cues than do their non-maltreated peers, over and above depression (Valentino, Toth, & Cicchetti, 2009). Interestingly, in Valentino and colleagues' (2009) study, younger relative to older children reported more OGM, highlighting the potential importance of developmental factors.

Children exhibiting PTSD manifest other memory difficulties. Indeed, PTSD is *characterized* by disturbances in memory, including gaps or impairments of voluntary memory and involuntary intrusions of aspects of the experience. Recent findings suggest that PTSD might disrupt a child's ability to provide a coherent narrative account of a traumatic experience, which is what Brewin (2011) found with adults. For example, Salmond and colleagues (2011) compared trauma narratives to narratives of unpleasant events in young people (aged 8 to 17 years) who had experienced a potentially traumatic event. Participants with *acute stress disorder* provided narratives containing more repetitions, expressions of uncertainty, confusion or non-consecutive chunks, and indicators of not comprehending what had occurred. Along with negative appraisals of the trauma experience, trauma narrative disorganization predicted higher levels of acute stress (Salmond et al., 2011; see also Kenardy et al., 2007; O'Kearney, Speyer, & Kenardy, 2007). It is unclear, however, whether this pattern also relates to attempts to avoid the arousal induced by narrating the experience (Salmond et al., 2011).

Although these findings suggest that psychological disorders are associated with particular patterns of memory impairment, a number of questions remain. For example, from a theoretical perspective, the extent to which memory factors either play a causal role in the development of psychopathology (that is, a predisposing factor), serve to maintain the individual's difficulties (a perpetuating factor), or both (Brewin, 2011) remains unclear. More specifically, in the context of eyewitness testimony, very little research has directly investigated the influence of psychopathology on children's reports. Given the prevalence of psychopathology amongst maltreated children, further research is clearly needed.

***Insecure attachment.*** For the vast majority of affected children, maltreatment is associated with significant disruptions to relationship styles (Aspelmeier, Elliott, & Smith, 2007; Trickett et al., 2011; Valentino, 2011). Attachment security is proposed to mediate the child's response to attachment-relative stressors. For example, secure mother–child attachment buffers children from exhibiting activation of the hypothalamic-pituitary-adrenal (HPA) axis and from an increase in glucocorticosteroids to threatening stimuli even when the children exhibit shyness and behavioral inhibition, whereas disturbances in attachment tend to provoke the reverse pattern (Wiik & Gunnar, 2009). Systems such as the HPA axis become activated, and glucocorticosteroids (e.g. cortisol) increase, when children are exposed to emotionally negative, especially stressful, experiences. Moreover, recent theory and supporting evidence demonstrate that attachment is associated with information processing style across the lifespan. As proposed by Dykas and Cassidy (2011) and others (e.g. Thompson, 2006), the internal working model of relationships developed through early attachment experiences may influence the extent to which individuals use biased rules to process social information. Specifically, insecure relative to secure individuals are expected to use these rules to filter out (from conscious awareness) attachment-relevant social information that would cause excessive emotional pain. These processes again reflect a balance between arousal and regulation.

Attachment security influences information processing (e.g. looking times) even in infancy. The mixed findings of the relatively few studies suggest that insecure children and adolescents either process attachment-relevant information negatively or avoid it, whereas secure children are able to process both negative and positive emotional information (for a review, see Dykas & Cassidy, 2011). Of direct relevance to children's eyewitness testimony is a strong body of work by Goodman and colleagues that shows that attachment influences children's memory and suggestibility for negative emotional events (for a review, see Chae, Ogle, & Goodman, 2009). Thus, parents with an avoidant rather than secure attachment style have children who manifest poorer recall of stressful medical procedures such as an x-ray of the kidneys, a VCUG or inoculations, particularly if the children had been highly distressed (Alexander et al., 2002). Moreover, over and above their level of distress, children of avoidant parents show greater suggestibility when recalling a VCUG (Goodman et al., 1994; Goodman et al., 1997; for a review, see Bruck & Melnyk, 2004). The association between attachment avoidance and poorer recall has also been replicated in adults who experienced abuse as children (Edelstein et al., 2005). Parents with an avoidant attachment style are less responsive to their children during a stressful medical procedure and their children manifest greater distress; this, in turn, may also be because they lack effective emotion-regulation strategies (e.g. Alexander et al., 2002).

***Impoverished parent-child conversation.*** The way in which parents, particularly mothers, talk about everyday experiences with their young children plays a critical role in the development of the children's autobiographical memory skill. This is now well-established by convergent findings of research using observational, longitudinal, experimental and training paradigms (e.g. Fivush, Haden, & Reese, 2006; McGuigan & Salmon, 2004; Nelson & Fivush, 2004; Ornstein, Haden, & Hedrick, 2004; Reese & Newcombe, 2007; Van Bergen, Salmon, Dadds, & Allen, 2009). Thus, parents who engage their child in discussion, and who elicit and expand upon their child's contributions to that discussion, have children who, across the preschool years and into mid-childhood, provide more detailed accounts of their personal experiences with their parents and independent adults (for reviews, see Fivush et al., 2006; Wareham & Salmon, 2006). Moreover, findings show that the style and content of mother–child reminiscing, particularly about negative emotional experiences, is an important context for children's understanding of self, minds and emotions (their labels, causes and strategies for regulation; Van Bergen et al., 2009; Nelson & Fivush, 2004). Although relatively little research has investigated parental reminiscing in the context of child maltreatment or psychopathology, preliminary findings suggest that conversations between maltreating mothers and their children, when they occur, lack key dimensions that promote socioemotional competence generally and the child's ability to provide a comprehensive account of personal experiences, more specifically (Shipman & Zeman, 1999; for a review, see Wareham & Salmon, 2006). Attachment style may be a mediator of this association, given findings that mothers of children who are securely attached are more elaborative during reminiscing, and their children participate to a greater extent in the conversations (Laible, 2004).

## Child factors

**Temperament and reactivity.** Given our emphasis on arousal and regulation, children's *temperament*, that is "individual differences in emotional, motor, and attentional reactivity and self regulation" (Rothbart, Ellis, Rueda, & Posner, 2003, p. 1114), might be expected to influence how children recall specific events. Indeed, all dimensions of temperament have hypothesized physiological concomitants that may well be associated with patterns of arousal and regulation (Nigg, 2006). Yet relatively little research has investigated the associations between memory and temperament in children. Of the research that has been conducted, some report null findings (e.g. Imhoff & Baker-Ward, 1999) or modest associations between aspects of temperament (e.g. approach/withdrawal and emotionality) and children's recall (Gordon et al., 1993). In a review of findings relating to the associations between temperament and suggestibility, Bruck and Melnyk (2004) found very little support for a consistent association.

From a theoretical perspective, associations between temperament and children's recall might be expected for the dimension of effortful control, defined by Rothbart and colleagues (2003, p. 114) as "the ability to suppress a dominant response in order to perform a subdominant response." Findings suggest that higher levels of effortful control are associated with better coping during a stressful medical procedure, possibly because these children are able to flexibly shift and refocus their attention as a means of distraction (Salmon et al., 2002). There is a positive relationship between effortful control and young children's recall (Alexander et al., 2002). Noteworthy in the context of maltreatment is that although effortful control emerges as a dimension of temperament early in life (having moderate coherence at around 22 months), its development is impaired by negative parenting practices. such as maternal power assertion (Kochanska & Knaack, 2003).

Children's level of stress reactivity is also relevant to their response to, and recall of, the to-be-remembered event. We cover this in our section on precipitating factors.

***Intellectual ability.*** Maltreatment might also influence children's episodic memory via its impact on cognitive and educational achievement. All forms of maltreatment are associated with heightened risk of academic failure (Cicchetti & Toth, 2005; Trickett et al., 2011). Sexually abused females, on average, acquire receptive language skills at a slower rate than do their peers, and continue to score at a lower level. More generally, they also perform less well relative to their peers on tests of crystallized and fluid intellectual ability (Trickett et al., 2011). Yet findings to date suggest that maltreatment per se is not the critical factor. For example, regardless of abuse status, higher intelligence predicted better memory, although associations tended to be relatively low and not always straightforward (Brown & Pipe, 2003; Eisen et al., 2002; Gignac & Powell, 2006; Howe et al., 2011; Roebers & Schneider, 2001).

Children with intellectual disabilities (ID) are more than twice as likely to experience maltreatment of all subtypes (Kendall-Tackett, Lyon, Taliaferro, & Little, 2005); intellectual functioning, in turn, influences all aspects of information processing, including understanding of an experience and the concomitant strength and organization of the event representation as well as the efficiency with which the information may be retrieved (Brown & Pipe, 2003). Although children with an ID can perform similarly to children matched for mental age and can also provide accurate, forensically relevant information, there is also evidence that, relative to chronological age- and mental age- matched groups, they report less correct information and are less accurate in their responses to questions about a staged event, a difference more marked for moderate than mild ID (e.g. Agnew & Powell, 2004; Gordon, Jens, Hollings, & Watson, 1994; Henry & Gudjonsson, 2003, 2005; Michel, Gordon, Ornstein, & Simpson, 2000).

***Language ability.*** Recent studies demonstrate significant but relatively modest associations between typically developing children's level of language skill and their recall, but findings, again, are not straightforward. It is possible, for example, that language ability plays a more important role in recall under some circumstances and not others. Thus, as for intellectual ability, language may play a stronger role when it is developing or relatively weak. For example, in the preschool years, the association between language and recall is stronger for younger than older children (McGuigan & Salmon, 2004; see also Burgwyn-Bailes, Baker-Ward, Gordon, & Ornstein, 2001), and preschoolers with better language skill manifest more detailed recall of a staged event (Boland, Haden, & Ornstein, 2003). The association between language skill and suggestibility is not necessarily straightforward, however, with both lower (Burgwyn-Bailes et al., 2001; Imhoff & Baker-Ward, 1999; Clarke-Stewart,

Malloy, & Allhusen, 2004) and higher (Roebers & Schneider, 2005) language associated with vulnerability to misleading information. Relatively few studies have included children beyond the preschool years, however.

Children with a specific language impairment constitute between 2 percent and 8 percent of preschool-aged children (Beeghly, 2006), and they provide narratives that are less sophisticated in topic maintenance, event sequencing and explicitness, compared with control groups matched on language ability and age (Miranda, McCabe, & Bliss, 1998). To our knowledge, however, no research has investigated this issue in the context of eyewitness memory.

*Precipitating factors*

According to Herve and colleagues' (2007) eyewitness memory model, *precipitating factors* are "specific to the circumstances of the event and, based on the parameters set by predisposing factors, further fine-tune memory formation" (p. 57). The specific event circumstance that is of concern here is degree of "stressfulness" of the to-be-remembered event. However, as noted previously, events are not in themselves stressful, but their stressfulness depends on how an individual responds to the event. Although there are other event characteristics that impact memorability, characteristics such as whether the child participated in the event or simply observed (e.g. Gobbo, Mega, & Pipe, 2002; Roberts & Blades, 1998; Tobey & Goodman, 1992) or whether caregivers engaged in elaborative talk during the stressful event (e.g. Boland et al., 2003, Low & Durkin, 2001; Tessler & Nelson, 1994), such features likely make their mark by influencing the degree of arousal and regulation experienced. In this section, the focus is on the "stressfulness" of the to-be-remembered event, as measured by the child's degree of behavioral and physiological arousal, whereas coping ability will be left for the next section.

A child's degree of arousal during stressful events has typically been measured in one of two ways, behaviorally or physiologically. The most common method has been to obtain self-report or observer ratings of children's behavior (e.g. parent, medical staff). As expected, because studies using such measures vary on a number of predisposing and methodological factors, behavioral measures of arousal have been associated with better memory, poorer memory, both better and poorer memory within the same study, or have not been associated with memory at all (e.g. Alexander et al., 2002; Brown et al., 1999; Goodman et al., 1991; Merrit et al., 1994; Shrimpton, Oates, & Hayes, 1998). For example, Brown et al. (1999) examined the impact of stress from two medical events, a pediatric assessment and the VCUG. The VCUG was rated as more stressful by a pediatrician-observer. Although the children who experienced the VCUG remembered more than did the children who underwent the pediatric examination, they also made more errors. Differences across studies also appear to depend on when arousal is experienced. For example, Quas et al. (1999) found that being more upset during a VCUG was associated with decreases in the amount of information provided in free recall, but being more upset before the VCUG procedure was related to less susceptibility to misleading questions.

Because of concerns about relying on behavioral measures of stress (Wallin et al., 2009), some researchers have turned to measuring stress via arousal, as driven by specific physiological systems. Unfortunately, the role of physiological arousal in children's memory has been basically overlooked (Wallin et al., 2009). There are a handful of studies investigating the relationship between physiological arousal, as measured by heart rate, and children's memory, again with varying results (e.g. Bugental et al., 1992; Chen, Zelter, Craske, & Katz, 2000; Quas & Lench, 2007). However, as Wallin et al. (2009) pointed out, a change in heart rate is likely a poor measure of experienced distress, as there are many reasons for increased heart rate (e.g. novelty, physical activity). They argued that to better understand how physiological stress responses relate to children's memory, it is necessary to directly study the systems driving children's experience of distress or arousal, namely the sympathetic and parasympathetic branches of the autonomic nervous system and the HPA axis. Recall that these systems become activated when children are exposed to emotionally negative, especially stressful, experiences.

Regarding the sympathetic system and children's memory, although Quas, Bauer and Boyce (2004) did not find an association between young children's sympathetic arousal and their memory for a fire alarm, Quas, Carrick, Alkon, Goldstein and Boyce (2006), with a larger sample of children across a wider age range, found that greater sympathetic activation predicted enhanced memory for a fire alarm. They comment on the consistency of their findings with those found in the adult and animal literatures, which indicate a reliable association between sympathetic activation and memory for emotional information. Quas et al. (2004, 2006) are also the only investigators to examine the relationship between the parasympathetic system and memory in children, with both studies finding a significant association between parasympathetic responses and children's memory for the fire alarm (this was the case only for the older children in the 2006 study).

A number of adult and animal studies find a significant relationship between HPA axis activity and enhanced memory. Wiik and Gunnar (2009), summarizing the research in this area, stated that glucocorticoids (of which cortisol is the most important) impact learning, consolidation and retrieval differently, depending on the timing of the increase in glucocorticoids. It appears that high levels of glucocorticoids typically impair memory, but there are exceptions, such as when the to-be-remembered information is emotional in nature. Wiik and Gunnar concluded that it is important to know more about how glucocorticoids and the HPA axis influence children's processing, retention and retrieval of emotional information.

Few studies have measured children's arousal via cortisol levels. Price (2007), for example, examined children's recall for an instance of a repeated anxiety-provoking event, private swimming lessons for beginners. These lessons were stressful for some children but not others, because some children fear water. Whereas self-reported stress was not related to memory, greater cortisol reactivity was associated with enhanced memory. Neither Chen et al. (2000) nor Merritt et al. (1994) found a significant relationship between cortisol levels and children's memory for highly distressing medical procedures, lumbar punctures or VGUGs, respectively. However, as Wallin et al. (2009) pointed out, both studies had relatively small sample sizes, leading to low power. Conversely, in Quas et al.'s (2004) study of children's memory for a fire-alarm incident, HPA axis reactivity was positively associated with children's memory for the alarm. Similarly, Quas, Yim, Edelstein, Cahill and Rush (2011) had children and adults complete an impromptu speech and math task and collected cortisol samples and self-reported stress ratings during the tasks. Greater cortisol reactivity, but not self-reported stress, was associated with enhanced memory, especially in children.

Given other individual difference factors, such as the predisposing factors described above, that contribute to variability in arousal and regulation, it is important to determine how these factors influence stress reactivity. Currently, only a handful of studies have examined how predisposing factors affect children's arousal levels during stressful events. For example, as we have noted previously, attachment style has been particularly important in predicting children's memory for stressful events, over and above measures of stress (e.g. Goodman et al., 1997). Alexander et al. (2002) found that memory and suggestibility measures were largely unrelated to children's stress regarding an inoculation until parental attachment style was considered; greater parental avoidance was associated with greater levels of stress in children, with both factors interacting to predict memory performance (see also our earlier discussion of Eisen et al., 2007, for another example of the type of work needed in this area). These findings support Goodman et al. (1997), who noted the importance of taking individual differences into account in order to clarify the relationship between stress and children's memory. This relationship becomes even more complex when we consider that a number of perpetuating factors also influence children's arousal and emotion regulation after an event, impacting what children report about these experiences.

## Perpetuating factors

According to Herve et al. (2007), *perpetuating factors* "follow the to-be-remembered event and act to either increase or decrease the quantity and quality of memory" (p. 63). Perpetuating factors influence how, why and when recall occurs. In addition to the predisposing and precipitating factors described above, factors present at the time of recall, such as coping, post-event processing, emotional state at retrieval, recall delay, repeated recall, recall context and interview format can influence what children remember and report.

*Coping.* What we recall is not random but is influenced by our motives and goals, as well as by our deliberate attempts to control how we feel (our post-event arousal levels) and what we remember (Baddeley, Eysenck, & Anderson, 2008). Different coping responses have different effects on memory. Compas et al. (2009) describe the detrimental effect on memory of the broad category of disengagement coping, such as avoidance, denial and wishful thinking. These avoidance strategies may thwart the storage of a complete and fully integrated memory (e.g. Brewin, Dalgleish, & Joseph, 1996; Ehlers & Clark, 2000). In fact, measures of intrusive thoughts, thought suppression and repressive coping style among nontraumatized adults are negatively related to memory specificity (Hermans et al., 2005; Raes et al., 2006; Wessel, Merckelbach, & Dekkers, 2002). Regular use of avoidance or stop-thinking strategies (e.g. denial, mental disengagement) may weaken the links and associations to specific event details (e.g. Wegner, Quillian, & Houston, 1996), which may affect retrieval of detailed information. As alluded to earlier, intrusive ruminative thoughts about traumatic experiences, and efforts to avoid these thoughts, drain cognitive resources and end the memory search process prematurely before a specific memory has been accessed (Kuyken & Brewin, 1995). Anderson et al. (2004) found that adults who stop unwanted memories by suppressing retrieval unwittingly engaged inhibitory processes, thereby reducing hippocampal activity. They argued that such findings indicate that it is possible to intentionally regulate hippocampal activation so as to disengage recollection, and thus regulate awareness of unpleasant memories (Anderson & Weaver, 2009).

Few developmental studies examine the role of coping on children's memories of stressful events, especially the effects of avoiding the processing of emotional information. Conroy, Salmon and O'Meara (2007) did find that children who reported avoiding discussions, emotions and activities regarding an emergency hospital visit had poorer memory for their experience than did children who reported using avoidance to a lesser degree, but we know little about how children forget experiences that they would prefer not to think about or remember, whether the forgetting is intentional or not, nor about the impact that this has on memory for those experiences. As research on *directed forgetting* in children indicates (e.g. Harnishfeger & Pope, 1996; Wilson & Kipp, 1998; Zellner & Bauml, 2004), young children have difficulties with such tasks; intentional forgetting does not reach adult-like levels before the end of elementary school. However, children appear to be susceptible to unintentional forms of forgetting, such as *retrieval-induced forgetting*

(RIF; e.g. Conroy & Salmon, 2005; Ford, Keating, & Patel, 2004; Williams, Wright, & Freeman, 2002) whereby the act of retrieving some information from memory causes the forgetting of related, but unretrieved, information (Anderson, Bjork, & Bjork, 1994). Generating diversionary thoughts can engage such forgetting, as can focusing on only some aspects of stressful events. For example, Marche, Briere and von Baeyer (2011) found that the negative aspects of children's pain-related memories can be inhibited through repeated retrieval of positive aspects of that same memory. Adults engage processes such as directed forgetting and RIF to forget both positive and negative personal experiences (e.g. Barnier, Conway, Mayoh, & Speyer, 2007; Joslyn & Oakes, 2005). Thus, forgetting may be an effective means of coping with past trauma and negative experiences (e.g. Hutchinson, 2010). More research is needed, however, to understand the role of coping and forgetting on children's recall.

*Post-event processing.* Baker-Ward, Ornstein and Starnes (2009) describe how the knowledge-based reasoning and interpretive constructive processes that lead to the initial representation of an experience can be extended in time and how they can produce further changes in the understanding and interpretation of that experience (Greenhoot, 2000). Both *endogenous* (e.g. reflection and rumination) and *exogenous* (e.g. conversation and exposure to misleading information) factors can influence the extended encoding of an experience, especially emotional experiences such as those accompanied by self-conscious emotions (e.g. pride or guilt). While few studies examine the impact of such constructive processing on children's memory for emotional events, Baker-Ward, Eaton and Banks (2005) did find that children who won a soccer game rated their performance significantly better at a second interview than at the first. However, the children who lost the game rated themselves as having played significantly more poorly after the delay. The relationship between understanding and remembering over time then appears to be a dynamic one (Baker-Ward et al., 2009). Further study is definitely needed.

*Emotional state at retrieval.* According to the Herve et al.'s (2007) eyewitness memory model, the nature and degree of one's emotional reaction during recall can affect what is reported. It is possible that some children may be more likely to be overtaken by affect when reporting and recalling an emotionally negative event, and feelings such as anxiety, embarrassment or shame may also impact recall (Saywitz, Goodman, Nicholas, & Moan, 1991). Although some research indicates that reinstating children's original emotional reaction can serve as an effective retrieval cue (see Liwag & Stein, 1995, study with preschoolers), there is little research examining the effects of negative emotion (e.g. shame, embarrassment, anxiety) on recall. Rapport is typically viewed as an essential part of the forensic interview, and it can help the child relax in a potentially stressful situation. However, there has been a lack of empirical attention given to the impact of rapport building on children's memory recall. The vantage point from which children recount their memories may also affect the degree of arousal and regulation experienced during recall, subsequently affecting what is remembered. For example, McIsaac and Eich (2004) found that adults with PTSD reported feeling less stress and anxiety when they recalled their traumatic experiences as if the experience had happened to someone else and they had only observed (observer perspective) than those who recollected the event (field perspective). There were also marked differences in the content of the memories. Research is needed that examines the forensic, as well as clinical, implications of field versus observer memories in children, as well as the impact that emotional intensity and arousal at retrieval has on children's reports.

*Delay.* The research on children's memory for emotional experiences following significant delays (e.g. years) is mixed. Children's recall can be extremely accurate for events that took place years earlier, especially for special events or stressful events (e.g. Alexander et al., 2005; Burgwyn-Bailes et al., 2001; Fivush et al., 2004; Peterson, 1999; Peterson & Walen, 2001). Sometimes, memory has even been found to increase in the recall of accurate detail over long delays (Fivush et al., 2004). However, the time between experiencing an event and recalling that event can have an adverse effect on memory in: (a) completeness of recall (e.g. Dent & Stephenson, 1979; Goodman, Batterman-Faunce, Schaaf, & Kenney, 2002; Jones & Pipe, 2002); (b) amount of correct information recalled (e.g. Flin, Boon, Knox, & Bull, 1992; Ornstein et al., 2006; Pipe & Salmon, 2009; Sales, Fivush, Parker, & Bahrick, 2005; Shrimpton et al., 1998; Quas et al., 1999); (c) spontaneous incorrect recall (e.g. Ornstein et al., 1998); (d) degree of misleading information recalled (e.g. Gobbo et al., 2002; Shapiro, Blackford, & Chen, 2005); (e) valence or degree of emotionality ascribed to the event (e.g. Baker-Ward et al., 2005; Sales et al., 2005); and (f) type of event details, central or peripheral, that are forgotten (e.g. Gobbo et al., 2002; Shapiro et al., 2005). A number of differences across these studies likely account for the different effects of delay on recall.

*Repeated recall.* Although some decline in recall over time is typical, forgetting can be reduced if an earlier additional interview precedes a later interview (Principe, Ornstein, & Baker-Ward, & Gordon, 2000; Shrimpton et al., 1998; Warren & Swartwood, 1992; however, see Ornstein et al., 2006), and can strengthen resistance to suggestion (Goodman et al., 1991). Repeatedly interviewing children in a non-misleading manner may improve recall through rehearsal (Brainerd & Ornstein, 1991; Howe, 1991) or through memory reinstatement (Howe, Courage, & Bryant-Brown, 1993). Similarly, as we have noted previously, parent–child reminiscing about children's past negative emotional experiences, opens discussions about emotion-related memories, and an elaborative conversational style positively affects how children come to understand, cope with and remember stressful events (Chae et al., 2009; Conroy & Salmon, 2006; Laible & Panfile, 2009; Leichtman et al., 2000; McGuigan & Salmon, 2004; Peterson, Sales, Rees, & Fivush, 2007; Sales, 2009; Sales & Fivush, 2005). However, repeated interviews or discussions with children with ID (e.g. Henry & Gudjonsson, 2003), or interviews that contain misleading suggestions, can lead to impairment in memory reports (e.g. Bruck, Ceci, Francoeur, & Barr, 1995), even after just one suggestive interview (e.g. Garvin, Wood, & Malpass, 2000; for a review see Bruck & Ceci, 2004). As Goodman and Quas (2008) pointed out, it is not the number of times children are interviewed that matters most, but when and how they are interviewed. Therefore, the specific questions asked and language used during the interview, as well as particular predisposing factors, are more important determinants of children's memory and suggestibility than are the frequency of interviews.

*Recall context.* Nathanson and Saywitz (2003) examined the effects of the courtroom context on children's memory and anxiety and found that children questioned in a mock courtroom showed poorer memory performance and greater heart rate variability, indicative of greater stress, than did children who were interviewed in a small, private room. Others have found that playroom environments can have a negative effect on recall, distracting children from answering interviewer's questions (Aldridge & Wood, 1998), encouraging fantasy and make-believe (Lamb, Sternberg, & Esplin, 1994; for a review, see Pipe & Salmon, 2009, for a review), and producing errors in children's reports (Salmon & Pipe, 1997). Furthermore, children recall more information, without decreasing accuracy, if they are interviewed where an event occurred rather than elsewhere, such as in a courtroom (e.g. Gee & Pipe, 1995; Orbach et al., 2000; Priestley, Roberts, & Pipe, 1999; however, see Shrimpton et al., 1998, for contradictory findings).

*Interview format.* There is a quite a bit of evidence for specific interview factors related to children's memory and suggestibility. These include the supportive atmosphere of the interview, the comprehensiveness of the interview, the language used and questions asked during interviews, and the use of repeated questioning, among others (for reviews, see Eisen, Goodman, Qin, & Davis, 1998). The atmosphere of the interview, how comfortable the child is made to feel and how much mnemonic support there is for retrieval makes a difference for recall. Children remember more information and are less suggestible when retrieval is examined under supportive, as opposed to non-supportive, examination conditions (e.g. Goodman et al., 1991; Edelstein et al., 2005; Quas & Lench, 2007; Quas et al., 2005). For example, Davis et al. (1998) found that when children are interviewed by a cold, professional interviewer, children of insecurely attached parents were more suggestible than were children whose parents were securely attached. Wiik and Gunnar (2009) argue that the supportive versus non-supportive interviewer effect on retrieval might be due to the effects that glucocorticoids appear to have on memory retrieval. Research conducted with young women indicates that when glucocorticoids are administered in a relaxed testing environment, the negative effects of glucocorticoids on memory retrieval are eliminated (Kuhlmann & Wolf, 2006).

The degree of retrieval support, such as props and interview techniques, can also affect children's recall. Recall can, under some circumstances, be enhanced with the use of anatomically detailed or regular dolls (e.g. Goodman & Aman, 1990; Goodman et al., 1997). For young children, in particular, dolls either do not facilitate recall or increase errors in children's accounts, and their use is not generally recommended (Poole, Bruck, & Pipe, 2011; Salmon, Pipe, Malloy, & Mackay, 2011; Thierry, Lamb, Orbach, & Pipe, 2005). Human figure drawings can enhance children's recall of personally experienced events, although, again, findings with respect to their impact on the amount of information reported and its accuracy are mixed (e.g. Aldridge et al., 2004; Butler, Gross, & Hayne, 1995; Gross & Hayne, 1998, 1999; Poole et al., 2011). Asking children to draw can produce reports that are less accurate under suggestive interviewing conditions (Bruck, Melnyk, & Ceci, 2000) and can increase the chances of false reports (Strange, Garry, & Sutherland, 2003). Cognitive techniques such as mental context reinstatement can be useful for helping children recover as much accurate information as possible (e.g. Hershkowitz et al., 2001), as can interviewing techniques such as the cognitive interview and narrative elaboration (e.g. Camparo, Wagner, & Saywitz, 2001; Holliday, 2003; Holliday & Albon, 2004; Saywitz & Snyder, 1996).

Another important feature of how children are interviewed that may impact what is recalled is the extent to which the interview inquires about all that is forensically relevant. RIF can have important implications for how witnesses should be questioned (Shaw, Bjork, & Handal, 1995). Simply discussing an experience with someone can affect whether people will remember what was omitted. In Conroy and Salmon's (2006) study, children in a discussion group recalled the non-discussed elements less well than did a control group of children who engaged in no discussion at all. Conroy and Salmon raised the possibility that children's memory of their childhood can be shaped by how parents and family members reminisce, with non-discussed aspects growing considerably less accessible with time. What role RIF mechanisms play in determining what children recall during an interview and across repeated interviews needs further examination.

The language used and the manner in which questions are asked, as well as the specific questions asked, also influence what is recalled. For example, when the language of the interview is developmentally inappropriate or too complex for a particular child, children are more likely to assent to an interviewer's question (e.g. Fritzley & Lee, 2003). The developmentally inappropriate language used in court (Evans, Lee, & Lyon, 2009), as well as the style of questioning (Zajac & Hayne, 2003, 2006), may also hamper children's ability to give reliable testimony and may influence trial outcome. Child witness investigations unfortunately involve suggestive interviewing techniques (e.g. Ceci & Bruck, 1993; Cederborg, 2004), and we know the negative impact that leading questions can have on children's recall, especially younger children (e.g. Cassel & Bjorklund, 1995; Roebers & Schneider, 2000); they can be led to report entirely fictitious emotional events that never occurred (e.g. Loftus & Pickrell, 1995; Pezdek, Finger, & Hodge, 1997; Pezdek & Hodge, 1999). Specific questions such as yes/no and wh- questions (e.g. Ceci & Bruck, 1993; Krackow & Lynn, 2003; Lamb et al., 2007; Peterson & Biggs, 1997; Peterson, Dowden, & Tobin, 1999; Peterson & Grant, 2001; Poole & Lamb, 1998; Poole & White, 1991; Rocha, Marche, & Briere, 2011), as well as incomprehensible questions (Fritzley & Lee, 2003), can be problematic, especially with younger children (Okanda & Itakura, 2010). Repeating specific questions during a single interview has been found to increase errors in children's reporting (e.g. Poole & White, 1991). However, informing children of this possibility beforehand can help them avoid changing their initial response (Saywitz & Moan-Hardie, 1994). Guidelines for good interviewing practice recommend avoidance of specific questions (Poole & Lamb, 1998; Yuille, 1988). There is now a wealth of information and research on appropriate interviewing procedures (see Lamb et al., 2007, and Chapter 8 of this volume).

## Conclusion

Typically, children involved in the legal system are asked to recall highly emotional and negative information. Children who are victims of abuse, or who witnessed abuse or murder, may be asked to relate the details of their experiences to police officers, lawyers or jurors, and they may be under significant emotional distress when encoding and retrieving these details. As we have discussed, recent theory and research suggests some general patterns in individuals' memory for emotionally charged experiences, particularly negative experiences. Yet the extant literature on children's recall of negative emotional experiences is replete with mixed and apparently contradictory findings. The answer to the question of whether high levels of emotion or stress experienced during an event enhance or impair memory for that event is not a simple one. That is, there is no single effect of stress on memory. Different studies find different relationships between stress and memory because of differences in the factors examined in these studies and because of methodological and design differences, such as what kind of information is being assessed (e.g. central v. peripheral details of an event), how emotion is measured (e.g. self-report v. physiological measures), or whether measures of stress are taken before, during or after the to-be-remembered event.

It has been argued here that the particular interaction of biological, psychological and social factors relating to the child, his/her experience and the circumstances of the forensic interview(s) that influence the child's arousal and emotion regulation are especially important for children's memory. Following Herve et al. (2007), we have conceptualized these overlapping factors as predisposing (those that delimit the child's response to the event/s and interview and therefore constrain what is encoded), precipitating (those that influence the child's immediate response) and perpetuating (post-event factors that further influence memory). Children's recall is influenced by factors that sway children to interpret and respond to events in particular ways (e.g. child maltreatment, problematic attachment relationships, temperament and intellectual ability) and affect how they respond during emotionally negative events (e.g. stress reactivity), as well as by factors that influence their memory retention and reconstruction (e.g. coping ability, knowledge and understanding, recall and interview context). Thus, there are multiple pathways through which individual differences in arousal and subsequent regulation attempts affect children's memories for distressing events in their lives. Emotionality is bestowed on the event by the individual experiencing that event, and thus varies across individuals and situations.

What, then, are the implications for children's eyewitness testimony? The first is that the potential effects on memory of some of the factors that we have discussed must not be taken to imply that child witnesses cannot provide a forensically relevant account of their experiences. Indeed, under some circumstances, such as where the anxious or maltreated child has a negative bias towards threatening information, the child's recall of core aspects might be superior to that of her non-anxious peer. That is, there are conditions under which stress and negative emotion might enhance children's recall. As we have discussed, however, some children may experience difficulties recalling emotionally negative experiences. For example, for diverse reasons, the narrative accounts of children with specific language impairments, ID or PTSD may be less organized and complete than those of other children, and children experiencing OGM may struggle, under conditions of free recall, to provide details of a specific experience. It is critical that experts who testify in court inform the triers-of-fact about the important predisposing, precipitating and perpetuating factors that influence children's memory for stressful experiences and their manifestations in children's accounts.

Second, it is clear that memory for negative emotional experiences is vulnerable to the same general memory principles as is memory for other kinds of events; thus, some children, even very young ones, can have very good memory for stressful events, and such events can be accurate and resistant to suggestion, especially for the central features of the event. Memory for such emotionally charged events is not always accurate and is subject to error, however, especially regarding non-central features. Delay, repeated interviewing and other factors that have been found to influence children's recall of non-emotional events may all compromise memory for emotional experiences. Third, developing a full understanding of the factors that influence children's accounts can provide guidance for optimal practice during forensic interviews. For example, children who are younger, insecurely attached, have intellectual impairments, various forms of psychopathology or who are sensitive to stress may need special interviewing. As we noted earlier, social support during an interview (a warm and supportive interviewer style) can aid children's recall after a delay and reduce suggestibility. Particularly promising are findings that a supportive interview can buffer children's memory reports from some of the potentially negative effects of maltreatment and its sequelae (e.g. insecure attachment style, lower working memory capacity, and higher physiological arousal; for a review, see Bottoms, Quas, & Davis, 2007). Understanding the range of factors that can influence children's reports might also include special attention to rapport-building at the beginning of the interview. Rapport is regarded as a critically important phase of the forensic interview, serving to help the child to relax in the potentially stressful situation and providing an opportunity to establish the interview parameters. Findings suggest, however, that it is relatively often conducted as a "mechanical" list of unrelated tasks rather than as a genuine relationship-building phase (Westcott & Kynan, 2006).

Given the forensic importance of the influence of emotion on memory, further study is needed to resolve some of the inconsistencies across studies regarding the role of physiological and emotional arousal on children's memory. Additional work is also needed to detail exactly how such arousal is moderated by the numerous variables considered here, and the regulatory strategies adopted to manage the arousal. There are also a number of issues that may influence children's memory for emotionally negative experiences that have not yet been studied much. These include factors that may affect children's arousal and emotion regulation (e.g. drug or stimulant use such as Ritalin), the effect of specific negative emotions (e.g. anger versus fear) on arousal and memory, whether feeling personally threatened matters, whether events are public or private (as abuse typically is), whether the stressful event is acute (unique, one-time event) or chronic (repeated event), and the influence of culture, gender socialization and response style (e.g. response to authority figures), to name a few. Findings from such studies have the potential to inform the forensic community, including police officers, attorneys, judges and jurors, about the reliability of children's testimony.

# References

Ackil, J. K., van Abbema, D. L., & Bauer, P. J. (2003). After the storm: Enduring differences in mother-child recollections of traumatic and nontraumatic events. *Journal of Experimental Child Psychology, 84*, 286–309.

Agnew, S. E. & Powell, M. B. (2004). The effect of intellectual disability on children's recall of an event across different question types. *Law and Human Behavior, 28*, 273–294.

Aldridge, J., Lamb, M. E., Sternberg, K. J., Orbach, Y., Esplin, P. W., & Bowler, L. (2004). Using a human figure drawing to elicit information from alleged victims of child sexual abuse. *Journal of Consulting and Clinical Psychology, 72*, 304–316.

Aldridge, M. & Wood, J. (1998). *Interviewing Children: A Guide for Child Care and Forensic Practitioners*. Chichester: John Wiley & Sons.

Alexander, K. W. & O'Hara, K. D. (2009). An integrated model of emotional memory: Dynamic transactions in development. In J. A. Quas & R. Fivush (Eds), *Emotion and Memory in Development: Biological, Cognitive, and Social Considerations* (pp. 221–255). Oxford University Press: New York, NY.

Alexander, K. W., Goodman, G. S., Schaaf, J. M., Edelstein, R. S., Quas, J. A., & Shaver, P. R. (2002). The role of attachment and cognitive inhibition in predicting children's memory for a stressful event. *Journal of Experimental Child Psychology, 83*, 262–290.

Alexander, K. W., Quas, J. A., Goodman, G. S., Ghetti, S., Edelstein, R. S., Redlich, A. D., Cordon, I. M., & Jones, D. P. H. (2005). Traumatic impact predicts long term memory for documented child sexual abuse. *Psychological Science, 16*, 33–40.

Anderson, M. C., Bjork, R. A., & Bjork, E. L. (1994). Remembering can cause forgetting: Retrieval dynamics in long-term memory. *Journal of Experimental Psychology: Learning, Memory, and Cognition, 20*, 1063–1087.

Anderson, M. C., Ochsner, K. N., Cooper, J., Robertson, E., Gabrieli, S. W., & Glover, G. H. (2004). Neural systems underlying the suppression of unwanted memories. *Science, 303*, 232–235.

Anderson, M. C. & Weaver, C. (2009). Inhibitory control over action and memory. In L. R. Squire (Ed.), *The New Encyclopedia of Neuroscience*. Oxford: Elsevier Ltd.

American Psychiatric Association (2000). *Diagnostic and Statistical Manual of Mental Disorders* (4th edn). Washington, DC: Author.

Aspelmeier, J. E., Elliott, A. N., & Smith, C. H. (2007). Childhood sexual abuse, attachment, and trauma symptoms in college females: The moderating role of attachment. *Child Abuse and Neglect, 31*, 549–566.

Ayoub, C. C., O'Connor, E., Rappolt-Schlichtmann, G., Fischer, K. W., Rogosch, F. A., Toth, S., & Cicchetti, D. (2006). Cognitive and emotional différences in young maltreated children: A translational application of dynamic skill theory. *Development and Psychopathology, 18*, 679–706.

Azar, S. T. & Wolfe, D. A. (2006). Child physical abuse and neglect. In E. J. Mash and R. A. Barkley (Eds), *Treatment of Childhood Disorders* (3rd edn, pp. 595–646). New York, NY: Guilford Press.

Baddeley, A., Eysenck, M. W., & Anderson, M. C. (2008). *Memory*. Hove, East Sussex: Psychology Press.

Bahrick, L. E., Parker. J. F., Fivush, R., & Levitt, M. (1998). The effects of stress on young children's memory for a natural disaster. *Journal of Experimental Psychology: Applied, 4,* 308–331.

Barnier, A. J., Conway, M. A., Mayoh, L., & Speyer, J. (2007). Directed forgetting of recently recalled autobiographical memories. *Journal of Experimental Psychology: General, 136,* 301–322.

Baker-Ward, L. E., Eaton, K. L., & Banks, J. B. (2005). Young soccer players' reports of a tournament win or loss: Different emotions, different narratives. *Journal of Cognition and Development, 6,* 507–527.

Baker-Ward, L. E., Ornstein, P. A., & Starnes, L. P. (2009). Children's understanding and remembering of stressful experiences. In J. A. Quas and R. Fivush (Eds), *Emotion and Memory in Development: Biological, Cognitive, and Social Considerations* (pp. 28–59). New York, NY: Oxford University Press.

Bauer, P. J. (2009). Complications abound: And why that's a good thing. In J. A. Quas and R. Fivush (Eds) *Emotion and Memory in Development: Biological, Cognitive, and Social Considerations* (pp. 374–393). New York, NY: Oxford University Press.

Bauer, P. J., Burch, M. M., Van Abbema, D. L., & Ackil, J. K. (2007). Talking about twisters: Relations between mothers' and children's contributions to conversations about a devastating tornado. *Journal of Cognition and Development, 8,* 371–399.

Beeghly, M. (2006). Translational research on early language development: Current challenges and future directions. *Development and Psychopathology, 18,* 737–757.

Bidrose, S. & Goodman, G. S. (2000). Testimony and evidence: A scientific case study of memory for child sexual abuse. *Applied Cognitive Psychology, 14,* 197–213.

Boland, A. M., Haden, C. A., & Ornstein, P. A. (2003). Boosting children's memory by training mothers in the use of an elaborative conversational style as an event unfolds. *Journal of Cognition and Development, 4,* 39–45.

Bottoms, B. L., Quas, J. A., & Davis, S. L. (2007). The influence of the interviewer-provided social support on children's suggestibility, memory, and disclosures. In M. E. Pipe, M. E. Lamb, Y. Orbach & A. C. Cederborg (Eds), *Child Sexual Abuse: Disclosure, Delay, and Denial* (pp. 135–157). Mahwah, NJ: Lawrence Erlbaum Associates Publishers.

Brainerd, C. J., Holliday, R. E., Reyna, V. F., Yang, Y., & Toglia, M. P. (2010). Developmental reversals in false memory: Effects of emotional valence and arousal. *Journal of Experimental Child Psychology, 107,* 137–154.

Brainerd, C. J., & Ornstein, P. A. (1991). Children's memory for witnessed events: The developmental backdrop. In J. Doris (Ed.), *The Suggestibility of Children's Recollections: Implications for Eyewitness Testimony* (pp. 10–23). Washington: American Psychological Association.

Brewin, C. (2011). The nature and significance of memory disturbance in posttraumatic stress disorder. *Annual Review of Clinical Psychology, 7,* 203–227.

Brewin, C. R., Dalgleish, T., & Joseph, S. (1996). A dual representation theory of posttraumatic stress disorder. *Psychological Review, 103,* 670–686.

Brown, D. & Pipe, M. E. (2003). Individual differences in children's event memory reports and the Narrative Elaboration Technique. *Journal of Applied Psychology, 88,* 195–206.

Brown, D. A., Salmon, K., Pipe, M. E., Rutter, M., Craw, S., & Taylor, B. (1999). Children's recall of medical experiences: The impact of stress. *Child Abuse and Neglect, 23,* 209–216.

Bruck, M., & Ceci, S. (2004). Forensic developmental psychology: Unveiling four common misconceptions. *Current Directions in Psychological Science, 13,* 229–232.

Bruck, M., Ceci, S. J., Francoeur, E., & Barr, R. (1995). "I hardly cried when I got my shot": Young children's reports of their visit to a pediatrician. *Child Development, 66,* 193–208.

Bruck, M., Melnyk, L., & Ceci, S. J. (2000). Draw it again Sam: The effect of drawing on children's suggestibility and source monitoring ability. *Journal of Experimental Child Psychology, 77*, 169–196.

Bruck, M., & Melnyk, L. (2004). Individual differences in children's suggestibility: A review and synthesis. *Applied Cognitive Psychology, 18*, 947–996.

Bugental, D. B., Blue, J., Cortez, V., Fleck, K., & Rodriguez, A. (1992). Influences of witnessed affect on information processing in children. *Child Development, 63*, 774–786.

Butler, S., Gross, J., & Hayne, H. (1995). The effect of drawing on memory performance in young children. *Developmental Psychology, 31*, 597–608.

Burgwyn-Bailes, E., Baker-Ward, L., Gordon, B. N., & Ornstein, P. A. (2001). Children's memory for emergency medical treatment after one year: The impact of individual difference variables on recall and suggestibility. *Applied Cognitive Psychology, 15*, S25–S48.

Camparo, L., B., Wagner, J. T., & Saywitz, K. J. (2001). Interviewing children about real and fictitious events: Revisiting the narrative elaboration procedure. *Law and Human Behavior, 25*, 63–80.

Cassel, W. S., & Bjorklund, D. F. (1995). Developmental patterns of eyewitness memory and suggestibility: An ecologically based short-term longitudinal study. *Law and Human Behavior, 19*, 507–532.

Ceci, S. J., & Bruck, M. (1993). Suggestibility of the child witness: A historical review and synthesis. *Psychological Bulletin, 113*, 403–439.

Cederborg, A. C. (2004). Factors influencing child witnesses. *Scandinavian Journal of Psychology, 45*, 197–205.

Chae, Y., Ogle, C. M., & Goodman, G. S. (2009). Remembering negative childhood experiences: An attachment theory perspective. In J. A. Quas, & R. Fivush (Eds), *Emotion and Memory in Development: Biological, Cognitive, and Social Considerations* (pp. 3–27). New York, NY: Oxford University Press.

Chen, E., Zelter, L. K., Craske, M. G., & Katz, E. R. (2000). Children's memory for painful cancer treatment procedures: Implications for distress. *Child Development, 71*, 931–945.

Christianson, S. (1992). Emotional stress and eyewitness memory: A critical review. *Psychological Bulletin, 112*, 284–309.

Christianson, S. A., & Loftus, E. F. (1991). Remembering emotional events: The fate of detailed information. *Cognition and Emotion, 5*, 81–108.

Cicchetti, D., & Dawson, G. (2002). Editorial: Multiple levels of analysis. *Development and Psychopathology, Special Issue: Multiple levels of analysis, 14*, 417–420.

Cicchetti, D., Rogosch, F. A., Howe, M. L., & Toth, S. L. (2010). The effects of maltreatment and neuroendocrine regulation on memory performance. *Child Development, 18*, 1504–1519.

Cicchetti, D., & Toth, S. L. (2005). Child maltreatment. *Annual Review of Clinical Psychology, 1*, 409–438.

Clarke-Stewart, K. A., Malloy, L. C., & Allhusen, V. D. (2004). Verbal ability, self-control, and close relationships with parents protect children against misleading suggestions. *Applied Cognitive Psychology, 18*, 1037–1058.

Compas, B. E., Campbell, L. K., Robinson, K. E., & Rodriguez, E. M. (2009). Coping and memory: Automatic and controlled processes in adaptation to stress. In J. A. Quas & R. Fivush (Eds), *Emotion and Memory in Development: Biological, Cognitive, and Social Considerations* (pp. 121–141). New York, NY: Oxford University Press.

Conroy, R. & Salmon, K. (2005). Selective postevent review and children's memory for nonreviewed materials. *Journal of Experimental Child Psychology, 90*, 185–207.

Conroy, R. & Salmon, K. (2006). Talking about parts of a past experience: The influence of elaborative discussion and event structure on children's recall of nondiscussed information. *Journal of Experimental Child Psychology, 95*, 278–297.

Conroy, R., Salmon, K. & O'Meara, M. (2007). *Attachment, avoidance, and children's recall of a stressful medical experience.* Unpublished manuscript.

Conway, M. A., & Pleydell-Pearce, C. W. (2000). The construction of autobiographical memories in the self-memory system. *Psychological Review, 107*, 261–288.

Davis, S. L., Bottoms, B. L., Guererro, R., Shreder, E., Krebel, A., Reyes, R., Rohacs, J., & Stein, A. (1998). *Attachment style, social support, and children's eyewitness reports.* Poster presented at the annual meeting of the Midwestern Psychological Association Convention, Chicago, IL.

Davidson, R. J. (2003). Affective neuroscience: A case for interdisciplinary research. In F. Kessel, P. L., Rosenfield, & N. B. Anderson (Eds), *Expanding the Boundaries of Health and Social Science: Case Studies in Interdisciplinary Innovation* (pp. 99–121). New York, NY: Oxford University Press.

Deffenbacher, K. A., Bornstein, B. H., Penrod, S. D., & McGorty, E. K. (2004). A meta-analytic review of the effects of high stress on eyewitness memory. *Law & Human Behavior, 28*, 687–706.

Dent, H. R., & Stephenson, G. M. (1979). An experimental study of the effectiveness of different techniques of questioning child witnesses. *British Journal of Social and Clinical Psychology, 18*, 41–51.

Drummond, L. E., Dritschel, B., Astell, A., O'Carroll, R. E., & Dalgleish, T. (2006). Effects of age, dysphoria, and emotion-focusing on autobiographical memory specificity in children. *Cognition and Emotion, 20*, 488–505.

Dykas, M. J., & Cassidy, J. (2011). Attachment and the processing of social information across the life span: Theory and evidence. *Psychological Bulletin, 137*, 19–46.

Dyregrov, A., Gjestad, R., & Raundalen, M. (2002). Children exposed to warfare: A longitudinal study. *Journal of Traumatic Stress, 15*, 59–68.

Edelstein, R. S., Ghetti, S., Quas, J. A., Goodman, G. S., Alexander, K. W., & Redlich, A. D., & Cordon, I. M. (2005). Individual differences in emotional memory: Adult attachment and long-term memory for child sexual abuse. *Personality and Social Psychology Bulletin, 31*, 1537–1548.

Ehlers, A., & Clark, D. M. (2000). A cognitive model of posttraumatic stress disorder. *Behaviour Research and Therapy, 38*, 319–345.

Eisen, M. L., Goodman, G. S., Qin, J., & Davis, S. (1998). Memory and suggestibility in maltreated children: New research relevant to evaluating allegations of abuse. In S. J. Lynn and K. M. McConkey (Eds), *Truth in Memory* (pp. 163–189). New York, NY: Guilford Press.

Eisen, M. L., Goodman, G. S., Qin, J., Davis, S., & Crayton, J. (2007). Maltreated children's memory: Accuracy, suggestibility, and psychopathology. *Developmental Psychology, 43*, 1275–1294.

Eisen, M. L., Qin, J., Goodman, G. S., & Davis, S. L. (2002). Memory and suggestibility in maltreated children: Age, stress arousal, dissociation, and psychopathology. *Journal of Experimental Child Psychology, 83*, 167–212.

Evans, A. D., Lee, K., & Lyon, T. D. (2009). Complex questions asked by defense lawyers but not prosecutors predicts convictions in child abuse trials. *Law and Human Behavior, 33*, 258–264.

Fivush, R., Haden, C., & Reese, E. (2006). Elaborating on elaborations: The role of maternal reminiscing style in cognitive and socioemotional development. *Child Development, 77*, 1568–1588.

Fivush, R., Sales, J. M., Goldberg, A., Bahrick, L., & Parker, J. (2004). Weathering the storm: Children's long-term recall of Hurricane Andrew. *Memory, 12*, 104–118.

Flin, R., Boon, J., Knox, A., & Bull, R. (1992). The effect of a five month delay on children's and adult's eyewitness memory. *British Journal of Psychology, 83*, 323–336.

Ford, R. M., Keating, S., & Patel, R. (2004). Retrieval-induced forgetting: A developmental study. *British Journal of Developmental Psychology, 22*, 585–603.

Fritzley, H. V., & Lee, K. (2003). Do young children always say yes to yes–no questions? A metadevelopmental study of the affirmation bias. *Child Development, 74*, 1297–1313.

Garvin, S., Wood, J. M., & Malpass, R. S. (2000). Allegations of wrongdoing: The effects of reinforcement on children's mundane and fantastic claims. *Journal of Applied Psychology, 85*, 38–49.

Gee, S. & Pipe, M. E. (1995). Helping children to remember: The influence of object cues on children's accounts of a real event. *Developmental Psychology, 31*, 746–758.

Gignac, G. E. & Powell, M. B. (2006). A direct examination of the nonlinear (quadratic) association between intelligence and suggestibility in children. *Applied Cognitive Psychology, 20*, 617–623.

Gobbo, C., Mega, C., & Pipe, M. E. (2002). Does the nature of the experience influence suggestibility? A study of children's event memory. *Journal of Experimental Child Psychology, 81*, 502–530.

Goodman, G. S. (2006). Children's eyewitness memory: A modern history and contemporary commentary. *Journal of Social Issues, 62*, 811–832.

Goodman, G. S., & Aman, C. (1990). Children's use of anatomically detailed dolls to recount an event. *Child Development, 61*, 1859–1871.

Goodman, G. S., Batterman-Faunce, J. M., Schaaf, J. M., & Kenney, R. (2002). Nearly 4 years after an event: Children's eyewitness memory and adults' perceptions of children's accuracy. *Child Abuse & Neglect, 26*, 849–884.

Goodman, G. S., Bottoms, B. L., Schwartz-Kenney, B. M., & Rudy, L. (1991). Children's testimony about a stressful event: Improving children's reports. *Journal of Narrative & Life History, 1*, 69–99.

Goodman, G. S., Ogle, C. M., Block, S. D., Harris, L. S., Larson, R. P., Augusti, E. E., Cho, Y. I., Beber, J., Timmer, S., & Urquiza, A. (2011). False memory for trauma-related Deese-Roediger-McDermott lists in adolescents and adults with histories of child sexual abuse. *Development and Psychopathology, 23*, 423–428.

Goodman, G. S. & Quas, J. A. (2008). Repeated interviews and children's memory: It's more than just how many. *Current Directions in Psychological Science, 17*, 386–390.

Goodman, G. S., Quas, J. A., & Ogle, C. M. (2010). Child maltreatment and memory. *Annual Review of Psychology, 61*, 325–331.

Goodman, G. S., Quas, J. A., Batterman-Faunce, J. M., Riddlesberger, M., & Kuhn, J. (1994). Predictors of accurate and inaccurate memories of traumatic events experienced in childhood. *Consciousness and Cognition, 3*, 269–294.

Goodman, G. S., Quas, J. A., Batterman-Faunce, J. M., Riddlesberger, M. M., & Kuhn, J. (1997). Children's reactions to and memory for a stressful event: Influences of age, anatomical dolls, knowledge and parental attachment. *Applied Developmental Science, 1*, 54–75.

Gordon, B. N., Jens, K. G., Hollings, R., & Watson, T. E. (1994). Remembering activities performed versus those imagined: Implications for testimony of children with mental retardation. *Journal of Clinical Child Psychology, 23*, 239–248.

Greenhoot, A. F. (2000). Remembering and understanding: The effects of changes in underlying knowledge on children's recollections. *Child Development, 71*, 1309–1328.

Gross, J., & Hayne, H. (1998). Drawing facilitates children's verbal reports of emotionally laden events. *Journal of Experimental Psychology: Applied, 4*, 163–179.

Gross, J., & Hayne, H. (1999). Drawing facilitates children's verbal reports after long delays. *Journal of Experimental Psychology: Applied, 5*, 265–283.

Hadwin, J. A., & Field, A. P. (2010). *Information Processing Biases and Anxiety: A Developmental Perspective*. England, UK: Wiley-Blackwell.

Hamm, A. O., Greenwald, M. K., Bradley, M. M., & Lang, P. J. (1993). Emotional learning, hedonic change, and the startle probe. *Journal of Abnormal Psychology, 102*, 453–465.

Hanna, K., Davies, E., Henderson, E., Crothers, C., & Rotherham, C. (2010). *Child witnesses in the New Zealand criminal courts: A review of practice and implications for policy*. Institute of Public Policy, Auckland University of Technology, New Zealand.

Harnishfeger, K. K., & Pope, R. S. (1996). Intending to forget: The development of cognitive inhibition in directed forgetting. *Journal of Experimental Child Psychology, 62*, 292–315.

Henry, L. A., & Gudjonsson, G. H. (2003). Eyewitness memory, suggestibility, and repeated recall sessions in children with mild or moderate intellectual disabilities. *Law and Human Behavior, 27*, 481–505.

Henry, L. A., & Gudjonsson, G. H. (2005). The effects of memory trace strength on eyewitness recall in children with and without intellectual disabilities. *Journal of Experimental Child Psychology, 98*, 53–71.

Hermans, D., Defranc, A., Raes, F., Williams, J. M. G., & Eelen, P. (2005). Reduced autobiographical memory specificity as an avoidant coping style. *British Journal of Clinical Psychology, 44*, 583–589.

Hershkowitz, I., Orbach, Y., Lamb, M. E., Sternberg, K. J., Horowitz, D., & Hovav, M. (2001). The effects of mental context reinstatement on children's accounts of sexual abuse. *Applied Cognitive Psychology, 15*, 235–248.

Herve, H., Cooper, B. S., & Yuille, J. C. (2007). Memory formation in offenders: Perspectives from a biopsychosocial model of eyewitness memory. In S. A. Christianson (Ed.), *Offenders' Memories of Violent Crimes* (pp. 37–74). West Sussex, England: John Wiley & Sons, Ltd.

Hipwell, A. E., Sapotichne, B., Klostermann, S., Battista, D., & Keenan, K. (2010). Autobiographical memory as a predictor of depression vulnerability in girls. *Journal of Clinical Child and Adolescent Psychology, 40*, 254–265.

Holliday, R. E. (2003). The effect of a prior cognitive interview on children's acceptance of misinformation. *Applied Cognitive Psychology, 17*, 443–457.

Holliday, R. E., & Albon, A. J. (2004). Minimizing misinformation effects in young children with cognitive interview mnemonics. *Applied Cognitive Psychology, 18*, 263–281.

Howe, M. L. (1991). Misleading children's story recall: Forgetting and reminiscence of the facts. *Developmental Psychology, 27*, 746–762.

Howe, M. L., Cicchetti, D., & Toth, S. (2006). Children's basic memory processes, stress, and maltreatment. *Development & Psychopathology, 18*, 759–769.

Howe, M. L., Cicchetti, D., Toth, S. L., & Cerrito, B. M. (2004). True and false memories in maltreated children. *Child Development, 75*, 1402–1417.

Howe, M. L., Courage, M. L., & Bryant-Brown, L. (1993). Reinstating preschoolers' memories. *Developmental Psychology, 29*, 854–869.

Howe, M. L., Goodman, G. S., & Cicchetti, D. (Eds) (2008). *Stress, Trauma, and Children's Memory Development: Neurobiological, Cognitive, Clinical, and Legal Perspectives*. New York, NY, US: Oxford University Press.

Howe, M. L., Toth, S. L., & Cicchetti, D. (2011). Can maltreated children inhibit true and false memories for emotional information? *Child Development, 82*, 967–981.

Hulse, L. M., Allan, K., Memon, A., & Read, J. D. (2007). Emotional arousal and memory: A test of the poststimulus processing hypothesis. *The American Journal of Psychology, 120,* 73–90.

Hutchinson, E. (2010). The psychological well-being of orphans in Malawi: "Forgetting" as a means of recovering from parental death. *Vulnerable children and Youth Studies, 6,* 18–27.

Imhoff, M. C. & Baker-Ward, L. (1999). Preschoolers' suggestibility: Effects of developmentally appropriate language and interviewer supportiveness. *Journal of Applied Developmental Psychology, 20,* 407–429.

Johnson, R. J., Greenhoot, A. F., Glisky, E., & McCloskey, L. A. (2005). The relations among abuse, depression, and adolescents' autobiographical memory. *Journal of Clinical Child and Adolescent Psychology, 34,* 235–247.

Jones, C. H., & Pipe, M. (2002). How quickly do children forget events? A systematic study of children's event reports as a function of delay. *Applied Cognitive Psychology, 16,* 755–768.

Joormann, J., Hertel, P. T., LeMoult, J., & Gotlib, I. H. (2009). Training forgetting of negative material in depression. *Journal of Abnormal Psychology, 118,* 34–43.

Joslyn, S. L., & Oakes, M. A. (2005). Directed forgetting of autobiographical events. *Memory and Cognition, 33,* 577–587.

Kagan, J., Reznick, J. S., & Gibbons, J. (1989). Inhibited and uninhibited types of children. *Child Development, 60,* 838–845.

Kagan, J., Reznick, J. S., & Snidman, N. (1987). The physiology and psychology of behavioural inhibition in children. *Child Development, 58,* 1459–1473.

Kearney, C. A., Wechsler, A., Kaur, H., & Lemos-Miller, A. (2010). Posttraumatic stress disorder in maltreated youth: A review of contemporary research and thought. *Clinical Child and Family Psychology Review, 13,* 46–76.

Kenardy, J., Smith, A., Spence, S. H., Lilley, P., Newcombe, P., Dob, R., & Robinson, S. (2007). Dissociation in children's trauma narratives: An exploratory investigation. *Journal of Anxiety Disorders, 21,* 456–466.

Kendall-Tackett, K., Lyon, T., Taliaferro, G., & Little, L. (2005). Why child maltreatment researchers should include children's disability status in their maltreatment studies. *Child Abuse & Neglect, 29,* 147–151.

Kensinger, E. A. (2009). Remembering the details: Effects of emotion. *Emotion Review, 1,* 99–113.

Kinzie, J. D., Sack, W. H., Angell, R. H., Manson, S. M., & Rath, B. (1986). The psychiatric effects of massive trauma on Cambodian children: I. The children. *Journal of the American Academy of Child Psychiatry, 25,* 370–376.

Kochanska, G. & Knaack, A. (2003). Effortful control as a personality characteristic of young children: Antecedents, correlates, and consequences. *Journal of Personality, 71,* 1087–1112.

Krackow E., & Lynn, S. J. (2003). Is there touch in the game of Twister (R)? The effects of innocuous touch and suggestive questions on children's eyewitness memory. *Law and Human Behavior, 27,* 589–604.

Kuhlmann, S., & Wolf, O. T. (2006). A non-arousing test situation abolishes the impairing effects of cortisol on delayed memory retrieval in healthy women. *Neuroscience Letters, 399,* 268–272.

Kuyken, W. & Brewin, C. R. (1995). Autobiographical memory functioning in depression and reports of early abuse. *Journal of Abnormal Psychology, 104,* 585–591.

Kuyken, W. & Dalgleish, T. (2011). Overgeneral autobiographical memory in adolescents at risk for depression. *Memory, 19,* 241–250.

Kuyken, W. & Howell, R. (2006). Facets of autobiographical memory in adolescents with major depressive disorder and never-depressed controls. *Cognition and Emotion. Special Issue: Autobiographical Memory Specificity and Psychopathology, 20,* 466–487.

Laible, D. (2004). Mother-child discourse in two contexts: Links with child temperament, attachment security, and socioemotional competence. *Developmental Psychology, 40,* 979–992.

Laible, D. & Panfile, T. (2009). Mother-child reminiscing in the context of secure attachment relationships: Lesson in understanding and coping with negative emotions. In J. A. Quas, & R. Fivush (Eds), *Emotion and Memory in Development: Biological, Cognitive, and Social Considerations* (pp. 166–195). New York, NY: Oxford University Press.

Lamb, M. E., Orbach, Y., Hershkowitz, I., Horowitz, D., & Abbott, C. B. (2007). Does the type of prompt affect the accuracy of information provided by alleged victims of abuse in forensic interviews? *Applied Cognitive Psychology, 21,* 1117–1130.

Lamb, M. E., Orbach, Y., Hershkowitz, I., Esplin, P. W., & Horowitz, D. (2007). A structured forensic interview protocol improves the quality and informativeness of investigative interviews with children: A review of research using the NICHD Investigative Interview Protocol. *Child Abuse and Neglect, 31,* 1201–1231.

Lamb, M., Sternberg, K. J., & Esplin, P. W. (1994). Factors influencing the reliability and validity of statements made by young victims of sexual maltreatment. *Journal of Applied Developmental Psychology, 15,* 255–280.

Lamb, M. E., Sternberg, K. J., Orbach, Y., Esplin, P. W., Stewart, H., & Mitchell, S. (2003). Age differences in young children's responses to open-ended invitations in the course of forensic interviews. *Journal of Consulting and Clinical Psychology, 71,* 926–934.

Laney, C., Heuer, F., & Reisberg, D. (2003). Thematically-induced arousal in naturally-occurring emotional memories. *Applied Cognitive Psychology, 17,* 995–1004.

Laor, N., Wolmer, L., Mayes, L. C., Gershon, A., Weizman, R., & Cohen, D. J. (1997). Israeli preschool children under scuds: A 30-month follow-up. *Journal of American Academy of Child and Adolescent Psychiatry, 36,* 349–356.

Leichtman, M. D., Pillemer, D. B., Wang, Q., Koreishi, A., & Han, J. J. (2000). When baby Maisy came to school: Mothers' interview styles and preschoolers' event memories. *Cognitive Development, 15,* 99–114.

Levine, L. J. & Edelstein, R. S. (2009). Emotion and memory narrowing: A review and goal-relevance approach. *Cognition and Emotion, 23,* 833–875.

Liwag, M. D. & Stein, N. L. (1995). Children's memory for emotion episodes: The importance of emotion enactment cues. *Journal of Experimental Child Psychology, 60,* 2–31.

Loftus, E. F. & Pickrell, J. E. (1995). The formation of false memories. *Psychiatric Annals, 25,* 720–725.

Low, J. & Durkin, K. (2001). Individual differences and consistency in maternal talk style during joint story encoding and retrospection: Associations with children's long-term recall. *International Journal of Behavioral Development, 25,* 27–36.

MacLeod, C. (2010). Current directions at the juncture of clinical and cognitive science: A commentary on the special issue. *Applied Cognitive Psychology. Special Issue: Current Directions at the Juncture of Clinical and Cognitive Science, 24,* 450–463.

Marche, T. A., Briere, J., & von Baeyer, C. (2011). *Individual differences in children's ability to remember and forget negative experiences.* Paper presented at the biannual meeting of the Society for Research in Child Development. Montreal, Quebec, Canada.

Mathews, A. & MacLeod, C. (2005). Cognitive vulnerability to emotional disorders. *Annual Review of Clinical Psychology, 1,* 167–195.

McMahon, S. D., Grant, K. E., Compas, B. E., Thurm, A. E., & Ey, S. (2003). Stress and psychopathology in children and adolescence: Is there evidence of specificity? *Journal of Child Psychology and Psychiatry, 44,* 107–133.

McGuigan, F., & Salmon, K. (2004). The time to talk: The influence of adult-child talk on children's event memory. *Child Development, 75*, 669–678.

McIsaac, H. K., & Eich, E. (2004). Vantage point in traumatic memory. *Psychological Science, 15*, 248–253.

Merritt, K. A., Ornstein, P. A., & Spicker, B. (1994). Children's memory for a salient medical procedure: Implications for testimony. *Pediatrics, 94*, 17–23.

Michel, M. K., Gordon, B. N., Ornstein, P. A., & Simpson, M. A. (2000). The abilities of children with mental retardation to remember personal experiences: Implications for testimony. *Journal of Clinical Child Psychology, 29*, 453–463.

Miranda, A. E., McCabe, A., & Bliss, L. S. (1998). Jumping around and leaving things out: A profile of the narrative abilities of children with specific language impairment. *Applied Psycholinguistics, 19*, 647–667.

Mitte, K. (2008). Memory bias for threatening information in anxiety and anxiety disorders: A meta-analytic review. *Psychological Bulletin, 134*, 886–911.

Moore, S. A. & Zoellner, L. A. (2007). Overgeneral autobiographical memory and traumatic events: An evaluative review. *Psychological Bulletin, 133*, 419–437.

Morgan, J. (2010). Autobiographical memory biases in social anxiety. *Clinical Psychology Review, 30*, 288–297.

Najarian, L. M., Goenjian, A. K., Pelcovitz, D., Mandel, F., & Najarian, B. (1996). Relocation after a disaster: Posttraumatic stress disorder in Armenia after the earthquake. *Journal of the American Academy of Child and Adolescent Psychiatry, 35*, 374–383.

Nathanson, R. & Saywitz, K. J. (2003). The effects of the courtroom context on children's memory and anxiety. *Journal of Psychiatry and Law, 31*, 67–98.

Nelson, K. & Fivush, R. (2004). The emergence of autobiographical memory: A social cultural developmental theory. *Psychological Review, 111*, 286–511.

Nigg, J. T. (2006). Temperament and developmental psychopathology. *Journal of Child Psychology and Psychiatry, 47*, 395–422.

Okanda, M. & Itakura, S. (2010). When do children exhibit a yes bias? *Child Development, 81*, 568–580.

O'Kearney, R., Speyer, J., & Kenardy, J. (2007). Children's narrative memory for accidents and their post-traumatic distress. *Applied Cognitive Psychology, 21*, 821–838.

Orbach, Y., & Lamb, M. E. (1999). Assessing the accuracy of a child's account of sexual abuse: A case study. *Child Abuse and Neglect, 23*, 91–98.

Orbach, Y., Hershkowitz, I., Lamb, M. E., Sternberg, K. J., & Horowitz, D. (2000). Interviewing at the scene of the crime: Effects on children's recall of alleged abuse. *Legal and Criminological Psychology, 5*, 135–147.

Ornstein, P. A., Baker-Ward, L., Gordon, B. N., Pelphrey, K. A., Tyler, C. S., & Gramzow, E. (2006). The influence of prior knowledge and repeated questioning on children's long-term retention of the details of a pediatric examination. *Developmental Psychology, 42*, 332–344.

Ornstein, P. A., Haden, C. A., & Hedrick, A. M. (2004). Learning to remember: Social-communicative exchanges and the development of children's memory skills. *Developmental Review. Special Issue: Memory Development in the New Millennium, 24*, 374–395.

Ornstein, P. A., Merritt, K. A., Baker-Ward, L. Furtado, E., Gordon, B. N., & Principe, G. F. (1998). Children's knowledge, expectation, and long-term retention. *Applied Cognitive Psychology, 12*, 387–405.

Park, R. J., Goodyer, I. M., & Teasdale, J. D. (2002). Categoric overgeneral autobiographical memory in adolescents with major depressive disorder. *Psychological Medicine: A Journal of Research in Psychiatry and the Allied Sciences, 32*, 267–276.

Peterson, C. (1999). Children's memory for medical emergencies: 2 years later. *Developmental Psychology, 35*, 1493–1506.

Peterson, C., & Bell, M. (1996). Children's memory for traumatic injury. *Child Development, 67*, 3045–3070.

Peterson, C., & Biggs, M. (1997). Interviewing children about trauma: Problems with "specific" questions. *Journal of Traumatic Stress, 10*, 279–290.

Peterson, C., Dowden, C., & Tobin, J. (1999). Interviewing pre-schoolers: Comparison of yes/no and wh-questions. *Law and Human Behavior, 23*, 539–535.

Peterson, C. & Grant, M. (2001). Forced-choice: Are forensic interviewers asking the right questions? *Canadian Journal of Behavioural Science, 33*, 118–127.

Peterson, C., Sales, J. M., Rees, M., & Fivush, R. (2007). Parent-child talk and children's memory for stressful events. *Applied Cognitive Psychology, 21*, 1057–1075.

Peterson, C. & Whalen, N. (2001). Five years later: Children's memory for medical emergencies. *Applied Cognitive Psychology, 15*, 7–24.

Peterson, C., Sales, J. M., Rees, M., & Fivush, R. (2007). Parent-child talk and children's memory for stressful events. *Applied Cognitive Psychology, 21*, 1057–1075.

Pezdek, K., Finger, K., & Hodge, D. (1997). Planting false childhood memories: The role of event plausibility. *Psychological Science, 8*, 437–451.

Pezdek, K. & Hodge, D. (1999). Planting false childhood memories in children: The role of event plausibility. *Child Development, 70*, 887–895.

Pipe, M. E., & Salmon, K. (2009). Memory development and the forensic context. In N. Cowan and M. Courage (Eds), *Development of Memory in Childhood* (2nd edn, pp. 241–282). Florence, KY: Psychology Press.

Pollak, S., & Tolley-Schell, S. A. (2003). Selective attention to facial emotion in physically abused children. *Journal of Abnormal Psychology, 112*, 323–338.

Poole, D. A., Bruck, M., & Pipe, M. E. (2011). Forensic interviewing aids: Do props help children answer questions about touching? *Current Directions in Psychological Science, 20*, 11–15.

Poole, D. A., & Lamb, M. E. (1998). *Investigative Interviews of Children: A Guide for Helping Professionals.* Washington, DC: American Psychological Association.

Poole, D. A., & White, L. T. (1991). Effects of question repetition on the eyewitness testimony of children and adults. *Developmental Psychology, 27*, 975–986.

Porter, C., Lawson, J. S., & Bigler, E. D. (2005). Neurobehavioral sequelae of child sexual abuse. *Child Neuropsychology, 11*, 203–220.

Price, H. L. (2007). A direct comparison of children's recall of stressful and non-stressful events. *Dissertation Abstracts International: Section B: The Sciences and Engineering, 68(3-B)*, p. 1955.

Priestley, G., Roberts, S., & Pipe, M. E. (1999). Returning to the scene: Reminders and context reinstatement enhance children's recall. *Developmental Psychology, 35*, 1006–1019.

Principe, G. F., Ornstein, P. A., Baker-Ward, L., & Gordon, B. N. (2000). The effects of intervening experiences on children's memory for a physical examination. *Applied Cognitive Psychology, 14*, 59–80.

Pynoos, R. S. & Nader, K. (1989). Children's memory and proximity to violence. *Journal of the American Academy of Child and Adolescent Psychiatry, 28*, 236–241.

Quas, J. A., Bauer, A. B., & Boyce, W. T. B. (2004). Emotion, reactivity, and memory in early childhood. *Child Development, 75*, 1–18.

Quas, J. A., Carrick, N., Alkon, A., Goldstein, L., & Boyce, W. T. (2006). Children's memory for a mild stressor: The role of sympathetic activation and parasympathetic withdrawal. *Developmental Psychobiology, 48*, 686–702.

Quas, J. A., & Fivush, R. (Eds) (2009). *Emotion and Memory in Development: Biological, Cognitive, and Social Considerations* (pp. 313–339). New York, NY: Oxford University Press.

Quas, J. A., Goodman, G. S., Bidrose, S., Pipe, M. E., Craw, S. & Ablin, D. S. (1999). Emotion and memory: Children's long-term remembering, forgetting, and suggestibility. *Journal of Experimental Child Psychology, 72*, 235–270.

Quas, J. A. & Lench, H. C. (2007). Arousal at encoding, arousal at retrieval, interviewer support, and children's memory for a mild stressor. *Applied Cognitive Psychology, 21*, 289–305.

Quas, J. A., & McAuliff, B. D. (2009). Accommodating child witnesses in the criminal justice system: Implications for death penalty cases. In R. F. Schoop, R. L. Wiener, B. H. Bornstein, and S. L. Willborn (Eds), *Mental Disorder and Criminal Law: Responsibility, Punishment, and Competence*. New York, NY: Springer.

Quas, J. A., & Sumaroka, M. (2011). Consequences of legal involvement on child victims of maltreatment. In M. E. Lamb, D. J. La Rooy, L. C. Malloy, & C. Katz (Eds), *Children's Testimony: A Handbook of Psychological Research and Forensic Practice* (pp. 323–350). Chichester, UK: John Wiley & Sons.

Quas, J. A., Wallin, A. R., Papini, S., Lench, H. & Scullin, M. H. (2005). Suggestibility, social support, and memory for a novel experience in young children. *Journal of Experimental Child Psychology, 91*, 315–341.

Quas, J. A., Yim, I. S., Edelstein, R. S., Cahill, L., Rush, E. B. (2011). The role of cortisol reactivity in children's and adults' memory of a prior stressful experience. *Developmental Psychology, 53*, 166–174.

Raes, F., Hermans, D., Williams, J. M. G., Demyttenaere, K., Sabbe, B., Pieters, G., & Eelen, P. (2006). Is overgeneral autobiographical memory an isolated memory phenomenon in major depression? *Memory, 14*, 584–594.

Reese, E. & Newcombe, R. (2007). Training mothers in elaborative reminiscing enhances children's autobiographical memory and narrative. *Child Development, 78*, 1153–1170.

Reid, S. C., Salmon, K., & Lovibond, P. F. (2006). Cognitive biases in childhood anxiety, depression, and aggression: Are they pervasive or specific? *Cognitive Therapy and Research, 30*, 531–549.

Reisberg, D., & Heuer, F. (2004). Memory for emotional events. In D. Reisberg & P. Hertel (Eds), *Memory and Emotion* (pp. 3–41). New York, NY: Oxford University Press.

Roberts, K. P., & Blades, M. (1998). The effects of interacting in repeated events on children's eyewitness memory and source monitoring. *Applied Cognitive Psychology, 12*, 489–503.

Rocha, E. M., Marche, T. A., & Briere, J. (2011). The effect of forced-choice interview questions on children's suggestibility. Manuscript submitted for publication.

Rocha, E. M., Marche, T. A., & von Baeyer, C. L. (2009). Anxiety influences children's memory for procedural pain. *Pain Research and Management, 14*, 233–237.

Roebers, C. M. & Schneider, W. (2000). The impact of misleading questions on eyewitness memory in children and adults. *Applied Cognitive Psychology, 14*, 509–526.

Roebers, C. M. & Schneider, W. (2001). Individual differences in children's eyewitness recall: The influence of intelligence and shyness. *Applied Developmental Science, 5*, 9–20.

Roebers, C. M. & Schneider, W. (2005). Individual differences in young children's suggestibility: Relations to event memory, language abilities, working memory, and executive functioning. *Cognitive Development, 20*, 427–447.

Rothbart, M. K., Ellis, L. K., Rueda, M. R., & Posner, M. I. (2003). Developing mechanisms of conflict resolution. *Journal of Personality, 71*, 1113–1143.

Sales, J. M. (2009). Creating a context for children's memory: The importance of parental attachment status, coping, and narrative skill for co-constructing meaning following stressful experiences. In J. A. Quas & R. Fivush (Eds), *Emotion and Memory in Development:*

*Biological, Cognitive, and Social Considerations* (pp. 196–217). New York, NY: Oxford University Press.

Sales, J. M. & Fivush, R. (2005). Social and emotional functions of mother-child reminiscing about emotional events. *Social Cognition, 23*, 66–88.

Sales, J. M., Fivush, R., Parker, J., & Bahrick, L. (2005). Stressing memory: Long-term relations among children's stress, recall and psychological outcome following Hurricane Andrew. *Journal of Cognition and Development, 6*, 529–545.

Salmon, K., & Bryant, R. A. (2002). Posttraumatic stress disorder in children: The influence of developmental factors. *Clinical Psychology Review, 22*, 163–188.

Salmon, K. & Pipe, M. E. (1997). Props and children's event reports: The impact of a 1-year delay. *Journal of Experimental Child Psychology, 65*, 261–292.

Salmon, K., Pipe, M. E., Malloy, A., & Mackay, K. (2011). Do non-verbal aids increase the effectiveness of "best practice" verbal interview techniques? An experimental study. *Applied Cognitive Psychology, 26*, 370–380.

Salmon, K., Price, M., & Pereira, J. K. (2002). Factors associated with young children's long-term recall of an invasive medical procedure: A preliminary investigation. *Journal of Developmental and Behavioral Pediatrics, 23*, 347–352.

Salmond, C. H., Meiser-Stedman, R., Glucksman, E., Thompson, P., Dalgleish, T., & Smith, P. (2011). The nature of trauma memories in acute stress disorder in children and adolescents. *Journal of Child Psychology and Psychiatry, 52*, 560–570.

Saywitz, K. J., Goodman, G. S., Nicholas, E., & Moan, S. F. (1991). Children's memories of a physical examination involving genital touch: Implications for reports of child sexual abuse. *Journal of Consulting and Clinical Psychology, 59*, 682–691.

Saywitz, K. J., & Moan-Hardie, S. (1994). Reducing the potential for distortion of childhood memories. *Consciousness and Cognition, 3*, 408–425.

Saywitz, K. J., & Snyder, L. (1996). Helping children tell what happened: A follow-up study of the narrative elaboration procedure. *Child Maltreatment, 1*, 200–212.

Schwartz, E. D. & Kowalski, J. M. (1991). Post-traumatic stress disorder after a school shooting: Effects of symptom threshold selection and diagnosis by DSM-III-R or proposed DSM-IV. *American Journal of Psychiatry, 148*, 592–597.

Shapiro, L. R., Blackford, C., & Chen, C. F. (2005). Eyewitness memory for a simulated misdemeanor crime: The role of age and temperament in suggestibility. *Applied Cognitive Psychology, 19*, 267–289.

Shaw, J. A., Applegate, B., & Schorr, C. (1996). Twenty-one-month follow-up study of school-age children exposed to Hurricane Andrew. *Journal of American Academy of Child & Adolescent Psychiatry, 35*, 359–364.

Shaw, J. S., Bjork, R. A., & Handal, A. (1995). Retrieval-induced forgetting in an eyewitness-memory paradigm. *Psychonomic Bulletin and Review, 2*, 249–253.

Shipman, K. L., & Zeman, J. (1999). Emotional understanding: A comparison of physically maltreating and nonmaltreating mother-child dyads. *Journal of Clinical Child Psychology, 28*, 407–417.

Shipman, K., Schneider, R., & Sims, C. (2005). Emotion socialization in maltreating and nonmaltreating mother-child dyads: Implications for children's adjustment. *Journal of Clinical Child and Adolescent Psychology, 34*, 590–596.

Shrimpton, S., Oates, K., & Hayes, S. (1998). Children's memory of events: Effects of stress, age, time delay and location of interview. *Applied Cognitive Psychology, 12*, 133–143.

Strange, D., Garry, M., & Sutherland, R. (2003). Drawing out children's false memories. *Applied Cognitive Psychology, 17*, 607–619.

Sumner, J. A., Griffith, J. W., & Mineka, S. (2011). Examining the mechanisms of overgeneral autobiographical memory: Capture and rumination, and impaired executive control. *Memory, 19*, 169–183.

Swales, M. A., Williams, J. M. G., & Wood, P. (2001). Specificity of autobiographical memory and mood disturbance in adolescents. *Cognition and Emotion, 15*, 321–331.

Tessler, M. & Nelson, K. (1994). Making memories: The influence of joint encoding on later recall by young children. *Consciousness & Cognition, 3*, 307–326.

Thierry, K. L., Lamb, M. E., Orbach, Y., & Pipe, M. E. (2005). Developmental differences in the function and use of anatomical dolls during interviews with alleged sexual abuse victims. *Journal of Consulting and Clinical Psychology, 73*, 1125–1134.

Thompson, R. A. (2011). Emotion and emotion regulation: Two sides of the developing coin. *Emotion Review, 3*, 53–61.

Thompson, R. A. (2006). Development and social regulation of stress neurobiology in human development: Implications for the study of traumatic memories. In N. Eisenberg, W. Damon, & R. M. Lerner (Eds), *The Development of the Person: Social Understanding, Relationships, Conscience, Self*. Hoboken, NJ: John Wiley & Sons Inc.

Trickett, P. K., Noll, J. G., & Putnam, F. W. (2011). The impact of sexual abuse on female development: Lessons from a multigenerational, longitudinal research study. *Development and Psychopathology, 23*, 453–476.

Tobey, A. E., & Goodman, G. S. (1992). Children's eyewitness memory: Effects of participation and forensic context. *Child Abuse and Neglect, 16*, 779–796.

Tyano, S., Iancu, I., Solomon, Z., Sever, J., Goldstein, I., Touvtana, Y., & Bleich, A. (1996). Seven-year follow-up of child survivors of a bus-train collision. *Journal of American Academy of Child and Adolescent Psychiatry, 35*, 365–373.

Vaish, A., Grossmann, T., & Woodward, A. (2008). Not all émotions are created equal: The negativity bias in social-emotional development. *Psychological Bulletin, 134*, 383–403.

Valentino, K. (2011). A developmental psychopathology model of overgeneral autobiographical memory. *Developmental Review, 31*, 32–54.

Valentino, K., Toth, S., & Cicchetti, C. (2009). Autobiographical memory functioning among abused, neglected, and nonmaltreated children: The overgeneral memory effect. *Journal of Child Psychology and Psychiatry, 50*, 1029–1038.

Valentino, K., Cicchetti, D., Rogosch, F. A., & Toth, S. L. (2008). True and false recall and dissociation among maltreated children: The role of self-schema. *Development and Psychopathology, 20*, 213–232.

Van Bergen, P., Salmon, K., Dadds, M. R., & Allen, J. (2009). The effects of mother training in emotion-rich, elaborative reminiscing on children's shared recall and emotion knowledge. *Journal of Cognition and Development, 10*, 162–187.

Vrielynck, N., Deplus, S., & Piilippot, P. (2007). Overgeneral autobiographical memory and depressive disorder in children. *Journal of Clinical Child and Adolescent Psychology, 36*, 95–105.

Wallin, A. R., Quas, J. A., & Yim, I. S. (2009). Physiological stress responses and children's event memory. In J. A. Quas, & R. Fivush (Eds), *Emotion and Memory in Development: Biological, Cognitive, and Social Considerations* (pp. 313–339). New York, NY: Oxford University Press.

Wareham, P., & Salmon, K. (2006). Mother-child reminiscing about everyday experiences: Implications for clinical interventions in the preschool years. *Clinical Psychology Review, 26*, 535–554.

Warren, A. R. & Swartwood, J. N. (1992). Developmental issues in flashbulb memory research: Children recall the *Challenger* event. In E. Winograd & R. Neisser (Eds), *Affect and Accuracy in recall: Studies of "Flashbulb" Memories* (pp. 95–120). New York: Cambridge University Press.

Westcott, H. L. & Kynan, S. (2006). Interviewer practice in investigative interviews for suspected child sexual abuse. *Psychology, Crime, and Law, 12,* 367–382.

Williams, S., Wright, D. B., & Freeman, N. H. (2002). Inhibiting children's memory of an interactive event: The effectiveness of a cover-up. *Applied Cognitive Psychology, 16,* 651–664.

Williams, J. M. G., Barnhofer, T., Crane, C., Hermans, D., Raies, F., Watkins, E., & Dalgleish, T. (2007). Autobiographical memory specificity and emotional disorder. *Psychological Bulletin, 133,* 122–148.

Wiik, K. L., & Gunnar, M. R. (2009). In J. A. Quas, & R. Fivush (Eds), *Emotion and Memory in Development: Biological, Cognitive, and Social Considerations* (pp. 256–277). New York, NY: Oxford University Press.

# CHAPTER 6

# Investigative Interviews of Children

DEBRA ANN POOLE AND JASON J. DICKINSON

Investigative interviewing of children is a specialty represented by three interrelated groups: An international community of scientists who study eyewitness testimony and interviewing, the policy groups that summarize evidence-based guidelines and coordinate dissemination, and the trained interviewers who elicit children's reports to support legal decision-making and child-protection efforts. The field began to coalesce in the late 1980s, when pressure mounted to respond to a set of social changes and challenges that had been unfolding for more than two decades – at somewhat different times and forms – in countries around the world. These influences included a growing awareness of child abuse (Myers, 2004), legislative changes that increased the number of abuse reports while removing barriers to children's participation in the legal system (Bottoms & Goodman, 1996; McGough, 1994), and widely publicized day-care cases that revealed the need for a systematic response to abuse allegations (Ceci & Bruck, 1993, 1995).

The concept of a systematic response came to involve two components. One is the investigative protocol, which specifies procedural details such as the professionals involved in various types of cases, how they coordinate activities, and the required time frames for responding to allegations. A second component is the interviewing protocol, which outlines procedures for conducting conversations with child witnesses. (For examples, see Governor's Task Force on Children's Justice and Department of Human Services, 1998, 2011.) Individual jurisdictions sometimes assemble these components into a single document, but protocols released by professional organizations and researchers are portable documents that contain little procedural information (e.g. APSAC Task Force on Investigative Interviews in Cases of Alleged Child Abuse, 2002; Lamb, Hershkowitz, Orbach, & Esplin, 2008). Numerous interviewing protocols have been produced from these sources (for a model,

157

see Home Office, 2007), with consultants adding additional training models (e.g. Lyon, 2005).

The volume of research on interviewing issues, along with the legion of guidance documents, makes it difficult to distill core knowledge in the field. This summary begins with a brief history of the protocol movement, which explains why multiple interviewing models currently coexist. Next, information about how adults typically speak to children illustrates why investigative interviewing is a specialized skill. This skill has an underlying framework consisting of two sets of "support beams": the three overarching characteristics of investigative interviews (that is, what makes some conversations investigative interviews) and the three skill sets interviewers need to conduct sound interviews. Finally, there are numerous advanced topics, of which five are discussed here: interviewing props, using physical evidence in interviews, interviewing children with disabilities, modifying criminally oriented protocols for broader child-protection purposes' and training interviewers.

## A brief history of interviewing protocols

Similarities among three early protocols drew international attention that ignited the fledgling field of investigative interviewing. The fact that guidelines produced in three countries converged on a set of core recommendations supported the growing conviction that eyewitness performance follows general principles of memory and social influence – and that these principles could be studied by isolating specific interviewing techniques.

Two early protocols for interviewing children were inspired by work from Germany and Sweden (Undeutsch, 1982; Steller & Köhnken, 1989; Trankell, 1972), and both were motivated by legislative changes that allowed video recorded interviews to supplement children's courtroom testimony. In Canada, psychologist John Yuille's collaboration with researchers in the United States and West Germany led him to advocate a phased interview structure, later called the Step-Wise Interview (now the Step-Wise Guidelines), in which initial conversations about neutral events are followed by an unpressured "client centered" free recall phase and then specific questions (Yuille, 1988; Yuille, Cooper, & Hervé, in press; Yuille, Hunter, Joffe, & Zaparniuk, 1993). In England, the Home Office asked psychologist Ray Bull and a lawyer, Di Birch, to draft the *Memorandum of Good Practice* (Home Office, 1992; see also 2007). This widely disseminated document emphasized numerous themes that remain central to investigative interviewing, including the concept of a hierarchy of question types and the notion that each interview phase has a purpose which is best accomplished when interviewers rely on some techniques and avoid others.

While these collaborations were producing child-oriented protocols, another effort was underway in the United States. Cognitive psychologist Ronald Fisher noticed that his style of talking to friends sometimes helped them remember where they had placed lost objects. After Edward Geiselman suggested that police officers would be interested in this skill, the two discovered that little was known about how to interview cooperative witnesses. With basic information about cognitive processes and memory in mind, they reviewed tapes from laboratory studies and investigative interviews to identify effective techniques, later searching a wide range of materials (e.g. books on oral history, medical interviewing) for testable ideas. The result was a set of strategies, called the Cognitive Interview (CI), that increased the amount of information in eyewitness reports by exploiting basic principles of social dynamics and communication, accompanied by memory-enhancing techniques (Fisher & Geiselman, 1992). From very different directions, the CI and abuse-oriented protocols had arrived in the same place: The conviction that effective interviewers encourage witnesses to narrate events instead of directing memory retrieval with a stream of specific questions (Fisher, Milne, & Bull, 2011; Fisher, Ross, & Cahill, 2010). Subsequent research on the usefulness of CI techniques with children confirmed the basic wisdom of this interviewing approach (e.g. Holliday, 2003; Holliday & Albon, 2004; McCauley & Fisher, 1995).

First-generation protocols were soon followed by approaches that repackaged and augmented a core set of techniques to solve newly discovered interviewing challenges. The most ambitious effort was undertaken by Michael Lamb, who developed collaborations in Israel to oversee field-based interviewing research. Due to the difficulty of training interviewers, Lamb and his colleagues developed a highly structured protocol, the National Institute of Child Health and Human Development (NICHD) protocol, which is continually revised to reflect new research findings (Lamb et al., 2008). There is considerable evidence that a structured protocol improves interviewers' behavior and the quality of information provided by children. For example, the longer narratives prompted by open-ended questioning yield more accurate credibility assessments of abuse allegations (Hershkowitz, Fisher, Lamb, & Horowitz, 2007) and produce a greater number of strong investigative leads (Lamb et al., 2008).

The efforts discussed thus far had a similar genealogy: All were produced by research psychologists accustomed to thinking about cognitive and social processes, and the development teams had access to the research facilities needed to promote evidence-based practice. Despite some differences, these early protocols shared an underlying design that has been called "standard" interviewing (Poole & Dickinson, 2011). These overlapping features form the consensus view of best-practice standards, and it is this content that reappears, in various forms, in policy documents around the globe.

But before standard interviewing guidelines were widely disseminated, front-line interviewers had to innovate to do their jobs, and they did so by developing approaches informed by ideas from social work and other clinically oriented professions. Because interviewers in the field rarely knew the accuracy of children's reports, honing skills on the job usually meant one thing: Using a technique and observing if children responded by providing information. Strategies that appeared to be child- and interviewer-friendly gained followers, even without information about whether children used these techniques as interviewers intended or whether the techniques performed better than alternative approaches. As a result, practice-based techniques developed that did not yet have (and might never have) research support, and the different worlds of interviewers and research psychologists muted the cross-talk that quickly generates relevant research. Over time, professionals who advocated practice-based models imported some evidence-based recommendations into their protocols (albeit sometimes in ways that differed from standard protocols; see Anderson et al., 2010) while also retaining favored but untested techniques. Thus, from the late 1980s to the present, the interviewing landscape has always included a mix of standard and practice-based approaches.

Policy-makers who try to sort through conflicting advice may find it hard to understand why conclusions derived from experiences on the job (i.e. "We've done this for years and it works") and research sometimes differ. Because this issue is critical to understanding what "evidence-based" means, interviewing workshops should include information about three topics. First is an explanation of why job experience alone does not provide the feedback needed to evaluate techniques (despite the fact that professionals tend to become increasingly wedded to their approaches; see Dawes, 1994). Second is a review of at least one well-loved intervention that produced harm, to drive home the message that popularity and longevity do not guarantee safety. (Lilienfeld, 2007, includes a short list of such interventions, including a trauma-focused therapy.) Finally, the relevance of these issues for investigative interviewing can be illustrated by discussing the rise and fall of an interviewing technique (e.g. anatomical dolls; Dickinson, Poole, & Bruck, 2005). As long as no restrictions prevent people from selling or training untested techniques, this background is the first step toward helping policy groups ask the right questions.

In sum, research-based approaches (a) were constructed from the ground up by assembling evidence on memory, social processing and communication to construct testable alternatives; (b) have been systematically studied; and (c) are publically available. Practice-based approaches originated from front-line interviewers who were less interested than researchers in cognitive issues but were more concerned about addressing the emotional needs of victimized children. It is likely that future research will fill gaps in knowledge that are preventing a speedy resolution of ongoing disagreements between these sets of approaches. In the meantime, the focus of this chapter is consensus practice.

## Why we need trained investigative interviewers

Investigative interviewing is a specialized skill because the way trained interviewers talk is not how adults usually talk. Daily conversations are guided by a set of biologically based tendencies that are honed by years of experience within our various cultural groups, but the habits that help us cooperate with others at home and in our communities do not always help us elicit the most useful information from them.

Consider a simple example: taking turns in conversation. Soon after babies start to babble ("da da mi ba ba ba"), adults can "converse" with them by getting close to their faces, babbling some gibberish ("Oh, what a PRETTY baby you are, yes ma ma ma ma"), and then standing silently. Often, babies will start a sequence of "conversational babbling," one in which babies and adults take turns making sounds, even though no one is actually saying anything at all.

Partly because children learn turn-taking so early, scientists believe that humans are neurologically wired to take turns in conversation (Lemasson et al., 2011; Stivers et al., 2009). This means that in cultures around the world, children and adults alike expect to say a little about something and then pass the ball to someone else. The expectation that "I'll say a little – but not too much – and then you'll say a little – but not too much" is the bane of investigative interviewing because witnesses rarely tell everything they know about a topic and interviewers have trouble suppressing the habit of talking. These two forces produce a dynamic in which inexperienced interviewers react by directing interviews with many specific questions, as in this reformatted example from transcripts of the McMartin Preschool case (Garven, Wood, Malpass, & Shaw, 1998, p. 348):

| Interviewer: | Who do you think played that game [horsey]? |
|---|---|
| Child: | Ray and Miss Peggy. |
| Interviewer: | Ray and Miss Peggy? Did Miss Peggy take her clothes off? |
| Child: | Yeah. |
| Interviewer: | I bet she looked funny didn't she? Did she have big boobs? |
| Child: | Yeah. |
| Interviewer: | Yeah. And did they swing around? |
| Child: | Yeah. |

Children's turn-taking abilities can lead interviewers to assume that young witnesses are more cognitively advanced than they actually are. In fact, children are still learning how to effectively search memory, tell a story and maintain conversational coherence. As a result, when meaningful conversations between adults and young children are sustained, it is usually because adults do the work. In one study, for example, mothers were good at managing a "turnabout" by addressing what the child said and then contributing something that invited the child to make a relevant response. The children, however, "rarely caught the ball and threw it back...they dropped it, or caught and kept it, or ignored it and threw a different ball back" (Kaye & Charney, 1981, p. 36). As the researchers explained, "the main goal in adult-adult conversations is getting one's turn, while the main goal of an adult in and adult-child conversation is getting the child to take his turn" (p. 47). Thus, children learn early to say something after an adult says something, but they come to interviewing environments expecting that adults will direct conversations.

To counter children's tendency to take little conversational turns and to drift off topic, best-practice standards include recommendations for keeping them talking and focused. A simple practice capitalizes on a trick children learn very early: "If I don't want to talk, I can repeat something the adult just said to turn the conversation back." An oft-cited example illustrates this tactic (Saywitz, 1988, pp. 38–39). Here a child is confused about kinship terms, which are notoriously difficult to master:

Attorney: When you were at your grandma's house with your daddy, whose mamma is your grandma?
Jenny: Grandma Ann. (gives grandma's name)
Attorney: Is she your daddy's mamma?
Jenny: Huh? (doesn't understand the question)
Attorney: Is she your daddy's mamma? (leading question requiring only a nod)
Jenny: Daddy's mamma.

Did the child answer the question? We don't know because the repetition could have been made to turn conversation back to the interviewer. Whenever the last utterance was not a question, another tactic for passing the conversational ball is to utter "facilitators," which are comments such as "Okay" and "Um hmmm" that take a short turn so others have permission to keep talking. Since children understand the purpose of partial repetitions and facilitators, interviewers can use these techniques to pass turns back to children, thereby keeping them talking about a topic without significant interruptions or interference (Roberts & Duncanson, 2011).

In sum, adults have years of experience that train them to dominate and direct conversations with children. As professionals become expert interviewers, they learn to inhibit some conversational habits and replace them with more effective techniques. Interviewers who keep children talking by interjecting facilitators are using their knowledge of language *pragmatics*: the social rules of language. Competent interviewing also involves knowledge of three other language topics. Information about *phonology* (the sound system of a language) helps interviewers understand children's speech, so experienced interviewers know that "some tain on my arm" is more likely to mean "something on my arm" than "some paint on my arm." Information about *semantics* (vocabulary development) helps interviewers avoid words children may not know, and information about *syntax* (grammar) helps them plan questions that children understand. (For overviews, see Poole & Lamb, 1998; Walker, 1999.) In addition to hundreds of details about language, expert interviewers know a lot about memory, suggestibility, and the broad social/communication factors (e.g. nonverbal behavior) that influence whether witnesses search their memories and talk – or not (Fisher & Geiselman, 1992).

A fail-safe way to convince policy-makers that interviewers need specialized training is to show them how professionals who do not know these things talk to children. Numerous studies on this issue have produced similar findings, which were wonderfully illustrated by an analysis of sexual abuse interviews from one U.S. state. Here is what Warren, Woodall, Hunt and Perry (1996) discovered when they compared the following interviewing guidelines to interviewers' behavior:

- *Build rapport with neutral conversation early in interviews.* "Warming up" children is an essential part of getting them to talk, yet over a quarter of the interviewers evaluated by Warren et al. made no attempt to build early rapport and, of those who did, many asked only a few questions about names of family members and number of siblings. Rather than encouraging children to talk, these interviewers talked three times as much as children during initial rapport-building (measured by number of words).
- *Explain ground rules for the interview* (e.g. "If I say something wrong, I want you to tell me I said something wrong"). Children believe they should be cooperative in conversation and answer any question asked – even if they do not know the answer or the interviewer said something wrong. Ground rules can ameliorate (although not eradicate) this problem, yet less than a third of the interviewers explained any ground rules.
- *Introduce the topic with the least suggestive prompt possible* (e.g. "Do you know why you are here today?"). Suggestive questions are more likely to elicit inaccurate information and less likely to elicit important but unanticipated information. Nonetheless, fewer than half of the interviewers followed

this advice. Most frequently, they introduced the topic by directly asking children whether they had ever been touched inappropriately or had seen inappropriate touching.

- *Avoid yes–no questions.* Children are notoriously inaccurate when answering yes–no questions, but the majority of questions during abuse-related portions of these interviews were this format.
- *Deliver one question at time.* Interviewers should give children ample time to respond, yet Warren et al. found 520 series of multiple questions in a subset of only 20 interviews.
- *Avoid introducing information the child has not already provided in the current interview.* Feeding children information – even if inadvertently – was the major issue in the contentious day-care cases that reignited interest in children's suggestibility. Yet the majority of interviewers (94 percent) introduced new information, averaging more than seven pieces of new information per interview.
- *Clarify new information mentioned by children.* It is common for children's reports to contain ambiguous information, so investigative interviewers need to ask questions that will clarify the intended meaning of any name, place, object or action mentioned. In this set of interviews, children often mentioned names that were ambiguous, but 43 percent of the time the interviewers never attempted to clarify the names.

These and other data paint a clear picture of how adults usually talk to children: They tend to jump to topics they are interested in without providing adequate time for children to feel at ease, fail to orient children to the rules for talking, rarely rely on open-ended questions to introduce the topic or to probe for information, and pepper children with a large number of specific (often yes–no) questions (sometimes delivering multiple questions without waiting for answers). In addition, interviewers often introduce new information and close interviews without clarifying critical information mentioned by children.

The way adults normally talk to children is a recipe for disaster when these conversational habits are combined with a well-known cognitive tendency: confirmation bias (also referred to as investigator bias). This bias is the strong tendency to seek information that will confirm a belief while overlooking information that might disconfirm the belief, as in the following example from Kelly Michael's case (Ceci & Bruck, 1995, p. 100):

Interviewer:   Do you think that Kelly was not good when she was hurting you all?

Child A:       Wasn't hurting me. I like her.

Interviewer:   I can't hear you, you got to look at me when you talk to me. Now when Kelly was bothering kids in the music room...

Child A:      I got socks off…
Interviewer:  Did she make anybody else take their clothes off in the music
    room?
Child A:      No.
Interviewer:  Yes?
Child A:      No.

Collectively, adults' natural language habits and confirmation bias, when combined with the architecture of children's minds, are the major reasons some cases go awry.

Interviewers in the field are at various levels of skill in avoiding undesirable behavior while also exploring topics that are crucial to those who will later evaluate the evidence. The volume of information needed to become an expert interviewer begs for an organizational framework to help professionals more easily grasp the underlying design of a sound investigative interview. One way to conceptualize this framework is to imagine two sets of support beams: the three characteristics of an investigative interview (that is, what makes a conversation an investigative interview) and the three skill sets required to conduct such an interview.

## The underlying design of investigative interviews

Imagine this familiar scenario. A mother prepares a snack for her 8-year-old son, who will soon return from school. When he walks in the door, she asks, "What did you do at school today?" After listening for a few minutes, she asks about a recent problem: "Did Sammy bother you at recess?", to which her son replies, "No."

This style of inquiry is a "story interview": The mother's goal was to prompt her son to recount the story of what happened at school today, and she was especially interested in whether he was safe at recess. She did not assume that her basic understanding of the situation might have another interpretation, so she did not ask questions to explore other possibilities. (For example, perhaps Sammy didn't bother her son because the bully was not at school that day, rather than because the situation was resolved.) Also, the mother did not invite her son to explain other issues he was having; instead, she quickly narrowed the conversation to her topic of concern. Nor did she ask who her son had played with at recess or which teacher had supervised that day, so she could potentially ask someone to verify her son's account. Mothers could conduct investigative interviews, but they usually do not.

Asking a child to tell a story – even when questions are neutral and non-suggestive – does not make an interview investigative. Three overarching characteristics, executed using three skill sets, are the hallmarks of expert practice.

## The three overarching characteristics of investigative interviews

Authors use different names for the characteristics of investigative interviews of children, but the characteristics themselves are part of the universal language of the field: hypothesis testing, a child-centered approach and exploration that supports the broader investigation.

Interviewers who take a hypothesis-testing approach have an open-minded, skeptical and objective perspective. When a specific allegation is on the table (e.g. that a mother wrenched her child's arm in anger), these interviewers realize that many things might have happened (i.e. they are open-minded), that the most obvious explanation for verbal reports or physical signs may not be the correct explanation (i.e. they are skeptical) and that it is important not to become emotionally involved in conclusions based solely on evidence collected thus far (i.e. they remain objective). John Yuille and his colleagues (in press) explain this approach as follows:

> Throughout the investigative process alternative explanations are generated for the emerging fact pattern. Similarly, throughout the interview of the child the interviewer is constantly creating alternative hypotheses to explain what the child is saying and the interviewer is weighing those hypotheses. At the end of the investigation the investigator develops a narrative to explain the existing facts. Once that narrative is developed the investigator then tries to disprove the narrative. Only if the narrative stands up to this challenge are any conclusions drawn about the case.

This summary describes two types of hypothesis testing. First are hypotheses about the events that triggered allegations or concerns, which investigative teams develop based on case-specific information and knowledge about the dynamics of similar cases. For example, if a mother alleges that her ex-husband sexually touched their daughter, the first hypothesis (i.e. possibility) is the allegation as stated: that the father sexually abused his daughter. Case features dictate what other possibilities are plausible. Examples are that the daughter was touched during routine care-giving (if she is young), that the mother interpreted vaginal redness as a sign of abuse due to concern for the daughter's safety, that the mother misinterpreted a comment her daughter made, that the mother questioned her daughter relentlessly after stumbling upon sex play, and that the mother is intentionally accusing the father (e.g. because she has been prevented from moving due to a joint custody agreement). Other hypotheses would be more appropriate for an older child or teenager, and new hypotheses might be warranted as additional evidence comes to light. Planning lines of questioning to address various possibilities is a critical part of preparation for an investigative interview (e.g. for examples, see Governor's Task Force on Children's Justice and Department of Human Services, 2011).

A second type of hypothesis testing occurs when interviewers test hypotheses about the details children provide during interviews. For example, if a child says that she watches her neighbors "have sex," the question, "What do they do when they have sex?" Could reveal that the child calls kissing "sex." Similarly, the statement "Jimmy does that too" should prompt questions to determine who Jimmy is and what the child means by "that." Exploring alternative hypotheses is one of the greatest challenges of investigative interviewing.

Meeting that challenge requires a child-centered approach. Here is how one protocol describes this second characteristic of investigative interviews (State of Maine Child and Family Services, 2010):

> Interviewers use open-ended questions to "transfer control" of conversations so children – not interviewers – are the information providers. Although interviewers direct the flow of conversation through a series of phases (steps), children determine the vocabulary and specific content of conversations as much as possible. Fact-finding interviewers are mindful to frame questions in ways that are developmentally and culturally sensitive. They choose techniques that empower children to be comfortable talking about potentially sensitive information.

While interviewers are collecting information to test hypotheses with developmentally appropriate techniques, they are also aware that an interview is only one part of a process involving other evidence-collection efforts. Interviewers demonstrate the third characteristic of investigative interviews – supporting the broader investigation – when they address topics that might lead to other evidence (e.g. physical evidence, other witnesses) and collect the information needed by decision-makers. Each reason for interviewing children (e.g. emotional abuse, sexual abuse, witness to violence, possible witness to an accidental death) involves specialized knowledge of the types of corroborating evidence that might be available and the needs of the professionals who will substantiate abuse, file criminal charges, or forward evidence garnered from the interview to support other types of decisions.

## The three skill sets of an investigative interviewer

Investigative interviewing is a complex skill, so it is likely that experienced interviewers differ from less-experienced interviewers in the same ways that experts in other fields differ from novices. Of course, experts know more than do non-experts, but the process of developing expertise has more far-reaching consequences. Experts spot patterns more rapidly than do novices, and their knowledge is organized around "big ideas." Expert knowledge is "conditioned," which means that experts are flexible thinkers who know when situations call for specific types of information and responses. After years of problem-solving within a particular domain of knowledge, experts have more rapid access to knowledge and routines, and this improved "automaticity" frees cognitive resources they can recruit to solve complex problems. Thus experts do not simply know more, they perceive information differently, organize it differently, retrieve it more effortlessly and solve problems more effectively (Bransford, Brown, & Cocking, 1999).

Research on the development of expertise suggests a way to think about and train interviewers. Because investigative interviewing requires people to suppress their usual communication habits, it is likely that new interviewers will need to be highly practiced on interviewing language – so these skills require little effort – before they can reliably anticipate where they might be directing the interview next. Similarly, they probably need to develop automaticity in directing a conversation through steps (or phases) before they can reliably engage in the on-the-spot problem-solving that yields case-specific information. Just as mathematics education involves a hierarchy of skills, with rapid math-fact retrieval supporting more complicated tasks, interviewing can also be broken down into skill sets. We call these skills the three "Cs": conversational habits, conventional content and case-specific exploration.

Many insights about conversational habits have a common origin: Someone noticed that an interviewer was particularly effective, evaluated what this person was doing and then conducted a study to test some target behaviors. For example, Roberts and Duncanson (2011) were struck by results from an interviewer who tolerated longer pauses between utterances, used more facilitators (e.g. okay, uh-huh), and sometimes paraphrased children (e.g. Child: "I went home first." Interviewer: "You went home first."). They constructed two interviewing conditions that were identical except for the following: In the "facilitative" condition, interviewers were required to wait 2–3 seconds after the last utterances (by the child or the interviewer) before speaking again, were encouraged to use facilitators and were required to paraphrase the child at least once every three prompts. Compared to children interviewed in the traditional way, those interviewed in a facilitative way reported more information but were just as accurate as children interviewed without these conversational habits.

Conversational habits include a wide range of techniques that build trust, reduce witnesses' anxiety levels, and encourage witnesses to search memory, continue talking and disclose sensitive information. Nonverbal techniques include selective mimicry (subtle mirroring of some witness behavior), body position and managing eye contact to appear engaged but not confrontative. Other habits are tolerating silence (pacing conversation), using open-ended questions whenever possible, and exploiting the ability of facilitators and partial repetitions to keep children talking. Interviewers can use these fundamental interviewing skills regardless of which specific protocol is in use or the purpose of an interview.

Once effective conversational habits are in place, interviewers are ready to learn the conventional content of an investigative interview. This content specifies how to direct an interview from start to finish according to the specific protocol in use. Conventional content includes information about how to execute the various interview phases (introduction, early rapport-building, etc.), the procedural issues involved in each phase (e.g. recording identifying information during an introduction phase), and recommendations about protocol flexibility and interviewer discretion (e.g. when it is appropriate to skip a phase or revisit an earlier phase).

Experienced interviewers also have mastered the third skill: case-specific exploration. This skill, which involves coordinating interview goals with the specifics of individual cases, is fraught with challenges. In their book *Made to Stick*, Heath and Heath (2007, p. 25) lead off with the military version of the problem: "No plan survives contact with the enemy." According to the Heaths, the limitation of a detailed battle plan, or any plan for expected behavior, is that unpredictable events render plans useless, leaving individuals without a course of action. In investigative interviewing, no interview plan survives contact with a 3-year-old, and few survive contact with a teenager.

The solution begins with simple commander's intent statements that represent "the desired end-state of an operation" (Heath & Heath, 2007, p. 26). Commander's intents are simple directives that help people make goal-relevant choices in complex situations. In the military, a commander's intent might be something such as "break the will of the enemy in the Southeast region" (Heath & Heath, p. 26); in child protection, commander's intent might be "determine if this child is safe."

Determining if children are safe requires interviewers to explore new information that is relevant to the commander's intent – even when this information is not about the precipitating allegation. For example, a concern about physical abuse may appear groundless after questioning, but if a child mentions that his mother recently started working outside the home, this new information should trigger questions to explore who is supervising the child. In this hypothetical case, an interviewer who asks how the child was bruised but fails to discover that he is unsupervised for long periods of time has not engaged in case-specific exploration. Similarly, closing a sexual abuse interview without realizing that the child has two uncles with the same name is a case-specific gap. (Imagine two uncles pointing fingers at each other.) In this situation, the commander's intent to "meet the needs of the charging authority" has clearly not been met.

Once interviewers are fluent in the conversational habits and conventional content of investigative interviewing, it becomes easier to jot down important details, pause to collect thoughts, and explore case-specific issues. While interviewers in the field work to improve these skills, researchers around the world are responding to interviewers' frustrations, questions and innovations by designing studies to fill gaps in our knowledge of interviewing. Many questions remain, including questions about the following five topics.

## Advanced topics

### Interview props

Few assumptions are more popular than the idea that concrete objects help adults and children communicate. Early guidance for interviewers included long lists of recommended supplies, including doll houses, family doll sets and anatomically correct dolls, art supplies, and even toy soldiers and zoo animals (e.g. Jones & McQuiston, 1988). As the realization spread that it is not productive to distract young children, uncluttered interviewing rooms gradually replaced playrooms. Yet even today, flipboards, markers, body diagrams (human figure drawings) and anatomical dolls are mentioned in some interviewing protocols, where these props occupy roles ranging from minor (e.g. paper available in case the child needs to draw a detail) to central (e.g. body diagrams used to elicit abuse disclosures).

The appropriateness of a prop depends on the purpose for its use and how it is used. In the RATAC® (also CornerHouse) interview protocol, for example, interviewers conduct early phases next to a flip board on which they write/draw information about themselves and the child (Anderson et al., 2010). This procedure is easy to train and helps interviewers feel comfortable, but does it have any drawbacks? To answer this question, one study compared research protocols with and without a flipboard. There was no positive or negative impact of the flipboard on numerous variables, including the number of verbal responses children made during early interview phases, whether topic introduction was successful, how much children talked during open-ended questioning, or the accuracy of their answers to a challenging set of source-monitoring questions (Poole & Dickinson, 2011).

But it is important to distinguish between props that make the interview room more inviting and props that alter the way interviewers elicit information from children. Using props as demonstration aids is problematic if children have difficulty understanding the relationship between the props and their real-world equivalents, if the props "pull" for responses that do not originate from searching memory, or if children's responses with the props are more likely than verbal reports to be misinterpreted by adults. In the aforementioned flipboard study, for example, children who answered questions about touching with a body diagram sometimes pointed to places that had just been labeled during a body identification procedure, and both touched and untouched children made these errors (Poole & Dickinson, 2011). The possibility that body diagrams encourage thoughtless pointing, along with a lack of evidence that diagrams provide benefits when added to verbal questions, has raised serious concerns about their use early in interviews (Poole, Bruck, & Pipe, 2011).

The lack of fit between children's minds and body diagrams is not an artifact of using non-memorable events in research because young children have difficulty reporting touches with props even when they have a visible reminder of an event that just occurred. To illustrate, a researcher individually showed 3-, 4-, and 5-year-olds three symbols – a body diagram, a doll and themselves – and pointed out some similarities between each prop and the child. For test trials, the researcher put a large sticker on the child and asked the child to use the prop (drawing/doll/adult) to show where the sticker was (e.g. "The big star is right here on you. Your job is to put the little star on the doll in just the same place as the big star is on you right now.") After removing the sticker, another trial commenced, for a total of four trials per prop. Errors were not uncommon, even though accuracy was liberally coded and left-right reversals were ignored. For example, 5-year-olds erred 5 percent of the time when they placed stickers on a body diagram, and error rates were alarmingly higher for younger children (21 percent and 55 percent for 4-year-olds and 3-year-olds, respectively; Ladd, London, & Bruck, 2011). Of course, these are error rates for a simple task that does not involve retrieval of information from memory.

Reviews are available for individuals interested in the impact of props on children's reports (Pipe & Salmon, 2009), some developmental reasons why props do not always improve children's performance (Poole, Bruck, & Pipe, 2011), and the risks associated with anatomical dolls (Dickinson et al., 2005). In-progress research is evaluating other issues, including the impact of props on children who have and have not previously disclosed touching and the influence of allowing children to freely draw/color (comfort drawing) during investigative interviews.

## Using physical evidence in interviews

Many children are reluctant to talk about maltreatment, and this is especially true of children who have not previously disclosed (London, Bruck, Ceci, &

Shuman, 2005). One technique for eliciting disclosures is to present children with physical evidence of abuse or neglect, such as medical photographs of bruises, photographs of a house (in neglect cases), camcorders (if a child was filmed), and photographs or video recordings of sexual abuse.

Michigan's forensic interviewing protocol provides guidelines for using physical evidence during investigative interviews (Governor's Task Force on Children's Justice and Department of Human Services, 2011). Informed by the experiences of FBI interviewers, these guidelines include questions the investigative team should ask before deciding whether to bring physical evidence to an interview (e.g. Is it necessary?), factors to consider when deciding which items or images to present (e.g. identification of other witnesses, needs of the charging authority), and how to tell a child about evidence while preserving the option of using or not using the materials (e.g. "I have some pictures I may want to show you and talk about today, but first I want to get to know you better," p. 40).

Due to laws governing the possession of sexually explicit material, issues regarding chain of custody, and concerns about the impact of revealing images to children, there are special considerations for obtaining, masking and documenting the use of photographs or recordings of children engaged in sexually abusive activity. It is important that interviewers interested in using physical evidence consult with local authorities, as it is risky to rely on advice produced for jurisdictions where different laws and procedures may apply.

## Interviewing children with disabilities

It is estimated that 6–10 percent of children in industrialized countries have a chronic health problem or a perceptual, movement, language, cognitive, or emotional disorder that interferes with the ability to perform some activities in a way that is within normal range for their age (Merrick & Carmeli, 2003). Clearly, interviewers should be prepared to factor special needs into their interview plans and to modify those plans, as needed, during interviews. Flexibility is key because many conditions manifest with varied levels of severity, and it is not uncommon for children to have more than one condition (U.S. Department of Education, 2009).

The limited time and resources available to prepare for investigative interviews typically preclude an individualized approach based on each child's pattern of strengths and difficulties. This is not usually an obstacle, though, because the overall interview process is the same for typical children and those with disabilities – with one exception: Because many disabilities produce the communication and behavioral challenges associated with younger children, practices that help young children participate in conversations also help many children with disabilities. Therefore, the first step towards accommodating diversity is to keep the following developmentally sensitive practices in mind:

- *Schedule the interview to maximize cooperation.* For example, children with vision impairments, attention-deficit disorder (ADD) or autism often have sleep disorders, and it is not uncommon for children to take medications several times a day or to require medical monitoring (e.g. blood-sugar monitoring for diabetes). As a result, special care should be taken when scheduling children with special needs.
- *Gather information about strengths and difficulties during rapport-building.* Interviewers can use early rapport-building and a practice interview to become accustomed to how children speak, to test children's ability to pay attention and answer simple factual questions, and to assess children's ability to describe personally experienced events.
- *Minimize distractions.* Some children with disabilities are highly distractible and bothered by visual clutter and noise. As a result, care should be taken to minimize sensory stimulation by keeping the interview room quiet and sparsely decorated.
- *Keep children on topic.* Children who are distractible, eager to please or confused by questioning are especially likely to stray from the topic of conversation by interjecting descriptions of unrelated events. Therefore, it helps to warn children of changes in the topic and to repeat the topic frequently.
- *Ignore irrelevant behavior that can be ignored.* Some children with disabilities have atypical mannerisms and behavior. For example, children with autism-spectrum disorder often avoid eye contact and may flap their hands, and children with visual impairments sometimes rock and press their eyes. Interviewers should maintain focus on the conversation by ignoring behaviors that do not interfere with asking questions and hearing the answers.
- *Emphasize open-ended questions and minimize specific, multiple choice and yes–no questions.* Many disabilities produce heightened suggestibility to focused questions, so interviewers should rely as much as possible on open-ended questions and follow focused questions with more open-ended prompts.
- *Use simple, direct questions.* Language concepts that are harder for typically developing children to master often develop later among children with disabilities, including those with vision, hearing or cognitive impairments. Therefore, interviewers should ask short, concrete questions that avoid pronouns, ambiguous terms and words with double meanings.
- *Double-check the meaning of children's answers.* Children with language and cognitive impairments are more likely to use language in unusual ways and to answer questions just to be cooperative. Interviewers should double-check that they heard children correctly, that children can answer consistently

and that answers mean what interviewers think they mean. (For more suggestions, see Shelton, Bridenbaugh, Farrenkopf, & Kroeger, 2008.)

## Customizing protocols for child protective services interviews

Most investigative protocols are designed for a variety of cases, but their emphasis has clearly been tilted towards investigations of sexual abuse allegations. One approach for correcting this bias is to include more varied examples. For instance, the current edition of Michigan's forensic interviewing protocol contains "Quick Guides" with sample questions for exploring concerns about physical abuse and neglect (Governor's Task Force on Children's Justice and Department of Human Services, 2011). Another approach is to construct a protocol specifically for child protective service workers. One example, from the State of Maine Child and Family Services (2010), is flexible enough to direct assessment interviews while also providing guidance for workers who monitor children in out-of-home care. In contrast to guidelines issued by national and international organizations, locally produced protocols have the advantage of packaging best-practice standards with language that reiterates broader agency values, culture and training goals, so interviewers do not feel they are walking into unfamiliar territory when they first confront a new interviewing model.

## Interviewer training

Because so much interviewing behavior involves engrained skills that develop through repetition over time, it is not surprising that training workshops alone tend not to improve interviewing (Lamb et al., 2008; Poole & Lamb, 1998). The field should not suspend workshops, however. Classroom-based training sessions, from two-day-long introductions to more intensive programs, educate interviewers about basic maltreatment dynamics, local procedures and fundamental interviewing skills. As a result, knowledge of facts improves after workshops, even if this knowledge does little to immediately increase the use of open-ended questions and other desired techniques.

Training workshops are most effective when combined with ongoing review (interview critiques) and booster training. For example, Rischke, Roberts and Price (2011) evaluated the work of investigative interviewers who averaged two years of interviewing experience. Interviewers submitted sample interviews before training and then weekly for two months after a two-day workshop that included child development principles, introduction to a structured protocol, and practice using pauses and open-ended questions. Throughout the post-training period, interviewers received written critiques and participated in phone conversations with a trainer. They then attended a two-day refresher training and continued to submit interviews for four additional months, including two months of post-refresher training (involving weekly or bi-weekly feedback) and two months of additional data collection (during which interviewers received feedback only on request). Evaluations of more than a hundred interviews provided the raw data to track progress during the various phases of training.

Confirming the results of previous studies, initial training did not produce meaningful changes in interviewing behavior: Many interviewers continued to omit preparatory interview phases (phases before abuse-related questioning), and there was no increased use of facilitators or open-ended questions. However, testifying to the value of training, ongoing supervision and practice, these interviewing skills did increase during the post-refresher period.

Research to discover the most effective interviewing strategies will do little to help children unless the interviewing community also invests resources to innovate and test cost-effective training models. Therefore, one goal for the future is to encourage partnerships between interviewing experts, curriculum designers and technology experts so teams can construct more effective training models that are affordable, responsive to new findings and sustainable in environments with high rates of staff turnover.

## Conclusion

Investigative interviewing of children involves more than a list of good questions or a series of interviewing phases. Interviewing guidelines are remedies for myriad problems that arise whenever adults (often unfamiliar adults) try to get children (often reluctant children) to talk about their lives and experiences. Interviews are problem-solving sessions, situated in broader investigations, in which interviewers juggle the needs of children, other fact-finders, and decision-makers who will determine the most reasonable interpretations of the evidence. Learning to interview well may be a lifelong process, one in which new research findings will continually challenge old assumptions about which practices best protect children.

## References

Anderson, J., Ellefson, J., Lashley, J., Miller, A. L., Olinger, A., Russell, A., Stauffer, J., & Weigman, J. (2010). The CornerHouse forensic interview protocol: RATAC®. *Thomas M. Cooley Journal of Practical and Clinical Law, 12,* 193–331.

APSAC Task Force on Investigative Interviews in Cases of Alleged Child Abuse (2002). *Investigative interviewing in cases of alleged child abuse.* Author.

Bottoms, B. L., & Goodman, G. S. (Eds) (1996). *International Perspectives on Child Abuse and Children's Testimony: Psychological Research and Law.* Thousand Oaks, CA: Sage.

Bransford, J. D., Brown, A. L., & Cocking, R. R. (Eds) (1999). *How People Learn: Brain, Mind, Experience, and School.* Washington, DC: National Academy Press.

Ceci, S. J., & Bruck, M. (1993). Suggestibility of the child witness: A historical review and synthesis. *Psychological Bulletin, 113,* 403–439.

Ceci, S. J., & Bruck, M. (1995). *Jeopardy in the Courtroom: A Scientific Analysis of Children's Testimony.* Washington, DC: American Psychological Association.

Dawes, R. (1994). *House of Cards: Psychology and Psychotherapy Built on Myth.* New York: Free Press.

Dickinson, J. J., Poole, D. A., & Bruck, M. (2005). Back to the future: A comment on the use of anatomical dolls in forensic interviews. *Journal of Forensic Psychology Practice, 5,* 63–74.

Fisher, R. P., & Geiselman, R. E. (1992). *Memory-enhancing Techniques for Investigative Interviewing: The Cognitive Interview.* Springfield, IL: Thomas.

Fisher, R. P., Milne, R., & Bull, R. (2011). Interviewing cooperative witnesses. *Current Directions in Psychological Science, 20,* 16–19.

Fisher, R. P., Ross, S. J., & Cahill, B. S. (2010). Interviewing witnesses and victims. In P. A. Granhag (Ed.), *Forensic Psychology in Context: Nordic and International Approaches* (pp. 56–74). Devon, UK: Willan Publishing.

Garven, S., Wood, J. M., Malpass, R. S., & Shaw, J. S. (1998). More than suggestion: The effect of interviewing techniques from the McMartin Preschool case. *Journal of Applied Psychology, 83,* 347–359.

Governor's Task Force on Children's Justice and Department of Human Services (1998). *A model child abuse protocol: Coordinated investigative team approach.* Retrieved from http://www.michigan.gov/documents/dhs/DHS-Pub-794_206830_7.pdf

Governor's Task Force on Children's Justice and Department of Human Services (2011). *Forensic interviewing protocol.* Retrieved From http://www.mi.gov/documents/dhs/DHS-PUB-0779_211637_7.pdf

Heath, C., & Heath, D. (2007). *Made to Stick: Why Some Ideas Survive and Others Die.* New York: Random House.

Hershkowitz, I., Fisher, S., Lamb, M. E., & Horowitz, D. (2007). Improving credibility assessment in child sexual abuse allegations: The role of the NICHD investigative interview protocol. *Child Abuse & Neglect, 31,* 99–110.

Holliday, R. E. (2003). Reducing misinformation effects in children with cognitive interviews: Dissociating recollection and familiarity. *Child Development, 74,* 728–751.

Holliday, R. E., & Albon, A. (2004). Minimising misinformation effects in young children with cognitive interview mnemonics. *Applied Cognitive Psychology, 18,* 263–281.

Home Office (1992). *Memorandum of good practice on video recorded interviews with child witnesses for criminal proceedings.* London: Author.

Home Office (2007). *Achieving best evidence in criminal proceedings: Guidance on interviewing victims and witnesses, and using special measures.* London: Author.

Jones, D. P. H., & McQuiston, M. G. (1988). *Interviewing the Sexually Abused Child.* London: Gaskell.

Kaye, K., & Charney, R. (1981). Conversational asymmetry between mothers and children. *Journal of Child Language, 8,* 35–49.

Ladd, N. E., London, K., & Bruck, M. (March 2011). *Children's developing understanding of dolls and drawings as symbols to map body touch.* Paper presented at the meeting of the American Psychology-Law Society, Miami, FL.

Lamb, M. E., Hershkowitz, I., Orbach, Y., & Esplin, P. W. (2008). *Tell Me What Happened: Structured Investigative Interviews of Child Victims and Witnesses*. West Sussex, England: Wiley.

Lemasson, A., Glas, L., Barbu, S., Lacroix, A., Guilloux, M., Remeuf, K., & Koda, H. (2011). Youngsters do not pay attention to conversational rules: Is this so for nonhuman primates? *Scientific Reports, 1.*

Lilienfeld, S. O. (2007). Psychological treatments that cause harm. *Perspectives on Psychological Science, 2*, 53–70.

London, K., Bruck, M., Ceci, S. J., & Shuman, D. W. (2005). Disclosure of child sexual abuse: What does the research tell us about the ways that children tell? *Psychology, Public Policy, and Law, 11*, 194–226.

Lyon, T. D. (2005). *Ten step investigative interview*. Retrieved from http://works.bepress.com/thomaslyon/5/

McCauley, M. R., & Fisher, R. P. (1995). Facilitating children's eyewitness recall with the revised Cognitive Interview. *Journal of Applied Psychology, 80*, 510–516.

McGough, L. S. (1994). *Child Witnesses: Fragile Voices in the American Legal System*. New Haven, CT: Yale University Press.

Merrick, J., & Carmeli, E. (2003). A review on the prevalence of disabilities in children. *Internet Journal of Pediatrics and Neonatology, 3*(1). Retrieved from http://www.ispub.com/ostia/index.php?xmlFilePath=journals/ijpn/vol3n1/prevalence.xml.

Myers, J. E. B. (2004). *Child Protection in America: Past, Present, and Future*. New York: Oxford University Press.

Pipe, M.-E., & Salmon, K. (2009). Dolls, drawings, body diagrams, and other props: Role of props in investigative interviews. In K. Kuehnle & M. Connell (Eds), *The Evaluation of Child Sexual Abuse Allegations: A Comprehensive Guide to Assessment and Testimony* (pp. 365–395). Hoboken, NJ: Wiley.

Poole, D. A., Bruck, M., & Pipe, M.-E. (2011). Forensic interviewing aids: Do props help children answer questions about touching? *Current Directions in Psychological Science, 20*, 11–15.

Poole, D. A., & Dickinson, J. J. (2011). Evidence supporting restrictions on uses of body diagrams in forensic interviews. *Child Abuse & Neglect, 35*, 654–669.

Poole, D. A., & Lamb, M. E. (1998). *Investigative Interviews of Children: A Guide for Helping Professionals*. Washington, DC: American Psychological Association.

Rischke, A. E., Roberts, K. P., & Price, H. L. (2011). Using spaced learning principles to translate knowledge into behavior: Evidence from investigative interviews of alleged child abuse victims. *Journal of Police and Criminal Psychology, 26*, 58–67.

Roberts, K., & Duncanson, S. (March 2011). *Enhancing children's testimony with the facilitative interview technique*. Paper presented at the meeting of the American Psychology-Law Society, Miami, FL.

Saywitz, K. J. (1988). The credibility of child witnesses. *Family Advocate, 10*(3), 38–41.

Shelton, K., Bridenbaugh, H., Farrenkopf, M., & Kroeger, K. (2008). *Project ability: demystifying disability in child abuse interviewing*. Portland, OR: CARES Northwest. Retrieved from http://www.oregon.gov/DHS/children/committees/cja/proj-abil.pdf?ga=t.

State of Maine Child and Family Services (2010). *State of Maine Child and Family Services Fact-Finding Child Interview Protocol*. Author.

Steller, M., & Köhnken, G. (1989). Criteria-based statement analysis. In D. Raskin (Ed.), *Psychological Methods in Criminal Investigation and Evidence* (pp. 217–245). New York: Springer.

Stivers, T., Enfield, N. J., Brown, P., Englert, C., Hayashi, M., Heinemann, T., Hoymann, G., Rossano, F., De Ruiter, J. P., Yoon, K. -E., Levinson, S. C. (2009). Universals and cultural variation in turn-taking in conversation. *Proceedings of the National Academy of Science,* *106,* 10587–10592.

Trankell, A. (1972). *Reliability of Evidence.* Stockholm: Beckmans.

Undeutsch, V. (1982). Statement reality analysis. In A. Trankell (Ed.), *Reconstructing the Past: The Role of Psychologists in Criminal Trials* (pp. 27–56). Deventer, the Netherlands: Kluwer.

U.S. Department of Education, Office of Special Education and Rehabilitative Services, Office of Special Education Programs (2009). *Annual report to Congress on the implementation of the Individuals with Disabilities Education Act, 2006* (Volume 1). Washington, D.C. Author.

Walker, A. G. (1999). *Handbook on Questioning Children: A Linguistic Perspective* (2nd edn). Washington, DC: American Bar Association Center on Children and the Law.

Warren, A. R., Woodall, C. E., Hunt, J. S., & Perry, N. W. (1996). "It sounds good in theory, but...": Do investigative interviewers follow guidelines based on memory research? *Child Maltreatment, 1,* 231–245.

Yuille, J. C. (1988). The systematic assessment of children's testimony. *Canadian Psychology,* *29,* 247–262.

Yuille, J. C., Cooper, B. S., & Hervé, H. H. F. (in press). The Step-Wise guidelines for child interviews: The new generation. In M. Casonato & F. Pfafflin (Eds), *Handbook of Pedosexuality and Forensic Science.*

Yuille, J. C., Hunter, R., Joffe, R., & Zaparniuk, J. (1993). Interviewing children in sexual abuse cases. In G. S. Goodman & B. L. Bottoms (Eds), *Child Victims, Child Witnesses: Understanding and Improving Testimony* (pp. 95–115). New York: Guilford.

# CHAPTER 7

# The Law and Science of Children's Testimonial Competency

J. Zoe Klemfuss and Stephen J. Ceci

In recent years, it has become increasingly likely that a young child's testimony will be admitted in court. This is partially due to an increased awareness of the seriousness and prevalence of crimes against children, and partially due to growing confidence in young children's ability to provide testimony. Because of the increasing reliance on children's testimony, the legal system has a vested interest in determining which children should be believed.

Part of determining the believability of a witness involves establishing their competence to provide testimony. In the most general sense, testimonial competency refers to a person's ability to provide useful testimony on the stand. A child's testimonial competency is considered separately from the accuracy and completeness of her testimony and from subjective opinions about the quality of her testimony, though theoretically all three concepts are related.

Generally, competency standards are undemanding: child witnesses are deemed competent in the United States if they are sufficiently intelligent to observe, recollect and recount an event, and if they have a moral sense of obligation to speak the truth. In England, Wales and Canada, the requirements are less stringent. Thus, most children, even preschoolers, can potentially be viewed as competent by courts. (In fact, some infrahuman primates can fulfill this requirement!). There are two main factors in the determination of competency – a cognitive one that concerns memory, perception and language, and in the United States (and previously in England, Wales and Canada), a moral one concerning the impiety of speaking falsehoods. In practice, courts are inept at distinguishing between these two factors, because the determination of a child's moral status is heavily influenced by the child's cognitive ability: that is, questions a judge or lawyer might ask of a child to probe the ability to understand the duty to tell the truth are dependent on a certain level of cognitive ability and, lacking this level of development, the child may appear morally incompetent when the real problem is their limited cognitive and linguistic ability. If interviewed in a developmentally sensitive manner, cognitive and linguistic limitations can be overcome to enable an honest child to provide the court with valuable information.

To understand the current state of testimonial competency determinations, it is useful to consider both the law regarding testimonial competency and the recent empirical literature on the topic. This chapter will also cover evidence that points to discrepancies between competence determination, accuracy, and credibility.

## Competence law in the United States, England and Canada

In 1779, a five-year-old girl named Mary Harris told her mother that a man sexually assaulted her while she was on her way home (1 Leach 199, 168 E.R. 202 (1779)). In the resulting landmark case of *King v. Brasier* (1 Leach, 1779), Harris's mother testified on her behalf. However, the English appellate court found that Harris's "testimony" could not be considered at trial because it was not taken under oath. The decision hinged on the issue of testimonial competency:

> an infant, though under the age of seven years, may be sworn in a criminal pros-
> ecution, provided such infant appears, on strict examination by the Court, to
> possess a sufficient knowledge of the nature and consequences of an oath...

In other words, the decision not to include Harris's out-of-court testimony was based on the decision that knowledge about the oath, and not a child's age, should be considered when deciding testimonial competency.

On 2 January 1895, George L. Wheeler was found guilty of murder (*Wheeler v. United States*, 1895). The 4-year-old son of the deceased man witnessed the murder and provided pivotal testimony at trial that resulted in a death sentence for Wheeler. Wheeler appealed the decision and his attorney argued that the boy's testimony should not be considered because he was only 5 years old when he testified. The original decision was affirmed with the following argument:

> That the boy was not by reason of his youth, as a matter of law, absolutely dis-
> qualified as a witness is clear. While no one should think of calling as a witness
> an infant only two or three years old, there is no precise age which determines
> the question of competency. This depends on the capacity and intelligence of

the child, his appreciation of the difference between truth and falsehood, as well as of his duty to tell the former. (p. 523)

This decision influenced competence law in two pivotal ways. First, it provided support for the *King v. Brasier* ruling in a U.S. court. Second, it established some long-standing guidelines for determining testimonial competency in the U.S., English and Canadian courts.

## Competence law in the United States

The majority of this chapter focuses on U.S. competence law, which retains a significant portion of the English common law regarding children's competency. Despite the passage of nearly twelve decades since Judge Whitney's decision in *Wheeler v. U.S.*, and several decades of empirical research on eyewitness testimony, testimonial competency standards in the United States have remained relatively untouched. The only adjustment to the content of the rules is that the standard requiring "sufficient intelligence" has been expanded to include two related standards of cognitive capacity. While competency standards vary from state to state, today the most expansive competency standards require that a person (1) understand and answer simple interview questions, (2) have the capacity to observe and recall events, (3) understand the difference between the truth and a lie, and (4) understand the obligation to tell the truth.

The United States Federal Rules of Evidence (FRE) state that everyone is considered competent to testify if they can prove that they have personal knowledge of the event in question and if they understand and take an oath to be truthful on the stand. Proving personal knowledge of the event can be as simple as providing first-hand testimony about what transpired – so everyone who witnessed the event meets this standard. The requirement of the oath has been adapted in the most recent rules so that it no longer requires the specific language that we think of when we imagine a courtroom scenario. Instead, courts have the flexibility to use any wording they think is most appropriate for the witness. This adaptation is in line with empirical evidence demonstrating that the classic legalese in the oath was not appropriate for some witnesses, including, specifically, child witnesses (McGough, 1994).

Historically, courts have moved between extremes of allowing child testimony. Previously, children were not allowed to testify as witnesses because they were not believed competent as a group. However, today children as young as 3 years of age are presumed competent in most courts. unless a particular child's competence is brought into question in a case (*Child Victims and Child Witnesses Rights Act*, 1990; Myers, 1992). According to Rule 601 of the Federal Rules of Evidence, age alone may not be considered a compelling reason to question a person's competency.

If a child's competence is in question, the trial judge or counsel can probe that child's competence in the presence of the jury. If a child seems particularly incompetent, this could result in a competency hearing with only the judge, lawyers, court reporter and a supportive adult, for the welfare of the child present. Both legal parties may submit questions to be used in the competency examination, as long as all questions asked directly assess the child's ability to provide testimony and use child-appropriate language. Competency examinations are designed to only assess a child's general ability to provide testimony and, therefore, no issues relating to the trial can be discussed during the exam. The judge can also request evidence from another witness or request counsel from a psychologist or social worker, but the final decision is made by the judge (Gershman, 2001; Myers, 1997).

The Federal Rules of Evidence state that in most cases testimonial competency should be decided according to state law. Therefore, competency standards can vary from state to state within the U.S. Table 7.1 gives basic information about competency requirements for the ten most populated states in the United States at the 2009 Census. While most states are relatively consistent with each other, and with federal standards, there is some variation in competency requirements. For example, while federal standards specify that a child's age can no longer be considered as the *sole* determinant of her ability to provide legal testimony, in many states age still plays a role. Six out of

**Table 7.1** Competency considerations for the ten most populated US states

| Pop. Rank[a] | State | Language | Memory | Truth/Lie | Immaturity |
|---|---|---|---|---|---|
| 1 | California | Yes | Indirectly[b] | Yes | No |
| 2 | Texas | Indirectly[c] | Indirectly[c] | No | Yes |
| 3 | New York | Indirectly[d] | Indirectly[d] | Yes | Yes |
| 4 | Florida | Yes | Indirectly[e] | Yes | No |
| 5 | Illinois | Yes | Indirectly[f] | Yes | No |
| 6 | Pennsylvania | Yes | Yes | Yes | Yes |
| 7 | Ohio | Yes | Yes | Yes | Yes |
| 8 | Michigan | Indirectly[g] | Indirectly[g] | Yes | No |
| 9 | Georgia | No | No | Yes | Yes |
| 10 | North Carolina | Yes | Indirectly[h] | Yes | Yes |

*Notes:* [a] Population ranks according to the 2009 US census.
[b] Incompetent: "incapable of expressing himself or herself concerning the matter so as to be understood."
[c] Competent: "sufficient intellect to relate transactions."
[d] Competent: "sufficient intelligence or capacity."
[e] Incompetent: "incapable of expressing himself or herself concerning the matter in such a manner as to be understood."
[f] Incompetent: "incapable of expressing himself or herself concerning the matter so as to be understood."
[g] Competent: "sufficient physical and mental capacity or sense of obligation to testify truthfully and understandably."
[h] Incompetent: "incapable of expressing himself concerning the matter as to be understood."

10 of the states listed consider a witness's level of maturity when determining competency, and sometimes age is considered explicitly. In New York State, children under the age of 9 must demonstrate their understanding of the oath before being allowed to testify, and in Ohio, children under the age of 10 are subject to special competency scrutiny. However, the competency standards in most states are similar to the federal competency guidelines.

While full competency hearings have become less common, trial judges make other legal decisions that previously would have fallen into the category of competency determination (Myers, 1986–1987). The competency requirements discussed so far determine whether or not a child can be heard in court. However, competency-like decisions can be made at any point in the trial process and can result in a child's testimony being nullified. For example, a trial judge can exclude a child's testimony because it is not relevant or because the child lacks sufficient "personal knowledge" of the case. The judge can also decide to reserve a child's testimony and use it only if it is necessary to the case, or offer warnings about a child's testimonial abilities that may decrease the child's credibility in the eyes of the court. These alternate decisions are legal, even given Rule 601, but they can be used to reach the same end of excluding a child's testimony because of perceived incompetence. In short, "competency" decisions are more ubiquitous than they seem at first glance, because legal loopholes allow judges to make competency decisions without conducting official competency hearings.

## Competence law in England & Wales

Relatively recent legal reform in England and Wales has had a major impact on how courts receive children's testimony (*Youth Justice and Criminal Evidence Act*, 1999). First, both the semantic and moral tests regarding truths and lies have been eliminated from the exam. In other words, children are not required to demonstrate truth and lie competence before testifying. In fact, children under the age of 14 are not required to testify under oath. Instead, juries are admonished to consider children's unsworn testimony with the same weight that they would consider sworn testimony. There is also no explicit memory component to the competency exam. In sum, a child's testimonial competency boils down to whether or not he is able to "understand questions put to him as a witness, and give answers to them which can be understood" (c. 23, s. 53(3)).

Second, courts liberally allow courtroom accommodations for child witnesses in order to reduce stress and enhance children's testimonial abilities. Most of these accommodations are available to other countries, including the United States, but they are far more likely to be utilized in England and Wales.

These accommodations include shielding the child so that she is unable to see the defendant while testifying, allowing children to provide testimony via closed-circuit television, testifying in private, removal of robes and wigs, and allowing videotaped testimony as evidence. These types of accommodations are discussed later in further detail.

## Competence law in Canada

The Child Witness Project is a group of Canadian researchers who have contributed to major recent reforms in Canadian competence law through systematic research and advocacy (see below for a discussion of the empirical literature). Their work focuses on the truth and lie components of testimonial competency, which previously took center stage in Canada (and is still the focus of competency determinations in the United States). In 2006, on advice from the Child Witness Project, the truth and lie components of the competency exam were removed from Canadian law, though, unlike in England and Wales, the oath is still required. This distinction is of critical importance, as will become clear in the empirical discussion below.

## General discussion

No matter what legal mechanism is used to exclude a child's testimony, the final decision is always made by the court, who often has no special training involving children or in developmental research (Cashmore & Bussey, 1996; Myers, 1992). To compound this issue, there are no empirically validated tests of testimonial competence currently used in courts (Cashmore & Bussey, 1996; Seton Hall L. Review, 2010).

Further, as will be discussed in detail below, there are few standards for the administration of competency exams, and there are few studies examining the predictive value of these exams. What little research there is suggests that current exams are not predictive of the quality of children's testimony (e.g. London & Nunez, 2002; Leach et al., 2004). That is, children who pass competency exams are no more likely to accurately report their experiences than are children who fail them. Interestingly, cross-examination does not appear to help. Several experiments (e.g. Zajac & Hayne, 2006) show that children are as likely to change their formerly accurate answers during cross-examination as they are to change their previously inaccurate answers. With young children, cross-examination does not appear to be the great legal engine driving the truth-seeking process that Wigmore (1923) famously described.

In sum, children's performance on competency interviews is not predictive of their cognitive accuracy in perceiving and recalling experienced events, and this may be because the typical competency questions are developmentally uninformed.

# Recent legal cases in the United States

Next, we review in detail several recent legal cases involving an appeal in which the defendant challenged the competency of a preschool-aged witness. These cases demonstrate how legal decisions about young children's testimonial competency are made.

### Everette v. Lewis (2011)

In 1988, Larry Anthony Everette was convicted of three counts of first degree rape and three counts of first-degree sexual offense against his 3-year-old stepdaughter and was sentenced to five concurrent life terms and one consecutive life term of imprisonment. In March 2010, he filed a *habeas* petition (a petition demanding a prisoner's release), in which one of his claims was that his stepdaughter had been incompetent to testify about prior incidents. The petition was denied because more than 20 years had elapsed since the trial and the statute of limitations had expired.

### Reyes v. Blacketter (2010)

In 2001, Juan Manuel Reyes was convicted of sexually abusing his three nieces, who were 2, 4, and 5 years old. In 2008, Reyes filed a federal *habeas corpus*. Amongst his complaints was the claim that his counsel was ineffective because they did not object to the inclusion of hearsay testimony from two of the alleged child victims, both of whom were found incompetent to testify. His appeal was denied because the judge found that Reyes' lawyer acted in accordance with the law at the time, which was more lax regarding admission of hearsay evidence. Later, we revisit the issue of hearsay.

### Vaughn v. State (2011)

The defendant was found guilty of multiple charges against two child witnesses, including child molestation. The younger victim testified at trial when she was 4 years old about events that occurred when she was 2 years old. Vaughn appealed the conviction, claiming that his counsel was ineffective for not challenging the witness's competency. However, the case was tried in Georgia, where all child witnesses in criminal cases are automatically presumed competent to testify. Further, she demonstrated knowledge of the difference between the truth and a lie, and promised to tell the truth before providing testimony. The original judgment was affirmed.

## Claywell v. State (2010)

Claywell appealed the use of a 4-year-old child's testimony in a prior trial against him. He claimed that the child witness was not competent because his testimony was "contradictory and confused." The judge in the original trial questioned the witness about the difference between the truth and a lie, and asked him to promise to tell the truth. Further, issues with the consistency and quality of a child's testimony are considered issues of credibility to be decided by the court and are not considered relevant to competency. Therefore, the appeals court supported the original decision regarding the witness's competency.

## L.M. v. State (2010)

L.M. was a juvenile who was convicted of the equivalent of child molestation. He appealed the decision by claiming that the court did not sufficiently examine the 3-year-old witness's competency prior to trial and that her testimony at trial demonstrated incompetence. The appeals court affirmed the decision of the trial court because (1) there was evidence that the child witness met the truth and lie requirements for competency; (2) because L.M. did not object during the original trial, in which case the judge would have conducted a more thorough competency exam; and (3) because, "To be qualified to testify, a child need not be a model witness, have an infallible memory, or refrain from making inconsistent statements." *Id.* (quoting *Casselman v. State*, 582 N.E.2d 432, 435 (Ind. Ct. App. 1991)). Instead, these points are reserved as issues of credibility to be decided by the trial court.

## Commonwealth v. Patton (2010)

In *Commonwealth v. Patton*, the petitioner claimed that a 4-year-old child's hearsay testimony should not have been admitted because the child was not competent to testify. However, the basic requirements for reliability of the hearsay were met. The hearsay was a videotaped forensic interview taken soon after the alleged event took place. The accused also did not object to the testimony before it was given, which is the appropriate time to request a competency decision. Finally, the judge screened the child's videotaped statement and found that:

> There was evidence that the child understood that she could receive a spanking if she told a lie. The child was able to describe her experience in detail, and she repeated the detail several times with consistency. She demonstrated sufficient cognitive and communication skills and memory. Based on this record, there was sufficient evidence to conclude that the child was competent.

Thus, within the videotaped statement, the judge found that the child demonstrated sufficient language, memory and truth/lie competency.

## State v. Mateo (2011)

Mateo was convicted of several counts of endangering the welfare of a child, abuse of a child and a count of assault. He argued on appeal that the child victim, who was 3 years old at the time of the crimes, and 4 years old at the time he provided testimony, was not competent to provide testimony at trial. The primary argument was that the oath was not administered to the child prior to his testimony. Because of the nature of the charges, the law in the state of Missouri states that all children are competent to testify unless they are "mentally incapacitated." The appeals court found that because the trial court established that the child witness understood his obligation to tell the truth in court, it was not necessary to administer the oath.

# Alternate means of providing testimony

What happens when a child is unable to provide sworn testimony? Even if a child meets the legal standards for competency, she may be too intimidated to speak in a courtroom, particularly in front of the accused. Because children are more likely than adults to be intimidated into silence or found incompetent to testify in court, they are more likely to provide evidence using alternate means. A child who is deemed incompetent to provide testimony in court may be allowed to make statements via closed-circuit television or prior videorecording, or a competent adult may testify about the child's prior statements.

Though these options are rarely available to children in the United States, in England and Wales they are frequently used to encourage and enhance child testimony (Troxel et al., 2009).

Testifying via closed-circuit television is reserved for children who meet the testimonial competence requirements, but who experts believe would be unable to provide testimony in the stressful court environment. For example, a child who is likely to be paralyzed by the fear of facing the accused might be allowed to sit in a separate room in the courthouse and answer questions via closed-circuit television. This method allows for live questioning of the child without direct confrontation with the accused. In the United States, because the confrontation clause of the 6th Amendment to the Constitution requires that defendants be allowed to face their accusers, and closed-circuit television denies them this right, it is only permitted in extreme circumstances.

Providing testimony via closed-circuit television minimizes the stress of the trial process on the child, and likely maximizes the odds that a child will testify at his or her peak competence level, particularly in cases where the child is crippled by fear or anxiety (Goodman et al., 1998). However, as will be discussed in the section on credibility, jurors are less swayed when testimony is provided remotely and are less likely to decide in favor of the child complainant. Therefore, while allowing some children to testify via closed-circuit television may be a necessary measure to protect their psychological well-being and to improve their testimonial abilities, it infringes on the rights of the defendant, and may decrease the weight of the child's testimony. Courts are probably wise to reserve this measure only for special circumstances unless at least the latter limitation can be remedied, for example by regarding the child's statements as non-testimonial albeit admissible if examined by a trained professional in the presence of counsel for both sides, a position recently advocated by some legal scholars, such as Friedman (see Friedman & Ceci, in preparation). However, the research which has demonstrated that providing evidence remotely decreases the weight of children's testimony has largely been conducted in the United States, where these measures are rare and unexpected. It is possible that there may be reduced stigma surrounding remote testimony, and, therefore, reduced impact on credibility ratings in the UK.

The next two categories of testimony fall under the umbrella of *hearsay* according to U.S. law. Hearsay refers to "... a statement, other than one made by the declarant while testifying at the trial or hearing, offered in evidence to prove the truth of the matter asserted" (FRE 801). Hearsay is generally not allowed in U.S. courts, but some important exceptions are sometimes made for child witnesses, particularly if they have been found incompetent to testify in court.

There are two primary methods of providing hearsay in the place of a child's in-court testimony. The first method is to show a videotaped interview in which a child made statements relevant to the case, and the second method is to allow a competent adult to report disclosures the child made outside of the courtroom. In a case in which a child was able to provide relevant statements on tape while being interviewed by law enforcement or a forensic interviewer, but is unable to communicate in the courtroom environment, the videotaped interview might be submitted as evidence in lieu of in-court testimony. This form of testimony is more frequently allowed in courts in England and Wales.

Witnesses can also talk about disclosures or other relevant statements child witnesses made to them if a videotaped interview is not available. For example, in *White v. Illinois* (502 U.S. 3xx, 1992), 3-year-old Nathan Siler made statements to an officer investigating the murder of his mother. Although Nathan did not appear agitated in his conversation with the officer, his statements incriminating his father in the murder were admitted under the hearsay exception of an "excited utterance," allowing the officer to testify in Nathan's absence. Meaning, the court decided that Nathan was still in a state of shock or stress resulting from the murder when he made the statement. Hearsay testimony can also supplement a videotaped interview or in-court statement.

# Empirical literature on testimonial competency

In the following sections, we will review the extant empirical literature on the components of testimonial competency. The first three sections review literature in the general area of children's abilities to understand and answer simple interview questions, observe and recall important events and information, and understand truths and lies. Finally, we will discuss some preliminary findings specifically concerning testimonial competency exams.

## Understanding and answering simple interview questions

When a child's testimonial competence is called into question, their ability to understand and answer simple interview questions is generally assessed through a short interview with the presiding judge, with or without council or jury present (Myers, 1997). There is also some empirical evidence that children with higher language scores have more accurate memory reports about past events (e.g. Kulkofsky, 2010; Kulkofsky, Wang, & Ceci, 2008).

The problem is, however, that as basic as this competency may seem, the ability to effectively communicate in a legal setting is extremely complex, and can be challenging even for competent children (Korkman, Santtila, Drzewiecki, & Sandnabba, 2008; Saywitz & Goodman, 1996; Saywitz, Snyder, & Nathanson, 1999; Walker, 1993).

Walker (1985, 1993) has analyzed court transcripts with an eye to the linguistic complexities involved in a standard case involving child witnesses. Her findings illustrate that the language used in court is "informal, illogical, ungrammatical...full of blunders and grievous errors and mutations...and characterized by endless sentences, false starts...and other crudities" (Walker, 1985, p. 115). Walker (1993) provides a detailed case analysis in which she examines the full court transcripts from interviews with a 5-year-old girl. She gives concrete examples of instances of semantic, syntactic and pragmatic complexity that are far beyond the developmental level of a preschool-aged child. In a particularly dramatic example of syntactic complexity, the girl was asked, "Do you also recall driving in a car a day or two after Doug – you found out that Doug – that something had happened to him and telling and pointing out houses as being the place where the people or one of the people who hurt Doug lived" (p. 68). As phrased, many adults would likely have difficulty unpacking the intent and providing a meaningful response. Recently, Angela Evans and her colleagues have demonstrated with actual trial transcripts that confronting children with complex syntax can boomerang, causing defense attorneys, but not prosecutors, to lose verdicts (Evans, Lee, & Lyon, 2009).

When the language of the interview is developmentally inappropriate or too complex for a particular child, children are likely to try to answer the question anyway. Fritzley and Lee (2003) asked preschool-aged children questions that were answerable, and questions that were nonsensical to see whether they would respond in predictable ways. Overall, children rarely answered "I don't know" to the nonsensical questions, and the youngest children exhibited a tendency to acquiesce to the experimenter. This finding suggests that when children's language skills limit their understanding of questions posed to them, they are still likely to attempt and answer, and thus their responses are likely less accurate overall.

The developmentally inappropriate language used in court (see Evans et al., 2009) makes it difficult for any child to provide reliable testimony, no matter what their relative competence at understanding and answering questions may be. However, competency examinations may still be helpful in determining which children can provide quality testimony, and to what degree, in instances where they are asked developmentally appropriate questions. In addition, competency determinations could potentially guide well-trained forensic interviewers to ask questions at appropriate levels of complexity in interviews that occur outside of court. Children with low language scores may require interviewers to be particularly mindful of the vocabulary and structure used in interview questions. These interviews can be critical pieces of evidence in cases involving child witnesses and in some cases out of court testimony may be the only evidence from a child witness (see Hall & Sales, 2008).

Validly and reliably determining individual differences in children's abilities to understand and answer simple interview questions is a daunting task. Children are often interviewed by professionals with experience interviewing children at some point in the pre-trial process, and these professionals are advised in the literature to make note of children's communicative abilities (ex: Myers, 1992, p. 52). However, these evaluations are merely recommendations to the court, and are not necessarily deciding factors in a child's competency determination. Moreover, these reports of children's language competence are seldom based on validated normative scales, forcing the court to infer what the child's linguistic status means in the context of the case at bar. The guidelines for judicial competency examinations are also extremely open-ended. Although courts have the responsibility to assess a child's ability to understand and answer questions, they are not given specific questions or tests to administer. Cashmore and Bussey (1996) found that there was a wide range of techniques used by judges to determine competency. While this study was conducted with Australian courts, the reliability issue is applicable to the United States, Canada, England and Wales. Because there is no standard test of children's communicative competency to be used in legal settings, we are limited in determining the validity of these tests, and communicative competency determinations are not likely to be reliable. Courts are in need of a practical, valid, and reliable test of communicative competency.

## Observing and recalling important events and information

Here, we briefly review the limited research on individual differences in children's memory and reporting abilities. The most consistent individual difference in memory ability and suggestibility is age. On average, older children and adults remember more accurate information and are less suggestible than are young children. However, competency decisions are not, and should not be, made solely on the basis of age, because there are wide individual differences in accuracy within age groups and because, in some contexts, young children are more accurate than are young children and adults. This insight appears to have been held by courts for centuries. In the *R v. Brasier* case mentioned earlier, involving the alleged assault of a young child, the Twelve

Judges, a group of common law judges who informally deliberated questions of law in eighteenth- and nineteenth-century England (Oldham, 2011), wrote that:

> there is no precise or fixed rule as to the time within which infants are excluded from giving evidence; but their admissibility depends upon the sense and reason they entertain of the danger and impiety of falsehood, which is to be collected from their answers to questions propounded to them by the Court.

There is limited research which explores individual differences in children's memory skills (Bauer, 2004). While it is clear that children vary considerably in their abilities to remember and to accurately report those memories at any given instance, there is little research which examines whether children have stable differences in memory abilities. In other words, few studies have examined whether a child's general memory skills are predictive of the accuracy of their recall in a given instance.

A majority of the limited research on memory as an individual difference variable has focused on forensic issues such as suggestibility (Bauer, 1996). For example, Leichtman and Ceci (1995) biased a group of children with stereotypes and interviewed the children repeatedly and suggestively to examine the effects on the children's memory reports. While some children eventually incorporated all four suggested, stereotype-consistent items into their memory reports, some children resisted all attempts at suggestion. Therefore, while some children are prone to incorporating suggestive details, not all children are suggestible. There are also reliable tests of individual differences in suggestibility which indicates that susceptibility to suggestion is a quantifiable individual difference, and that suggestibility in one domain appears to predict suggestibility in unrelated domains (Gudjonsson, 1984, 1987; Scullin & Ceci, 2001). Bruck and Melnyk (2004) published a thorough review of the literature on individual differences and suggestibility and found that while the cognitive factors that were most consistently related to suggestibility were language ability and creativity, there was some mixed evidence that general memory skills were also predictive of children's resistance to suggestion.

Not only is there evidence that there are individual differences in memory accuracy and resistance to suggestion within age groups, but there is also a body of recent evidence demonstrating that in some contexts young children may be *more* accurate than their older counterparts. For example, children's limited knowledge of semantic associations has been shown to limit their suggestibility when the suggestions concern items that are semantically related to true items. Older children and adults are more susceptible to these types of suggestions than are younger children who lack this knowledge (Brainerd &

Reyna, 2007; Brainerd, Reyna, & Ceci, 2008; Ceci, Papierno, & Kulkofsky, 2007). Therefore, younger children are not always more suggestible than older children and adults.

In summary, there is significant variability in preschool-aged children's abilities to provide accurate testimony and to resist suggestion. Because of the breadth of individual differences in children's abilities to recall events, predicting children's competency in this domain could prove critical in order to ensure a fair trial. However, the determination of a child's ability to observe and recall the events relevant to a case currently suffers from the same limitations in reliability and validity as the assessment of a child's ability to understand and answer interview questions. Additionally, the empirical literature on the topic is especially limited. Judges have the freedom to determine competence using their own discretion and are provided with only skeletal guidelines with which to make those assessments. This process necessarily leads to inconsistencies in assessment (Cashmore & Bussey, 1996).

## Knowledge about truths and lies

In order to provide accurate testimony, children must not only meet a threshold of language and memory skills, but they must also be motivated to provide accurate testimony – they must be honest. In England, honesty is not examined in competency decisions; new Canadian policy relies on the oath to enhance children's honesty; and in the United States, children are regularly still required to demonstrate knowledge about truths and lies as was required by the Brasier Court in 1779, "... [children's] admissibility depends upon the sense and reason they entertain of the danger and impiety of falsehood, which is to be collected from their answers to questions propounded to them by the Court" 1 Leach, 1779, 202–203. Research has amply demonstrated that young children can, and will lie to adults for multiple reasons. Children will sometimes lie to avoid punishment, to sustain a game, to keep a promise/protect a loved one, to achieve personal gain or to avoid embarrassment (see Ceci & Bruck, 1995, for a review). Importantly, Lyon, Malloy, Quas and Talwar (2008) found that children are susceptible to coaching by a parent to conceal the parent's transgression. In fact, some research paradigms rely on lying behaviors in preschool-aged children (London & Nunez, 2002; Talwar & Lee, 2008; Talwar, Lee, Bala, and Lindsay, 2002). A paradigm used by London and Nunez (2002), Talwar et al. (2002) and Talwar & Lee (2008) to examine contextual effects on lying behavior involves instructing children not to peek at a concealed object or toy when the interviewer leaves the room. The room is surveyed by a hidden video camera to observe children's behaviors. In these studies, the lying rates for the children who peeked were as high as 90 percent.

The most frequently studied components of testimonial competency are children's ability to distinguish truths from lies and children's understanding of their moral obligation to tell the truth. While the debate about how early children are capable of lying is long-standing (Piaget, 1932), the relationship of their understanding of truth-telling and their truth-telling behavior has only recently been empirically tested. The research on children's truth and lie competency has taken two approaches. The first is designed to assess the predictive power of current competency exams for children's behavior, and the second strives to enhance the validity of the current exams.

It appears that from an early age, children have a basic grasp of what it means to tell the truth and an understanding that it is good to tell the truth (Pipe & Wilson, 1994). In fact, young children often have more rigid defini-tions of morality than do adults (Kohlberg, 1963; Piaget, 1932). Haugaard, Repucci, Laird and Nauful (1991) showed preschool-aged children a video in which a young girl is coached by her mother to lie to the police, or a video in which she is not coached. The children were then interviewed to see whether they thought the girl lied when she told the police incorrect information. The authors hypothesized that because of immature knowledge of what it means to lie, and because of children's susceptibility to social pressure by authority figures, children would not consider the false information provided by the mother as a lie. However, they found that even the preschoolers said that the girl was lying if she told the police incorrect information. It did not matter whether the girl in the video was instructed to lie by her mother. The authors also read children a vignette in which one child lied to protect a friend from punishment and they found that nearly every child (91 percent) agreed that saying something that was untrue was a lie even if it was to protect a friend.

It has been demonstrated that if children are interviewed in an age-appro-priate manner, they can be competent at answering questions testing their understanding of the truth/lie distinction and their understanding of the importance of telling the truth (Pipe & Wilson, 1994). Interviews that are appropriate for young children reduce the need for conceptual description of terms and rely on concrete demonstrations of truths and lies. For example, preschool-aged children are generally accurate at answering questions such as, "If I told you I had purple hair, would that be the truth or a lie?" On the other hand, young children have difficulty answering questions that call for abstract conceptualizations, such as, "What is the difference between the truth and a lie?" The downside to these types of competency questions is that they may underestimate young children's appreciation of truth/lie dis-tinctions. Children can also be accurate when answering simple, concrete questions about the morality of lying. For example, they are often accurate at answering a question such as, "Is it good/bad to tell the truth/a lie?" (Myers, 1997). The downside to these latter types of competency exams, however, is that they involve exclusively closed-ended and forced-choice questions, which are often more leading than the open-ended variety (e.g. Fritzley & Lee, 2003).

Empirical work has failed to find a clear relationship between these competency tests and children's lie-telling behavior. While most children are able to pass the truth and lie sections of legal competency exams, their performance on these exams does not often predict whether they will lie or tell the truth. It is unclear whether this is an artifact of the methods employed to test children's knowledge, or whether children's behavior simply does not reflect their knowledge in this context.

Talwar et al. (2002) interviewed 3–7-year-old children using hypothetical scenarios, where either the child or an imaginary character had the opportunity to lie or tell the truth about a transgression. Nearly every child demonstrated knowledge of truths and lies, indicated that the imaginary character should not lie to conceal a transgression, and that they would not lie to protect themselves. However, performance on these measures did not predict truth-telling performance. Many of the children lied to conceal their own transgression, despite successfully passing the competency exam.

Talwar et al. (2002) engaged children in a conceptual discussion about lies and truths and gave them the opportunity to lie. For half the children the conceptual discussion came first, and for half the children the opportunity to lie came first. The authors found that the order of presentation did not matter. This implies that truth and lie components of competency exams do not predict behavior, and further, that having these conversations does not make children more truthful. However, when children promised to tell the truth, their truth-telling behavior increased. Therefore, Talwar et al. (2002) suggest that taking the oath is more likely to increase children's truthfulness than is measuring their understanding of truth v. lies, or their understanding of the morality of lying. It is also more likely to influence their truth-telling behavior than is having a discussion about truths and lies.

London and Nunez (2002) similarly tested the relationship between children's truth-telling knowledge and performance. They found that children's performance on competency exams did not predict their truth-telling behavior but that children who participated in these discussions were less likely to lie to experimenters about minor transgressions. Thus, neither Talwar et al. (2002) nor London and Nunez (2002) found a relationship between truth/lie competency and truth-telling performance. However, there is a discrepancy in their respective findings concerning the benefits of truth/lie discussions. Talwar et al. (2002) found that truth/lie discussion had no impact on children's truth-telling behavior and London and Nunez (2002) found that the discussion improved children's memory performance. This is likely because the truth-lie discussions in London and Nunez (2002) included requests for children to tell the truth, which is similar to the beneficial effect of taking the oath in the Talwar et al. (2002) study. Therefore, it may be the case that it was the oath alone that led to increased accuracy in the London and Nunez (2002) results. In fact, in a study with 8–16-year-olds, Evans and Lee (2010) found that this was the case. In Study 1, they found reduced lying behavior when children had a moral discussion about lying and promised to be honest, and in Study 2, they found that it was the promise alone that enhanced truthful behavior. Based on this body of research, it appears that the updated Canadian policy which requires children to promise to be truthful, but not to demonstrate knowledge of the distinction between truths and lies or to demonstrate knowledge of the moral obligation to be truthful, is the most empirically valid.

## Previous research on testimonial competence

There have been some efforts to develop reliable tests of children's competence. In an unpublished pilot, Hansen (1990) designed a functional test of two components of competency, (1) *understanding of the obligation of an oath*, and (2) *sufficient intelligence and capacity*. The test was piloted on a non-representative sample of 17 children including 1st–4th graders, and 7th graders. The test had high inter-rater reliability and high internal consistency on all measures. However, attempts at external validity were not successful, and the pilot did not include measures of predictive validity.

The second study examined a number of child variables, including language ability, as predictors of testimonial performance (Jacobson, 2002). The outcome variables for the study included factors relating to the narrative quality of children's responses as well as child demeanor on the stand and case outcome. Because court transcripts were examined instead of controlled staged-events, the accuracy of the children' reports could not be directly examined. The competency ratings had no relationship with case outcomes. Children's verbal skills were associated only with the confidence children demonstrated on the stand, and not with the quality of testimony. While this in-depth study of children's testimonial abilities provides insight into the qualities of children's in-court testimony and provides high ecological validity, it cannot address the issue of predictive validity.

Lyon and Saywitz (1999, 2000) have developed a theoretically reliable test of children's knowledge of truths and lies, and understanding of the distinction between truths and lies. For each task, children are presented with four images with accompanying stories. For example, to test children's knowledge of the distinction between the truth and a lie, children see an image of two children who are looking at a truck. Speech bubbles above the children's heads indicate that one child says that the truck is a truck and the other child says it is an airplane. Participants are then asked which child is telling the truth. This is repeated four times, each with different scenarios.

The process for testing understanding of the consequences of lying is quite similar. Participants are shown images in which two children are standing in front of an adult authority figure. For example, in one scenario, they both stand in front of a judge. Children are told that one of the children told the truth to the judge and the other child told a lie to the judge, and are then asked which child would likely get into trouble. Children's passing scores require that they answer questions about all four scenarios correctly. These tests are useful because they reduce children's reliance on language and passing scores on the tests mean that children scored significantly above chance because they respond to four different scenarios rather than a single yes–no question.

## Children's credibility as witnesses

> No mental or moral qualifications for testifying as a witness are specified. Standards of mental capacity have proved elusive in actual application. A leading commentator observes that few witnesses are disqualified on that ground. Discretion is regularly exercised in favor of allowing the testimony. A witness wholly without capacity is difficult to imagine. The question is one particularly suited to the jury as one of weight and credibility, subject to judicial authority to review the sufficiency of the evidence. (Advisory committee note to FRE 601)

Because of the limited research and limited guidelines for assessing testimonial competency, some legal commentators and even the Advisory Committee for the Federal Rules of Evidence (above) have suggested that competency assessments be used infrequently or not at all. The argument is that children should be presumed to be as competent as an adult witness would be and that it would be up to the jury to decide how much weight and credibility to assign to the child's testimony (see McLain, 2012). This decision shifts the burden from a decision by the judge to a decision by a jury, and requires that a child provide testimony before the decision about the child's testimonial ability is made.

Judging a child's credibility is no simple task. In fact, even professionals who are trained and experienced in credibility assessment (i.e. customs officers trained to detect child abductions) are often no better than chance at establishing whether a particular child has provided accurate testimony (Leach et al., 2004). This is especially true if a child's report has been tainted by suggestion (Bruck & Ceci, 1999). There are very few differences between the memory narrative of a child who has incorporated suggestions into their report and that of a child who is accurate.

However, research has identified some child characteristics and some situational characteristics that jury-eligible adults use to make decisions about a child's credibility. While there is a potentially infinite list of factors that might influence credibility ratings of a child witness, we will discuss some of the more commonly studied factors. Child age is one individual difference which tends to influence credibility ratings. However, the directionality of the relationship is unclear. Some work has demonstrated that adults tend to have less faith in the credibility of young children, while others have found that adults generally find young children more credible than adults.

Goodman, Golding, Helgeson, Haith and Michelli (1987) presented adult participants with trial descriptions in which the eyewitness to the crime was either 6, 10, or 30 years old. In addition to age, the authors varied the type of crime witnessed, the manner in which the trial description was presented (written or video) and the population of adults who participated (college students or the general population). They found that the only significant variable was child age. Adults rated older witnesses as more credible than they did younger witnesses.

Ross, Dunning, Toglia and Ceci (1990) conducted a similar study, but had the opposite result. In one experiment, adult participants viewed a video of a staged trial involving either an 8-year-old witness or an adult witness. In the second experiment, the adults read transcripts of the same trial, again involving either a child or adult witness. The dialogue in the videos and transcripts was the same in each condition, except that the witness was presented as either a child or an adult. The authors found that children were rated higher than were adults on several measures of credibility (e.g. confidence and honesty were higher for children in both the video and transcript conditions, and children were rated higher on general credibility in the video condition only). There were no differences in convictions based on the age of the child witness. Several studies have found similar results (e.g. Nightingale, 1993; Ruva & Bryant, 2004).

Often, studies that present the witness as a bystander have found that credibility increases with age, as in the Goodman et al. (1987) study, and studies that present the witness as a victim have found the opposite result. However, this is not always the case. For example, Ross et al. (1990) above found that children were viewed as more credible when they were presented as having been the witness in a case about cocaine possession. Another possible factor may be the jurors' implicit beliefs about the role of ulterior motives and the likelihood that a young child would harbor such motives.

Related to this point, Ross et al. (1990) point out that on the one hand, adults tend to believe that children have poorer memory and are more vulnerable to suggestion, when compared to older children and adults. On the other hand, adults generally perceive young children as being more honest than adults. They argue that, therefore, in studies that emphasize memory accuracy, adults view children as less credible, and in studies that emphasize honesty, adults view children as more credible. A potential example of this is that in cases where a witness could have a motive to lie, adults should be more prone to trust the testimony of a young child over the testimony of an adult, whereas in cases where the principal consideration is accuracy, adults should perceive other adults more favorably than children.

To take the examples described above, in the Goodman et al. (1987) study, the witness had no motive to lie because he was not personally invested in the outcome of the case. Instead, memory was paramount in describing the circumstances of the two cases presented – a vehicular homicide case and a murder case. In the Ross et al. (1990) study, the witness had more motive to lie because he was testifying against someone familiar – either a friend or parent, depending on the age of the witness. Therefore, the results obtained in the above studies are not surprising, based on the assumption that adult raters think adults have more accurate memories and are less honest than are children.

Several studies have demonstrated that honesty and cognitive ability such as memory are components that jury-eligible adults look for when assessing credibility. McCauley and Parker (2001) gave adult participants simulated court transcripts in which the victim was either described as 6 or 13 years of age. They found that participant assessments of honesty and memory ability predicted both adult ratings of child credibility, and participant assessments of what the length of sentence should be for the defendant.

Ross et al. (2003) directly tested the idea that adults focus on honesty and cognitive ability as the factors of interest when determining child credibility. Mock jurors watched a video in which a 10-year-old testified that she had been sexually abused. Mock jurors did, in fact, focus on the child's cognitive ability and honesty in their assessments of credibility. Adults who rated the girl more positively on these factors (higher cognitive ability and more honest) also rated the girl as more credible.

However, honesty and cognitive ability are not the only factors which have been demonstrated to affect adult ratings of child credibility. The way in which a child is interviewed also appears to influence perceptions of the child's credibility (Castelli, Goodman, & Ghetti, 2005; Ruva & Bryant, 2004; Tubb, Wood, & Hosch, 1999; Ross, Lindsay, & Marsil, 1999). This is a particularly important point for legal professionals and interviewers who are responsible for providing testimony to consider.

One difference in interviewing practice that influences credibility is that children who are interviewed in a leading or suggestive manner appear less credible to adults. Tubb et al. (1999) presented participants with written transcripts of a trial involving inappropriate touching. The transcripts varied only in that one-third of the transcripts were suggestive, one-third of them were focused, and one-third were open-narrative. Adult raters found that the children in the suggestive group were less credible, honest, competent, and intelligent, and participants were less likely to convict. Castelli et al. (2005) had similar results. Adults rated children's testimony as less credible when it was elicited by more suggestive techniques, even though children's responses were controlled so they provided the same information in the low-suggestive, medium-suggestive, and highly suggestive interview scenarios. Therefore, in these studies, child credibility was significantly determined by interviewer characteristics. As discussed above, recent evidence demonstrates that poor interviewing techniques can sometimes have the opposite result. Evans et al. (2009) demonstrated that when attorneys used more-complex language to interview child victims, jurys were *more* likely to convict.

Another contextual feature that influences credibility ratings is the physical means by which testimony is presented. Clinical work has studied the ways in which video deposition, remote testimony and testimony via closed-circuit television may be psychologically beneficial or harmful in individual cases in which children are asked to provide testimony (Hall & Sales, 2008). The flip-side to this is the research which examines the impact of these alternate means of testimony on the credibility of the child providing testimony. Both factors must be weighed when deciding the means by which a child will testify. While some researchers have found that there are no differences in credibility ratings based on means of presentation of testimony (e.g. Ross et al., 1994), most have found that alternative presentation modes significantly decrease ratings of child credibility and may even decrease conviction rates (Eaton, Ball, & O'Callaghan, 2001; Goodman et al., 2006; Luus, Wells, & Turtle, 1995).

For example, Eaton et al. (2001) found that when children provided evidence either through video deposition or live in court, they were seen as more credible than if they provided evidence through videolink. Guilt ratings were significantly higher when children provided evidence in court rather than through video deposition or videolink. This implies that contextual factors outside of the testimony itself contribute to juror perceptions of child credibility.

Goodman et al. (2006) staged mock trials in which children gave evidence live, on videotape, or through hearsay evidence (via a social worker). A detailed path analysis demonstrated that increased exposure to child witnesses increased adult credibility ratings of the child witnesses. They found that live testimony was the most credible format tested, and, unlike Eaton et al. (2001), it was more credible than video deposition. This finding replicates and expands on Goodman et al.'s (1998) results that children's live testimony is more credible than is closed-circuit testimony.

As discussed briefly above, adults are generally quite poor at determining whether a child's testimony is accurate. The studies which do show that adults can distinguish between accurate and inaccurate children generally involve comparing children who are telling the truth and children who are spontaneously lying. Therefore, it is often the anxiety about lying that distinguishes the accurate from inaccurate children. However, children who are inaccurate through mistaken memory or suggestion are extremely difficult to distinguish from accurate children, especially over time (Ceci & Bruck, 1993; Bruck, Ceci, & Hembrooke, 1998). Shao and Ceci (2011) demonstrated that adults had a very difficult time discriminating between truths and inaccuracies when the latter were the product of suggestive interviews. Therefore, in many cases, the factors that adults use to distinguish child credibility are likely not useful for distinguishing child accuracy. However, there is some evidence that a subset of the variables adults use to decide credibility may also predict accuracy.

Our review of the child credibility literature has focused on variables associated with child age and variables associated with courtroom interviewing conditions. First, we noted that jurors make assumptions about memory abilities, suggestibility and honesty based on the witness' age, and that they then use those factors to establish credibility. We have already reviewed the literature pointing to a slow developmental trajectory for memory skills. On the whole, younger children tend to have poorer memory skills than do older children and adults. We have also discussed that, on the whole, resistance to suggestion increases with age. However, we reviewed evidence that honesty does not decrease with age, and, in fact, young children are often less honest than are their older counterparts. Therefore, it appears that two out of three of these lay conceptions about child witnesses are accurate.

The second link in the chain between child witness age and juror credibility decisions involves the relationships between memory, suggestibility, honesty and witness accuracy. We have already examined these relationships in the sections on the empirical literature on differences in competency. A child must be able to remember an event in order to provide accurate testimony about the event. However, as of yet, there is little to no evidence linking children's individual differences in general memory abilities and their accuracy in describing a specific event.

Therefore, while the lay adult is correct to assume that children's memory skills increase through adulthood, and there is some evidence that they are correct to use memory skills as a gauge of the child's accuracy, the latter argument requires more investigation. There is considerably more evidence demonstrating that young children are more suggestible than are older children and adults. While not all children are vulnerable to suggestion, on average, suggestibility decreases with age (though there are some important exceptions). Therefore, the assumption that children are more suggestible than are adults is generally correct. Further, a person who is vulnerable to suggestion is by definition, vulnerable to inaccurate reporting when they are subjected to suggestion. So, jurors are correct to assume that because children are more likely to be suggestible, they are more likely to provide inaccurate reports *if* they have been subjected to suggestion.

Jurors' assumptions about children's honesty, however, appear misguided and potentially damaging. We have reviewed evidence that a) young children are capable of lying for various reasons and b) young children can be *less* honest than older children and adults. Also by definition, less-honest reports are less accurate. Therefore, the lay juror's assumption that young children will be *more* honest when giving testimony about issues that may present motivation for dishonestly is counter-intuitively backward.

Support for jurors' perceptions about interviewing method and credibility is also mixed. There is support for the assumption that leading, suggestive and overly complex questions lead to inaccurate reports, but not for the assumption that children's remote testimony is less credible than in-court testimony. The countless studies involving suggestive interviewing paradigms generally have non-suggested children as a control group (see Bruck & Melnyk, 2004, for a review of some suggestibility literature). Exposure to leading and suggestive techniques in these studies increases false reports and, therefore, decreases report accuracy. On average, jurors are correct to assign lower credibility to testimony elicited through suggestive questioning. However, the finding that jurors are more likely to convict when child victims are asked complex questions at trial is not in line with evidence about child accuracy. As we discussed in *Understanding and Answering Simple Interview Questions,* children often attempt to answer incomprehensible questions rather than indicate that they do not understand. This behavior can lead to inaccurate reporting.

However, limited evidence suggests that jurors' credibility assessments for children who provide testimony remotely compared with in-court are in opposition to the accuracy literature. Goodman et al. (1998) found that young children who testified via closed-circuit television in a series of mock trials incorporated fewer suggested details into their reports compared with children who were interviewed in mock court. The difference in presentation mode also had no influence on jurors' abilities to detect accurate statements. Though most studies on this topic are not experiments, and thus cannot speak to children's accuracy, the general trend seems to be that children who testify remotely have memory reports that are at least equal in quality to reports from children live in court (Hall & Sales, 2008).

The research on credibility assessments suggests that we should be cautious about relying on juror's decisions about the weight and credibility of child testimony. While there is currently little research to guide courts in decisions about children's testimonial competency, the research also suggests that adults may not be making meaningful credibility assessments, so it may not be appropriate to rely on these assessments. Further, research findings suggest that adults might be swayed by children's testimony even if they decide it is not credible. A highly replicated finding in the memory literature demonstrates that people forget the source of information long before forgetting the information itself (Schachter, 2001). Therefore, particularly in long trials, the gist of a child's testimony may subconsciously sway jurors even if they consciously decided to give little weight to it. Effective competency screening can avoid this bias, because children who are incapable of providing useful testimony would not be allowed to testify in court.

## Recommendations

The limited data on children's testimonial competence suggests that competency standards are in need of revision and refinement. No research directly assesses the relationship between types of questions that are typically used to measure children's ability to understand and answer interview questions, or those used to estimate children's memory skills. However, above we have reviewed evidence that individual differences exist in these domains, and have reviewed the recent work on the truth and lie components of the competency exam. These data suggest that establishing a child's understanding of truths and lies and morality about lying is at best measured inappropriately in the current system and at worst an unnecessary and misleading component to the exam. Instead, requiring children to take a child-friendly oath may accomplish more than would including these components on a competency exam (McGough, 1994).

The research thus far presents us with some limited recommendations about best practice when conducting competency assessments. We discussed a wide range of individual differences which can potentially predict testimonial accuracy. Many of the cognitive differences can be directly assessed in a competency exam. Components regarding psychological fitness can be assessed through testimony from therapists where applicable.

To determine a child's ability to understand and answer interview questions, it may be helpful to measure the child's language abilities, such as verbal skills, language comprehension skills, and narrative quality. There is extensive psychometric data on several tests of children's language abilities (receptive, expressive, syntactic, pragmatic and semantic), and these tests could be applied to competency determinations. Assessments of narrative skills can be taken from the literature and applied to narratives elicited from a child prior to testimony, or to recordings of children's testimony to police or social service workers before trial. In addition, a child's willingness to ask for clarification or admit ignorance may also be helpful as a demonstration that the child is monitoring their responses for accuracy.

There are also several standardized exams which measure young children's general memory skills. Adaptations of these exams could provide evidence of individual children's abilities to "observe and recall" relevant events. Although suggestibility is not formally included in competency determinations, Scullin and Ceci (2001) have demonstrated that suggestibility is an individual difference that can be quantified. Inclusion of children's scores on the Video Suggestibility Scale for Children may prove useful, particularly given research which demonstrates the suggestive nature of questions used in court (Ceci & Bruck, 1993).

Evidence concerning best practices for the truth and lie components to the competency exam continues to grow. Hansen (1990) and Lyon and Saywitz (2000) offer compelling new tests of children's abilities in this domain and if these tests are validated, they could prove assets to the legal system. However, currently, it appears that simply asking children to take the oath may be the most effective means of reducing lying on the stand.

## Conclusion

The effect of unreliable and non-validated competency exams is that incompetent children may be put on the stand and competent children may miss their opportunity for justice. These effects are particularly dangerous in cases of child abuse. In most cases of physical and sexual abuse, the only evidence of abuse lies in children's testimony. Only in rare cases are other witnesses or physical evidence available. Unreliable competence exams can result in the prosecution of innocent people on the one hand and under-prosecution of child-abusers on the other hand.

Identifying the disconnects between legal practice and empirical research is only a first step in improving the legal process. We also need to improve communication between the legal and research communities to address these discrepancies. Since the early 1980s, this communication has improved considerably. As one example, based on recommendations from the research, the trend in the past few decades has been to deemphasize the use of competency exams for young children. In many states within the United States, even very young children are presumed competent unless there is a compelling written argument for a competency assessment of a particular child. Age alone is no longer a legal argument for competency assessment based on federal law (*Child Victims and Child Witnesses Rights Act,* 1990). This allows more cases involving child victims to be heard in court; however, it forces reliance on credibility assessments, which are often flawed estimations of testimonial accuracy. We have also discussed how competence law in England and Wales has shifted in recent years to be more in line with empirical research and how research on child development has directly impacted competence law in Canada. The area of children's testimonial competency requires extensive empirical inquiry to help guide legal professionals in the daunting task of assessing children's testimony.

# References

1 Leach 199, 168 E.R. 202 (1779).

40 Seton Hall L. Rev. 1169 (2010).

Bauer, P. J. (1996). What do infants recall of their lives? Memory for specific events by one- to two-year-olds. *American Psychologist, 51(1)*, 29–41.

Bauer, P. J. (2004). Event memory. In William Damon, Richard M. Lerner, Deanna Kuhn, & Robert S. Siegler (Eds), *Handbook of Child Psychology* (Volume 2, pp. 267–297). Hoboken, NJ: John Wiley & Sons, Inc.

Brainerd, C. J. & Reyna, V. F. (2007). Explaining developmental reversals in false memories. *Psychological Science*, 18(5), 442–448.

Brainerd, C. J. & Reyna, V. F., & Ceci, S. J. (2008). Developmental reversals in false memory: A review of data and theory. *Psychological Bulletin, 134*(3), 343–382.

Bruck, M. & Ceci, S. J. (1999). The suggestibility of children's memory. *Annual Reviews, 50*, 419–439.

Bruck, M., Ceci, S. J. & Hembrooke, H. (1998). Reliability and credibility of young children's reports: From research to policy and practice. *American Psychologist, 53*, 136–151.

Bruck, M. & Melnyk, L. (2004). Individual differences in children's suggestibility: A review and synthesis. *Applied Cognitive Psychology, 18*(8). Special issue: Individual and Developmental Differences in Suggestibility, 947–996.

Cashmore, J. & Bussey, K. (1996). Judicial perceptions of child witness competence. *Law and Human Behavior, 20*, 313–334.

Castelli, P., Goodman, G. S., & Ghetti, S. (2005). Effects of interview style and witness age on perceptions of children's credibility in sexual abuse cases. *Journal of Applied Social Psychology, 35*, 297–319.

Ceci, S. J. & Bruck, M. (1993). The suggestibility of the child witness: A historical review and synthesis. *Psychological Bulletin, 113*, 403–439.

Ceci, S. J., & Bruck, M. (1995). *Jeopardy in the Courtroom: A Scientific Analysis of Children's Testimony*. Washington, DC: American Psychological Association.

Ceci, S. J., Papierno, P. B., & Kulkofsky, S. C. (2007). Representational constraints on children's memory and suggestibility. *Psychological Science, 18*(6), 503–509.

Child Victims and Child Witnesses Rights Act of 1990, 18 U.S.C. 3509 (2008).

Claywell v. State, 929 N.E.2d 268, 2010 Ind. App. LEXIS 1213 (Ind. Ct. App. 2010).

Commonwealth v. Patton , 458 Mass. 119, 934 N.E.2d 236, 2010 Mass. LEXIS 686 (2010).

Eaton, T. E., Ball, P. J., & O'Callaghan, M. G. (2001). Child-witness and defendant credibility: Child evidence presentation mode and judicial instructions. *Journal of Applied Social Psychology, 31*, 1845–1858.

Evans, A.D., & Lee, K. (2010). Promising to tell the truth makes 8- to 16-year-olds more honest. *Behavioral Sciences & the Law, 28,* 801–811.

Evans, A. D., Lee, K., & Lyon, T. (2009). Complex questions asked by defense lawyers but not prosecutors predicts convictions in child abuse trials. *Law and Human Behavior, 33,* 258–264.

Everette v. Lewis, 2011 U.S. Dist. LEXIS 16180 (E.D.N.C. Feb. 17, 2011).

Fritzley, V. H. and K. Lee (2003). Do young children always say yes to yes-no questions? A metadevelopmental study of the affirmation bias. *Child Development, 74,* 1297–1313.

Gershman, Bennett L. (2001) Child witnesses and procedural fairness. *Pace Law Faculty Publications.* Paper 127. Available at http://digitalcommons.pace.edu/lawfaculty/127.

Goodman, G. S., Golding, J. M., Helgeson, V. S., Haith, M. M. & Michelli, J. (1987). When a child takes the stand: Jurors perceptions of children's eyewitness testimony. *Law and Human Behavior, 11,* 27–40.

Goodman, G. S. Myers, J. E. B., Qin, J., Quas, J. A., Castelli, P., Redlich, A. D., & Rogers, L. (2006). Hearsay versus children's testimony: Effects of truthful and deceptive statements on jurors decisions. *Law and Human Behavior, 30*(3), 363–401.

Goodman, G. S., Tobey, A. E., Batterman-Faunce, J. M, Orcutt, H., Thomas, S., Shapiro, C., & Sachsenmaier, T. (1998). Face-to-face confrontation: Effects of closed-circuit technology on children's eyewitness testimony and jurors' decisions. *Law and Human Behavior, 22*(2), 165–203.

Gudjonsson, G. H. (1984). A new scale of interrogative suggestibility. *Personality and Individual Differences, 5,* 303–314.

Hall, S. R., Sales, B. D. (2008). *Courtroom Modifications for Child Witnesses: Law and Science in Forensic Evaluations.* Washington, D.C.: American Psychological Association.

Hansen, D. A. (1990). The development of an instrument to test the testimonial competence of children: A pilot test of the Hansen competency test for children (HCTC). *Dissertation Abstracts International,* 50(8-B), 3697.

Haugaard, J. J., Repucci, N. D., Laird, J. & Nauful, T. (1991). Children's definitions of the truth and their competency as witnesses in legal proceedings. *Law and Human Behavior, 15,* 253–271.

Jacobson, L.G. (2002). Psychological predictors of children's competency as witnesses in sexual abuse trials. *ETD Collection for Wayne State University.* Paper AAI3047558.

Kohlberg, L. (1963). The development of children's orientations toward a moral order: I. Sequence in the development of moral thought. *Vita Humana,* 6(1–2), 11–33.

Korkman, J., Santtila, P., Drzewiecki, T., & Sandnabba, N. K. (2008). Failing to keep it simple: Language use in child sexual abuse interviews with 3–8-year-old children. *Psychology, Crime, & Law, 14,* 41–60. DOI: 10.1080/10683160701368438.

Kulkofsky, S. (2010). The effects of verbal labels and vocabulary skill on memory and suggestibility. *Journal of Applied Developmental Psychology, 31,* 460–466.

Kulkofsky, S. C., Wang, Q., & Ceci, S. J. (2008). Do better stories make better memories? Narrative quality and memory accuracy in preschool children. *Applied Cognitive Psychology, 22,* 21–38.

L.M. v. State , 928 N.E.2d 905, 2010 Ind. App. LEXIS 1178 (Ind. Ct. App. 2010).

Leach, A. M., Talwar, V., Lee, K., Bala, N., & Lindsay, R. C. L. (2004). "Intuitive" lie detection of children's deception by law enforcement officials and university students. *Law and Human Behavior, 28,* 661–685.

Leichtman, M. D. & Ceci, S. J. (1995). The effects of stereotypes and suggestions on preschoolers' reports. *Developmental Psychology, 31,* 568–578.

London, K. & Nunez, N. (2002). Examining the efficacy of truth/lie discussions in predicting and increasing the veracity of children's reports. *Journal of Experimental Child Psychology, 83,* 131–147.

Luus, C. A. E., Wells, G. I., & Turtle, J. W. (1995). Child eyewitnesses: Seeing is believing. *Journal of Applied Psychology, 80*, 317–326.

Lyon, T. D., Malloy, L. C., Quas, J. A., & Talwar, V. (2008). Coaching, truth induction, and young maltreated children's false allegations and false denials. *Child Development, 79*, 914–929.

Lyon, T. D. & Saywitz, K. J. (1999). Young maltreated children's competence to take the oath. *Applied Developmental Science, 3*, 16–27.

Lyon, T. D., & Saywitz, K. J. (2000). Qualifying Children to Take the Oath: Materials for Interviewing Professionals. Practitioners guide retrieved from: http://works.bepress.com/thomaslyon/9/

McCauley, M. R. & Parker, J. F. (2001). When will a child be believed? The impact of the victim's age and jurors gender on children's credibility and verdict in a sexual-abuse case. *Child Abuse and Neglect, 25*, 523–539.

McLain, L. (2012). "Sweet childish days": Using developmental psychology research in evaluating the admissibility of out-of-court statements by young children. *Maine Law Review, 64*(1), 78–117.

McGough, L. (1994). *Child Witnesses: Fragile Voices in the American Legal System*. New Haven, CT: Yale University Press.

Myers, J. E. B. (1986–1987). The testimonial competence of children. *Journal of Family Law, 25*, 287–356.

Myers, J. E. B. (1992). *Legal Issues in Child Abuse and Neglect*. Newbury Park, CA: Sage.

Myers, J. E. B. (1997). *Evidence in Child Abuse and Neglect Cases*. New York, NY: John Wiley & Sons.

Nightingale, N. N. (1993). Juror reaction to child victim witnesses: Factors affecting trial outcome. *Law and Human Behavior, 17*, 679–694.

Oldham, J. (2011). Informal lawmaking in England by the twelve judges in the late eighteenth and early nineteenth centuries. *Law and History Review, 29*, 181–220. doi: doi:10.1017/S0738248010001252

Piaget, J. (1932). *The Moral Judgment of the Child*. New York: Harcourt, Brace.

Pipe, M. E. & Wilson, J. C. (1994). Cues and secrets: Influences on children's event reports. *Developmental Psychology, 30*, 515–525.

Reyes v. Blacketter, 2010 U.S. Dist. LEXIS 134099 (D. Or. Sept. 16, 2010)

Ross, D., Dunning, D., Toglia, M., and Ceci, S. J. (1990). The child in the eyes of the jury: Assessing mock jurors' perceptions of the child witness. *Law and Human Behavior, 14*, 5–23.

Ross, D. F., Hopkins, S., Hanson, E., & Lindsay, R. C. L., Hazen, K. & Eslinger, T. (1994). The impact of protective shields and videotape testimony on conviction rates in a simulated trial of child sexual abuse. *Law and Human Behavior, 18*, 553–566.

Ross, D. F., Lindsay, R. C. L., & Marsil, D. F. (1999). The impact of hearsay testimony on conviction rates in trials of child sexual abuse: Toward balancing the rights of defendants and child witnesses. *Psychology, Public Policy, and Law, 5*. Special issue: Hearsay testimony in trials involving child witnesses, 439–455.

Ruva, C. L. & Bryant, J. B. (2004). The impact of age, speech style, and question form on perceptions of witness credibility and trial outcome. *Journal of Applied Social Psychology, 34*, 1919–1 944.

Saywitz, K. J., & Goodman, G. S. (1996). Interviewing children in and out of court: Current research and practice implications. In J. Briere, L. Berliner, A. J. Bulkley, C. Jenny, T. Reid (Eds), *The APSAC Handbook on Child Maltreatment* (pp. 297–318). Thousand Oaks, CA, US: Sage Publications, Inc.

Saywitz, K. J., Snyder, L., & Nathanson, R. (1999). Facilitating the communicative competence of the child witness. *Applied Developmental Science, 3*, 58–68.

Schachter, D. L. (2001). *The Seven Sins of Memory: How the Mind Forgets and Remembers.* New York, NY: Houghton Mifflin.

Scullin, M., & Ceci, S. (2001). A suggestibility scale for children. *Personality and Individual Differences, 30*, 843–856.

Shao, Y. & Ceci, S. J. (2011). Adult credibility assessments of misinformed, deceptive and truthful children. *Applied Cognitive Psychology, 25*, 135–145.

State v. Mateo, 335 S.W.3d 529, 2011 Mo. App. LEXIS 164 (Mo. Ct. App. 2011)

Talwar, V., & Lee, K. (2008) Socio-cognitive correlates of children's lying behavior: Conceptual understanding of lying, executive functioning, and false beliefs. *Child Development, 79*, 866–881.

Talwar, V., Lee, K., Bala, N., & Lindsay, R. C. L. (2002). Children's conceptual knowledge of lying and its relation to their actual behaviors: Implications for court competence examinations. *Law and Human Behavior, 26*(4), 395–415.

Troxel, N. R., Ogle, C. M., Cordon, I. M., Lawler, M. J., & Goodman, G. S. (2009). Child witnesses in criminal court. In B. L. Bottoms, C. J. Najdowski, & G. S. Goodman (Eds), *Children As Victims, Witnesses, and Offenders: Psychological Science and the Law.* New York, NY: Guilford Press.

Tubb, V. A., Wood, J. M., & Hosch, H. M. (1999). Effects of suggestive interviewing and indirect evidence on child credibility in a sexual abuse case. *Journal of Applied Social Psychology, 29*, 1111–1127.

U.S. Census Bureau, Cumulative Estimates of Resident Population Change for the United States, Regions, States, and Puerto Rico and Region and State Rankings: April 1, 2000 to July 1, 2009 (NST-EST2009–02), December 2009.

Vaughn v. State, 307 Ga. App. 754, 706 S.E.2d 137, 2011 Ga. App. LEXIS 70, 2011 Fulton County D. Rep. 293 (2011)

Walker, A. G. (1993). Questioning young children in court: A linguistic case study. *Law and Human Behavior, 17*, 59–81.

Walker, A. G. (1985). From oral to written: The "verbatim" transcription of legal proceedings. University Microfilms International, Ann Arbor, Mich.

Wheeler v. United States, 159 U.S. 523 (1895).

Wigmore, J. H. (1923). *A Treatise on the Anglo-American System of Evidence in Trials at Common Law: Including the Statutes and Judicial Decisions of All Jurisdictions of the United States and Canada* (2nd edition). Boston: Little, Brown.

*Youth Justice and Criminal Evidence Act 1999* (U.K.), 1999, c. 23

Zajac, R., & Hayne, H. (2006). The negative effect of cross-examination style questioning on children's accuracy: Older children are not immune. *Applied Cognitive Psychology, 20*, 3–16.

# CHAPTER 8

# Child Eyewitness Person Descriptions and Lineup Identifications

JOANNA D. POZZULO

She described him as a white man, the height of her brother Charles (5'8"), about 30- or 40-years-old, wearing light-colored clothing and a golf hat (Smart, Smart, & Morton, 2003). He had dark hair, dark hair on his arms and on the back of his hands. He had a gun. She thought his voice was familiar. This description was provided by Mary Katherine Smart, Elizabeth Smart's 9-year-old sister, who witnessed Elizabeth being taken from their bedroom in the middle of the night on 4 June 2002. How accurate was Mary Katherine's description? Was the perpetrator, in fact, familiar to Mary Katherine? Could she identify him? These are some of the questions that plagued investigators and members in the tight-knit Salt Lake City community. Researchers alike wonder about the accuracy of children's descriptions of perpetrators and their ability to identify the correct person.

In October 2002, Mary Katherine remembered from where she knew the abductor's voice. She stated the voice belonged to "Immanuel" (Smart, Smart, & Morton, 2003). Immanuel, as he called himself, was one of the homeless people that the Smarts would hire for short periods to work around the house. Immanuel was Caucasian, 5'8", with dark hair, and about 45-years-old. The Smarts hired a sketch artist to help draw Immanuel's face from Mary Katherine's memory. This sketch was shown on *Larry King Live* and *America's Most Wanted*. Immanuel's family recognized this sketch and reported that, in fact, the man's name was Brian David Mitchell. On 12 March 2003, Mitchell was spotted travelling with two other people. Police were contacted and the three were brought in for questioning. One of the women with Mitchell was Elizabeth Smart, who had been wearing a disguise. Mitchell and his companion, Wanda Barzee, were arrested and charged with kidnapping, sexual assault and burglary. According to Elizabeth, Mitchell was wearing sweats, a sweatshirt, a stocking cap and tennis shoes the night he abducted her. He had put a knife to her neck, threatening to kill her and her family if she did not leave quietly with him.

The above case is just one example where a child had to describe a perpetrator and later go on to identify him. Numerous crimes occur, however, where a child may be an eyewitness (Pozzulo, 2007). For example, children may witness thefts, vandalism and be victims of sexual assault. An eyewitness will need to describe the perpetrator and then attempt an identification from a lineup (e.g. a set of photos), provided a suspect is found. The focus of this chapter will be on children's abilities to describe "strangers" (i.e. a person they are unfamiliar with). The quantity, accuracy and nature of these person descriptions will be examined. In addition, the accuracy and reliability of children identifying the stranger from a lineup will be explored in this chapter.

## Describing the perpetrator

Perpetrator descriptions alert the public to individuals with those characteristics for which they should be on the lookout. Unfortunately, the descriptions provided by children (and adults) are often vague and could apply to a number of people. Consider the number of white males, 5'8" with dark hair, approximately 40 years of age you know. Most likely, there are a few that you can think of (but hopefully none have committed a crime).

In order to assess person descriptions, two methods have been used: archival reviews and laboratory studies (Schooler, Meissner, & Sporer, 2007). Archival reviews consist of researchers examining descriptions provided by actual witnesses to real crime. Accuracy is estimated by comparing the description provided by the witness(es) with the appearance of the arrested/convicted offender. Archival reviews have, for the most part, been concerned with person descriptions provided by adult witnesses. Few studies have examined the person descriptive abilities of children. The few studies available, however, have been primarily of a "laboratory" nature.

Laboratory studies entail exposing participants to an unfamiliar individual(s) or face(s). The exposure may be a live target or presented via slide/video. Participants are unaware that they will need to describe the individual or the face once it is no longer in view. With the "target" out of sight, the participant is asked to describe the target, using an open-ended format, and/or the participant might be asked a series of questions about the target's appearance. For example, the participant might be asked to rate the target's skin tone using a scale from light to dark, or to state how much the target weighed, or

whether the target had any markings/tattoos. Below is a review of the literature on person descriptions by child witnesses.

## Nature and quantity of person descriptors

Pozzulo, Dempsey and Crescini (2009) evaluated the person descriptions
provided by preschool aged children ($M$ age = 59.10 months). Preschoolers
interacted with a female experimenter to make a mask for approximately 20
minutes. After a delay of 20–30 minutes, children were asked to describe
the mask-making teacher using a free recall question (i.e. "Remember the
mask-making teacher, what did she look like?"). Hair color was the descriptor most often reported (by 58 percent of participants). This descriptor was
followed in frequency by clothing color (47 percent), hair length (20 percent)
and clothing type (17 percent). Other descriptors less often reported included
height (7 percent), complexion (6 percent), eyes (1 percent) and accessories (1
percent). On average, the preschoolers reported 1.57 descriptors. In an early
study examining children's person descriptions, Dent and Stephenson (1979)
found that some children reported no descriptors to describe a target when
a free recall format was used. In another study, Davies, Tarrant and Flin
(1989) asked younger (6–7-year-olds) and older children (10–11-year-olds)
to describe a stranger using a free recall format. Younger children recalled
fewer items ($M$ = 1.00 descriptor) than older children ($M$ = 2.21 descriptors).
As can be seen, few descriptors are provided by child witnesses when they are
asked an open-ended question to describe the "target."

How does the amount of person descriptive information provided by child
witnesses compare to adult eyewitnesses, however? We can only compare
descriptive information from studies that included both a child and adult
comparison group. In one such paper, Pozzulo and Warren (2003) conducted
two studies comparing free recall person descriptions provided by youths
(10–14-year-olds) and adults. In their first study, youths provided significantly fewer descriptors ($M$ = 7.61) than did adults ($M$ = 9.85) overall. More
specifically, youths reported significantly fewer descriptors than did adults
across three descriptor categories: exterior face, such as hair items ($M$ = 1.71
v. $M$ = 2.22); interior face, such as eye color ($M$ = 1.00 v. $M$ = 2.38); and
body, such as weight ($M$ = .97 v. $M$ = 1.35). Conversely, adults reported significantly fewer accessories, such as belts and necklaces ($M$ = .05) compared
with youths ($M$ = .16), though neither reported many items in this category.
Youths and adults reported a similar number of clothing descriptors ($M$ =
2.73 v. $M$ = 2.67). In the second study, once again, overall the youths provided significantly fewer descriptors ($M$ = 3.64) than did adults ($M$ = 8.09).
Specifically, youths reported significantly fewer descriptors than did adults

across five categories: exterior face ($M$ = 1.58 v. $M$ = 2.66), interior face ($M$= .24 v. $M$ = .82), body ($M$ = .49 v. $M$ = 1.23), clothing ($M$ = 1.03 v. $M$ = 2.66) and accessories ($M$ = .13 v. $M$ = .34). Overall, youths appear to report few descriptors and fewer descriptors than did adults.

Why do children provide fewer descriptors than did adults? It is important to note that children may have more person descriptive information available but perhaps due to a limited vocabulary, when a free recall prompt is provided, children report less information than adults. A verbal description via free recall is a verbal task that requires linguistic ability and this ability increases with age (e.g. Holliday, 2003). Children simply may not have the words to describe the person. It would be interesting to examine alternative modes of providing a person description. For example, using a pictorial format. Another possibility for why children provide fewer person descriptors than adults may be the encoding strategies they used. For example, children may use a less-effective encoding strategy (somewhat like a novice) than do adults (somewhat like an expert) and produce less information. These ideas are discussed in greater detail below.

## Accuracy of person descriptors

The exterior feature of hair seems to be a dominant descriptor reported by both children and adults (Ellis, Shepherd, & Davies, 1980; Sporer, 1996). Davies, Tarrant and Flin (1989) found that hair was described most often by both younger and older children. Also, Pozzulo and Warren (2003) found that exterior facial descriptors were predominately and accurately reported by youths and adults. King and Yuille (as cited in Davies, 1996) found that hair descriptors, presence of facial hair and glasses were likely to be reported by children. Pozzulo, Dempsey and Crescini (2009) found that preschoolers had a 60 percent accuracy rate for the person descriptors they reported. An example of a description error would be the target's shirt being described as red when it was yellow. Only 6 percent of person descriptions by preschoolers contained confabulations where preschoolers described an item that was not present. Overall, hair is a predominate and accurately reported descriptor by children. Unfortunately, however, hair can change quite easily and may be of limited use forensically, if a long lapse has occurred between the time the perpetrator was witnessed and a suspect is apprehended. Pozzulo and Balfour (2006) found that children (as well as adults; Pozzulo & Marciniak, 2006) have difficulty identifying a perpetrator who has undergone a change in appearance.

Although interior features are less likely to change and may be unique in helping facilitate narrowing of the suspect search, these features may not be accurately reported by children or youths. Various explanations are possible for children's difficulty with interior facial features. For one, exterior features may be more salient and, hence, garner more attention by younger versus older individuals. With increasing age, finer discriminations are made where interior facial features are observed, encoded and recalled (in addition to exterior features) (e.g. Pozzulo & Warren, 2003). Alternatively, there may be more descriptor words for some features such as hair compared to others (e.g. nose). Interior features may be more difficult to describe, requiring a richer vocabulary (e.g. stating that she had almond-shaped eyes may be more accurate than stating that her eyes were round). Furthermore, in order to describe interior features, one may need to consider the relation between features (e.g. a nose may appear larger on a smaller face) that may only occur later in childhood (e.g. Carey & Diamond, 1977).

Height, weight and age do not appear to be reported often by children (e.g. Pozzulo & Warren, 2003), however, they are often key descriptors that police request. Unfortunately, height, weight and age can be particularly problematic for children and youths. Davies, Stevenson-Robb and Flin (1988) found that children/youths (7–12-year-olds) were inaccurate when asked to report the height, weight and age of an unfamiliar visitor. Also, Goetze (as cited in Davies, 1996) found that the accuracy of height, weight and age estimates increased with the age of the participants (8-year-olds v. 11-year-olds v. 13-year-olds). Janssen and Horowski (as cited in Sporer, 1996) examined height estimates by participants aged 10–18-years-old and found that the accuracy of these descriptors increased with age. Brigham, Van Verst and Bothwell (1986) found that children had difficulty with weight estimates. Dent (1982) found that age was the most inaccurate descriptor provided by children. Flin and Shepherd (1986) reported that a participant's height (adult participants) was related to height estimates of others. Furthermore, it has been suggested that a witness's self-characteristics may influence reports of others (Clifford & Bull, 1978). Pozzulo and Warren (2003) found that youths had greater difficulty accurately reporting body descriptors, such as height and weight, than did adults. They also found that age was unlikely to be reported by youths or adults using a free recall format.

Children and youths may be inaccurate with height and weight estimates because of a lack of knowledge and/or experience with these descriptors. Understanding the relation between height and weight is necessary to provide accurate body estimates. For example, taller people are heavier than shorter people with a similar girth. The development of these relations may not occur until the middle teen years, when youths become more interested in body image and health. Children's and youths' difficulty with age estimates may be due to an in-group age bias, such that people are more accurate when reporting the ages of others who are similar in age to themselves and have difficulty with estimating ages of those who are younger or older. The studies reviewed above have used adult targets (e.g. Pozzulo & Warren, 2003).

Of greater concern to police may be child witnesses' limited descriptions, rather than the accuracy of those descriptions. Children report very few person descriptors when asked to recall what the 'stranger' looked like. It is unlikely that the few descriptors that children provide would be successful at narrowing the suspect search. In addition, with so few descriptors available, it is unclear whether these items would be sufficient to help select lineup members for the identification task (discussed in greater detail below). Efforts should be concentrated on developing procedures that increase the number of descriptors children report. Kask, Bull, Heinla and Davies (2007) examined whether the use of a "standard" for comparison would increase accuracy on some of the descriptors children have difficulty with, such as age and body descriptors of height and weight. Children approximately 7-year-old were asked to use the experimenter as the standard for comparison when describing the previously witnessed person. For example, the experimenter would ask, "My hair is this long. How long was his hair?" Unfortunately, the standard was not consistently helpful; however, the data suggested that if a standard is going to be successful, the standard should be the same gender as the target.

Moreover, it is important to establish how much person information can be elicited by children without compromising accuracy. Interview type (e.g. cognitive interview, narrative elaboration) may help to increase the amount of information reported without the expense of losing accuracy (e.g. Camparo, Wagner, & Saywitz, 2001; Holliday, 2003; Holliday & Albon, 2004; Saywitz & Snyder, 1996). It is important to consider the pitfalls of asking leading questions, yes/no questions, and wh-questions (e.g. Ceci & Bruck, 1993; Saywitz & Camparo, 1998; Waterman, Blades, & Spencer, 2004), especially with younger children (i.e. under 5 years old) who have difficulty with providing accurate responses to these types of questions.

## A real-life description by an adolescent

Based on the research available above, how accurate and credible do you find the following description to be? It was provided by a 16-year-old female who alleged she had been sexually assaulted in a suburb of Ottawa, Canada (CBC News, 2011). The teen claimed to have been abducted at gunpoint while on her way to school during the mid-morning. She described her abductor as a male in his 40s, about 5'6", light-brown- or olive-skinned, speaking English with a French accent, with a slightly protruding stomach and dark, shaggy ear-length hair. She also described the abductor wearing a beige suede coat, blue jeans, black work boots, glasses with thin black rims, and a gold wedding band. The teen described the car as an older, red, four-door SUV with winter tires, no hub-caps, and no front license plate. She described the car as having two front bucket seats but the rear seats had been removed. Although the teen provided quite a few descriptors and detail, was the teen accurate regarding this very specific description? In fact, a few days after the investigation of the alleged crime, the teen reported that she fabricated the assault and all the details. There was no abductor.

## Identifying the perpetrator

A mother was violently raped and murdered while her 6-year-old and 2-year-old children were in the apartment (www.innocenceproject.org). Danny Brown was the victim's boyfriend for some months prior to the victim's murder. The victim's 6-year-old son identified Danny as one of two men that were in the apartment the evening of the murder. The 6-year-old said he was awakened by a loud noise and saw Danny come into the building through a window. Danny then got into an argument with his mother. The boy ran to his room and hid under his bed, falling asleep there. The boy picked out Danny from a lineup and this was the primary evidence used to convict Danny Brown, even though Danny Brown had numerous alibi witnesses accounting for his whereabouts when the murder had occurred. Was the 6-year-old correct in the identification of his mother's murderer? After serving more than 18 years in prison, Danny Brown was excluded from having committed the crime through DNA testing.

Identifying the suspect as the perpetrator increases the likelihood that the suspect is indeed the perpetrator, above and beyond the description provided by the witness (Wells, 1993). A number of alternatives exist for obtaining an identification from a witness. Essentially, however, for a lineup identification, the witness is presented with a set of photos (or video or live individuals) that includes a photo of the suspect (who may or may not be guilty) and photos of foils/fillers/distracters who are known to be innocent for the crime in question.

Greater attention has been paid in the literature to understand and assess children's ability to identify perpetrators, compared to the work on person descriptions. To understand children's identification evidence, two approaches have been taken: one in a more "cognitive" tradition and one in a more "social" tradition. The term "recognition" typically is used in the cognitive domain and the term "identification" is typically used in the social domain. Differences between these two literatures are described below, as well as the conclusions that would be reached for children's abilities based on these works.

# Recognition versus identification studies

Although identification from lineups is an application of face recognition, the paradigm used to study face recognition differs in important ways from research using an eyewitness paradigm.

From the cognitive psychology arena, a face recognition paradigm typically exposes a participant to a series of faces (e.g. 20), often with no other visual details, via slides or computer presentation. Participants may (or may not) be informed that they will need to remember these faces for a later recognition task. Participants may experience a delay and/or a distracter. Lastly, participants are given the recognition test where "old" faces (those initially seen) are interspersed with "new" faces (e.g. an additional 20) and participants must indicate the old faces. Some studies have participants examine a set of faces simultaneously and the participants need to indicate which face was the previously seen target.

The "hit rate" or the proportion of faces that were correctly recognized as previously seen is most often used as the measure of recognition accuracy. Also a measure of accuracy is the "true negative" rate or the proportion of faces correctly labeled as not previously seen. The true negative rate is rarely discussed in the literature, however. Two types of error are measured: "false-alarm" rate, or the proportion of faces incorrectly labeled as previously seen when they in fact were not; and the "miss" rate, or the proportion of faces incorrectly labeled as not previously seen when in fact they were. Estimates of children's ability to correct identify perpetrators was based on this work up until the mid-1980s, when a number of researchers noted several differences between the "face recognition paradigm" and the "eyewitness context." Social and cognitive psychologists developed an ecologically valid paradigm to better understand identification evidence. In addition to a difference in methodology, a difference in terminology (e.g. identification v. recognition) to be used when discussing eyewitness identification was developed. Researchers conducted eyewitness identification studies in the laboratory or field. Unsuspecting participants would find themselves exposed to a target under the guise that they were participating in some other activity. This exposure could be live or via slide sequence/videotape. Following the "event", participants, now witnesses, would be informed of the true nature of the study/task that in fact, they would be asked to identify the target seen earlier. A brief delay of 20–30 minutes or a longer delay of days could be imposed. Note that participant-witnesses are exposed to one target. For the identification phase, witnesses would be shown a lineup task to assess their ability to identify the target/perpetrator. The lineup would be composed of a set of photos (e.g. six) that would either contain a photo of the target (to simulate when the suspect is guilty) or contain a replacement photo for the target (to simulate when the suspect is innocent). The lineup photos would be selected to have some resemblance to the target as well as to the descriptors provided by the witness (Luus & Wells, 1991).

As mentioned, two types of lineups are used in identification research to simulate the situation when a suspect is guilty (target-present) and when the suspect is innocent (target-absent). With each of these lineups, three identification decisions are possible. When examining a target-present lineup, witnesses can make a correct identification by identifying the guilty suspect, they can make a foil identification by identifying one of the known to be innocent lineup members, or witnesses can make a false rejection by rejecting the lineup and not identify the guilty suspect. The only correct decision with a target-present lineup is a *correct identification*. For example, a correct identification occurs when the witness picks out the guilty suspect. When examining a target-absent lineup, witnesses can make a *correct rejection* by rejecting the lineup and not identify any lineup member. For example, the witness states the perpetrator is not present when the police have an innocent suspect. Witnesses can make a *foil identification* by identifying a known to be innocent lineup member. For example, the witness picks out one of the fillers the police used to create the lineup. Finally, witnesses can make a *false identification* by identifying the innocent suspect. For example, the witness identifies the suspect, who is in fact innocent. The only correct decision with a target-absent lineup is a correct rejection. All other decisions with target-present and -absent lineups are errors. In many studies, there is an individual in the target-absent lineup who the experimenter has deemed to be the innocent suspect, generating a false identification rate. Recently, researchers in the field are combining false identifications and foil identifications from target-absent lineups and referring to them as the false-positive rate (Lindsay et al., 1997).

The face recognition and eyewitness identification paradigms present a number of differences. First, the number of targets differs. Face recognition studies use a relatively large number of targets (e.g. 20) and several attempts or trials for recognition, whereas identification studies typically use one target and one attempt or trial (i.e. one lineup) for identification. Second, in face recognition studies, the same photographs can be used when initially displaying the photograph (i.e. encoding) and testing recognition. Eyewitness identification studies use different images and mediums for encoding and identification. For example, the target may be seen live and the identification task may use photographs. Lastly, recognition studies use only target-present recognition trials. In contrast, identification studies use target-present and target-absent conditions. It is critical to use a target-absent lineup in order to assess the rate of false identification. It is not possible to determine the rate at which a witness will identify an innocent suspect from a target-present lineup because the suspect in a target-present lineup is guilty.

Overall, the research questions posed by face recognition studies differ from eyewitness identification questions. Face recognition studies ask theoretical questions, such as how are faces encoded and what are the brain structures involved for memory. Eyewitness identification studies ask applied questions such as what are the best procedures for police to use in order to increase accurate identification evidence. Next in this chapter, face recognition studies will be discussed.

## Face recognition studies

What do we know about the recognition abilities of children? Not surprisingly, as with many abilities, face recognition accuracy increases with increasing age. Face recognition studies have generally found that the proportion of hits, and, thus, the level of accuracy, increases with participants' age (Blaney & Winograd, 1978; Carey, Diamond, & Woods, 1980; Chance, Turner, & Goldstein, 1982; Cross, Cross, & Daly, 1971; Ellis, Shepherd, & Bruce, 1973; Feinman & Entwistle, 1976; Flin, 1980). Between the ages of 5 and 12 years old, a significant increase in recognition accuracy is found (Blaney & Winograd, 1978; Carey, 1981; Carey, Diamond, & Woods, 1980; Flin, 1980; Goldstein & Chance, 1964). For example, Chance and Goldstein (1984) reported hit rates between 35 percent and 40 percent for 4- to 5-year-olds, between 50 percent and 58 percent for 6- to 8-year-olds, between 60 percent and 70 percent for 9- to 11-year-olds, and between 70 percent and 80 percent for 12- to 14-year-olds. Adult performance has been found to be similar to that of 12- to 14-year-olds (Goldstein, 1977). In a meta-analysis by Shapiro and Penrod (1986), age was found to yield a large effect size for hits. In terms of false-alarm rates, some, but not all, face recognition studies report this pattern of findings. Of the studies reviewed, not surprisingly, false alarms have been found to decrease with age (Chance et al., 1982; Cross et al., 1971; Ellis et al., 1972; Flin, 1980). Chance and Goldstein (1979) found false-alarm rates comparable from 12-years-old to adult ($M = 36$ years; 11 percent and 7 percent, respectively).

*How are faces processed? The featural versus holistic debate.* Perhaps, hits increase and false alarms decrease as a result of how faces are processed. Faces may be encoded featurally or holistically, or by a combination of both strategies. Featural encoding involves focusing on individual features such as the eyes or mouth. In contrast, holistic encoding involves representing the entire face, not just its parts (Farah, Wilson, Drain, & Tanaka, 1998). Moreover, with holistic encoding, the relationship between features is considered such as the distance from the nose to the mouth rather than just the individual features (Schwarzer, 2000). The ability to discriminate between faces increases when one considers the relations between features rather than simply the features (Bartlett & Searcy, 1993; Bradshaw & Wallace, 1971; Diamond & Carey, 1986; Farah, Tanaka, & Drain, 1995; Rhodes, 1988; Sergent, 1984).

Carey and Diamond (1977; see also Carey Diamond, & Woods, 1980) conducted a face inversion study to test the prediction that a shift occurs from featural processing to holistic processing in late childhood. This face inversion paradigm involves presenting faces in an upright position for encoding and then presenting the faces inverted for recognition. The logic behind this paradigm is that if faces are represented by features, inverting the face should not influence recognition. On the other hand, if faces are represented holistically, inverting the face would distort the pattern of the face and thus make recognition more difficult. Adults are believed to process faces holistically and are found to have more difficulty recognizing inverted than upright faces (Hochber & Galper, 1967; Scapinello & Yarmey, 1970; Yin, 1969). Overall, younger children (e.g. 7- to 8-year-olds) seemed unaffected by face pattern when the face was inverted as would be predicted for featural encoding. Adults, on the other hand, did have difficulty with the inverted faces suggesting a greater reliance on holistic encoding.

To further explore encoding strategies, Baenninger (1994) examined whether wearing paraphernalia, such as a hat, would influence recognition. Results showed that if targets were not wearing their paraphernalia for the recognition task, children missed the target believing the target was not there when he/she was. Further, Hay and Cox (2000) found that 6- to 7-year-olds were better at recognizing individual facial features compared to 9- to 10-year-olds.

In another line of research examining encoding, Ellis and Flin (1990) used delay and exposure duration. Ellis and Flin (1990) argued that younger children may encode fewer features at encoding compared to older children, so that a longer delay would be less detrimental to younger children's memories because there were fewer details to remember. Recognition accuracy by 7-year-olds was not influenced by delay. In contrast, lower recognition accuracy was observed for 10-year-olds following a one-week delay. In a second study examining exposure duration, Ellis and Flin (1990) speculated that increasing exposure duration from two to six seconds would be beneficial for older but not younger children because of advanced encoding strategies of the older group. Once again, recognition accuracy did not differ for 7-year-olds as a function of exposure duration but for 10-year-olds, recognition accuracy increased with the longer duration. Thus, older children may be able to encode more information during a given time period, or they may have better strategies to help them integrate this newly encoded information while still presented with the target. Alternatively, the few features that younger children will encode may not require as much time to process as the more complicated relational information used by older children and adults.

Based on the above lines of research, children between the ages of 10- and 12- year-old appear to process faces holistically, whereas, younger children appear to encode faces featurally. However, there is a tendency for some of the developmental increases in recognition to decrease or plateau around the ages of 10-, 12-, and 14-year-old. Carey et al. (1980) observed that over-all performance in face encoding declined slightly after the age of 10-year-old and improved again until the age of 16-year-old. Chung and Thomson (1995) demonstrated an inferior performance in face recognition with 12- to 14-year-olds compared with 6-, 8-, 10-, and 16-year-olds. On the other hand, Diamond and Carey (1977) found that between 10- and 16-year-old, accuracy in recognition tended to remain stable rather than decline. Researchers disagree as to whether this decline occurs and if so, the age at which it occurs. Moreover, an adequate explanation for this effect has yet to be provided.

Disagreement exists regarding the processing abilities of children; however, many would agree that the ability to recognize faces increases with age (Tanaka et al., 1998). For example, it has been suggested that if children can be taught to use a holistic approach or be given holistic encoding instructions, this may improve their recognition performance to adult level (Chung & Thomson, 1995). If we consider this suggestion, children may be able to encode faces holistically but prefer to use a featural approach until later childhood. An experiment by Blaney and Winograd (1978) examined the effect of holistic versus featural encoding instructions on children's memory for unfamiliar faces. Children in grades 1, 3, and 5 were presented with 20 male faces. One-third of the children were asked if the man had a big nose (i.e. featural instruction, one-third of the children were asked if the man looked nice (i.e. holistic instruction), and the final third were told to look carefully at the faces and try to remember them (i.e. use their "normal" strategy). Holistic instructions improved recognition for each age group. Thus, even young children seem able to encode faces holistically.

Tanaka et al. (1998) examined 6-year-olds and 10-year-olds when they were presented with parts of a face that were either placed within the whole face or placed in isolation for the recognition phase. Consistent with the notion that children are capable of holistic encoding, all three age groups of children recognized the parts of a face more accurately when they were presented within the whole. To follow up these results, Tanaka et al. (1998) added inverted faces at the recognition phase. They found that the whole-face advantage was only present when the face was upright for recognition.

Furthermore, Baenniger (1994) compared the recognition of intact faces versus scrambled faces in 8- and 11-year-olds and adults. Baenniger hypothesized that if children processed faces featurally, then recognition accuracy would not differ across conditions. This hypothesis was not supported. All groups were less accurate at recognizing faces when they were scrambled versus intact. Friere and Lee (2001) found that 4-year-olds were able to recognize target faces that had the same features but whose spacing differed, suggesting that children were processing faces as a whole. In a study by Tanaka, Kay, Grinnell, Stansfield and Szechter (1998; also Tanaka & Farah, 1993), a target face was presented and identified by name for encoding (e.g. This is Tom). For recognition, some children were shown the target face and a foil face that differed from the target by only one feature (eyes, nose) and asked which face was Tom (holistic condition). Other children were presented with one feature from the target face and one feature from the foil face and asked which one was Tom's nose, for example (feature condition). The inversion paradigm also was employed. Six-, 8-, and 10-year-olds were each increasingly more accurate with whole faces that were presented upright compared with features. This effect was not present for inverted faces. Thus, given upright faces were more accurately recognized than features for each age group, it is suggestive that even young children can and do encode faces holistically.

Although there is debate regarding children's face processing abilities, some general conclusions are accepted. First, children's ability to accurately recognize unfamiliar faces increases with age between 5- and 10-year-old (e.g. Goldstein & Chance, 1964; Carey et al., 1980; Baenninger, 1994). Second, younger children have greater difficulty with recognizing faces when they do not match their appearance from encoding (e.g. Diamond & Carey, 1977; Ellis, 1992). A number of questions remain ambiguous, however. For example, do young children naturally use holistic processing with unfamiliar faces? At what age do children reach an adult level of face recognition accuracy? Does a decrease in face recognition occur before adult-level accuracy is reached and, if so, why?

## What would our conclusions of child witnesses be, based on face recognition studies?

Based on the research reviewed above, we may conclude that children are more accurate witnesses with increasing age. When presented with a lineup (identification task), we would expect 6-year-olds to be less accurate at identifying the perpetrator than would 8-year-olds or adults. Moreover, we would expect 10- to 12-year-olds to have an adult level of identification accuracy. Studies using an eyewitness methodology suggest a different picture of children's identification abilities. Next, the results of identification studies are discussed.

# Lineup identification studies

The early work on identification accuracy used target-present lineups exclusively. In one of the first studies examining children's and adults' identification abilities, Marin, Holmes, Guth and Kovac (1979) used a live target with various aged children (5- to 6-year-olds, 8- to 9-year-olds, 12- to 13-year-olds) and adults, followed by an identification from a simultaneous lineup. Surprisingly, a significant increase in correct identification rates was not found across the various age groups. All groups produced comparable rates of correct identification. In another early study, Goodman and Reed (1986) examined children (3- to 4-year-olds, 6- to 7-year-olds) and adults who were exposed to an unfamiliar individual. Shown a simultaneous lineup, 6- to 7-year-olds and adults produced a similar correct identification rate (.94 v. .75, respectively). The younger children (3- to 4-year-olds) had a significantly lower correct identification rate (.38) than did the older children and adults. Producing a somewhat different pattern of results, Brigham, Van Verst and Bothwell (1986) exposed 4th, 8th, and 11th graders to a live staged theft. A six-person simultaneous lineup was used to test identification accuracy. Fourth graders produced a significantly lower correct identification rate than did 8th and 11th graders (68 percent v. 93 percent v. 88 percent, respectively). Eighth and 11th graders did not differ in their correct identification rates. Based on these data, correct identification rates are fairly flat from about 5-year-old.

Target-absent lineups provide a fuller picture of children's abilities. For example, Parker and Carranza (1989) examined the abilities of 9- to 10-year-olds and adults. Participants were shown a slide sequence. A six-person target-present or target-absent simultaneous lineup was used to examine identification accuracy. Shown a target-present lineup, children produced a higher correct identification rate than did adults (.33 v. .08). Shown a target-absent lineup, children produced a lower correct rejection rate than did adults (.42 v. .67).

In an attempt to clarify children's identification abilities compared to adults, Pozzulo and Lindsay (1998) conducted a meta-analysis. The identification abilities of four groups of children (4-year-olds, 5- to 6-year-olds, 9- to 10-year-olds, and 12- to 13-year-olds) were compared with those of adults. In addition, moderator variables that may differentially influence the identification accuracy of children and adults were examined (e.g. presence v. absence of target; method of lineup presentation). Pozzulo and Lindsay (1998) found that preschoolers (i.e. 4-year-olds) produced a significantly lower correct identification rate than did adults (.47 v. .67, respectively). With studies contrasting the performance of children between 5- and 6-year-olds and adults, correct identification rates differed but not in the expected direction (.71 v.

.54, respectively). Children made significantly more correct identifications than did adults. In a comparison of older children (9- to 10-year-olds) with adults, similar correct identification rates were observed between the two groups (.47 v. .48, respectively). Adolescents (i.e. 12- to 13-year-olds) also maintained adult-level performance in terms of correct identification. Thus, children over 5-year-old produced correct identification rates comparable to those of adults. Preschoolers had more difficultly than adults at picking out the target from a lineup that contained the target.

In terms of correct rejections, children of all ages were less likely than adults to correctly reject lineups that did not contain the target (Pozzulo & Lindsay, 1998). More specifically, preschoolers were significantly less likely to correctly reject a target-absent lineup (.39 v. .98). Although not significant, young children (5- to 6-year-olds) made fewer correct rejections than adults (.57 v. .65, respectively). Older children were significantly less likely to correctly reject a target-absent lineup compared with adults (.41 v. .70, respectively). Adolescents also were significantly less likely to correctly reject target-absent lineups (.48 v. .74, respectively). Thus, all children had difficulty with target-absent lineups, choosing to select a lineup member as the target rather than reject the lineup as not containing the target.

## Why do children produce more false positives than do adults with target-absent lineups?

### Demand

Beal, Schmitt and Dekle (1995) suggested that identification errors made by children may not be primarily a result of poor memory of the events but rather could reflect other factors, such as social pressure. Raskin and Yuille (as cited in Ricci, Beal, & Dekle, 1996) suggested that the mere presentation of a lineup may suggest to the child that the presenter expects the child to make a choice (i.e. why else would a lineup be shown?). Further, Wells and Luus (1990) likened the lineup task to a social psychology experiment. Just as there are social demands that are experienced by the participant in an experimental task, so, too, does the witness experience similar demands when examining a lineup. The mere presentation of a lineup suggests a "selection" is being requested. Making no selection (or rejecting the lineup) may be viewed as a "non response" and a participant not willing to complete the task. For example, both participant and witness may want to please the experimenter/police officer by choosing the "right person". The participant may try to guess the experimenter's hypothesis. The witness may guess who the police suspect and who the officer wants the witness to choose. Moreover, the social demands associated with a lineup task may be more pronounced for the younger child. For example, the experimenter/police officer is an authority figure who is older than the child. There is an implicit demand to make a selection when shown a lineup; why else would you be shown a lineup if not to pick someone out? The child may worry about getting into trouble if no selection is made because this behavior would suggest non-compliance. For example, Pozzulo and Lindsay (1997) found that children were less likely to use an "I don't know" response compared to adults, even when this response option was made salient. Thus, children's higher false positive rates compared to adults may occur because of a greater sense to make a selection/identification when shown a lineup (e.g. Parker & Ryan, 1993; Pozzulo & Lindsay, 1998). A target-present lineup elicits a correct response because children see the target, select the target and make an identification. A target-absent lineup elicits an incorrect response because children think they need to make an identification and, consequently, select a lineup member. The perceived pressure to pick someone may be lower for adults, or adults may be better able to resist such pressure. Thus, adults are less likely to make an identification than children when shown a target-absent lineup.

In one study examining authority via clothing worn by the lineup administrator, Lowenstein, Blank and Sauer (2010) had 9- to 10-year-olds make a lineup identification from a target-present or -absent lineup where the administrator wore a uniform or plain clothing. Correct identification rates were not influenced by the administrator's clothing. However, children made more false positive identifications from target-absent lineups when the administrator wore a uniform versus plain clothing. The uniform may have increased the pressure to make a selection, leading to greater false positives in the absent condition. The demand characteristics of the lineup task is one explanation for why children produce a higher false positive rate than do adults.

## Processing strategy

Borrowing from the face recognition literature, children may process faces using a "featural" strategy, whereas adults may be more likely to use a holistic approach (Carey & Diamond, 1977; Diamond & Carey, 1977). Differences in processing strategies may explain differences in identification rates (Bower & Karlin, 1974; Wells & Hryciw, 1984; Winograd, 1976). Consider that using a few features to encode and process a face may lead to accuracy with a target-present lineup but inaccuracy with a target-absent lineup. For example, if a child focuses on hairstyle, when examining a target-present lineup, the child matches his/her memory of the target's hairstyle to one of the lineup members. It is likely that the child's memory will match most closely the target's hairstyle in the lineup and, thus, a correct identification ensues. With a target-absent lineup, holistic processing is more likely to lead to accuracy because matching a single feature will result in inaccuracy because the target is not present so any match on a feature will be wrong. Thus, other facial information is necessary to make a correct decision with a target-absent lineup. If children are not using a holistic approach, it is likely that they will reach an erroneous decision with a target-absent lineup. Differences in processing strategy may be an explanation for children's higher false positive rates compared to adults.

## Memory Trace

Differences in encoding also may lead to differences in memory strength, such that memory strength increases with age (e.g. Holliday, Douglas & Hayes, 1999; Marche, 1999) and declines in later years, as seen in the elderly (Holliday et al., 2012). A weaker memory trace may lower the threshold for a match between memory and lineup member. A lineup member who resembles the target "somewhat" is selected and identified. In the target-present lineup condition, this lower threshold still results in a correct identification because the target is sufficiently similar to the child's memory. In the target-absent lineup condition, this lower threshold leads to an error and false positive identification because any "match" will be an error. Differences in memory trace may provide an alternative explanation for children's higher false positive rate compared to adults (see Brainerd & Reyna, 1995).

Few studies have been conducted to understand the reason for children's higher false positive rate. In one study focused on demand characteristics, Pozzulo and Dempsey (2006) examined biased and neutral lineup instructions. Past research examining lineup instructions has demonstrated that one condition that increases an adult's sense of pressure to make an identification is biased lineup instructions (i.e. implying that the perpetrator is present; Malpass & Devine, 1981; Steblay, 1997). Adults' greater sense of pressure with biased instructions is manifested with greater false-positive responding (in the target-absent condition). If children "normally" feel pressure to make a selection, children's choosing behavior should be similar across neutral (i.e. stating that the perpetrator may or may not be present) and biased lineup instructions. Pozzulo and Dempsey (2006) conducted two experiments where "pressure" was treated as a dichotomous variable and was manipulated via lineup instructions (i.e. neutral or biased). Children and adults were included in both experiments. As predicted, children produced a lower correct rejection rate compared to adults. Also in both experiments as predicted, adults produced a lower correct rejection rate when given biased versus neutral instructions. Intriguingly, children also produced lower correct rejection rates with biased versus neutral instructions. However, children maintained their higher false positive rate compared to adults. False positives increased at a similar rate for children and adults with biased instructions. In other words, the absolute difference in false positive rate between children and adults was maintained from neutral to biased instructions. These data suggest that children's greater propensity to make false-positive identifications (with a target-absent lineup and neutral instructions) compared to adults may be driven by a factor other than or in addition to pressure.

To shed further light on the issue of demand, Pozzulo, Dempsey, Bruer and Sheahan (2011) hypothesized that a lower cognitive demand lineup task (i.e. a lineup that results in 100 percent identification accuracy) that produces false positives would have to be driven more by social factors than by cognitive factors. Pozzulo et al. used familiar cartoon characters as the lower cognitive demand lineup, and unfamiliar adults as the higher cognitive demand lineup. Both children (4–5-year-old) and adults were examined. Not surprisingly, children (and adults) showed 99 percent accuracy for the cartoon targets in the target-present lineup. However, children produced a higher false positive rate compared to adults for both the cartoon characters and human targets. Even though children knew the cartoon characters and could pick them out when present, they were more likely than adults to identify an erroneous character (and erroneous human target) suggesting that demand may be driving false positive responding in children after all.

More research is needed to specifically examine the causes of higher false positive responses in children compared with adults using an eyewitness paradigm before definitive conclusions can be reached.


## Consequences of identification errors

Identification errors have varying consequences for the eyewitness, the suspect and the community. A foil identification with a target-present or -absent lineup suggests that the witness has a poor memory. Other crime details provided by this eyewitness may be considered cautiously, given that a known error was made. A false rejection may have a guilty suspect back into the community to commit further crime. A false identification can lead to an innocent person being charged and convicted of a crime he/she did not commit, while the real perpetrator remains at large to commit further crime. Consider the case of Larry Youngblood, who was convicted of child molestation, sexual assault and kidnapping of a 10-year-old boy who was abducted in Pima County, Arizona, in 1983 (www.innocenceproject.org). The 10-year-old boy was repeatedly sexually assaulted by his abductor. The boy described his abductor as having a disfigured eye. The boy identified Larry Youngblood as the abductor, which was the main evidence used to convict. After serving nine years in prison, Larry Youngblood was exonerated through DNA testing. Using the national DNA database for convicted offenders, there was a DNA match for a Walter Cruise, who was blind in one eye (and incarcerated in Texas at the time the match occurred). Cruise was convicted for the crimes against the 10-year-old boy in August 2002 and was sentenced to 24 years in prison.

Given the consequences of identification errors, researchers have examined a number of alternatives to increase children's correct rejection rates.

# Attempts to increase children's correct rejection rates

## The role of training

In an attempt to increase children's identification accuracy and, more specifically, children's correct rejection rate, a number of researchers have examined the use of practice lineups and/or identification training (Davies, Stevenson-Robb, & Flin, 1988; Goodman, Bottoms, Schwartz-Kenney, & Rudy, 1991; Parker & Myers, 2001; Parker & Ryan, 1993; Pozzulo & Lindsay, 1997). Training has typically consisted of giving children a practice lineup followed by feedback on the accuracy of their response. For example, Davies et al. (1998) showed children two- and three-person simultaneous lineups: a target-present lineup for practice, followed by a target-absent lineup for the actual identification test. The experimenter was the target for the practice lineup. Unfortunately, this practice did not help children's correct rejection rates.

In another attempt to increase correct rejections, Pozzulo and Lindsay (1997) used a number of different forms of practice. For example, they used a demonstration video of accurate decision-making with a six-person simultaneous lineup or a handout illustrating accurate decision-making with a six-animal simultaneous lineup. Although correct rejection rates were not increased, surprisingly, the correct identification rates increased for children. It is possible that simply clarifying the lineup task removes ambiguity for the child, leading to a higher correct identification rate when the child sees the target and wants to pick the target.

Parker and Myers (2001) examined practice with sequential lineups. In an elaborate design, participants either practiced themselves or the practice was modeled by the experimenter. These conditions were crossed with the content of the practice lineups. That is, practice lineups consisted of either two target-absent sequential lineups or a target-absent and a target-present sequential lineup. Moreover, data were divided by gender. As was the case in Pozzulo and Lindsay's study (1997), practice improved the correct identification rate but only for females. Correct rejection rates did not increase with practice for females or males. In contrast to these findings of unsuccessful practice for increased correct rejection rates, Goodman et al. (1991) used three practice lineups, two target-present and one target-absent, and found a reduction in false positives from target-absent lineups.

Training was examined in the meta-analysis by Pozzulo and Lindsay (1998). They found that children (9–14-year-old) who were given practice were not more likely to correctly reject target-absent lineups compared to children who were not given practice. Intriguingly, 9- to 10-year-olds who received training were more likely to make a correct identification than children who did not receive training. The effect size was small, however ($d = .29$). Although practice may not be effective at increasing children's correct rejection rates, it may have some positive effects for increasing correct identification rates. Further research should more clearly delineate the type of practice that may be beneficial for increasing correct identification rates and the mechanisms that are involved. Once again, these results may suggest that correct identifications and correct rejections are driven by different processes (Pozzulo & Lindsay, 1998). Greater understanding of these mechanisms may explain why practice is not effective at increasing correct rejections.

## Mr. Nobody/Wildcard

A number of researchers have attempted to increase children's correct rejection rates by providing a salient graphic to represent "no-one" (e.g. Pozzulo & Lindsay, 1997; Zajac & Karageorge, 2009). Researchers have speculated that children may perceive the correct response to a lineup task as making a selection (i.e. demand characteristics). By providing children with a salient alternative, a silhouetted photo for example, children may be more inclined to choose this option if they do not see the perpetrator. In one study employing such an option, Davies, Tarrant and Flin (1989) provided children with a "Mr. Nobody" card that was a line drawing, in addition to the lineup of photos. Children could point to Mr. Nobody if they did not see the target. Unfortunately, the use of this option did not increase correct rejections. Beal, Schmitt and Deckle (1995) also had a salient rejection option in the form of a "Not Here" card. This option had limited success, as well. In a recent study, Zajac and Karageorge (2009) examined the identification accuracy of 8- to 11-year-old children with the inclusion of a silhouetted figure with a superimposed question mark as an additional option to the lineup faces. Zajac and Karageorge found that including this "wildcard" option increased correct rejections compared to when no such visual option was available. Several details are noteworthy here. First, without an adult comparison group, it is hard to know whether including a "wildcard" increases correct rejections to an adult level. Second, it is fairly common practice to use some form of graphic "not here" response in eyewitness studies. Even with the inclusion of a salient rejection option, children produce lower correct rejection rates than adults (Pozzulo & Lindsay, 1998). Third, it is not clear what these options represent and whether a child is selecting this alternative to indicate that the target is not present or that they are unsure if the target is not present. This distinction is critical in a criminal justice context, as each response will have different consequences for the suspect. Rejecting a lineup would suggest to police that they may have an innocent suspect, whereas a witness who is unsure of whether the perpetrator is present does not provide evidence of suspect guilt or not guilt.

Future research with lineups should continue to use some form of a graphical "not here" option as standard practice, given that by *not* providing such an option the demand characteristics of the task may be heightened. Further to this point, it has been found with adult participants, that not including an instruction that the perpetrator may not be present increases false positive responding in the target-absent condition (Malpass & Devine, 1981; Steblay, 1997). As previously mentioned, most lineup identification research with children and adults includes a salient "not here" response. The current data do not appear to suggest that this option would increase children's correct rejection rates to adult level.

## Sequential lineup procedure

The sequential lineup is an alternative to the simultaneous lineup (i.e. all lineup members are presented at one time to the witness). Lindsay and Wells (1985) suggested that the simultaneous lineup encourages a relative judgment where the person who looks most like the perpetrator is identified. In the target-present condition, it is most likely that the perpetrator will look most like himself/herself leading to a correct identification. Unfortunately, in the target-absent condition, the person who looks most like the perpetrator is *not* the perpetrator, leading to a false positive identification. Lindsay and Wells (1985) suggested that if lineup members were displayed individually and sequentially, witnesses would be inclined to use an absolute judgment strategy where the lineup member is compared with the witness' memory of the perpetrator. Witnesses would not be able to move forward in the sequence or review a previously seen photo, rather, witnesses would have to indicate for each photo shown whether it was or was not the perpetrator. The sequential lineup procedure reduces false positive responding compared to simultaneous presentation for adult witnesses (Lindsay & Wells, 1985). This pattern however has not been found for child witnesses (Pozzulo & Lindsay, 1998).

In the meta-analysis by Pozzulo and Lindsay (1998), simultaneous lineup presentation compared to sequential lineup presentation increased the child-adult gap for correct rejections. More specifically, for children, the sequential lineup typically produced higher false positives than the simultaneous lineup. In contrast, the sequential procedure decreased false positives compared to simultaneous presentation for adults. It is important to note that the sequential lineup procedures used in the studies reviewed in the meta-analysis (Pozzulo & Lindsay, 1998) differed from the recommend practice outlined by Lindsay and Wells (1985). For example, the participants should be unaware of the number of photographs to be shown. This element can be critical to the sequential procedure, because once witnesses are aware that they are running out of pictures, they are more likely to identify someone (Lindsay, Lea, & Fulford, 1991). The sequential procedures used in some of the child studies in the meta-analysis did not conceal the number of photos to be shown. Although this procedural modification did not seem to hinder adult performance, it may have had a greater impact on child performance. That is, assuming that children perceive a greater pressure than did adults that they should identify someone (Ceci, Toglia, & Ross, 1987), knowing there are few pictures left may increase this pressure and, thus, increase choosing.

*Elimination lineup procedure.* Designed specifically for children, Pozzulo and Lindsay (1999) developed the elimination lineup procedure to reduce children's feelings of pressure and demand. Pozzulo and Lindsay (1999) postulated a two-judgment theory of identification accuracy. First, witnesses make a relative judgment. This judgment is followed by an absolute judgment. Children are less likely to engage the second judgment resulting in a higher false positive rate in target-absent lineups. With a target-absent lineup, a relative judgment is sufficient to result in a correct decision. With a target-absent lineup, a relative judgment will lead to a false positive identification because the most similar-looking lineup member (in a target-absent lineup) is not the target. Children may be less likely to engage an absolute judgment compared to adults because of a feeling of pressure to having to make a selection that is greater than for adults. Children may stop their decision-making once a relative judgment is made. Moreover, the traditional lineup instructions may be too subtle for children to understand that they only should make an identification, if the person is the perpetrator. Based on these notions, Pozzulo and Lindsay (1999) developed the elimination lineup procedure whereby two decisions are explicitly requested from the child witnesses; first, witnesses are shown a simultaneous lineup and then are asked to pick out the person who looks most like the criminal. Once this person is selected, all other lineup members are removed and children are asked whether the person selected is in fact the criminal. Witnesses are reminded that the criminal may or may not be present. The elimination procedure was found to increase children's correct rejection rate to a level comparable to adults' correct rejection rate (Pozzulo & Lindsay, 1999). Moreover, the elimination procedure produced correct rejection rates comparable to levels previously obtained with adults shown a sequential lineup (Pozzulo & Lindsay, 1999).

The elimination procedure has been tested with different-aged witnesses and under varying conditions demonstrating that the procedure is robust and effective (e.g. Pozzulo et al., 2008; Pozzulo & Balfour, 2006). For example, preschoolers were exposed to a live target and following a 45-minute delay were then shown either a target-present or target-absent lineup presented using either the simultaneous or elimination procedure (Pozzulo, Dempsey, & Crescini, 2009). Preschoolers produced a significantly higher correct rejection rate with the elimination procedure. Intriguingly, the elimination also appeared helpful with increasing the correct identification rate.

Currently, the elimination procedure appears effective at increasing correct rejection rates for children at levels comparable to adults while maintaining comparable correct identification rates. Moreover, the elimination procedure seems effective for adults as well producing correct identification and rejection rates comparable to simultaneous and sequential procedures.

## Lineup size

Although there are similarities across North America when it comes to lineup identification practices, one obvious difference between Canada and the United States concerns the number of lineup members shown to an eyewitness. It is common to have six-person lineups in the United States, whereas Canada is likely to show witnesses a 12-person lineup. With adult witnesses, this increase in lineup members is negligible in terms of identification accuracy. Specifically, Nosworthy and Lindsay (1990) found that lineups containing up to 20 members did not produce differences in correct identification or rejection. For child witnesses, however, the increase in lineup members may be more taxing cognitively or may produce greater social demands such that identification accuracy rates are influenced. Pozzulo, Dempsey and Wells (2010) compared six- and 12-person lineups with participants who were 8- to 13-year-old. The elimination lineup procedure was used to present the lineups (Pozzulo & Lindsay, 1999). Both correct identification and correct rejection rates did not differ significantly as a function of lineup size. Children produced comparable rates of accuracy for the six- and 12-person lineups.

## Technology and lineups

As the use of online or video imaging increases, it is not surprising that photographic lineups may move to a digital format. In the United Kingdom, video parades are common for identification. Havard, Memon, Clifford and Gabbert (2010) compared the abilities of 7- to 9-year-olds and 13- to 15-year-olds to make identifications from video versus static photo lineups. Participants witnessed a live event and then following a two- to three-day delay were shown either a target-present or -absent lineup in one of the two formats. Correct identification rates did not differ between the two age groups or the two formats. Correct rejection rates were higher for adolescents compared to the younger children when video lineups were used. There was no difference in the correct rejection rate as a function of age for the photographic lineups. These data suggest that video identification procedures can be used with children without losing accuracy compared to the more traditional photographic lineup.

## Are children ever more accurate than adults?

In an intriguing, large-scale study, Ross, Marsil, Benton, Hoffman, Warren, Lindsay and Metzger (2006) examined 5- to 12-year-olds who watched a videotape of a teacher having her wallet stolen. The video either did or did not include a bystander. For some children, the lineup contained a photo of the bystander but not the thief. Eleven- to 12-year-olds were more likely to misidentify the bystander compared to children who did not see the bystander. For 5- to 10-year-olds, however, this effect was *not* found. The authors concluded that "the relationship between a child's age and witness accuracy is context dependent. The legal system should consider not only the age of the witness but the other factors present when trying to evaluate the capabilities of the witness" (p. 256). Numerous individuals present during an event may elicit transference and witnesses of different ages may be more or less sensitive to this.

## Identification accuracy across childhood for familiar others

All the research reviewed thus far has focused exclusively on the identification of unfamiliar targets. The studies reviewed have used targets that were seen for the first time during the "exposure phase." Often, the exposure is brief, lasting approximately a minute or so. Much of the crimes against children, however, may involve perpetrators that the child has seen on a previous occasion or may have some experience with. Consider the case of Elizabeth Smart outlined at the beginning of this chapter. The perpetrator was not a complete stranger. In fact, the perpetrator was someone hired by the Smarts and seen by the witness Mary Katherine Smart (Elizabeth's sister) on previous occasions at the house. Also, consider cases where the perpetrator may be a staff member at a school, or someone who lives in the neighborhood, or even a mother's new boyfriend. Limited research is available to assess children's abilities with more "familiar" targets than "stranger" targets. What does children's identification accuracy look like in these situations?

In one study by Cain, Baker-Ward and Eaton (2005), children aged 19-months to 5-year-old were exposed to volunteer caregivers for a total of 20 hours over a six- to eight-week period. The youngest children (mean 34 months old) performed at chance level, that is, their identification of the caregivers were comparable to making a selection randomly. The older children, however, were significantly better, performing above chance. In an applied context, it is not uncommon for children to be exposed to repeated questioning and even repeated lineups. Lewis, Wilkins, Baker and Woobey (1995) found that with repeated questioning, 3- to 4-year-olds may change a correct identification decision to an incorrect identification decision. Overall, few studies have examined the identification of familiar others and consequently, firm conclusions cannot be drawn regarding children's abilities in this context. Also, it is important to note that the term "familiar" may have various definitions across studies. In addition to familiarity, other factors may come into play, such as the interest/preference the child has in something or someone that may increase or decrease their identification accuracy (Cain, Baker-Ward, & Eaton, 2005).

Far more research in the domain of the identification of a "familiar-stranger" is critical, given many crimes involving children are of perpetrators children have had some previous exposure to.

## Age, description and identification

As mentioned at the beginning of this chapter, person descriptions tend to be limited and vague. These types of descriptions may suggest that the witness did not get a good look at the perpetrator or has a poor memory of the perpetrator. Unfortunately, brief descriptions are characteristic of children and youths. The criminal justice system may perceive children and youths as bad witnesses who should not attempt an identification. However, the relation between description and identification may be tenuous for a variety of reasons (for witnesses of all ages).

Providing a description is a recall task dependent on verbal ability, whereas identification is a recognition task that is almost independent of linguistic demands (other than being able to understand the task instructions). Wells (1984) has suggested that recall and recognition tasks may be driven by different processes. Ellis (1984) suggests that verbal processes may be irrelevant to encoding and the recognition of faces (also Chance & Goldstein, 1976; Goldstein, Johnson, & Chance, 1979; Malpass, Lavigueur, & Weldon, 1973). Also, it has been suggested that retrieval cues for recall tasks may differ from those for recognition tasks (Flexser & Tulving, 1978). In examination of the relation between description accuracy and identification accuracy for adults, a significant relation has not been found (Cutler, Penrod, & Martens, 1987; Pigott & Brigham, 1985; Pigott, Brigham, & Bothwell, 1990). However, Sporer (1996) reported a significant relationship between description length (number of descriptors) and correct identification decisions for adults. Witnesses who made a correct decision reported more descriptors ($M = 6.52$) than witnesses who made an incorrect decision ($M = 5.16$).

Pozzulo and Warren (2003) found that youths (10–14-year-old) provided fewer descriptors than did adults, regardless of identification accuracy. Description length did not predict the identification accuracy from a youth witness. Description length also did not appear to be a good marker for identification accuracy from adults. Pozzulo, Dempsey, Crescini and Lemieux (2009) also examined the relation between eyewitness recall and recognition for children aged 9- to 12-year-olds and adults across two studies. Not surprisingly, children recalled fewer crime details and perpetrator descriptors than did adults, although accuracy for descriptors was comparable between the two groups. Across both studies, there was no evidence that participants who made accurate lineup decisions recalled more details than participants who made inaccurate identification decisions. Also, there was no evidence that witnesses who made accurate identification decisions were more likely to be accurate in their recall than were witnesses who made inaccurate identification decisions.

## Conclusion

Reliable descriptive and identification evidence is possible from child witnesses, provided developmentally appropriate procedures are used. Unfortunately, person descriptions are limited for both child and adult witnesses. Although generally accurate, greater person descriptions would be helpful to narrow suspect searches. Methods to increase person descriptions should be examined for both children and adults. The literature for developmentally appropriate interview protocols may be helpful to increase descriptive information of the perpetrator. It is important not to infer the accuracy of identification evidence from the quantity or accuracy of person descriptions.

Attempts to increase children's correct rejection rates have resulted in promising avenues to increase correct identifications. Further research should explore whether increases in correct identifications can be found consistently. The elimination lineup procedure appears effective at maintaining correct identifications while increasing correct rejections for children (and adults). This procedure has been investigated under various conditions and appears successful. For example, in a recent investigation, Humphries, Holliday and Flowe (2011) examined the identification abilities of children (5- to 6-year-olds, and 9- to 10-year-olds) and adults using video lineups with the following procedures: simultaneous, sequential and elimination. The rate of correct identification using simultaneous and elimination procedures did not differ as a function of age. The sequential lineup produced a lower correct identification rate for all aged participants. In terms of correct rejection rates, the elimination procedure led to a higher rate for adults. Correct rejection for both groups of children was not influenced by identification procedure. Currently, the elimination procedure may be effective for numerous aged witnesses and under various conditions.

# References

Baenninger, M. (1994). The development of face recognition: Featural or configural processing? *Journal of Experimental Child Psychology, 57*, 377–396.

Bartlett, J. C., & Searcy, J. (1993). Inversion and configuration of faces. *Cognitive Psychology, 25*, 281–316.

Beal, C. R., Schmitt, K. L., & Deckle, D. J. (1995). Eyewitness identification of children: Effects of absolute judgments, nonverbal response options, and event encoding. *Law and Human Behavior, 19*, 197–261.

Blaney, R. L., & Winograd, E. (1978). Developmental differences in children's recognition memory for faces. *Developmental Psychology, 14*, 441–442.

Bower, G. H., & Karlin, M. B. (1974). Levels of processing: A framework for memory research. *Journal of Verbal Learning and Verbal Behavior, 11*, 671–684.

Bradshaw, J. L., & Wallace, G. (1971). Models for the processing and identification of faces. *Perception & Psychophysics, 9*, 443–448.

Brainerd, C. J., & Reyna, V. F. (1995). *The Science of False Memory.* Oxford University Press: New York, NY.

Brigham, J. C., Van Verst, M., & Bothwell, R. K. (1986). Accuracy of children's eyewitness identifications in a field setting. *Basic and Applied Social Psychology, 7*, 295–306.

Cain, W. J., Baker-Ward, L., & Eaton, K. L. (2005). A face in the crowd: The influences of familiarity and delay on preschoolers' recognition. *Psychology, Crime, & Law, 11*, 315–327.

Camparo, L. B., Wagner, J. T., & Saywitz, K. J. (2001). Interviewing children about real and fictitious events: Revisiting the narrative elaboration procedure. *Law and Human Behavior, 25*, 63–80.

Carey, S. (1981). The development of face perception. In G. Davies, H. Ellis, & J. Shepherd (Eds), *Perceiving and Remembering Faces* (pp. 9–38). New York: Academic Press.

Carey, S., & Diamond, R. (1977). From piecemeal to configurational representation of faces. *Science, 195,* 312–314.

Carey, S., Diamond, R., & Woods, B. (1980). Development of face recognition: A maturational component? *Developmental Psychology, 16,* 257–269.

CBC News (February 2, 2011). *Barrhaven Sexual Assault Never Happened: Police.* Retrieved from http://www.cbc.ca/news/canada/ottawa/story/2011/02/02/ottawa-sexual-assault-unfounded.html on June 23, 2011.

Ceci, S. J., & Bruck, M. (1993). Suggestibility of the child witness: A historical review and synthesis. *Psychological Bulletin, 113,* 403–439.

Ceci, S. J., Toglia, M. P., & Ross, D. F. (1987). *Children's Eyewitness Memory.* New York: Springer-Verlag.

Chance, J., & Goldstein, A. (1976). Recognition of faces and verbal labels. *Bulletin of the Psychonomic Society, 7,* 384–387.

Chance, J., & Goldstein, A. (1979). Reliability of face recognition performance. *Bulletin of the Psychonomic Society, 14,* 115–117.

Chance, J., & Goldstein, A. (1984). Face-recognition memory: Implications for children's eyewitness testimony. *Journal of Social Issues, 40,* 69–85.

Chance, J., Turner, A., & Goldstein, A. (1982). Development of differential recognition of own- and other-race faces. *Journal of Psychology, 112,* 29–37.

Chung, M., & Thomson, D. M. (1995). Development of face recognition. *British Journal of Psychology, 86,* 55–87.

Clifford, B. R., & Bull, R. (1978). *The Psychology of Person Identification.* London: Routledge & Kegan Paul.

Cross, J. F., Cross, J., & Daly, J. (1971). Sex, race, age, and beauty as factors in recognition of faces. *Perception and Psychophysics, 10,* 393–396.

Cutler, B. L., Penrod, S. D., & Martens, T. K. (1987). Improving the reliability of eyewitness identifications: Putting context into context. *Journal of Applied Psychology, 72,* 629–637.

Davies, G. (1996). Children's identification evidence. In S. Sporer, R. Malpass, & G. Koehnken (Eds), *Psychological Issues in Eyewitness Identification* (pp. 233–258). Mahwah, NJ: Lawrence Erlbaum Associates.

Davies, G., Stevenson-Robb, Y., & Flin, R. (1988). Tales out of school: Children's memory for a simulated health inspection. In M. Gruneberg, P. Morris, & R. Sykes (Eds), *Practical Aspects of Memory: Current Research and Issues.* Volume 1, *Memory in Everyday Life* (pp. 122–127). Chichester, England: Wiley.

Davies, G., Tarrant, A., & Flin, R. (1989). Close encounters of the witness kind: Children's memory for a simulated health inspection. *British Journal of Psychology, 80,* 415–429.

Dent, H. (1982). The effect of interviewing strategies on the results of interviews with child witnesses. In A. Trankell (Ed.), *Reconstructing the Past* (pp. 279–298). Dordrecht, the Netherlands: Kluwer.

Dent, H., & Stephenson, G. (1979). An experimental study of the effectiveness of different techniques of questioning child witnesses. *British Journal of Social and Clinical Psychology, 18,* 41–51.

Diamond, R., & Carey, S. (1977). Developmental changes in the recognition of faces. *Journal of Experimental Child Psychology, 23,* 1–22.

Diamond, R., & Carey, S. (1986). Why faces are and are not special: An effect of expertise. *Journal of Experimental Psychology: General, 115,* 107–117.

Ellis, H. D. (1984). Practical aspects of face memory. In G. L. Wells & E. F. Loftus (Eds), *Eyewitness Testimony: Psychological Perspectives* (pp. 12–37). New York: Cambridge University Press.

Ellis, H. D. (1992). The development of face processing skills. *Proceedings of the Royal Society Series B, 335,* 105–111.

Ellis, H. D. & Flin, R. H. (1990). Encoding and storage effects in 7-year-olds' and 10-year-olds' memory for faces. *British Journal of Developmental Psychology, 8,* 77–92.

Ellis, H. D., Shepherd, J. W., & Bruce, A. (1973). The effects of age and sex upon adolescents' recognition of faces. *Journal of Genetic Psychology, 123,* 173–174.

Ellis, H. D., Shepherd, J. W., & Davies, G. M. (1980). The deterioration of verbal descriptions of faces over different delay intervals. *Journal of Police Science and Administration, 8,* 101–106.

Farah, M. J., Tanaka, J. W., & Drain, H. M. (1995). What causes the face inversion effect? *Journal of Experimental Psychology: Human Perception and Performance, 21,* 628–634.

Farah, M. J., Wilson, K. D., Drain, H. M., & Tanaka, J. W. (1998). What is "special" about face perception? *Psychological Review, 105,* 482–498.

Feinman, S., & Entwistle, D. R. (1976). Children's ability to recognize other children's faces. *Child Development, 47,* 506–510.

Flexser, A. J., & Tulving, E. (1978). Retrieval independence in recognition and recall. *Psychological Review, 85,* 153–171.

Flin, R. H. (1980). Age effects in children's memory for unfamiliar faces. *Developmental Psychology, 16,* 373–374.

Flin, R. H., & Shepherd, J. W. (1986). Tall stories: Eyewitnesses' ability to estimate height and weight characteristics. *Human Learning, 5,* 29–38.

Friere, A., & Lee, K. (2001). Face recognition in 4- to 7-year-olds. Processing of configural, featural, and paraphernalia information. *Journal of Experimental Child Psychology, 80,* 347–371.

Goldstein, A. G. (1977). The fallibility of the eyewitness. Psychological evidence. In B. D. Sales (Ed.), *Psychology in the Legal Process.* New York: Spectrum.

Goldstein, A. G., & Chance, J. (1964). Recognition of children's faces. *Child Development, 35,* 129–136.

Goldstein, A. G., Johnson, K. A., & Chance, J. E. (1979). Does fluency of face description imply superior face recognition. *Bulletin of the Psychonomic Society, 13,* 15–18.

Goodman, G. S., Bottoms, B. L., Schwartz-Kenney, B., & Rudy, L. (1991). Children's memory for a stressful event: Improving children's reports. *Journal of Narrative and Life History, 1,* 69–99.

Goodman, G. S., & Reed, R. (1986). Age differences in eyewitness testimony. *Law and Human Behavior, 10,* 317–332.

Hay, D. C., & Cox, R. (2000). Developmental changes in the recognition of faces and facial features. *Infant and Child Development, 9,* 199–212.

Havard, C., Memon, A., Clifford, B., & Gabbert, F. (2010). A comparison of video and static photo lineups with child and adolescent witnesses. *Applied Cognitive Psychology, 24,* 1209–1221.

Hochberg, J., & Galper, E. (1967). Recognition of faces: An exploratory study. *Psychonomic Society, 9,* 619–620.

Holliday, R. E. (2003). Reducing misinformation effects in children with cognitive interviews: Dissociating recollection and familiarity. *Child Development, 74,* 728–751.

Holliday, R. E., & Albon, A. J. (2004). Minimising misinformation effects in young children with cognitive interview mnemonics. *Applied Cognitive Psychology, 18,* 263–281.

Holliday, R. E., Douglas, K., & Hayes, B. K. (1999). Children's eyewitness suggestibility: Memory trace strength revisited. *Cognitive Development, 14*, 443–462.

Holliday, R. E., Humphries, J. E., Milne, R., Memon, A., Houlder L., Lyons, A., Bull, R. (2012). Reducing misinformation effects in older adults with cognitive interview mnemonics. *Psychology & Aging, 27*(4).

Humphries, J. E., Holliday, R. E., & Flowe, H. (2011). Faces in motion: Age-related changes in eyewitness identification performance in simultaneous, sequential, and elimination video lineups. *Applied Cognitive Psychology.* DOI:10.1002/acp.1808.

Innocence Project (2011). *Know the Cases.* Retrieved from www.innocenceproject.org on June 22, 2011.

Kask, K., Bull, R., Heinla, I., & Davies, G. (2007). The effect of a standard to improve person descriptions by children. *Journal of Police and Criminal Psychology, 22*, 77–83.

Lewis, C., Wilkins, R., Baker, L., & Woobey, A. (1995). "Is this man your dadday?": Suggestibility in children's eyewitness identification of a family member. *Child Abuse and Neglect, 19*, 739–744.

Lindsay, R. C. L., Lea, J. A., & Fulford, J. A. (1991). Sequential lineup presentation: Technique matters. *Journal of Applied Psychology, 76*, 741–745.

Lindsay, R. C. L., Pozzulo, J. D., Craig, W., Lee, K., & Corber, S. (1997). Simultaneous lineups, sequential lineups, and showups: Eyewitness identification decisions of adults and children. *Law and Human Behavior, 21*, 391–404.

Lindsay, R. C. L., & Wells, G. L. (1985). Improving eyewitness identifications from lineups: Simultaneous versus sequential lineup presentations. *Journal of Applied Psychology, 70*, 556–564.

Lowenstein, J. A., Blank, H., & Sauer, J. D. (2010). Uniforms affect the accuracy of children's eyewitness identification decisions. *Journal of Investigative Psychology and Offender Profiling, 7*, 59–73.

Luus, C. E. & Wells, G. L. (1991). Eyewitness identification and the selection of distractors for lineups. *Law and Human Behavior, 15*, 43–57.

Malpass, R. S., & Devine, P. G. (1981). Eyewitness identification: Lineup instructions and the absence of the offender. *Journal of Applied Psychology, 66*, 482–489.

Malpass, R. S., Lavigueur, H., & Weldon, D. E. (1973). Verbal and visual training in face recognition. *Perception and Psychophysics, 14*, 285–292.

Marche, T. A. (1999). Memory strength affects reporting of misinformation. *Journal of Experimental Child Psychology, 73*, 45–71.

Marin, B. V., Holmes, D. L., Guth, M., & Kovac, P. (1979). The potential of children as eyewitnesses. *Law and Human Behavior, 3*, 295–305.

Meissner, C. A., Sporer, S. L., & Schooler, J. W. (2007). Person descriptions as eyewitness evidence. In R. C. L. Lindsay, D. F. Ross, J. D. Read, & M. P. Toglia (Eds), *Handbook of Eyewitness Psychology* (pp. 3–34). Mahwah, NJ: Lawrence Erlbaum and Associates.

Nosworthy, G., & Lindsay, R. C. L. (1990). Does nominal lineup size matter? *Journal of Applied Psychology, 75*, 358–361.

Parker, J. F., & Carranza, L. E. (1989). Eyewitness testimony of children in target-present and target-absent lineups. *Law and Human Behavior, 13*, 133–149.

Parker, J. F., & Myers, A. (2001). Attempts to improve children's identifications from sequential presentation lineups. *Journal of Applied Social Psychology, 21*, 796–815.

Parker, J. F., & Ryan, V. (1993). An attempt to reduce guessing behavior in children's and adults' eyewitness identifications. *Law and Human Behavior, 17*, 11–26.

Pigott, M. A., & Brigham, J. C. (1985). Relationship between accuracy of prior description and facial recognition. *Journal of Applied Psychology, 70*, 547–555.

Pigott, M. A., Brigham, J. C., & Bothwell, R. K. (1990). A field study on the relationship between quality of eyewitnesses' descriptions and identification accuracy. *Journal of Police Science and Administration, 17,* 84–88.

Pozzulo, J. D., & Balfour, J. (2006). The impact of change in appearance on children's eyewitness identification accuracy: Comparing simultaneous and elimination lineup procedures. *Legal and Criminological Psychology, 11,* 25–34.

Pozzulo, J. D., & Dempsey, J. (2006). Biased lineup instructions: Examining the effect of pressure on children's and adults' eyewitness identification accuracy. *Journal of Applied Social Psychology, 36,* 1381–1394.

Pozzulo, J. D., Dempsey, J., Bruer, K., & Sheahan, C. (2011). The culprit in target-absent lineups: Understanding young children's false positive responding. *Journal of Police and Criminal Psychology.* doi:10.1007/s11896–011–9089–8.

Pozzulo, J. D., Dempsey, J., Corey, S., Girardi, A., Lawandi, A., & Aston, C. (2008). Can a lineup procedure designed for child witnesses work for adults: Comparing simultaneous, sequential, and elimination lineup procedures. *Journal of Applied Social Psychology, 38,* 2195–2209.

Pozzulo, J. D., Dempsey, J., & Crescini, C. (2009). Preschoolers' person description and identification accuracy: A comparison of the simultaneous and elimination lineup procedures. *Journal of Applied Developmental Psychology, 30,* 667–676.

Pozzulo, J. D., Dempsey, J., Crescini, C., & Lemieux, J. (2009). Examining the relation between eyewitness recall and recognition for children and adults. *Psychology, Crime, and Law, 15,* 409–424.

Pozzulo, J. D., Dempsey, J., & Wells, K. (2010). Does lineup size matter with child witnesses. *Journal of Police and Criminal Psychology, 25,* 22–26.

Pozzulo, J. D., & Lindsay, R. C. L. (1997). Increasing correct identifications by children. *Expert Evidence, 5,* 126–132.

Pozzulo, J. D., & Lindsay, R. C. L. (1998). Identification accuracy of children versus adults: A meta-analysis. *Law and Human Behavior, 22,* 549–570.

Pozzulo, J. D., & Lindsay, R. C. L. (1999). Elimination lineups: An improved identification procedure for child eyewitnesses. *Journal of Applied Psychology, 84,* 167–176.

Pozzulo, J. D., & Marciniak, S. (2006). Comparing identification procedures when the perpetrator has changed appearance. *Psychology, Crime, and Law, 12,* 429–438.

Pozzulo, J. D., & Warren, K. (2003). Descriptions and identifications of strangers by child and adult witnesses. *Journal of Applied Psychology, 88,* 315–323.

Ricci, C. M., Beal, C. R., & Dekle, D. J. (1996). The effect of parent versus unfamiliar interviewers on children's eyewitness memory and identification accuracy. *Law and Human Behavior, 20,* 483–500.

Rhodes, G. (1988). Looking at face: First-order and second-order features as determinants of facial appearance. *Perception, 17,* 43–63.

Ross, D. F., Marsil, D. F., Benton, T. R., Hoffman, R., Warren, A. R., Lindsay, R. C. L., & Metzger, R. (2006). Children's susceptibility to misidentifying a familiar bystander from a lineup: When younger is better. *Law and Human Behavior, 30,* 249–257.

Saywitz, K., & Camparo, L. (1998). Interviewing child witnesses: A developmental perspective. *Child Abuse and Neglect, 22,* 825–843.

Saywitz, K. J., & Snyder, L. (1996). Narrative elaboration: Test of a new procedure for interviewing children. *Journal of Consulting and Clinical Psychology, 64,* 1347–1357.

Scapinello, K. F., & Yarmey, A. D. (1970). The role of familiarity and orientation in immediate and delayed recall of pictorial stimuli. *Psychonomic Society, 21,* 329–330.

Schwarzer, G. (2000). Development of face processing: The effect of face inversion. *Child Development, 71,* 391–401.

Sergent, J. (1984). An investigation into component and configural processes underlying face perception. *The British Journal of Psychology, 75,* 221–242.

Shapiro, P. N., & Penrod, S. (1986). Meta-analysis of facial identification studies. *Psychological Bulletin, 100,* 139–156.

Smart, E., Smart, L. & Morton, L. (2003). *Bringing Elizabeth Home: A Story of Faith and Hope.* New York: Doubleday.

Sporer, S. L. (1996). Psychological aspects of person descriptions. In S. Sporer, R. Malpass, & G. Koehnken (Eds), *Psychological Issues in Eyewitness Identification* (pp. 53–86). Mahwah, NJ: Lawrence Erlbaum Associates.

Steblay, N. M. (1997). Social influence in eyewitness recall: A meta-analytic review of lineup instruction effects. *Law and Human Behavior, 21,* 283–297.

Tanaka, J. W., & Farah, M. J. (1993). Parts and wholes in face recognition. *Quarterly Journal of Experimental Psychology, 46,* 225–245.

Tanaka, J. W., Kay, J. B., Grinnell, E., Stansfield, B., & Szechter, L. (1998). Face recognition in young children: When the whole is greater than the sum of its parts. *Visual Cognition, 5,* 479–496.

Waterman, A., Blades, M., & Spencer, C. (2004). Indicating when you do not know the answer: The effect of question format and interviewer knowledge on children's "don't know" response. *British Journal of Developmental Psychology, 22,* 135–148.

Wells, G. L. (1984). The psychology of lineup identifications. *Journal of Applied Social Psychology, 14,* 89–103.

Wells, G. L. (1993). What do we know about eyewitness identification? *American Psychologist, 48,* 553–571.

Wells, G. L., & Hryciw, B. (1984). Memory for faces: Encoding and retrieval operations. *Memory & Cognition, 12,* 338–344.

Wells, G. L., & Luus, E. (1990). Police lineups as experiments: Social methodology as a framework for properly-conducted lineups. *Personality and Social Psychology Bulletin, 16,* 106–117.

Winograd, E. (1976). Recognition memory for faces following nine different judgments. *Bulletin of the Psychonomic Society, 8,* 419–421.

Yin, R. K. (1969). Looking at upside-down faces. *Journal of Experimental Psychology, 81,* 141–145.

Zajac, R., & Karageorge, A. (2009). The wildcard: A simple technique for improving children's target-absent lineup performance. *Applied Cognitive Psychology, 23,* 358–368.

# CHAPTER 9

# The Psychology of the Missing: Missing and Abducted Children

JAMES MICHAEL LAMPINEN, CHRISTOPHER S. PETERS,
VICKI GIER, AND LINDSEY N. SWEENEY

This chapter focuses on the problem of missing and abducted children. It takes as its guiding principle the idea that addressing this problem requires a focused empirical research effort to better understand the root causes of how children go missing, the consequences of children going missing, and what can be done to ameliorate that problem. In this regard, the chapter focuses on a growing body of research on the topic of *prospective person memory* (Lampinen, Arnal, & Hicks, 2009a). Prospective person memory refers to people's ability to recognize an individual they have been asked to be on the lookout for, and to take appropriate action if the individual is spotted. In missing child cases, prospective person memory involves contacting the authorities if one sees a child whose picture has been shown on a missing child poster, AMBER Alert or other public notification system. Missing child notification systems also rely on *retrospective person memory* (Lampinen, Miller, & Dehon, 2011). Retrospective person memory refers to situations where a member of the general public has encountered a missing or wanted person in the past, and later encounters an alert concerning the person.

We organize the chapter along the following lines. First, we describe some definitional and conceptual issues and address the scope of the missing child problem. In this regard, we will primarily rely on incidence and prevalence data from the United States, since this is the data we are most familiar with. Second, we describe characteristics of people who commit these kinds of crimes against children, and characteristics of children who are most often victimized. Third, we discuss research on the physical and psychological harm caused to children and their families in missing child cases. Finally, we discuss approaches to ameliorating the problem.

## How big a problem is it?

It has been estimated that around 800,000 children are reported missing annually in the United States (Flores, 2002). This is a very large number and is the source of the claim that a child goes missing in the United States every 40 seconds (AmberView, 2009). It is important to look at this number more closely so as to have a proper perspective on the true scope of the missing child problem. The number comes from a series of large U.S. Department of Justice-funded studies that randomly sampled U.S. households and asked parents about cases where a child may have gone missing, for even relatively brief periods of times (Finkelhor, Hotaling, & Sedlak, 1990; Flores, 2002). The studies are known as the National Incidence Studies of Missing, Abducted, Runaway and Thrownaway Children (NISMART). Two separate NISMART studies were conducted, approximately 10 years apart. The data we discuss in this chapter is based on the more recent study, NISMART-2 (Sedlak, Finkelhor, Hammer, & Schultz, 2002).

Beyond merely providing incidence and prevalence data, the NISMART studies contributed to the literature by making important conceptual distinctions (Finkelhor et al., 1990). NISMART researchers noted the concept of *child abduction* and the concept of *missing children* are only partially overlapping categories. Children can go missing for a number of reasons, only some of which involve abduction. NISMART (Flores, 2002) classified missing child cases into five broad categories: (1) Runaways/throwaways; (2) Family Abductions; (3) Non-family Abductions; (4) Missing Involuntarily, Lost or Injured; (5) Missing for Benign Explanations. Just as not all missing child cases involve abductions, not all abductions involve a child who is missing. In some cases, especially family abductions, the child's caretaker may know the child's whereabouts even though they are unable to gain access to the child. Or a child may be abducted, but only held for an hour or two. In these cases, the parents may not become aware of the abduction until it is over. In fact, a surprisingly large proportion of missing children are never even reported to the police (Sedlak et al., 2002).

### Runaways/Throwaways

According to NISMART-2, the most common reason why children go missing is because they run away from home or are forced out of their home by their caregiver (Sedlak et al., 2002). Children who decide to leave home are called "runaways", whereas children who are forced out of their homes are called "throwaways" (Adams, Gullotta, & Clancy, 1999). In practice, it is sometimes difficult to decide whether any particular case constitutes a runaway or throwaway episode. The parent may consider the child to be a runaway and the child may consider themselves to have been forced out of the home. Many episodes have both runaway and throwaway characteristics. For this reason, NISMART-2 did not attempt to distinguish between these categories empirically, and treated runaway/throwaway as one broad category. (Hammer et al., 2002a).

Approximately 1.68 million U.S. youth are involved in runaway/throwaway incidents annually (Hammer, Finkelhor & Sedlak, 2002a). Out of this number, only 539,100 cases were reported to police. It is important to note that not all runaways are actually missing. For example, a child may run away from home and move into the house of a friend. The parents may know that's where their child is, but may not be able to secure the child's return. The vast majority of runaways are in their late teens with males and females being equally likely to runaway. Runaway incidents occur nearly twice as often in the summer, with the majority of youth traveling between 10 and 50 miles away from home, and being away from home for less than a week.

## Family abductions

Although the public tends to think of child abductions in the context of abductions by complete strangers, most child abductions are actually committed by family members, most often parents (Sedlak et al., 2002). NISMART defines family abduction quite broadly to include abductions by parents, other biological relatives, and even non-family members who are playing parental roles (such as live-in boyfriends or girlfriends; Hammer, Finkelhor, & Sedlak, 2002b). NISMART also distinguishes between "takings" and "keepings". As the name implies, a *taking* occurs when one person has legal control of a child and another person takes the child away from that person. A *keeping* occurs when a person has legal control of a child, but refuses to allow access to the child when legally required to do so. Although one would typically assume that abductions are perpetrated by the non-custodial parent, custodial parents can also commit child abductions. This follows from the fact that, in most custody settlements, both parents retain some custody or visitation rights. Violations of those rights are treated as family abductions under the NISMART rubric.

Under these broad definitions, NISMART-2 found that there were 203,100 family abductions in 1999 (Hammer et al., 2002b). In 117,200 of those cases, the parents did not know their child's whereabouts, for at least part of the time – that is, the child was missing. These cases resulted in 56,500 missing child reports being submitted to law enforcement agencies. Oftentimes, these matters are resolved by the parties themselves or through the civil court system rather than through law enforcement. Most family abduction cases are resolved with the child's safe return; however, about one in five cases takes more than a month to be resolved.

## Non-family abductions

When most people think of child abductions, they think of cases in which a complete stranger forcefully takes a child. The term *stereotypical kidnappings* has been used to describe this type of cases (Finkelhor, Hammer, & Sedlak, 2002). Stereotypical kidnappings are formally defined as abductions committed by strangers, where the victim is moved by 50 miles or more, the perpetrator uses force or threat of force, and where the perpetrator intends to keep the child, hold the child for ransom or kill the child. Although such cases represent the public stereotype of child abductions, only around 100 such cases occur in the United States every year. Stereotypical kidnappings are a subset of a larger category of abductions called *broadscope non-family abductions*. Formally, a broadscope abduction is defined as a situation where a child is moved by force or threat of force, and the child is held for an hour or more. Cases where a young child is lured or enticed to go with the abductor also fit under the definition of broadscope abduction. These cases can include situations that fit the pattern of the stereotypical kidnapping, but may also include cases where the child is held in the context of another crime, oftentimes sexual assaults. NISMART-2 found that there were 58,200 non-family abductions in the United States in 1999. Of these cases, only 33,000 involved cases where the caretaker was aware that the child had been missing, and only 12,100 of the cases were reported to the police. Most non-family abductions are resolved in under a day, with only a fraction of a percent leading to long-term missing child cases.

In most non-family abductions, the abductor is someone known to the child (Finkelhor et al., 2002). However, this does not mean we should be entirely unconcerned about abductions of children by strangers. Stranger abductions account for approximately 37 percent of the 58,200 non-family abductions that occur every year in the United States – 21,534 cases annually. In the year that data was collected for NISMART-2, there were about 81,000,000 children in the United States (Federal Interagency Forum on Child and Family Statistics, 2011), so that amounts to approximately 1 in 3,761 children who are victimized in stranger abductions every year in the

United States. About 80 percent of non-family abductions involve children over the age of 12 – which suggests approximately 17,000 stranger abductions occur annually in this age group in the United States.[1] In the year that the data for NISMART-2 were collected, there were 24 million children in this age range in the United States (Federal Interagency Forum on Child and Family Statistics, 2011). That implies a 1 in 1,411 chance of being a victim of a stranger abduction for children in this age range. Most non-family abductions involve girls (69 percent; Finkelhor et al., 2002), and so we can estimate that around 12,000 stranger abductions of girls over age 12 occur every year in the United States. This results in an estimate of a 1 in 1,000 chance of a girl over 12 years old being abducted by a stranger in any particular year.

The above only involves cases where the abduction attempt was successful. We would guess that most parents teach their children to take reasonable precautions when approached by strangers. If so, then the correct index of the potential risk posed by strangers is not completed abductions, but attempted abductions. Evidence in the United States indicates that as many as 100,000 attempted but unsuccessful stranger abductions may occur every year (Finkelhor, Hotaling, & Asdigian, 1995). A more recent study in Britain found that at least 6.7 percent of children between the ages of 9–16 in one sample had been a victim of an attempted or completed sexual assault or abduction by a stranger in the past year (Gallagher, Bradford, & Pease, 2008). For girls it was closer to 10 percent. About one in five of these cases involved an attempted or completed abduction (about 1.3 percent of children in that age range). For older children, the risk was greater.

It is certainly a mistake to exaggerate the danger posed by stereotypical kidnappings. Doing so risks creating a sense of panic in parents and children, and it risks seriously misallocating resources (Hahn-Holbrook, Holbrook, & Bering, 2010). Yet the above data also argue against public policy options which completely minimize the danger posed to children by strangers.

## Missing involuntarily, lost, or injured (MILI)

Children may go missing because the child got lost or got hurt. NISMART-2 found that 204,500 missing children fit into this category (Sedlak, Finkelhor, & Hammer, 2005). Note that this number far exceeds the number of non-family abductions and is comparable to the number of family abductions, yet research on cases where children are missing because they are lost or injured

---

[1] This assumes the relative proportion of stranger abductions to non-stranger abductions is uniform across age groups.

is extremely limited. Of the 204,500 missing children in this category, 68,100 were reported to authorities. An estimated 43,700 were missing due to an injury, with only 10,200 being reported to the authorities. Children in this category were disproportionately white, male and older, often times getting lost or injured while playing in wooded areas or parks away from their caretakers. The numbers for NISMART-2 are lower in this category compared to NISMART-1, possibly due to the increase in cell phone use by children and their caretakers.

## Missing for Benign Explanation (MBE)

Many times when a child is reported missing, the child was not actually in any danger. NISMART categorizes these cases as "missing for benign explanations – MBE" (Sedlak et al., 2005). For the child to be considered missing in the MBE category, the caretaker had to have contacted a local law enforcement agency or missing children's agency, or have spent at least one hour looking for the child. There are multiple reasons that a child may fit into this category, especially in an era where the family unit is no longer the center of a child or adolescence's daily routine. With parents working more than at any other time in history, and children in multiple after-school activities, it is easy to see how this hectic lifestyle could lead to miscommunications about where and when caretakers expect their children to arrive home. Sometimes, caretakers forget to tell each other who is picking up which child after school or a sporting event, or the caretaker, busy with his/her own work schedule, forgets to pick the child up. Other life incidents must be taken into account, such as being late due to a flat tire, or missing the school bus home, helping friends with their homework, or playing at a friend's house and losing track of time. NISMART-2 found that 374,700 children were reported in the missing benign explanation category in the year data was collected. This number represented 43 percent of all missing children. Teenagers were disproportionately overrepresented in the MBE category and, interestingly, there were significantly higher numbers of children in the MBE category in the Midwest relative to their prevalence in the child population.

When considering the figure that close to 800,000 children are reported missing in the United States every year, it is important to have some perspective on the issue. Most children who go missing are recovered relatively quickly, oftentimes within a day. Moreover, very few missing child cases are represented by the stereotypical kidnapping that get so much media attention. Indeed, more than 40 percent of reported missing child cases are simply false alarms. Despite this, it is important to note that a substantial number of very serious missing child cases do occur, and children in these cases can be in serious psychological and physical danger.

# Characteristics of perpetrators and victims

Although children go missing for a variety of reasons, a great deal of public attention is focused on cases of child abductions. Abduction cases are of particular interest to forensic psychologists because these cases involve a perpetrator who is operating outside the bounds of the law and morality. As a consequence, these people are important to understand. It is also important to know something about the victimology of abduction scenarios. Particularly, what are the characteristics of children who are abducted and how can that information be used to help protect these children?

## Family abductions

In a family abduction, the perpetrator is often the parent or someone very close to the parent (for example romantic partner or relative). In this section, we review research describing the perpetrators and victims of family abductions.

### Characteristics of the perpetrator of family abductions

In terms of general demographics, the overwhelming vast majority (78 percent) of abductors in family abductions are biological parents (Hammer et al., 2002b). This is followed by biological grandparents (14 percent); other blood-related kin, such as the parents' siblings or older siblings of the child (5 percent); and lastly, by non-blood related romantic partners (4 percent). Male family members (66 percent) accounted for almost two times as many family abductions as female family members. This fact may be partly due to the fact that mothers are generally more likely to receive custody than are fathers in divorce settlements (Gender Bias Study Committee, 1990). Forty-five percent of family abductors are between the ages of 30–39 (Hammer et al., 2002b). Many familial child abductors do not view the abduction as wrongful and feel justified in their actions (Johnston & Girdner, 2001).

Johnston and Girdner (2001) described six distinct, but overlapping, profiles for individuals at risk of attempting a family abduction. The first profile consists of parents who consistently threaten or attempt to abduct the child in question. A great deal of distrust exists between the two parents, which may be justified given the attempts/threats of one or both parents to illegally remove the child from the other parent's custody. Often, the abducting parents are unemployed, lack ties to the area, and have external resources or support from sympathetic allies (such as other family members) which will aid in their ability to hide from authorities.

The second profile involves parental abductors who suspect or believe that the other custodial parent is abusing or neglecting the child and feels that law enforcement has been ineffective in preventing the abuse. This often occurs when instances of previous abuse or neglect (either towards the spouse or children) has occurred or is believed to have occurred in the past. It is possible that these concerns are sometimes warranted. The custodial parent may, in truth, be currently neglecting or abusing the child, but insufficient evidence exists to prove the claims in court. Abductors that fit this profile typically view their actions as not only justified, but necessary to protect the safety of their children. Furthermore, they often have the support of other family members or friends to support their beliefs (Johnston & Girdner, 2001).

The third profile consists of parental abductors who suffer from paranoid delusions. Many of these delusions are so incredible that there is no question that they are unfounded (for example, believing that the custodial parent is actually an alien). As a result, these abductors also believe they are acting out of necessity to protect the child from harm. However, unlike the second profile, these individuals do not typically have the support of others in their actions, nor do they feel the need for outside support. Psychotic abductors are among the most dangerous of familial abductors, as their actions can be unpredictable and potentially violent. This type of profile, however, is thankfully rare, accounting for only 4 percent of all family abductions (Johnston & Girdner, 2001).

The fourth profile of parental abductors involves parents with severe psychopathic tendencies. Such individuals have a significant lack of regard for societal rules and a disregard for the concerns or feelings of others. To the psychopathic abductor, the child is merely a pawn to obtain something else they value or to get revenge on the custodial parent. Abductors with this profile are also dangerous, as they would not hesitate nor feel remorse for causing harm to the child. Like the third profile, abductors with severe psychopathic tendencies are also thankfully rare (Johnston & Girdner, 2001).

The fifth profile consists of abductors who were previously members of a mixed-culture marriage and are citizens of a foreign country. These abductors typically idealize their native culture and have a desire to raise the child in the values of their native culture, instead of the culture of their former spouse. Abductors with this profile typically have a number of resources and/or family members in their native country. Unfortunately, given the high variability of international laws regarding child custody, it is often difficult to recover the child when they have been absconded to foreign countries – especially if the country is not a signatory of the Hague Treaty (Johnston & Girdner, 2001).

The final profile consists of abductors who feel alienated from the legal system for some reason. This profile could include parents who have previous criminal records, are poorly educated or feel the legal system has somehow failed them in the past. People who meet this profile may not trust the legal system to treat them fairly or act in the best interests of the child. Therefore, the abductor chooses to take measures into their own hands. This profile accounts for a substantial proportion of familial abductors. Nearly, 50 percent of all parental abductors have a previous criminal record (Johnston & Girdner, 2001).

## Characteristics of the victim of family abductions

Both male and female children are equally likely to be abducted by a family member (Hammer et al., 2002b). Over three-quarters (79 percent) of children taken in family abductions are younger than 11 years old. Meanwhile, only a small percentage (~4 percent) were older teens between the ages of 15 and 17. Hammer et al. (2002) speculate that this may be due to the fact that older teens were more able to think for themselves and make their own decision regarding which parent to stay with. However, it is also consistent with the fact that most divorces occur approximately seven years into the marriage, and most family abductions occur in the context of a recent separation or divorce (Finkelhor, Hotaling, & Sedlak, 1991; Plass, Finkelhor, & Hotaling, 1997a). The majority (59 percent) of abducted children were of Caucasian non-Hispanic ethnicity; however, the abduction numbers tend to very closely resemble the overall population distribution in the United States (Hammer et al., 2002b).

## Non-family abductions

Non-family abductions include abductions by both acquaintances and strangers. Although in many cases these two groups are lumped together, Miller et al. (2008) suggest that it may be more appropriate to examine the two groups in isolation. In the following section, these two groups will be examined together; however, differences between them will also be explained.

## Perpetrators of non-family abduction

Approximately one-third of non-family abductions are perpetrated by strangers with the rest involving family friends or acquaintances (Finkelhor et al.

& Sedlak, 2002). The main motivation for non-family abductions is sexual assault. Approximately three-quarters of non-family abductions are perpetrated by men. Over half (54 percent) of perpetrators are in their twenties or thirties; however, approximately a quarter of perpetrators are juveniles or young adults between the ages of 13 and 19 themselves.

Lord, Boudreaux and Lanning (2001) created profiles of child abductors based on the ages of the children they abducted and the motivations for the abductions. The youngest age involves adults whom abduct newborn infants which consists of two motivation profiles. The first of these is what the authors term "maternal desire" abductors. These individuals are predominately female, and are attempting to abduct the child to raise as their own. In some cases, the perpetrator may see the abduction of the child as a way to save a failing relationship or to satisfy some personal desire to have children. These types of abductors typically have intricate well-thought-out plans, such as faking a pregnancy and abducting the infant from the hospital.

The second profile involves individuals that abduct the infant to inflict emotional distress on the parents or other significant individuals. That being said, the most common individual to perpetrate these crimes is actually the mother herself. These abductors have a high risk of impulsively murdering the infant. Given the impulsiveness of the act, little planning is involved and the perpetrators are extremely unpredictable (Lord et al., 2001).

The next age group consists of perpetrators who abduct toddlers. Similar to the previous group, the primary motivation for these perpetrators is to inflict emotional distress. There is a subset of abductors targeting this age group that have a sexual motivation; however, it is rare (Lord et al., 2001). The third age group consists of perpetrators who abduct preschool-aged children. These perpetrators are less likely to abduct a child for purposes of inflicting emotional distress, however, are more likely than previous age groups to abduct for sexual motivations. Males begin to far outweigh females in this age group and the victims are primarily females. The vast majority of the offenders at this phase are acquaintances rather than strangers (Lord et al., 2001).

The next age group includes abductors who target elementary and middle school-aged children. The majority of offenders are males who select female victims to abduct. The abductors at this level are primarily motivated by sexual desires and view the children as mature enough to be sexually attractive, but young enough to be easily controlled or manipulated. For elementary children, acquaintances and strangers abduct the children about equally. For middle school children, however, stranger abductions predominate. Abductors usually live near the site of the abduction or victim, and the victimization will typically occur close by. In some cases, however, the child is transported miles away from the site. Abductions motivated by attempts at causing emotional distress are very rare at this age (Lord et al., 2001).

The final age group consists of perpetrators who abduct high school-aged teenagers. At this age, abductions motivated for profit increase dramatically. In many cases, these profit motivated abductions occur in the course of other risky behaviors like drug trafficking. They are perpetrated by male strangers or acquaintances equally and typically involve male victims. Those abducted for sexual motivations or emotional distress tend to resemble adult abduction cases. In many cases, they are perpetrated by a scorned lover or significant other and are often proceeded by threats or stalking. Most abductors live near the victim, however, in some cases the victim is transported large distances (Lord et al., 2001).

## Victims of non-family abduction

The majority of victims of non-family abductions were female (over 65 percent). Victims of non-family abductions tended to be older than victims of family abductions, with nearly two-thirds of victims being between the ages of 15–17 and another quarter between the ages of 12–14 (Finkelhor et al., 2002). For stranger abductions, the race of the victim appears to be in line with the overall U.S. population; however, for acquaintance abductions, African Americans are disproportionately overrepresented. Approximately 42 percent of acquaintance abduction victims were African American, compared to only 15 percent in the normal U.S. population.

# Damage done

In this section, we provide a brief review of the damage that can be done to children and their families when children go missing. To examine these issues, it is important to keep in mind that different classes of missing child cases are associated with their own sets of consequences.

## Runaways

Runaways are often troubled youth to begin with and often have home lives that are far from ideal (McGarvey et al., 2010). Consequently, it is sometimes difficult to separate whether a particular problem (e.g. drug use) caused the child to run away, or was a consequence of the child running away, or both (Mallett, Rosenthal, & Keys, 2005). There is also a great deal of variability in the living conditions faced by teen runaways. Some teens who runaway are domiciled with a friend or relative, some find abandoned houses or apartments to live in, others spend nights in a homeless youth shelters and others on the streets (Whitbeck, Johnson, Hoyt, & Cauce, 2004). A runaway, over the time period they are gone, may have a number of different living arrangements.

In U.S. studies, it has been found that 71 percent of runaways could be subcategorized as "endangered runaways because they were exposed to drugs, criminal activity, and / or physical or sexual assault" (Flores, 2002). Runaways are at a substantially increased risk of violent crime, including both physical or sexual assaults (Baron, 2003; Kipke, Simon, Montgomery, Unger, & Iversen, 1997; Tyler, Whitbeck, Hoyt, & Cauce, 2004). Runaways often experience health problems related to poor hygiene, lack of adequate nutrition and lack of regular medical care (Deisher & Rogers, 1991; Ensign & Santelli, 1997). Runaways are more likely to engage in unprotected sex, may engage in survival sex (i.e. sex in exchange for lodging, food or drugs), have high rates of HIV and other sexually transmitted diseases, and high pregnancy rates with little prenatal care (Bailey, Camlin, & Ennett, 1998; Greene, Ennett, & Ringwalt, 1991; Rotheram-Borus, Koopman, Haignere, & Davies, 1991; Thompson, Bender, Lewis, & Watkins, 2008). Runaways also suffer from a range of mental health problems, including depression, anxiety, suicidal ideation, conduct disorder, dissociation and post-traumatic stress disorder (Molnar, Shade, Kral, Booth, & Watters, 1998; Slesnick & Prestopnik, 2005a, b; Whitbeck, Johnson, Hoyt, & Cauce, 2004). Runaway youth often have difficulties at school to begin with and runaway experiences exacerbate those problems (Thompson et al., 2002). Despite these serious dangers faced by runaways, it is not uncommon for people to minimize these dangers. Runaways are typically older children and are seen by many as being "voluntarily missing" (Hammer et al., 2002a). It should be clear from the above that this is a serious misunderstanding of the challenges runaways may face.

## Family abductions

Family abductions typically do not pose a physical danger to the abducted child. The NISMART studies found that physical abuse was reported in only 4 percent of cases and sexual abuse was reported in 1 percent of cases (Finkelhor et al., 1990). However, family abductions may involve the use of physical force against other adults in order to obtain access to the child (about 7 percent of the time )(Hammer et al., 2002b). About 40 percent of U.S. family abductions are serious enough to require the intervention of law enforcement (Plass, Finkelhor, & Hotaling, 1997b).

Although family abductions do not typically involve physical violence perpetrated against the child, this does not mean that family abductions do not harm the child. In fact, research indicates that family abductions can be psychologically harmful for the child, the left-behind parent, and the parent–child relationship (Lampinen, Arnal, Culbertson-Faegre, & Sweeney, 2010, for a review). Interviews with parents suggest that psychological harm to the child occurs in approximately 40 percent of all family abductions (Finkelhor et al., 1991). Symptoms experienced by children include depressive symptoms, anxiety disorders, conduct disorders, psychosomatic symptoms, difficulty sleeping and clinging behaviors (Schetky & Haller, 1983; Senior, Gladstone, & Nurcombe, 1982). The risk of psychological harm is exacerbated the longer the child remains missing (Plass et al., 1997b). Family abductions also produce extreme distress on the part of the left-behind parent. Parents experience symptoms such as feeling loss, sleep disorders, eating disorders, anxiety disorders, depressive symptoms, and anger (Greif & Hegar, 1991).

## Non-family abductions

Although non-family abductions are much less common than family abductions, these cases represent the greatest danger to the child in terms of physical harm, sexual abuse or even death (Finkelhor et al. 1990). In considering these dangers, it is important to distinguish between broadscope abductions and stereotypical kidnappings. Broadscope abductions typically occur in the context of another crime such as sexual assault, robbery, car-jackings, revenge plots and dating violence (Asdigian et al., 1995). Sexual assaults occur in approximately half of broadscope abductions, and physical assaults are also extremely common (Finkelhor et al., 2002).

Although stereotypical kidnappings occur only about 100 times per year in the United States, they are extremely dangerous crimes. Sexual assaults occur in approximately half of stereotypical kidnappings and these cases often also involve physical aggression, including the use of weapons in their commission (Finkelhor et al., 2002). About 40 percent of these cases involve the murder of the child and 4 percent of cases remain unsolved. In cases where the child is murdered, the murder usually occurs in within three hours of the abduction (Brown, 2007). Of those cases where the child is murdered, they are usually killed before they are even reported missing. These results suggest that, despite the fact that these cases are rare, law enforcement needs empirically tested tools for addressing these cases when they do occur.

## Ameliorating the problem

The problem of missing children is not a single problem, but rather a set of loosely related problems. Given the focus of the current volume on forensic issues, we focus in what follows on responses to children who go missing as a consequence of abduction. This in no way gainsays the dangers posed in other types of missing child cases or the need to systematically address those problems.


## Family abductions

Family abductions are far more common than are stranger abductions, and although they rarely result in physical harm to the child, they can produce considerable emotional distress on both the child and the left-behind parent (Lampinen et al., 2010, for a review). For that reason, dealing with the issue of parental abductions is very important.


### *Prevention*

Most family abductions occur in the context of custody disputes that occur in the course of the dissolution of a marriage or domestic partnership (Hammer et al., 2002b). The end of a marriage is, of course, stressful for all parties involved and can be tremendously acrimonious (Clarke-Stewart & Brentano, 2006). Moreover, many parental abductions occur because the non-custodial parent feels as if they were not treated fairly by the divorce courts (Johnston & Girdner, 2001). Thus, ensuring that these disputes are handled professionally and amicably, with all sides being adequately represented and all sides being treated fairly, is important. However, even when the utmost care is taken to ensure the procedural fairness of custody hearings, it is unavoidable that parents who lose custody may feel aggrieved. For these reasons, Johnston and Girdner (1998) have proposed that parents take the following steps to prevent parental abductions.

• Make sure that they have a copy of the custody and visitation order on hand. That way, if they need to contact law enforcement, they can quickly provide proof that the other parent has violated the court order.
• Flag children's passports so that these documents cannot be used without the permission of both parents.
• Have a current photograph of the child showing what the child typically looks like.
• If the potential abductor has psychological problems, make sure that the court is aware of these problems, so that an assessment of risk can be undertaken.

Counseling of couples during the dissolution of their marriage can also decrease the risk of parental abductions (Johnston & Girdner, 1998). In one program, couples who were at risk for abduction underwent therapy that helped them work through their disagreements, focus on their children first, and taught them the potential legal ramifications of parental abductions. Cases of custodial interference in these couples dropped to 10 percent, compared to 44 percent for couples in a control condition. Of course, even with all of these steps being taken, one can never entirely prevent the risk of an abduction by a parent, especially because under most circumstances, both parents retain some custody or visitation rights giving potential abductors easy access to the child.

## Legal protections

Historically, abductions by parents have been seen by society as less of a problem than abductions by non-family members (Spangler, 1982). These cases were seen as part of the natural consequence of divorce and were treated legally as a civil matter to be decided by lawyers, not a criminal matter to be resolved by law enforcement. In fact, when the U.S. Federal Government passed the *Federal Anti-Kidnapping Act*, it excluded kidnapping if committed by parents (Johnston & Sagatun-Edwards, 2002). Because law enforcement generally took a hands-off approach, parents who lost custody in one state court would sometimes abduct the child, take the child to another state, and then try to obtain a favorable custody order in that state – often successfully (Spangler, 1982).

In the 1980s, state governments in the United States began to address this problem by passing tougher laws, making parental abductions a felony offense (Agopian, 1980). Making these cases felonies aided in enforcement because U.S. law allows federal law enforcement to pursue fugitives who cross state lines in felony cases but not in misdemeanor cases (Chiancone, Girdner, & Hoff, 2001). However, even with these state laws in place, federal law enforcement was initially hesitant to get involved in what were seen as private family matters (Spangler, 1982).

Another important change in many states was the adoption of model legislation that held that state courts should abide by the custody decisions of the child's home state (National Conference of Commissioners of Uniform State Laws, 1997). So, for instance, if a child had been living in Oregon, but a parent takes the child to Illinois, it's the Oregon court that gets to make the custody decision not the Illinois court. These changes did a great deal to limit the forum shopping that had been so prevalent previously. In 1980, the U.S. Congress passed the *Parental Kidnapping Prevention Act* (Spangler, 1982). This made it federal law that state courts had to respect the custody decisions of other state courts. It also made quite clear that federal law enforcement could track and apprehend parents across state lines who abduct their child.

Similar problems can arise internationally (Chiancone, Girdner, & Hoff, 2001). If a couple is made up of parents of different national origins and they decide to get a divorce, the parent who loses the custody decision may decide to take the child back to his or her country of origin. Typically this is done because the parent hopes to be granted custody by the courts in his or her home country. To help alleviate this problem, the Hauge Convention was adopted by more than 50 nations. The basic idea behind the Hauge Convention is that if a child is abducted by a parent and taken to another country, the courts in that country will abide by the decision of the courts in the child's home country (i.e. the country that they were more recently living in). If there is already a decision in the home country's courts, the courts in the country where the child has been taken are required to honor their decision. If custody has not yet been resolved in the child's home country, the matter has to be sent back to those courts for adjudication. The Hauge Convention is a very important protection for parents and children in international abduction cases. However, there are still problems. One obvious problem is that not all countries are signatories. Thus a strategy of some abductors may be to take the child to a country that is not a signatory of the Hauge Convention.

## Non-family abductions

Non-family abductions are the least common type of missing child case, but nothing strikes as much fear in the heart of parents as these cases (Kidscape, 1993; Muris, Merckelbach, Ollendick, King, & Bogie, 2001; Stickler, Salter, Broughton, & Alario, 1991). Stereotypical kidnappings, in particular, receive a great deal of attention, partly because the outcome in these cases is often the most severe (Best, 1988).

### Perpetrator-based approaches

One approach to addressing non-family abductions involves attempting to limit the access potential abductors have to children. Because non-family abductions often have a sexual abuse component, these laws typically focus on making it more difficult for convicted sex offenders to re-offend. Indeed, in many of the best-known child abduction cases, the perpetrator is someone who has a prior history of sexual offenses against children. For example, in the United States, Jaycee Dugard was recently recovered after 18 years of being held by her abductor (Netter, 2009). She was 11 years old when she was taken. Her abductor, Phillip Craig Garrido, had a history of sex offenses.

Understandably, when crimes like this occur, the public wants to know why someone with such dangerous proclivities has been allowed out of prison where they can harm children (Levenson, Brannon, Fortney, & Baker, 2007). This sentiment has led to a number of laws in the United States to control such defendants. For instance, following the abduction and murder of Polly Klaas, California and other U.S. states passed laws that sentenced a person to life in prison if they were convicted of three or more felony offenses – the Three Strikes laws (Forquer, 1995). Other U.S. states passed laws providing for the death penalty for offenders who commit especially heinous sexual assaults against children, even if the child is not murdered (Bays, 2007). The U.S. Supreme Court later ruled that these death penalty statutes were unconstitutional (*Kennedy v. Louisiana*, 2008), although public support for such laws is widespread (Sweeney & Lampinen, 2010). Laws exist in many states which allow for the civil commitment of sex offenders after they have served their full sentence, if it can be shown that they show a substantial danger of re-offending (Levenson, 2004). The United States also has laws which require sex offenders to register with local authorities (*Jacob's Law*) and to make that information available to the general public (*Megan's Law*; *Walsh Act*) (Salerno et al., 2010a, 2010b).

## Abduction-prevention education

Another approach to dealing with non-family abductions involves providing skills training to potential victims designed to teach them how to avoid being victimized (Carroll-Rowan & Miltenberger, 1994; Holcombe, Wolery, & Katzenmeyer, 1995; Johnson et al., 2005; Johnson et al., 2006; Marchand-Martella, Huber, Martella, & Wood, 1996; Miltenberger & Olsen, 1996; Olsen-Woods, Miltenberger, & Foreman, 1998). Johnson et al. (2005) tested one such program designed for preschoolers. With their parents' knowledge and consent, children underwent a series of baseline assessment trials. On each of the trials, children were approached by a confederate who was previously unknown to them, and the confederate tried to get the children to leave with him or her. Four different types of lures were examined, with each child being exposed to all of the lures randomly across the baseline, training, and follow-up trials. The *simple lure* involved merely asking the child to go with, without providing any explanation. The *incentive lure* involved asking the child to go with and providing an incentive for doing so (e.g. "Would you like to go get some candy with me?") The *authority lure* involved telling the child that someone known to the child asked the stranger to get the child (e.g. "Your mom asked me to pick you up from school"). The *helping lure* involved telling the child that his or her assistance was needed by the confederate (e.g. "Will you come with me and help me find my puppy?"). Sixty-two percent of children agreed to go with confederates on at least some of the trials during baseline.

Children were then taught a series of abduction-prevention skills. These skills included learning about the different types of lures abductors might use and learning how to respond to those situations. In particular, children were taught that if a stranger approached and tried to get the child to go with him/her, that the child should (1) say "no", (2) immediately run away, and (3) tell an adult what happened. About 15 minutes after the behavioral skills training ended, children were approached by a new stranger using one of the lure types and the child's response was noted. If the children engaged in all of the target behaviors, they were praised. If not, they received corrective feedback (e.g. "Good job saying "no", but don't forget run as fast you can and find an adult you trust and tell what happened"). Follow-up tests occurred at two weeks, one month and three months. Children showed marked improvement, with most engaging in all three of the target behaviors during the two-week follow-up testing and maintaining those behaviors for up to three months.

The above suggests that children can learn appropriate safety skills for dealing with potential stranger abductions. There are, however, reasonable public policy questions about whether the programs are warranted. One question is whether these programs are even aimed at the right children. Most non-family abductions involve children over 12 years old, not the preschoolers tested in these studies (Finkelhor et al., 2002). Moreover, most non-family abductions are committed by someone known to a child, not a complete stranger (Finkelhor et al., 2002). To the extent that abduction-prevention education programs are pursued, it is important for educators and parents to weigh the relative costs and benefits of these programs to the children, in light of the risks posed by stranger abductions to children in this age range.

## Finding the missing

In many cases where a child goes missing, police will release the child's picture to the general public in hopes that the child will be spotted and that authorities will be contacted. Many of the most commonly used techniques used to find missing children rely on publicizing pictures of the children or pictures of potential abductors. Early efforts included putting pictures of missing children on product packaging, such as milk cartons (Sadler, 1986). Since 1996, the Wal-Mart Corporation has placed posters of missing children at the exits of its stores (Wal-Mart, 2011). The National Center for Missing Children (NCMEC) in the United States and Child Focus in the EU maintain searchable databases showing pictures of missing children, and NCMEC sends out pictures through direct mail advertisements (Child Focus, 2011; Girouard, 1990; Office of Juvenile Justice and Delinquency Prevention, 2004). In the U.S. authorities can put out AMBER Alerts to local media when a child goes missing under circumstances which suggest that the child is in imminent danger (NCMEC, 2010). The key question is how effective are these techniques, and more importantly, how can the success of these techniques be improved.

Lampinen, Arnal and Hicks (2009a) argued that such situations often rely on a special type of event-based prospective memory that they called *prospective person memory*. In prospective person memory people are shown the picture of a wanted or missing individual and are asked to contact authorities if this person is seen. In one early field study, Lampinen et al. (2009a) showed students pictures of two individuals and told the students that these individuals might appear on campus at some point in the future. Students were told that if they spotted either individual and contacted their instructor, they could win a cash prize. Two days later, one of the men walked into the classroom, put down a stack of papers, and said to the instructor, "Here are the copies you wanted." He then turned to the class, said, "Good morning!" and walked out of the class. Only 5 percent of students identified the target. Other experiments have produced similar identification rates (Lampinen et al., 2009a; Lampinen et al., 2012).

Prospective person memory has obvious implications for cases of finding missing children. However, missing children may also be recovered if people encounter a child and then later encounter alerts concerning the child – what, Lampinen, Miller and Dehon (2011b) have termed *retrospective person memory*. Collectively, prospective person memory and retrospective person memory are key competencies that need to be addressed when designing campaigns to help find missing children. Since missing child alerts are likely seen prior to encountering a child in some circumstances and subsequent to encountering a child in other cases, common sense suggests that public policy should focus on maximizing both types of recognition. Indeed, we believe designing programs aimed specifically at increasing rates of prospective person memory and retrospective person memory have the potential to make a major contribution to efforts to recovery missing children.

## Missing child posters

In the United States, the NCMEC, through its corporate sponsors, has programs to display posters depicting missing children at the exits of participating stores (NCMEC, 2011). There are similar projects in Europe (Missing Children Europe, 2011). These programs have met with some success. For instance, Wal-Mart Corporation reports that its missing children program has been involved in the recovery of hundreds of missing children since it was first initiated (Wal-Mart, 2011). However, research also indicates that there is substantial room to increase customer memory and attention for these posters. Lampinen et al. (2009b) set up eight posters of missing children on a bulletin board at the exit of a local grocery store. As shoppers left the store, they were approached by a trained survey researcher and were asked to complete a two-page survey. On one side of the survey, they were asked for demographic information, were asked whether they thought the problem of missing children was an important problem, and were asked the degree to which they looked at the posters in the supermarket. On the other side of the survey, they were shown pictures of 16 children and they were asked to circle the eight pictures that had been displayed on the bulletin board. Most customers thought that the problem of missing children was important. However, approximately 70 percent of customers reported that they did not look at the posters and most of those that did, looked only briefly. Recognition memory for the children shown in the posters did not differ significantly from chance.

In a follow-up study, Lampinen, Peters, Arnal & Hicks (in preparation) once again set up posters of missing children. In addition to the survey questions and memory questions, customers were also asked to describe in their own words what factors limited their attention to the posters. As in the previous study, most customers reported not looking at the posters, and those that did reported looking only briefly. Memory for the posters did not significantly differ from chance. Common reasons for not looking at the posters included being in a hurry (33.7 percent), failing to notice the posters as they made their way out of the store (40.22 percent) and simply not thinking to look at the posters (11.96 percent). In the next study, they created posters on foam posterboard that included pictures of six missing children. These posters were mounted facing the customer at the point of purchase – like, the cash register. Not only did the researchers find increased attention being paid to the posters, but they also found substantially better memory for the children's faces than in our previous studies. This finding is consistent with research in marketing psychology, showing that point of purchase advertising can increase product sales and memory for the advertising (Woodside & Waddle, 1975).

Factors influencing the effectiveness of missing child posters have also been studied in the laboratory. For instance, Lampinen, Peters and Gier (2012) examined the effect of array size on prospective person memory for missing children. In poster campaigns, stores sometimes place large numbers of posters at exits. For instance, poster templates used by Wal-Mart Corporation in the United States have room for 15 missing child posters. Lampinen et al. raised the issue of whether displaying this many posters might impair recognition for individual children. To examine this, participants were shown posters of either 12 children or four children. They then completed a computer-based prospective person memory task. In the task, participants were asked to imagine that they were camp counselors and that they were sorting children into two teams (P and Q). Participants were then shown pictures of a large number of children and were asked to press the P key to assign the children to the P team and the Q key to assign children to the Q team. They were also told that if at any point they saw one of the "missing" children, they should press the "H" key to alert authorities. Four children from the missing child posters were randomly interspersed among the pictures of children that the participants saw. Under free-study conditions, the 12 poster condition led to a small decrement in performance relative to the four-poster condition, but the authors noted that this cost was small relative to the benefits of publicizing more cases.

Missing child campaigns also sometimes include pictures of both the child and the likely abductor. There are two potential advantages to this approach. First, presenting an associated adult provides an additional avenue by which the child could be recovered. A person might recognize the adult and contact authorities. Second, compound cue models (Gillund & Shiffrin, 1984) suggest that including an associated adult might serve as a contextual cue that improves memory for the child if the adult is present. However, there are also potential costs. First, if a person only has a limited amount of time to look at a poster, including additional individuals decreases the amount of time that can be devoted to either picture individually. Second, if compound cue models are correct, including an associated adult may decrease memory for the child if the child is seen with a different adult (e.g. an accomplice). Research by Lampinen and Sweeney (submitted) examined this issue using the team-sorting task. Participants studied mock missing child posters showing either a child or both a child and an associated adult. During the team-sorting task, participants saw a large number of pictures showing children with adults. Half of the participants who studied posters showing associated adults ended up seeing the children with the same adults during the team-sorting task. The other half of the participants who saw posters with associated adults ended up seeing the children with different adults during the team-sorting task. Results showed that performance was best when the child was shown with an associated adult, but that including the wrong associated adult did not decrease performance relative to the child only condition. These results are consistent with the idea that presenting pictures of associated adults increases recognition opportunities.

## Age progression

Most children who go missing are returned home relatively quickly (Finkelhor et al., 2002; Hammer et al., 2002b; Sedlak et al., 2005). However, in a subset of cases, children may go missing and remain missing for many years. In fact, a recent review of cases listed on the website of the National Center for Missing and Exploited Children in the United States found that approximately a quarter of the cases involved a child who had been missing for at least one decade (Lampinen, Arnal, Culbertson-Faegre, & Sweeney, 2010). Children's appearances can change dramatically as they age, making identification attempts more difficult. In order to address this issue, authorities sometimes take outdated images of children and have them altered to reflect the child's current appearance. These photo alterations are known as age progressions and are used in approximately one-third of long-term missing child cases (Lampinen et al., 2010).

Age progression is not a single technique, but is rather a set of related techniques. Age progressions can be done by trained forensic artists – either by hand or using image manipulation software to alter the images – or can be done using specially developed computer algorithms (Taylor, 2001). Although computerized age progression holds promise, in practice most age progressions in actual cases are still done by human forensic artists. Both human artists and computer algorithms make use of two main types of information. First, all approaches make use of knowledge of typical growth patterns that occur with aging. Second, most approaches supplement information about growth patterns with pictures of biological relatives at both the target age and the age the child went missing. This has sometimes been called the *genetic approach* and is based on the idea that appearance is determined partly by shared genetic factors between the missing child and biological relatives (Sadler, 1986).

The basic premise behind age progression is a sensible one. If one knows the average facial growth rates of an appropriate subgroup of children, and one knows what a child looked like at a particular age, then it should be possible to apply the average growth rates to the last-known picture to get an estimate of the child's current appearance. Further, if one knows that a child bore a particular resemblance to one of his or hers biological relatives at a certain age, then it is not unreasonable to think that he or she will also bear a resemblance to that relative at a later age. However, despite the plausibility of the approach accurate age prediction is faced with three main hurdles that need to be overcome. First, for age progression to be considered a success it should produce more identifications than outdated photographs of the child, otherwise one could just rely on the outdated photographs (Lampinen et al., 2011a). The empirical evidence suggests that people do reasonably well at identifying a person at one age when presented with a picture of that person at an earlier age, even without sophisticated age progressed images being produced (Lampinen et al., 2011a; Lampinen et al., 2011b; Seamon, 1982). Second, although population averages can be used to predict what a child may look like, there is tremendous inter-individual variation in growth rates that make prediction in the case of a particular child difficult (Feik & Glover, 1998). Finally, although family resemblance can sometimes be used to predict what a child may look like, patterns of inheritance are randomly determined and may be difficult to predict (Sadler, 1986). Evidence also indicates that who a child is similar to at one age may not match who they are similar to at a later age (Alvergne, Faurie, & Raymond, 2007). All of these issues make accurate age progression a non-trivial technical problem.

Lampinen et al. (2011a) examined the effectiveness of age progressed images in the context of a prospective person memory task. Pictures of children at ages 7 and 12, as well as pictures of their biological relatives, were obtained by the researchers. Forensic artists recommended by law enforcement were then provided with the pictures of the children at age 7, as well as the pictures of the biological relatives, and were asked to age progress the images to age 12. The images were then used in the main experiment, in which participants were shown mock missing child posters and were asked to imagine that the children were missing. In the *current photo condition,* the posters showed the children at age 12 and indicated that the children were currently 12. In the *outdated photograph condition,* the posters showed the children at age 7 and indicated that the children were currently 12. In the *age progressed condition,* the posters showed the children at age 7 and an age progression to age 12, and indicated that the children were currently 12. Participants were told that if at any point in the experiment they saw one of the "missing children", they should press the "H" key on their computer to obtain "Help" from the authorities. Participants were then asked to imagine that they were camp counselors and that they were sorting children into two teams, the P team and the Q team. Forty-four pictures of children who were approximately 12 years old were presented in this task, including the four target children. All three conditions produced performance that was significantly better than chance. The current poster condition produced the best performance, but the age progressed and outdated poster conditions did not significantly differ from each other. Subsequent research confirmed these basic findings in prospective person memory tasks, retrospective person memory tasks, and in tasks in which other forensic artists and other age ranges were used (Lampinen et al., 2011b).

## AMBER alerts

When a child goes missing, police organizations will sometimes put on an emergency alert notifying the general public of the child's disappearance. In the United States, these systems are called AMBER Alerts. Similar alert systems have been developed in Europe (Missing Children Europe, 2011). Alert systems such as these rely on prospective person memory and retrospective person memory in an effort to find the missing child. The AMBER Alert program got its impetus with the abduction and murder of 9-year-old Amber Hagerman in Fort Worth, Texas, in 1996 (U.S. Department of Justice, 2010).

The little girl's abduction and murder rocked the Fort Worth community. Diana Simon, a mother living in the Fort Worth area, followed the case closely and this led her to propose an emergency alert plan to a local radio station. The program caught on in Texas and then the rest of the United States and eventually internationally. It was called the AMBER Alert program in honor of Amber Hagerman and also to serve as an acronym for "America's Missing Broadcast Emergency Response."

A key of the AMBER Alert system is that AMBER Alerts are designed to be issued selectively. AMBER Alerts are meant for the most serious of missing child cases, where there is imminent risk to the child's safety and it is believed by law enforcement that broadly notifying the public might produce good results (NCMEC, 2010). The specific guidelines used to decide when to issue an AMBER Alert include (a) the authorities have good reason to believe a child has been abducted, (b) the person abducted is under the age of 18, (c) there is imminent danger of death or serious bodily injury, and (d) the police know enough about the abduction that is it reasonable to believe that releasing the information to the public is likely to do some good. Once an AMBER Alert is issued, information about the case is released to the public through a variety of mechanisms, including radio and television news alerts, road signs, cells phones and internet systems (NCMEC).

The United States averages 232.8 AMBER Alerts per year, with the number of alerts declining somewhat in recent years (NCMEC, 2010). That averages out to around 4.66 AMBER Alerts per state, per year. However, there is a great deal of variability between U.S. states in terms of the issuance of AMBER Alerts. For instance, in 2009 there were 27 AMBER Alerts issued in the state of Michigan, 26 in Texas and 18 in California, all well above the national average (NCMEC, 2010). A plurality of AMBER Alert cases involve abductions by family members ($M_{2005-2009}$ = 114), followed closely by non-family abductions ($M_{2005-2009}$ = 88.2). AMBER Alerts in cases where the child is lost, injured or missing are rare ($M_{2005-2009}$ = 24.6) and AMBER Alerts for runaways happen only a handful of times per year ($M_{2005-2009}$ = 3.2).

The fact that family abductions represent such a large proportion of AMBER Alerts has sometimes been used as a criticism of the system (Griffin, 2010). According to this argument, AMBER Alerts are meant for cases where the child is in actual physical danger, and physical danger to the child is rare in family abduction scenarios. However, it is noteworthy that only an extremely small proportion of family abductions lead to an AMBER Alert (about 0.2 percent of family abductions) and although physical violence is rare in family abductions, there is a subset of family abductions which do pose a risk of physical harm to the child. On this last point, it is noteworthy that 15,000 family abductions per year involve use of force and 2,700 cases involve the use of a weapon.

Data published by NCMEC (2010) indicate that approximately 80 percent of cases in which an AMBER Alert was issued in 2009 ended in a live recovery of the missing child, another 4 percent ended with finding the child dead, 1.4 percent of cases were still active when the data were published, and the rest of the AMBER Alerts were either judged to be hoaxes or unfounded. NCMEC claims that approximately 21 percent of AMBER Alerts end with a recovery that was a direct consequence of the AMBER Alert being issued.

AMBER Alerts are a quintessential case where prospective person memory and retrospective person memory are potentially relevant to the recovery process. As we have seen, studies of prospective person memory typically find low rates of identification of individuals in realistic field settings (Lampinen et al., 2009a). However, it is important to note that even if the probability of a particular individual recognizing a missing child is low, these systems can still be successful if a large number of people are made aware of the fact that the child is missing and they encounter the child. In other words, if 100 people each see a missing child and each has a 5 percent chance of noticing the child, then the chance that *somebody* will notice the child will be high. This reasoning supports the practice of widespread notifications of as many people as possible in the relevant geographical area.

The success of an AMBER Alert system also depends on how the alerts are presented. Gier, Kreiner and Hudnell (2011) suggest that the pictures used in AMBER Alerts may at times be suboptimal. They showed participants a videotape of the U.S. television show *Criminal Minds*. Students were told that the video was taken directly from their professor's television and that the professor had not had time to edit out commercials or news breaks from the video. The researchers inserted a professional quality mock AMBER Alert into the video, leading participants to think it was a current AMBER Alert from their local area. Two of the photos were in the style of a typical school photograph, while two showed the children's faces dirty and bruised. The idea was that when AMBER Alerts are issued, authorities may use a recent school photograph, but that is unlikely to be how the child looks during the course of an abduction. Consistent with this hypothesis, recognition of children was better when the photograph in the mock AMBER Alert closely matched the photograph on the recognition memory test (see, Gier & Kreiner, 2009, for related work).

These findings suggest that recognition of missing children by members of the general public may be impaired by poor retrospective and prospective memory for missing children. Consistent with these findings, only 11 percent of all recoveries that occur due to AMBER Alerts occur because a member of the general public recognizes the child and contacts authorities (NCMEC, 2010). In more than one-third of the successful recoveries the AMBER Alert led to the recovery by spooking the perpetrator and leading the perpetrator to release the child. Improving prospective person memory and retrospective person memory may hold the key to improving the effectiveness of alert systems.

Although the AMBER Alert system is very popular in the United States it is not without its critics (Griffin, 2010; Griffin & Miller, 2008; Zgoba, 2004a, 2004b). These critics argue, in part, that the AMBER Alert system was designed for cases where a child is in imminent risk of bodily injury or death, but that the system is not well designed to meet these objectives. For instance, Griffin (2010) has argued that the AMBER Alert system is being used in situations that pose no imminent risk to the life or safety of the child. According to this argument, overuse of the AMBER Alert system dilutes its effectiveness because citizens end up tuning out the alerts (i.e. the car alarm effect). Recent field research in the prospective person memory paradigm provides some support for the view that overuse of an alert system can dilute its effectiveness. Lampinen et al. (2012) showed mock missing persons alerts to multiple sections of an introductory psychology class during a single semester. Each alert showed pictures of two college-aged individuals – one male and one female – and indicated that they had recently gone missing. Students were told that the individuals pictured in the alerts were not actually missing, but that they might appear on campus at some point in the future. They were told that if they saw one of the "missing" individuals and contacted their instructor, they would win a portion of a cash prize. In approximately half of the classes, students were shown one mock missing person alert per week for six straight weeks (six-video condition). For the other classes, students were shown a single mock missing person alert during the sixth week of the study (one-video condition). On the sixth week of the study, immediately after the class periods where the video was shown, the two target individuals were positioned outside of the classroom such that students were guaranteed to walk past one of them on their way out of the building. Students were dramatically more likely to make an identification in the single-video condition than the six-video condition. These results suggest that presenting missing person alerts too often can cause people to tune out the alerts and limit their effectiveness. However, it is not entirely clear how many alerts is too many during the course of a year. As noted above, the average number of alerts per state in the United States is about 4.66, but particular states may issue more than 20 alerts (NCMEC, 2010). Nor is it certain that the results would generalize to an actual missing persons case where the potential consequences are more dire. However, the results certainly indicate that AMBER Alerts and other types of missing persons alerts should be appropriately limited to cases where there is good reason to believe that the child is in considerable danger in order to maximize their effectiveness.

# Conclusion

Missing children represent an important social problem. Addressing the problem requires the development of a serious research-based approach. Yet that research base is seriously underdeveloped, especially with regards to developing approaches that are most likely to lead to recovery of children. Yet this significant gap in our scientific understanding is beginning to be addressed. What we are learning, hopefully, will lead to better prevention efforts and more successful recoveries when children go missing.

# References

Adams, G. R., Gullotta, T., & Clancy, M. A. (1999). Homeless adolescents: A descriptive study of similarities and differences between runaways and throwaways. In R. M. Lerner & C. M. Ohannessian (Eds), *Risks and Problem Behaviors in Adolescence* (pp. 315–324). Taylor & Francis: New York.

Agopian, M. W. (Fall 1980). Parental child stealing: California's legislative response. *Canadian Criminology Forum, 3*, 37–43.

Alvergne, A., Faurie, C., & Raymond, M. (2007). Differential facial resemblance of young children to their parents: Who do children look like more? *Evolution and Human Behavior, 28*, 135–144.

AmberView (2009). *Did you know?* Retrieved June 10, 2009, from http:// AmberView.com.

Asdigian, N. L., Finkelhor, D., & Hotaling, G. (1995). Varieties of nonfamily abductions of children and adolescents. *Criminal Justice and Behavior, 22*, 215–232.

Bailey, S. L., Camlin, C. S., & Ennett, S. T. (1998). Substance use and risk sexual behavior among homeless and runaway youth. *Journal of Adolescent Health, 23*, 378–388.

Baron, S. W. (2003). Street youth violence and victimization. *Trauma, Violence and Abuse, 4*, 22–44.

Bays, N. K. (2007). A rush to punishment: The Louisiana Supreme Court upholds the death penalty for child rape in the State v. Kennedy. *Tulane Law Review, 82*, 339–378.

Best, J. (1988). Missing children, misleading statistics. *Public Interest, 92*, 84–92.

Brown, J. J. (2007). Child abduction murders: Incidence and impact on social and public policy. Paper presented at the Annual Meeting of the American Society of Criminology, Atlanta, GA.

Carroll-Rowan, L. & Miltenberger, R. G.(1994). A comparison of procedures for teaching abduction prevention to preschoolers. *Education and Treatment of Children, 17*, 113–129.

Chiancone, J., Girdner, L., & Hoff, P. (2001). Issues in Resolving Cases of International Child Abduction. Office of Juvenile Justice and Delinquency Prevention. Washington, DC.

Child Focus (2011). Refer http://www.childfocus.be/.

Clarke-Stewart, A. & Brentano, C. (2006). *Divorce: Causes and Consequences.* Yale University Press: New Haven CT.

Deisher, R. W. and Rogers, W. M. (1991) The medical care of street youth. *Journal of Adolescent Health, 12*, 500–503.

Ensign, B. J. and Santelli, J. (1997) Shelter-based homeless youth: Health and access to care. *Archives of Pediatrics and Adolescent Medicine, 151*, 817–823.

Federal Interagency Forum on Child and Family Statistics (2011). Child population: Number of children (in millions) ages 0–17 in the United States by age, 1950–2010 and projected 2030–2050. Downloaded from http://www.childstats.gov/americaschildren/tables/pop1.asp.

Feik, S. A., & Glover, J. E. (1998). Growth of children's faces. In J. G. Clement & D. Ranson (Eds), *Craniofacial Identification in Forensic Medicine*. New York, NY: Oxford University Press.

Finkelhor, D., Hammer, H., & Sedlak, A.J. (2002). Non-family abducted children: National estimates and characteristics. *National Incidence Studies of Missing, Abducted, Runaway and Thrown Away Children*. U.S. Department of Justice, Office of Juvenile Justice and Delinquency Prevention: Washington D.C.

Finkelhor, D., Hotaling, G., & Asdigian, N.L. (1995). Attempted non-family abduction. *Child Welfare, 74*, 941–955.

Finkelhor, D., Hotaling, G., & Sedlak, A. (1990). *Missing, Abducted, Runaway, and Thrownaway Children in America*. U.S. Department of Justice, Office of Juvenile Justice and Delinquency Prevention.

Finkelhor, D., Hotaling, G., & Sedlak, A. (1991). Children abducted by family members: A national household survey of incidence and episode characteristics. *Journal of Marriage and Family, 53*, 805–817.

Flores, J. R. (2002). Highlights from the NISMART bulletins. *National Incidence Studies of Missing, Abducted, Runaway and Thrown Away Children*. U.S. Department of Justice, Office of Juvenile Justice and Delinquency Prevention: Washington D.C.

Forquer, L. (1995). California's three strikes law – Should a juvenile adjudication be a ball or a strike? *San Diego Law Review, 32*, 1297–1346.

Gallagher, B., Bradford, M., & Pease, K. (2008). Attempted and completed incidents of stranger-perpetrated child sexual abuse and abduction. *Child Abuse and Neglect, 32*, 517–528.

Gender Bias Study Committee (1990). Gender bias study of the court system in Massachusetts. *New England Law Review, 24*, 745.

Gier, V., & Kreiner, S.(2009). Memory of children's faces by adults: Appearance does matter. *Applied Cognitive Psychology, 23*, 972–986.

Gier, V. Kreiner, S., Hudnell, W. (2011). AMBER alerts: Are school-type photographs the best choice for identifying missing children? *Journal of Police and Criminal Psychology.* DOI 10.1007/s11896–011–9085-z

Gillund, G. & Shiffrin, R. M. (1984). A retrieval model for both recognition and recall. *Psychological Review, 91*, 1–67.

Girouard, C. (1990). *The National Center for Missing and Exploited Children*. Washington, DC: U.S. Dept. of Justice, Office of Justice Programs, Office of Juvenile Justice and Delinquency Prevention.

Greene, J. M., Ennett, S. T., Ringwalt, C. L. (1991). Prevalence and correlates of survival sex among runaway and homeless youth. *American Journal of Public Health, 89*, 1406–1409.

Greif, G. & Hegar, R. (1991). Parents whose children are abducted by the other parent: Implications for treatment. *American Journal of Family Therapy, 19*, 215–225.

Griffin, T. (2010). An empirical examination of AMBER Alert successes. *Journal of Criminal Justic, 38*, 1053–1062.

Griffin, T., & Miller, M. K. (2008). Child Abduction, AMBER Alert, and Crime Control Theater. *Criminal Justice Review, 33*, 159–176.

Hahn-Holbrook, J., Holbrook, C., & Bering, J. (2010). Snakes, spiders, strangers: How the evolved fear of strangers may misdirect efforts to protect children from harm. In J. M.

Lampinen & K. Sexton-Radek (Eds) *Protecting Children from Violence: Evidence Based Interventions*. New York: Psychology Press.

Hammer, H., Finkelhor, D., & Sedlak, A. J. (2002a). Runaway/thrownaway children: National estimates and characteristics. *National Incidence Studies of Missing, Abducted, Runaway and Thrownaway Children*. Washington, DC: U.S. Department of Justice.

Hammer, H., Finkelhor, D., & Sedlak, A. J. (2002b). Children abducted by family members: National estimates and characteristics. *National Incidence Studies of Missing, Abducted, Runaway and Thrownaway Children*. Washington, DC: U.S. Department of Justice.

Holcombe, A., Wolery, M., & Katzenmeyer, J. (1995). Teaching preschoolers to avoid abduction by strangers: Evaluation of maintenance strategies. *Journal of Child and Family Studies, 4*, 177–191.

Johnson, B. M., Miltenberger, R. G., Egemo-Helm, K., Jostad, C. M., Flessner, C., & Gatheridge, B. (2005). Evaluation of behavioral skills training for teaching abduction-prevention skills to young children. *Journal of Applied Behavior Analysis, 38*, 67–78.

Johnson, B. M., Miltenberger, R. G., Knudson, P., Egemo-Helm, K., Kelso, P., Jostad, C., & Langley, L. (2006). A preliminary evaluation of two behavioral skills training procedures for teaching abduction-prevention skills to schoolchildren. *Journal of Applied Behavior Analysis, 39*, 25–34.

Johnston, J., & Girdner, L. (1998). Early identification of parents at risk for custody violations and prevention of child abductions. *Family & Conciliation Courts Review, 36*, 392–409.

Johnston, J. R., & Girdner, L. K. (2001). Family abductors: Descriptive profiles and preventive interventions. Washington, DC: U.S. Department of Justice, Office of Justice Programs, Office of Juvenile Justice and Delinquency Prevention.

Johnston, J., & Sagatun-Edwards, I. (2002). Parental kidnapping: Legal history, profiles of risk and preventive interventions. *Child and Adolescent Psychiatric Clinics of North America, 11*, 805–822.

Kennedy v. Louisiana, 554 U.S. 407 (2008).

Kidscape (1993). How safe are our children? A Kidscape special report. Kidscape, London.

Kipke, M. D., Simon, T. R., Montgomery, S. B., Unger, J. B., & Iversen, E. F. (1997). Homeless youth and their exposure to and involvement in violence while living on the streets. *Journal of Adolescent Health, 20*, 360–367.

Lampinen, J. M., Arnal, J. D., Adams, J., Courtney, K., & Hicks, J. L. (2011b). Forensic age progression and the search for missing children. *Psychology, Crime, and Law*. DOI:10.108 0/1068316X.2010.499873.

Lampinen, J. M., Arnal, J. D., Culbertson-Faegre, & Sweeney, L. (2010). Missing and abducted children. In J. M. Lampinen & K. Sexton-Radek (Eds). *Protecting Children from Violence: Evidence Based Interventions* (pp. 129–165). New York: Psychology Press.

Lampinen, J. M., Arnal, J. D., & Hicks, J. L. (2009a). Prospective person memory. In M. Kelley (Ed.), *Applied Memory* (pp. 167–184). Hauppauge NY: Nova.

Lampinen, J. M, Arnal, J. D, & Hicks, J. L. (2009b). The effectiveness of supermarket posters in helping to find missing children. *Journal of Interpersonal Violence, 24*, 406–423.

Lampinen, J. M., Erickson, Peters, C. S. Sweeney, L. N., & Culbertson-Faegre, A. (2012). Car alarms and AMBER Alerts: Do repeated alerts impair prospective person memory. Presented at the Meeting of the American Psychology Law Society. San Juan Puerto Rico.

Lampinen, J. M., Miller, J. T., & Dehon, H. (2011). Depicting the missing: Prospective person memory for age progressed photographs. *Applied Cognitive Psychology*. DOI: 10.1002/acp.1819.

Lampinen, J. M., Peters, C. S., Arnal, J. D., & Hicks, J. L (in prep). Point of purchase displays and attention and memory for missing children. Manuscript in preparation.

Lampinen, J.M., Peters, C.S., & Gier, V. (2012). Power in numbers: The effect of target set size on prospective person memory in an analog missing child scenario. *Applied Cognitive Psychology*. DOI: 10.1002/acp.2848

Lampinen, J. M. & Sweeney, L. N. (submitted). Associated adults: Prospective person memory and retrospective person memory for family abducted children. Manuscript submitted for publication.

Let's Bring Them Home (2009). Children's Health and Safety Conference. Springdale AR.

Levenson, J. S. (2004). Sexual predator civil commitment: A comparison of selected and released offenders. *International Journal of Offender Therapy and Comparative Criminology*, 48, 638–648.

Levenson, J. S., Brannon, Y.N., Fortney, T., & Baker, J. (2007). Public perceptions about sex offenders and community protection policies. *Analyses of Social Issues and Public Policy*, 7, 1–25.

Lord, W. D., Boudreaux, M. C., & Lanning, K. V. (2001). Investigating potential child abduction cases: A developmental perspective. *FBI Law Enforcement Bulletin, 70,* 1–10.

Mallett, S., Rosenthal, D., & Keys, D. (2005). Young people, drug use and family conflict: Pathways into homelessness. *Journal of Adolescence, 28,* 185–199.

Marchand-Martella, N., Huber, G., Martella, R., & Wood, S. W.(1996). Assessing the long-term maintenance of abduction prevention skills by disadvantaged preschoolers. *Education and Treatment of Children, 19,* 55–59.

McGarvey, E. L., Keller, A., Brown, G. L., DeLonga, K., Miller, A. G., Runge, J. S., & Koopman, C. (2010). Parental bonding styles in relation to adolescent males' runaway behavior. *The Family Journal: Counseling and Therapy for Couples and Families, 18,* 18–23.

Miller, J. M., Kurlycheck, M., Hansen, J. A., & Wilson, K. (2008). Examining child abductions by offender type patterns. *Justice Quarterly, 25,* 523–543.

Miltenberger, R. G. & Olsen, L. A.(1996). Abduction prevention training: A review of findings and issues for future research. *Education and Treatment of Children, 19,* 69–82.

Missing Children Europe (2011). Stimulating the interconnection of child alert systems. Downloaded from http://www.missingchildreneurope.eu/index.php?option=com_content&view=article&id=71&Itemid=58 on October 18, 2011.

Molnar, B. E., Shade, S. B., Kral, A. H., Booth, R. E., & Watters, J. K. (1998). Suicidal behavior and sexual/physical abuse among street youth. *Child Abuse and Neglect, 22,* 213–222.

Muris, P., Merckelbach, H., Ollendick, T. H., King, N. J., & Bogie, N. (2001). Children's nighttime fears: Parent-child ratings of frequency, content, origins, coping behaviours and severity. *Behaviour Research and Therapy, 39,* 13–28.

National Center for Missing and Exploited Children (2006). Criminal Custodial Interference – State Statutes (Through July 2006). Downloaded from http://www.missingkids.com/en_US/documents/CriminalCustodialInterference.

National Center for Missing and Exploited Children (2010). *Analysis of AMBER Alert Cases in 2009.* Alexandria VA: NCMEC.

National Center for Missing and Exploited Children (2011). Corporate sponsors. Downloaded from http://www.missingkids.com/missingkids/servlet/PageServlet?LanguageCountry=en_US&PageId=2295 on October 11, 2011.

National Conference of Commissioners of Uniform State Laws (1997). Uniform Child Custody Jurisdiction and Enforcement Act. The 106th Annual Meeting of the National Conference of Commissioners of Uniform State Laws: Sacramento California.

Netter, S. (August 27, 2009). Jaycee Lee Dugard Found: Missing Girl Located After 18 Years – ABC News. ABCNews.com. Retrieved November 01, 2010, from http://abcnews.go.com/US/story?id=8426124.

Office of Juvenile Justice and Delinquency Prevention (May 2004). When Your Child is Missing: A Family Survival Guide. NCJ 204958. Washington D.C.: U.S. Department of Justice.

Olsen-Woods, L. A., Miltenberger, R. G, & Foreman, G.(1998). Effects of correspondence training in an abduction prevention training program. *Child and Family Behavior Therapy, 20*, 15–34.

Plass, P. S., Finkelhor, D., & Hotaling, G. T. (1997a). Risk factors for family abduction: Demographic and family interaction characteristics. *Journal of Family Violence, 12*, 333–348.

Plass, P. S., Finkelhor, D. & Hotaling, G. T. (1997b). Family abduction outcomes: Factors associated with duration and emotional trauma to children. *Youth and Society, 28*, 109–130.

Poly Klaas Foundation (2011). About the Foundation. Downloaded from http://www.klaaskids.org/pg-prog.htm.

Rotheram-Borus, M. J., Koopman, C., Haignere, C., & Davies, M. (1991). Reducing HIV sexual risk behaviors among adolescents. *Journal of the American Medical Association, 66*, 1237–1241.

Sadler, L. L. (1986) Scientific art and the milk carton kids. Paper presented at the 7th Annual Guild of Scientific Illustrators, Washington, DC.

Salerno, J. M., Stevenson, M. C., Wiley, T. R. A., Najdowski, C. J., Bottoms, B. L., & Schmillen, R. A. (2010a). Public attitudes towards applying sex offender registration laws to juvenile offenders. In J. M. Lampinen & K. Sexton-Radek (Eds), *Protecting Children from Violence: Evidence Based Interventions* (pp.193–218). New York: Psychology Press.

Salerno, J. M., Najdwoski, C. N., Stevenson, M. C., Wiley, T. R. A., Bottoms, B. L., Pimentel, P. S., & Vaca, R. (2010b). Psychological mechanisms underlying support for juvenile sex offender registry laws: Prototypes, moral outrage, and perceived threat. *Behavioral Sciences and the Law, 28*, 58–83.

Seamon, J. G. (1982). Dynamic facial recognition: Examination of a natural phenomenon. *American Journal of Psychology, 95*, 363–381.

Sedlak, A. J., Finkelhor, D., Hammer, H., & Schultz, D. J. (2002). National estimates of missing children: An overview. *National Incidence Studies of Missing, Abducted, Runaway Nd Throwaway Children*. Washington, D.C.: U.S. Department of Justice.

Sedlak, A. J., Finkelhor, D., Hammer, H. (2005). National estimates of children missing involuntarily or for benign reasons. *National Incidence Studies of Missing, Runaway and Throwaway Children*. Washington, D.C.: U.S. department of Justice.

Slesnick, N. & Prestopnik, J. (2005a). Dual and multiple diagnosis among substance using runaway youth. *The American Journal of Drug and Alcohol Abuse, 1*, 179–201.

Slesnick, N. & Prestopnik, J. L. (2005b). Ecologically based family therapy outcome with substance abusing runaway adolescents. *Journal of Adolescence, 28*, 277–298.

Spangler, S. (1982). Snatching legislative power: The Justice Department's refusal to enforce the parental kidnapping prevention act. *Journal of Criminal Law & Criminology, 73*(3), 1176–1203.

Stickler, M., Salter, M., Broughton, D. D., & Alario, A. (1991). Parents' worries about children compared to actual risks. *Clinical Pediatrics, 30*, 522–528.

Sweeney, L. N. & Lampinen, J. M. (2010). Arkansas' Attitudes Regarding the Use of the Death Penalty for Child Rape. Annual Convention of the Association for Psychological Science. Boston MA.

Taylor, K. T. (2001). *Forensic Art and Illustration*. Boca Raton, FL: CRC Press.

Thompson, S. J., Bender, K. A., Lewis, C., Watkins, R. (2008). Runaway and pregnant: Factors associated with pregnancy in a national sample of runaway/homeless females. *Journal of Adolescent Health, 43*, 125–132.

Thompson, S. J., Pollio, D. E., Constantine, J., Reid, D. & Nebbitt, V. (2002). Short-term outcomes for youth receiving runaway and homeless shelter services. *Research on Social Work Practice, 12,* 589–603.

Tyler, K. A., Whitbeck, L. B., Hoyt, D. R., & Cauce, A. M. (2004). Risk factors for sexual victimization among male and female homeless and runaway youth. *Journal of Interpersonal Violence, 19,* 503–520.

United States Department of Justice (Spring 2010). In the beginning: How the AMBER plan began. *The AMBER Advocate, 4(1),* 3–5.

Wal-Mart (2011). Missing children's network. Downloaded from http://walmartstores.com/ CommunityGiving/212.aspx on October 18, 2011

Whitbeck, L. B., Johnson, K. D., Hoyt, D. R., & Cauce, M. (2004). Mental disorder and comorbidity among runaway and homeless adolescents. *Journal of Adolescent Health, 35,* 132–140.

Woodside, A. G. & Waddle, G. L. (1975). Sales effects of in-store advertising. *Journal of Advertising Research, 15,* 29–34.

Zgoba, K. M. (2004a). AMBER Alert: The appropriate solution to preventing child abduction? *Journal of Psychiatry and Law, 32,* 71–88.

Zgoba, K. M. (2004b). Spin doctors and moral crusaders: The moral panic behind child safety legislation. *Criminal Justice Studies, 17,* 385–404.

# Chapter 10

# Conclusions and Next Steps for Researchers and Practitioners

Michael J. Lawler, Daniel Bederian-Gardner
and Gail S. Goodman

The science of child forensic psychology is well-documented in this book and reflects more than 30 years of research literature and the ongoing development of international practice standards. Drawing on noted experts and researchers, the book reconciles current practices in law, law enforcement, social work and psychology with some of the best-known scientific research and suggests areas of additional examination to refine research frameworks and evidence bases of practice. In this concluding chapter, we summarize and comment on the major points and themes of the book by chapter and add recommendations for future research.

## Chapter reviews and critiques

In the Introduction chapter, Holliday and Marche describe the book's goal of providing "(1) the current state of scientific knowledge of memory in children from infancy to adolescence, and (2) how that knowledge is applied practically to children's eyewitness testimony" (pp. 1). The central question posed concerns about the reliability of children's memories and testimony for witnessed or experienced events. The subsequent chapters prove the editors right in saying, about children's accuracy, that "It depends." Fortunately, the book achieves its goal of providing a current review of some of the key findings in the scientific study of memory development and child eyewitness memory.

A great strength of this book is the information provided about basic memory processes. Without such information, only a superficial understanding of children's eyewitness memory is obtained. Bauer's chapter provides an excellent overview of laboratory research on infant memory. Professor Bauer has performed some of the most innovative and compelling research on infant memory that exists today, including studies of the neuroscience of memory development. However, research with pre verbal infants is necessarily constrained by methodology. Given infants' lack of verbal skills, methodology that can tap memory is essential. New methods have revealed memory abilities that challenge earlier notions that infants lacked mnemonic skill. Bauer notes how recent advances in methodology have altered those notions: The view that infants can indeed remember the past has gained significant ground. An important distinction for understanding early developmental changes in memory is made between non-declarative memory, that is memory that is not consciously accessible but rather is evinced through changes in behavior, and *declarative memory*, that is memory that is consciously accessible, for example, through recognition or recall of facts or knowledge. The core issue addressed in Bauer's chapter is whether current behavioral and neuroscience tests reveal declarative memory in infancy.

The obvious barrier to recognizing infants' declarative memory skills was how to test their recognition or recall without using verbal methods. Methods such as visual paired comparison, habituation and operant conditioning provided the first evidence of young infants' memory; however, as Bauer notes, elicited and deferred imitation tasks have been key to questioning whether children were really as poor at remembering as had been thought. The advantage of deferred imitation is in its similarity to verbal reports. Three main ways are mentioned in the chapter in which imitation can be argued to be an early form of declarative memory. First, as with declarative memory, imitation can be learned rather rapidly and even after just one experience. Second, imitation paradigms often involve multiple steps, and once children become verbal they can talk about these learning experiences, including the multiple steps. Third, patients with declarative memory impairments have difficulty with imitation-based tasks. Results from imitation tasks arguably provide evidence that infants form an early version of declarative memory.

Through elicited and deferred imitation, researchers have studied infants' ability to remember events. Results have indicated that as early as 6 months of age infants can remember one step of a sequence for a full day but that they do not yet possess the ability to remember the step past 24 hours without reminders. The amount of information retained, the length of the retention interval, and the robustness of the memory continue to improve throughout infancy.

The chapter on infant memory provides a wonderful summary of infants' mnemonic abilities. Bauer also offers a framework for thinking about these advances by defining how the neural structures that develop to support declarative memory influence each of the main stages of memory (encoding, consolidation and retrieval). Bauer concludes that, by the second year of life, infants possess declarative memory that is long-term and robust.

Of particular direct importance to eyewitness memory is the last section of her chapter, concerning verbal accessibility of early event memories. In this section, Bauer describes compelling research showing that children of about 20 to 26 months of age who cannot describe an event due to lack of verbal skill can nevertheless put words to their memories many months later when language has been acquired (e.g. into the preschool years). The studies reviewed include Peterson and Rideout's (1998) important research on young children's memory for hospital emergency room procedures following accidents, thus addressing memory for traumatic events in childhood, and Hamond and Fivush's (1991) vital work showing the need for prompting of memory in preschoolers to enable the distant past to be recalled. As Bauer states, "... it now is clear that from early in life, the human organism stores information over the long term" (p. 30).

The "long term" is clearly the focus of the second chapter of the book. Professor Howe is one of the leading researchers in the world on memory development. Citing testimony from legal cases in the United States and the United Kingdom, Howe describes "memory feats" of recalled or reconstructed memory of adults allegedly abused as children, as presented in testimony during prosecutions of alleged perpetrators. The validity of these memories of abuse, often recalled decades after the alleged maltreatment, are questioned by Howe in relation to the scientific research that indicates less reliability of long-term memories in historical child sexual abuse cases, at least in the absence of other confirming evidence. Specifically, Howe reviews the research literature on memory in young children, concluding that "although young children can and do form memories, they are not the sorts of memories that are particularly enduring" (p. 46). He suggests that the scientific research does not fully support claims that narrative accounts of early childhood abuse are based on intact memories of abuse. Howe cites a report from the British Psychological Society (2010) that concludes the accuracy of memories from below the age of 7 years cannot be established without corroborating evidence and that only by ages 9 to 10 years do children have autobiographical memories similar to adults. To us, this seems like a rather conservative age cut-off, however, given that research increasingly shows that some adults (and children) can access memories of events that occurred well before the age of 7 years (e.g. Usher & Neisser, 1993). Moreover, one wonders if the corroborated cases might validate the accuracy of some early memories of abuse, which would provide valuable information about whether detailed memories of traumatic childhood experiences can be retained into adulthood. Note that cases with sufficient corroboration are likely plea bargained, at least in the United States, making the cases that come to experts' attention a potentially biased sample. Looking beyond child sexual abuse (which often has little in the way of physical evidence) to adult memory in child witness cases that are more likely to include physical evidence (e.g. domestic violence cases involving homicide), and that still at times involve long delays, would be of considerable interest. Take, for example, a current case going to trial in the United States in which a 2-year-8-month old child witnessed her mother's murder 16 years previously, but the suspect (the girl's father) was only recently apprehended. Considerable physical evidence in such cases often exists.

Howe addresses the emerging consensus in the research literature that traumatic experiences may be remembered better than more mundane events. However, he cautions readers that these traumatic memories are susceptible to the same errors of memory reconstruction that occur with all memories (e.g. memory decay, forgetting, interference and misinformation effects). In fact, some studies indicate that a subset of children who experienced higher levels of stress produce more memory errors than do those children who found the same event less stressful (e.g. Goodman & Quas, 1997). However, as Howe points out, stressful events are usually remembered at least as well, and sometimes better than, less-stressful, more-benign experiences.

According to Howe, false memories are not uncommon and can occur in relation to stressful events (and everyday experiences) for both adults and children. Although some would take issue with his generalizations to legal cases based on false memory findings from laboratory studies of word lists, Howe is well versed in memory development research generally, and his conclusions are, therefore, more broadly based than on this one paradigm. His overall point in the chapter is that memories from early childhood are prone to errors of reconstruction and cannot be assumed to be completely accurate, especially without corroborating evidence to validate events. Because there is often no hard test to assess accuracy of memory in real legal cases (Bernstein & Loftus, 2009; but see Paz-Alonso, Ogle, & Goodman, in press), Howe asserts that other evidence (e.g. medical reports of the abuse) must be available to confirm any testimony of maltreatment or abuse drawn from early memories.

Howe's general caution to the field about over-reliance on early memory testimony is supported by decades of scientific research. His assertions about the need for corroborating evidence to validate memory-based testimony are important for practitioners in law, social work, psychology and law enforcement to understand. We worry a bit, however, about the portrayal of some of the testimony and the individuals giving testimony based on memory (e.g. "miraculous feats of testimony"), which could be interpreted as questioning the veracity of individuals' statements and memories in advance of gathering other validating information. Providing testimony in court is often an emotional task for children and adults. We encourage professionals working in child forensic psychology to find ways to support the individuals testifying, while also properly verifying the details of memory-driven testimony.

The third chapter of the book, like the first chapter, concentrates on basic memory development, in particular on "false memory." It does so from Brainerd and Reyna's theoretical perspective, called fuzzy-trace theory (FTT). In the chapter, Corbin, Wilhelms, Reyna and Brainerd first summarize several theories of memory development, some of which may explain perplexing findings in the literature. Early theories of constructivism and schema-theory are reviewed mainly as backdrops for two currently prominent theories, the source-monitoring framework (SMF) and FTT. According to SMF, memories are judged to be true or false based on attributional processes concerning the source of the memory (e.g. was the source of the memory from experiencing an event or from imagination or interviewer misinformation). SMF predicts increases in memory for source with age and, in turn, false memory based on source misattribution would be expected to decrease. However, Corbin et al. assert that SMF cannot entirely account for the phenomenon of an age increase in "spontaneous false memory." One well-known paradigm that can produce spontaneous false memory is the Deese-Roediger-McDermott (DRM; Deese, 1959; Roediger & McDermott, 1995) paradigm, explained thoroughly in the chapter. Briefly, it involves presentation of a list of semantically associated words, after which (false) memory for a semantically related nonpresented word is assessed. In studies by Brainerd and Reyna, as well as others (e.g. Howe, 2006), adults produce greater error than do young children on this task, indicating a developmental reversal in false memory compared to the more typical developmental decrease in false memory, as found in suggestibility and misinformation studies. By being founded in dual-process theories of memory, FTT is well suited to explain how both true and false memory can increase through development.

As with almost any theory in psychology, FTT is not without criticism. FTT relies on the notion that two memory representations, gist memory and verbatim memory, are encoded independently and separately. However, the criticism has been levied in the consistency in which an item is considered a gist or verbatim trace. Is gist no more than an extra step in association activation? Howe (2006) has argued that associative activation can explain developmental reversals without reliance on a distinction between gist and verbatim traces as proposed in FTT.

There has been considerable debate about the link between FTT and forensic relevance, especially given FTT's current heavy reliance on the DRM paradigm. For example, on the face of it, it seems unlikely that memory performance for a word list would be analogous to memory of sexual abuse.

It was argued in the chapter that by connecting meaning, word lists can simulate eyewitness memory. This argument would be better supported if the link between connected-meaning paradigms and forensic situations could be bridged. Recent studies of more direct relevance to criminal courts, such as findings of developmental reversals in eyewitness identification (Ross et al., 2006), have helped create this bridge. Nevertheless, FTT has been difficult to test in an externally valid way that gives confidence to its generalizability to actual eyewitness situations concerning adults or children. Moreover, the many socioemotional factors (e.g. loyalty, embarrassment, psychopathology, trauma reactions) that can crucially affect children's eyewitness memory are not addressed by this theory. Still, the brilliant work by the senior authors of this chapter highlight many valuable points that are quite relevant to child eyewitness memory, such as the likelihood that developmental reversals in false memories can at times exist and that verbatim-like and gist-like traces may differentially affect memory and differ in developmental trajectories.

Odegard and Toglia present an historical overview of child witness research, using literature from the fields of psychology and law. The focus of the chapter is largely on children's suggestibility and false memory. The authors early on mention several of the high-profile alleged sexual and ritual abuse cases in the 1980s and 1990s that led to increased empirical research on children's eyewitness memory and suggestibility and, ultimately, to refinement of child interviewing practices. This review of historical development of child witness research literature and case law is focused in large part on children's suggestibility and false memory, and is especially useful for scientists and practitioners not already familiar with this history. Fortunately, new information is interspersed into this history providing useful kernels even for those who have read the former historical reviews (e.g. see Ceci & Bruck, 1993; Goodman, 1984; Sporer, 2008).

The authors argue that distorted recollections of the past by child witnesses stem from a mixture of internal and external factors. For this dichotomous view, they draw on the seminal work of Wells (1978), whose study of lineup identification produced a distinction between estimator and system variables. Similarly, Odegard and Toglia propose a framework of intrinsic and extrinsic factors that may affect children's eyewitness testimony. They suggest that intrinsic factors (e.g. child's age, prior knowledge of an event, gist extraction, and plausibility monitoring) provide a basis to evaluate reliability of child memory, whereas extrinsic factors (e.g. social factors, misleading questioning, repeated interviews and questions) form a foundation with which to assess the procedures used to interact with child witnesses. Thus, any efforts to help reduce memory distortions in child witnesses should pay close attention to both intrinsic and extrinsic factors. This is a useful dichotomy that can inform research and practice.

Child victims' progression through the entirety of a legal case can be affected by emotion at every phase and in several domains. The crime itself is emotional and therefore the nature of what is recounted at testimony can be affected by the emotional valence and traumatic force of the content and of the emotional arousal of children themselves. As emotion influences the children's testimony, judgments made by juries can in turn be influenced by the quality of the testimony and the children's emotional displays while testifying (Bederian-Gardner, 2012). The children's experiences during the legal case as well as the outcome can then impact the children's emotional well-being. Trying to understand the full effect that emotions have on child victims must rest on a proper understanding of the role emotion plays within each domain along the way.

Marche and Salmon tackle one of these important domains, namely children's memory for emotionally negative experiences, and do so with particular sensitivity, accuracy and breadth. If you only have time to read one chapter, and want to obtain an overall understanding of the child eyewitness memory research, read this one. Marche and Salmon expand on Herve, Cooper and Yuille's (2007) model of eyewitness testimony to ensure its relevance to child witnesses. The model emphasizes the notion that three factors interact to influence the formation of memories: predisposing factors, precipitating factors and perpetuating factors. Predisposing factors include child and child-experience factors that could potentially influence what is reported during interviewing. Precipitating factors relate to the event itself and how the child responds during the event. Perpetuating factors occur after the event and include the emotional state during retrieval, the recall context and the interview format. Marche and Salmon suggest that research on children's memory for emotional experiences has not included all the relevant factors and that this lack could explain the mixed findings within the literature.

As previously noted, emotion's influence can occur in many different ways, which renders the task of understanding its impact on all domains of children's involvement within the legal system difficult. Herve et al.'s model might also be appropriate as a framework within this larger context, much in the way it is proposed to frame research on memory for emotional events. For now, Marche and Salmon have left us with the intriguing idea that at least one area where emotion and forensic psychology intersect might well be served by such a model.

In a particularly lucid and well-written chapter, Poole and Dickinson describe the history and current science of investigative interview protocols. They outline the underlying framework for investigative interviews and describe a number of applications with various populations of children. Notably, they recognize that the proliferation of research and practice literature over the past 30 years makes it challenging to "distill core knowledge in

the field." Thus, in the chapter, the authors seek to describe "consensus practice." For practitioners who are actively engaged in child forensic interviewing, or who are about to become so, this chapter is a must read.

Recognizing that investigative interviewing is a complex skill that requires
attainment of new communication abilities while suppressing usual conversational habits, Poole and Dickinson identify three key skill areas (called the
three Cs) for effective interviewing: conversational habits, conventional content and case-specific exploration. Conversational habits include an array of
verbal and non-verbal techniques to build rapport with and lower child-witness anxiety while also supporting the disclosure of accurate information.
With developed conversational skills, interviewers can learn effective conventional content of evidence-based interview protocols, which include structured procedures and guidance for interviewer flexibility. Once interviewers
have built up developmentally appropriate competencies in conversational
skills and conventional context, they are better able to address case-specific
issues germane to individual children's needs or cases. In essence, the three
Cs describe a developmental approach to building investigative interviewer
expertise.

In what they describe as "advanced topics," Poole and Dickinson address
interviewing with props, using physical evidence in interviews, interviewing
children with disabilities, customizing protocols for child protective services
interviews and the need for interviewer training. These sections are helpful:
The information targets dangers of using props, such as anatomical dolls
and the legal risks associated with using physical evidence during interviews.
Developmentally sensitive skills are outlined for working with children with
developmental disabilities and suggestions are made for integrating protocols into local practices and laws. Finally, the authors affirm the need for
ongoing training and professional collaboration to strengthen interview skills
and knowledge of emerging best practices.

Poole and Dickinson achieve their goal of describing a consensus approach
to investigative interviewing. Although some of the research cited (e.g. regarding the use of human body drawings) is still in the relatively early stages and
thus is less than definitive, the chapter information generally is well supported
by citations from the empirical research literature relative to investigate interviews of children. They provide useful guidelines in a very accessible form.

Klemfuss and Ceci's chapter focuses on children's competency examinations. Professor Ceci has made vital contributions to research on children's
suggestibility and is well known as an international expert on the topic. Here,
he and Klemfuss tackle the thorny issue of the legal system's assessment of
children's competency rather than suggestibility. In the legal system, competence to testify is considered separately from testimonial accuracy, completeness of testimony, and the subjective quality of testimony. According to

Lyon (2011), the law recognizes two types of competency: basic competency and truth-lie competency. Klemfuss and Ceci note that if a child demonstrates he or she is sufficiently able to communicate memories and passes the truth-lie test (e.g. that the child understands the obligation to tell the truth), he or she is likely to be deemed competent to testify. As the legal examples presented in this chapter attest, truth-lie competency weighs quite heavy on the courts. Witnesses in general take an oath to tell the truth, but courts know that not everyone is honest when they take the stand. The courts also know that witnesses sometimes err due to perception and memory deficits. The courts (rightly) worry that, at least prior to trial, they cannot assess the accuracy of testimony of children or adults. Instead, they accept a minimal standard for competence to testify. In the past, children under certain ages (e.g. 10 years) were often *presumed* incompetent, and attorneys had to prove child competence. Many courts now take the opposite stance: Children are *presumed* competent unless shown otherwise.

By reviewing the relevant psychological literature and interspersing quotes from pertinent legal cases, Klemfuss and Ceci argue for revising and refining child witness competency standards. The traditional approach of a judge interviewing a child to determine the child's understanding of the difference between a truth and a lie appears to be insufficient and may actually be misleading in representing a child's capacity for truthful testimony. The authors recommend that determining a child's capacity to give accurate testimony should require individual assessments of a child's memory and suggestibility. For example, they suggest that evaluations of a child's cognitive and language skills through standard psychometric tests would help determine a child's capacity to understand and answer interview questions. However, the amount of variability in performance accounted for in psychological research based on such tests is fairly limited typically. Moreover, how well the tests' scores, such as for assessing suggestibility, generalize to actual child witness cases (e.g. involving traumatic events) has yet to be established. Thus, at present, considerable error would likely result in predicting the performance of any specific child witness. Although psychological science can provide important guidance, going to the "ultimate issue" of stating if a particular child is accurate or not based on standardized tests is typically problematic, and may be problematic as well for competence determinations. As Klemfuss and Ceci wisely conclude, it may be best now to adopt the Canadian approach, which is to simply have children promise to tell the truth.

For many crimes, children are the sole witnesses and are relied upon to identify perpetrators for law enforcement and in court. Pozzulo first focuses on the accuracy and nature of perpetrator description of strangers provided by child witnesses. To help understand the research literature on identification of offenders by children, the author differentiates between assessments of children's abilities to identify perpetrators from children's abilities to provide accurate person descriptions. Pozzulo points out that greater attention is paid in the literature to understanding children's abilities to identify perpetrators compared to person description capacity.

As described by Pozzulo, the paradigm used to study face recognition differs in important ways from that used to investigate perpetrator identification, the latter of which involves an eyewitness paradigm. The author summarizes these differences and asserts that research questions posed by face recognition studies are different from those in eyewitness identification studies. Specifically, using a cognitive psychology framework, face recognition studies address theoretical questions about how the brain processes memories of facial features. In contrast, eyewitness identification studies concern applied questions, such as how best law enforcement should collect forensic evidence to facilitate increased accuracy of identification evidence.

Although the research literature that suggests reliable identification evidence is possible from child witnesses, especially when developmentally appropriate interventions are applied, person descriptions are still not commonly obtained from actual child or adult witnesses. Pozzulo suggests person descriptions may help narrow suspect searches, and she encourages increased scientific examination of children's and adults' person description abilities. The author rightfully cautions against inferences of identification evidence based on person descriptions, suggesting the need for research on the integration of person description data with perpetrator identification procedures via developmentally appropriate interview protocols.

One promising approach to perpetrator identification involves the elimination lineup procedure (Pozzulo & Lindsay, 1999). The elimination lineup appears to effectively support correct identifications while also improving correct rejections by children and adults. Because the value of the procedure has held up when investigated under different conditions and with various populations, the lineup elimination procedure may be suitable for witnesses across a broad age range and across a variety of crime situations.

In an emerging area of social concern and scientific inquiry, Lampinen, Peters, Gier, and Sweeney discuss the problem of missing and abducted children. Although the practices of protecting or diligently searching for a missing child are relatively well known (e.g. AMBER Alerts), the research base for determining successful practices is underdeveloped. The authors review the available research and offer frameworks for future research relative to missing children.

Lampinen and colleagues outline two types of memory constructs in relation to missing person reports – prospective person memory and retrospective person memory. Prospective person memory involves individuals contacting authorities after seeing a child who has been shown to be missing in different media or public notice. Retrospective person memory occurs when a person encounters a child and later sees a public notice or media announcement about the child's disappearance. The authors argue that addressing both prospective person memory and retrospective person memory would help increase success rates for child recovery programs.

The authors describe several categories of missing children, including runaways, homeless youth and family/non-family abductions. Additionally, they describe different profiles of child abductors. As outlined in the chapter, the characteristics of the victims and perpetrators vary widely relative to different types of missing children. As the research base develops further, future books may be able to address the sub-populations each in different chapters to allow more detailed descriptions and analyses of the available research literature. For now, it is admirable that the editors included this important chapter and that Lampinen and his colleagues are conducting research on this important topic.

The authors' work on the effectiveness of public notices about missing children seems quite promising and may help steer future efforts relative to missing children searches. With a more developed research base as suggested and led by Lampinen and colleagues, new approaches to missing children prevention and safe recovery interventions should emerge.

## Future research

The excellent chapters in this informative book spawn a number of questions and ideas. Although we can't mention all of them here, we highlight a few that we consider particularly worth the mention.

Perhaps foremost among the questions for many readers is how to apply the findings of basic memory development theory and research (e.g. neuroscience as described in the Bauer chapter, FTT and/or DRM research as discussed in the Brainerd and Reyna chapter and in the Howe chapter) to the social services and legal arenas. Forensic interviewers and attorneys can take comfort in the work of high-level scholars like Deborah Poole, as well as Michael Lamb, Karen Saywitz, Ron Fischer, John Yuille and others, who are actively incorporating the basic research into forensic protocols. It is also possible for police and child protective services agencies to hire researchers as consultants to keep the agency informed about the latest research, as there are always new findings being published in journals and books and presented at scientific conferences. Then the researchers and practitioners can actively discuss one-on-one how the findings can inform practice.

Although the research on child witnesses is now vast, there is still much more to learn. As the book reflects, much of the current research concerns suggestibility and false memory. Marche and Salmon point out that research is also needed on such topics as how psychopathology affects children's memory reports, on children's forgetting of traumatic and stressful experiences, and on how children's negative emotions and coping mechanisms affect memory retention and retrieval. The idea to examine memory for events that pose a strong personal threat is also a good one. Although research on emotional word lists has considerable theoretical importance, it has yet to be proven that such research generalizes to situations in which a strong personal threat is present. Perhaps a future book to be edited by Holliday and Marche will present such findings, as the research base matures.

Pozzulo's chapter spurs many ideas for further research. For example, we know too little about children's person descriptions, and yet such descriptions play a crucial role in many investigations that involve child witnesses. The development of scientifically based techniques to bolster children's accuracy in both describing people and in identifying them (including for familiar people) would also be a wonderful contribution to the field. This is especially needed for preschoolers, who generally pose the greatest challenges to interviewers.

Lampinen and his colleagues are to be congratulated for their innovative efforts to bring science to the problem of missing children. Their work reminds us that there are many more topics about child victimization for researchers to tackle. There are few studies of child witness testimony, for example, aimed at missing children specifically. The child witness work by Leander and colleagues in Sweden (e.g. Leander, Christianson, & Granhag, 2007) is quite relevant, however, since it includes cases of children who were abducted and sexually abused. Future research on child witness testimony could be addressed to this important topic as well as to child custody cases, domestic violence cases, and physical abuse cases (see Greenhoot, McCloskey, & Glisky, 2005).

Child witness research provides great mutual benefits to science and practice. This is an area where, by coming together, considerable good can be achieved. Scientists have explored new vital topics and revised their theories; practitioners have refined their techniques and approaches. As long as the findings are carefully applied, the goal of helping society, child victims and science can be achieved.

# References

Bederian-Gardner, D. (March 2012). *Emotional display on the stand: How child victims of sexual abuse are perceived by potential jurors.* Paper presented at the American Psychology-Law Society Meetings, Puerto Rico.

Bernstein, D. M., & Loftus, E. F. (2009). How to tell if a particular memory is true or false. *Perspectives on Psychological Science, 4,* 370–374.

Ceci, S. J., & Bruck, M. (1993). Suggestibility of the child witness: A historical review and synthesis. *Psychological Bulletin, 113,* 403–439.

Deese, J. (1959). On the prediction of occurrence of certain verbal intrusions in free recall. *Journal of Experimental Psychology, 58,* 17–22.

Goodman, G. S. (1984). Children's testimony in historical perspective. *Journal of Social Issues, 40,* 9–31. doi: 10.1111/j.1540–4560.1984.tb01091.x

Goodman, G. S., & Quas, J. A. (1997). Trauma and memory: Individual differences in children's recognition of a stressful experience. In N. L. Stein, P. A. Ornstein, B. Tversky, & C. J. Brainerd (Eds), *Memory for Everyday and Emotional Events* (pp. 267–294). Mahwah, NJ: Erlbaum.

Greenhoot, A. F., McCloskey, L. M., & Glisky, E. (2005). A longitudinal study of adolescents' recollections of family violence. *Applied Cognitive Psychology, 19,* 719–743.

Hamond, N. R., & Fivush, R. (1991). Memories of Mickey Mouse: Young children recount their trip to Disneyworld. *Cognitive Development, 6,* 433–448.

Herve, H., Cooper, B. S., & Yuille, J. C. (2007). Memory formation in offenders: Perspectives from a biopsychosocial model of eyewitness memory. In S. A. Christianson (Ed.), *Offenders' Memories of Violent Crimes* (pp. 37–74). West Sussex, England: John Wiley & Sons, Ltd.

Howe, M. L. (2006). Developmentally invariant dissociations in children's true and false memories: Not all relatedness is created equal. *Child Development, 77,* 1112–1123.

Leander, L., Christianson, S. A., & Granhag, P. A. (2007). A sexual abuse case study children's memories and reports. *Psychiatry, Psychology and Law, 14,* 120–129.

Lyon, T. D. (2011). Assessing the competency of child witnesses: Best practice informed by psychology and law. In M. E. Lamb, D. La Rooy, L. C. Malloy, & C. Katz (Eds), *Children's Testimony: A Handbook of Psychological Research and Forensic Practice* (pp. 69–85). Sussex, UK: Wiley-Blackwell.

Memory and the Law Working Party (2010). *Guidelines on memory and the law: Recommendations from the scientific study of human memory.* Leicester, UK: The British Psychological Society. Retrieved from http://www.bps.org.uk/sites/default/files/documents/guidelines_on_memory_and_the_law_recommendations_from_the_scientific_study_of_human_memory.pdf.

Paz-Alonso, P. M., Ogle, C. M., & Goodman, G. S. (in press). Children's memory in scientific case studies of child sexual abuse: A review. In M. Ternes, D. Griesel, & B. Cooper (Eds), *Applied Issues in Investigative Interviewing, Eyewitness Memory, and Credibility Assessment.* New York: Springer.

Peterson, C., & Rideout, R. (1998). Memory for medical emergencies experienced by 1- and 2-year-olds. *Developmental Psychology, 34,* 1059–1072.

Pozzulo, J. D., & Lindsay, R. C. L. (1999). Elimination lineups: An improved identification procedure for child eyewitnesses. *Journal of Applied Psychology, 84,* 167–176.

Roediger, H. L., & McDermott, K. B. (1995). Creating false memories: Remembering words not presented in lists. *Journal of Experimental Psychology: Learning, Memory, and Cognition, 21,* 803–814.

Ross, D. F., Marsil, D. F., Benton, T. R., Hoffman, R., Warren, A. R., Lindsay, R. C. L., & Metzger, R. (2006). Children's susceptibility to misidentifying a familiar bystander from a lineup: When younger is better. *Law and Human Behavior, 30,* 249–257.

Sporer, S. L. (2008). Lessons from the origins of eyewitness testimony research in Europe. *Applied Cognitive Psychology, 22,* 737–757.

Usher, J. A., & Neisser, U. (1993). Childhood amnesia and the beginnings of memory for four early life events. *Journal of Experimental Psychology: General, 122,* 155–165.

Wells G. L. (1978). Applied eyewitness-testimony research: System variables and estimator variables. *Journal of Personality and Social Psychology, 36,* 1546–1557.

# Index